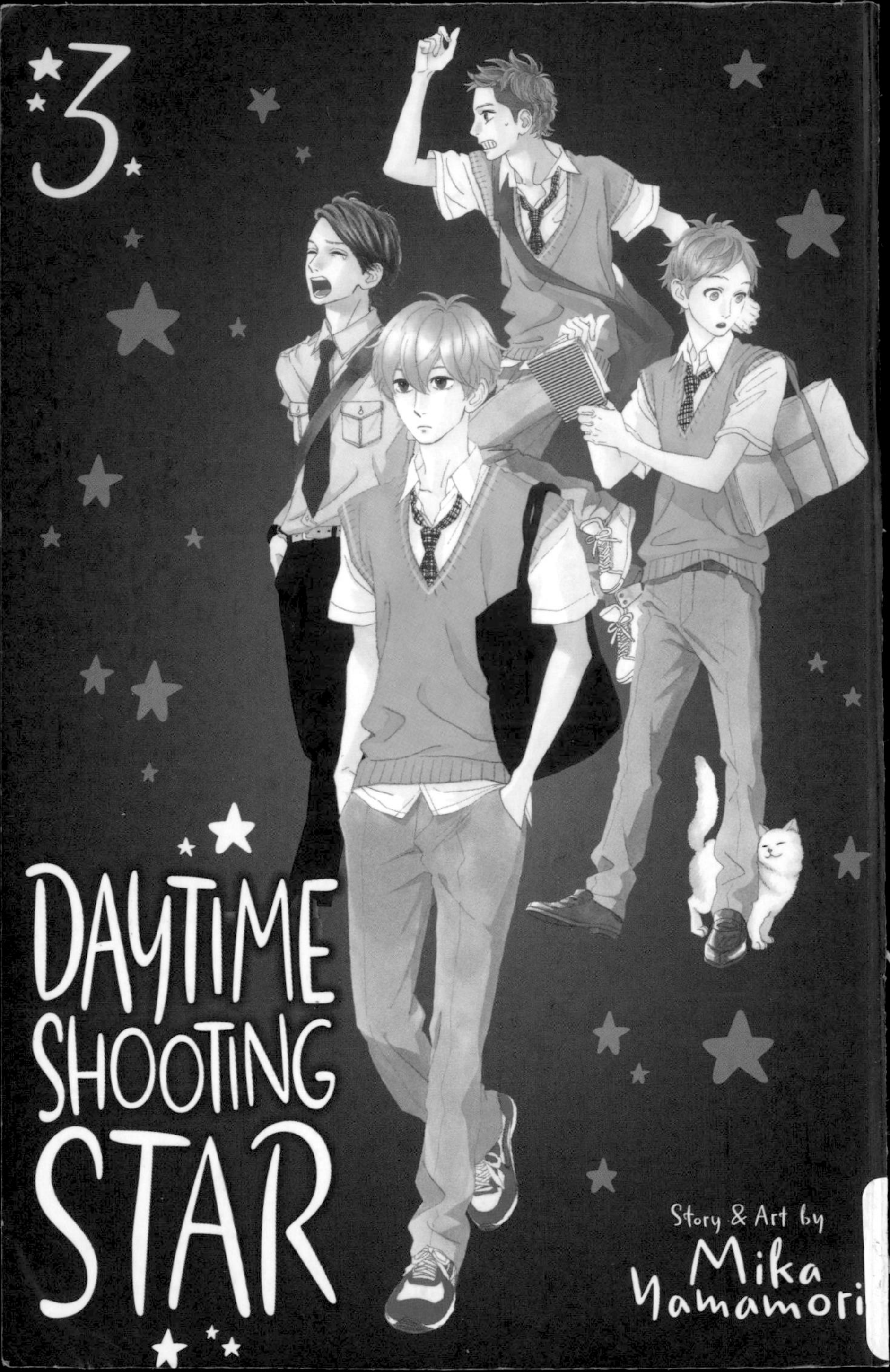
3
DAYTIME SHOOTING STAR
Story & Art by
Mika Yamamori

Shojo Beat

DAYTIME SHOOTING STAR

Story & Art by

Mika Yamamori

CONTENTS

STORY THUS FAR

Suzume Yosano is a first-year in high school. Born in the country, she grew up living a free and easy life. When she learns her father is being transferred abroad, she moves to Tokyo to live with her Uncle Yukichi. On her first day in the city, she gets lost and passes out, but a man carries her on his back to her uncle's home. A freckle on the back of his neck reminds Suzume of when she was lost as a child and a shooting star in broad daylight showed her the way home.

At her new school, she runs into the man again: he is her homeroom teacher, Mr. Shishio. As Suzume begins making friends, she is concerned about Yuyuka—who likes Mamura—because Mamura seems to like her instead. Suzume becomes aware of her growing feelings for Mr. Shishio.

One day, Mr. Shishio's ex-girlfriend Tsubomi appears. Suzume's heart aches as she sees how friendly they are. When Suzume finds him asleep in the infirmary and hears him mutter her nickname, she hears herself uttering the unbidden words "I love you."

And so...

We've reached volume 3 already!! Yay! KLAP KLAP KLAP
I'm so grateful.
In the previous volume, I said I'd gotten used to having two deadlines a month, but...

THAT WAS A LIE. TWICE A MONTH IS AWFUL.

I feel like I'm DROWNING each time.

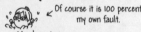

Me, drowning.
Of course it is 100 percent my own fault.

Will I ever get accustomed to these twice-a-month deadlines? Well, be that as it may, I hope you enjoy this volume of *Daytime Shooting Star*.

ME BEFORE MY DEADLINES.

(This is strictly in my own imagination.)

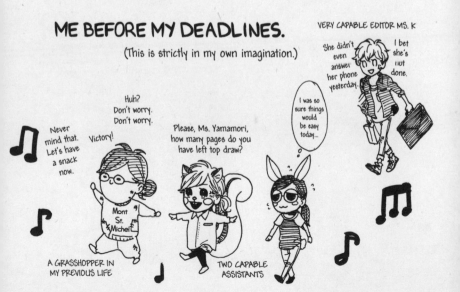

VERY CAPABLE EDITOR MS. K
I bet she's not done.
She didn't even answer her phone yesterday.
I was so sure things would be easy today...
TWO CAPABLE ASSISTANTS
Please, Ms. Yamamori, how many pages do you have left top draw?
Huh? Don't worry. Don't worry.
Victory!
Never mind that. Let's have a snack now.
Mont St. Michel
A GRASSHOPPER IN MY PREVIOUS LIFE

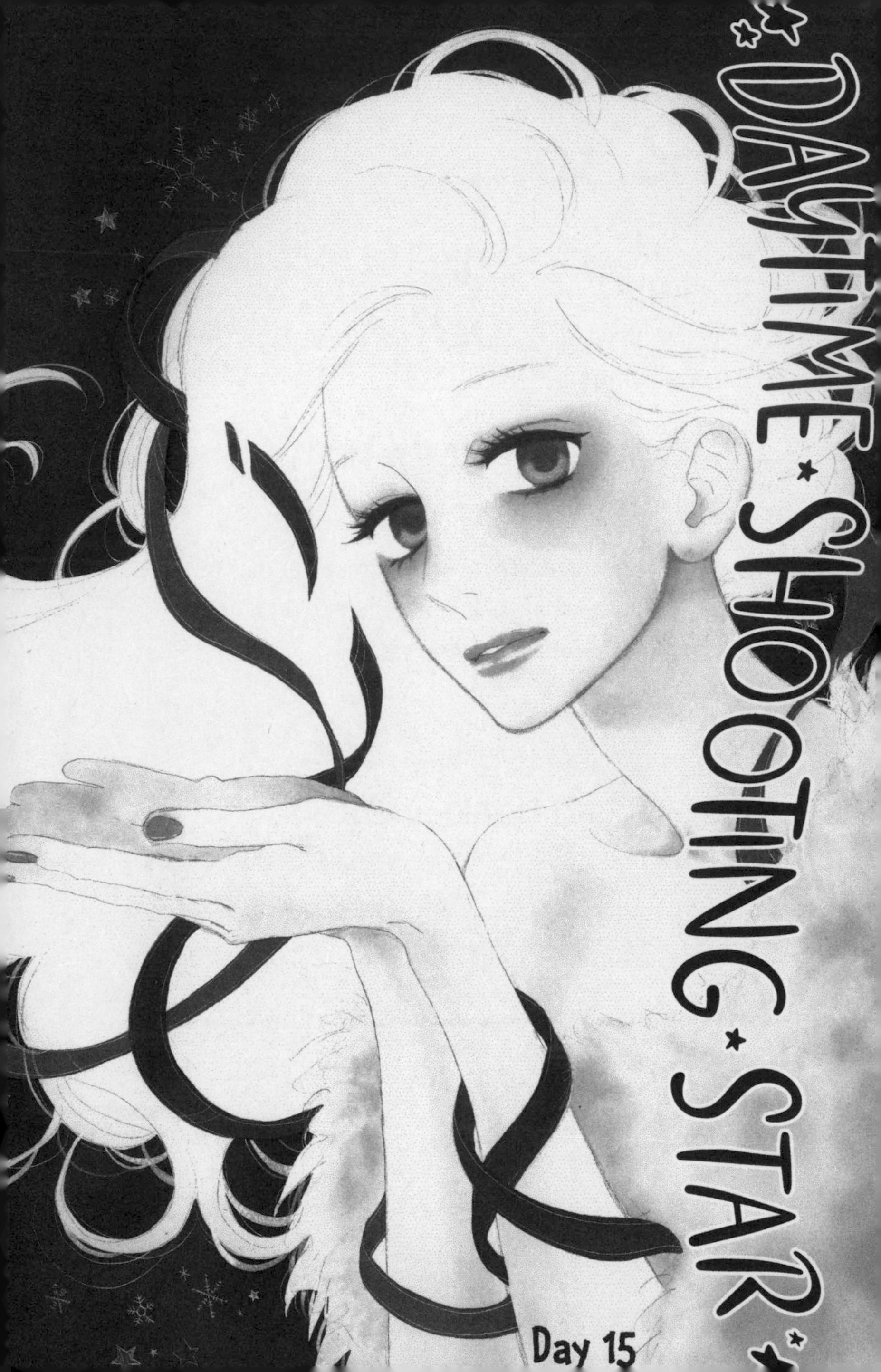
DAYTIME SHOOTING STAR
Day 15

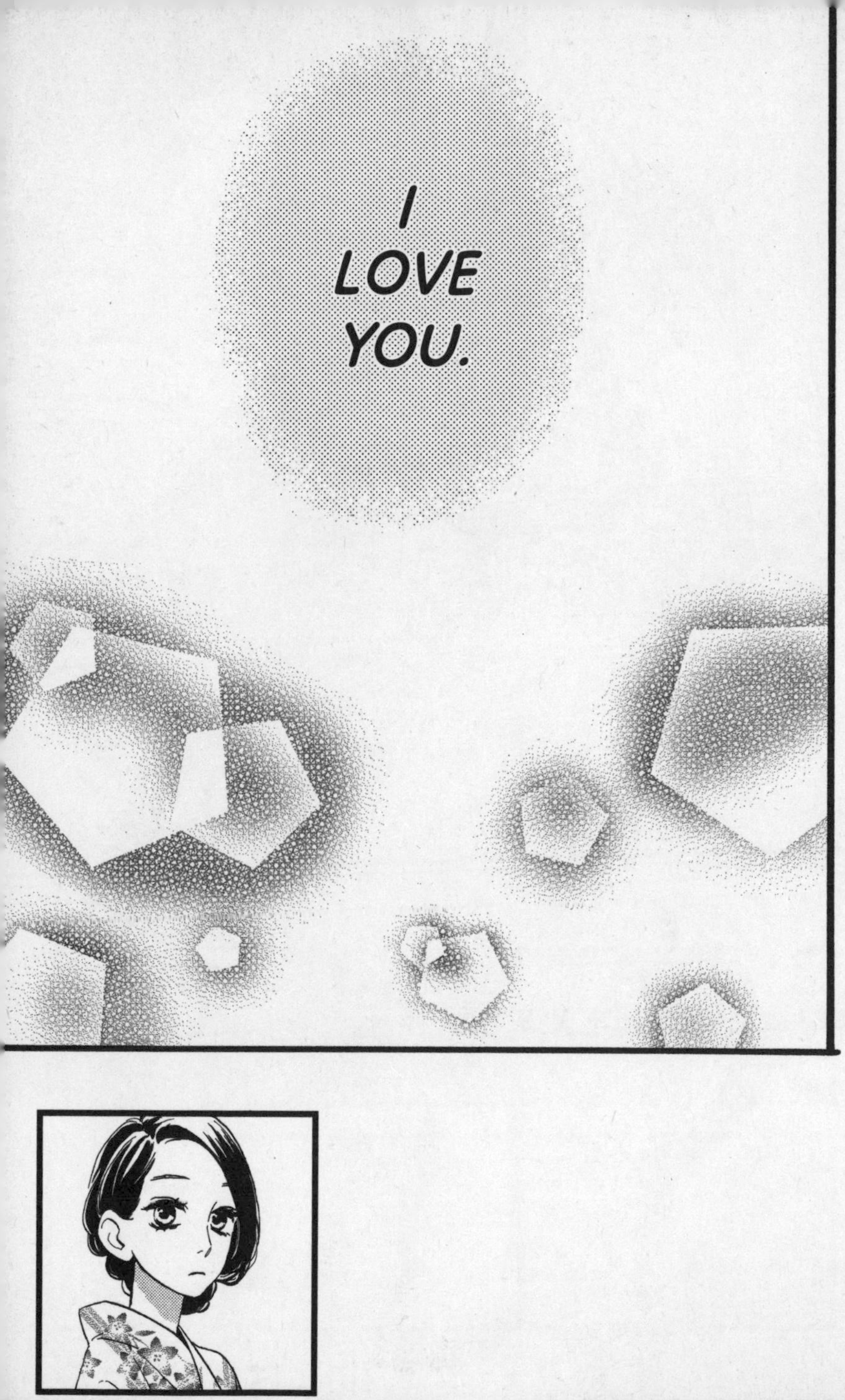
I LOVE YOU.

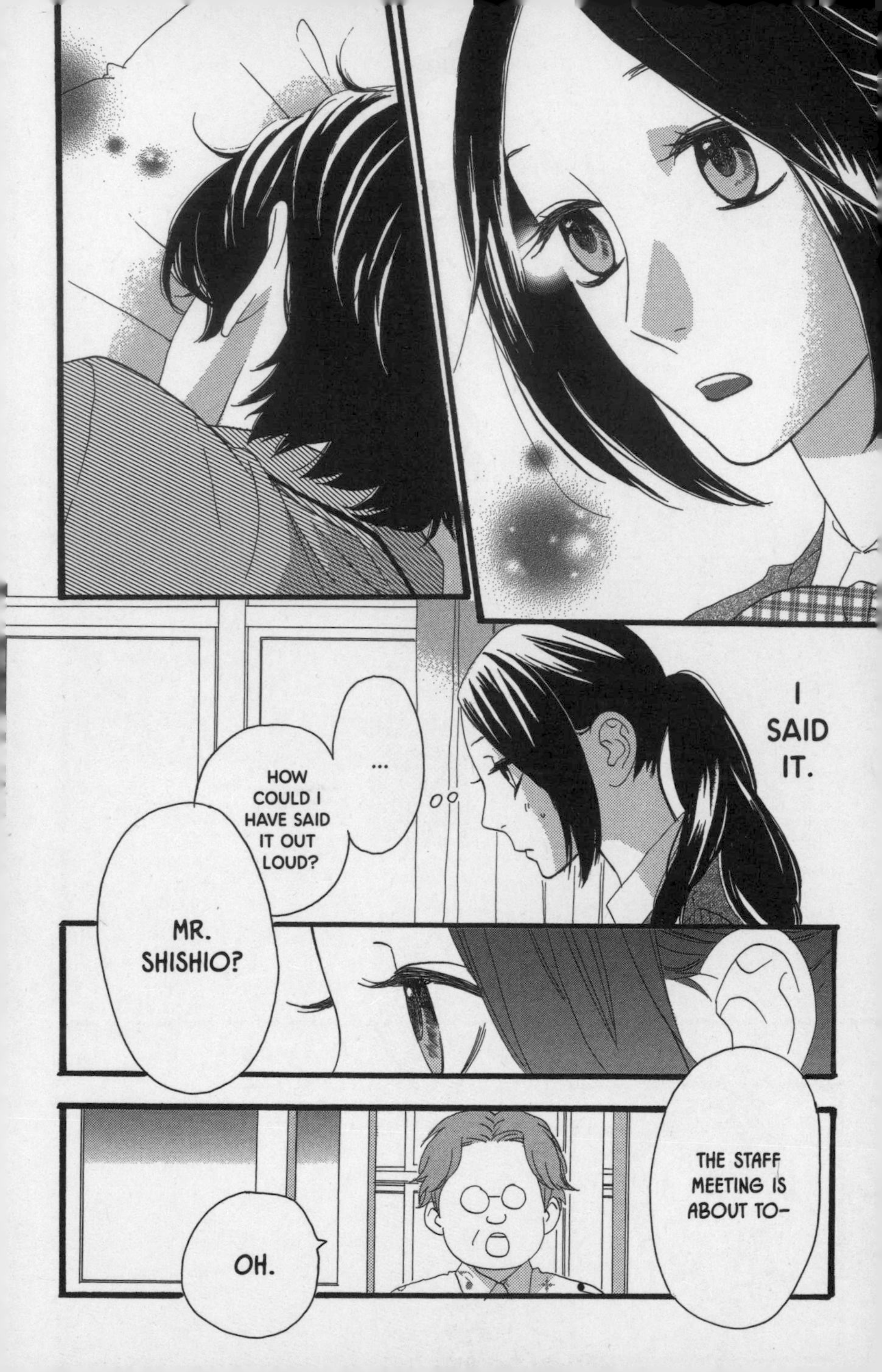
I SAID IT.
...
HOW COULD I HAVE SAID IT OUT LOUD?
MR. SHISHIO?
THE STAFF MEETING IS ABOUT TO–
OH.

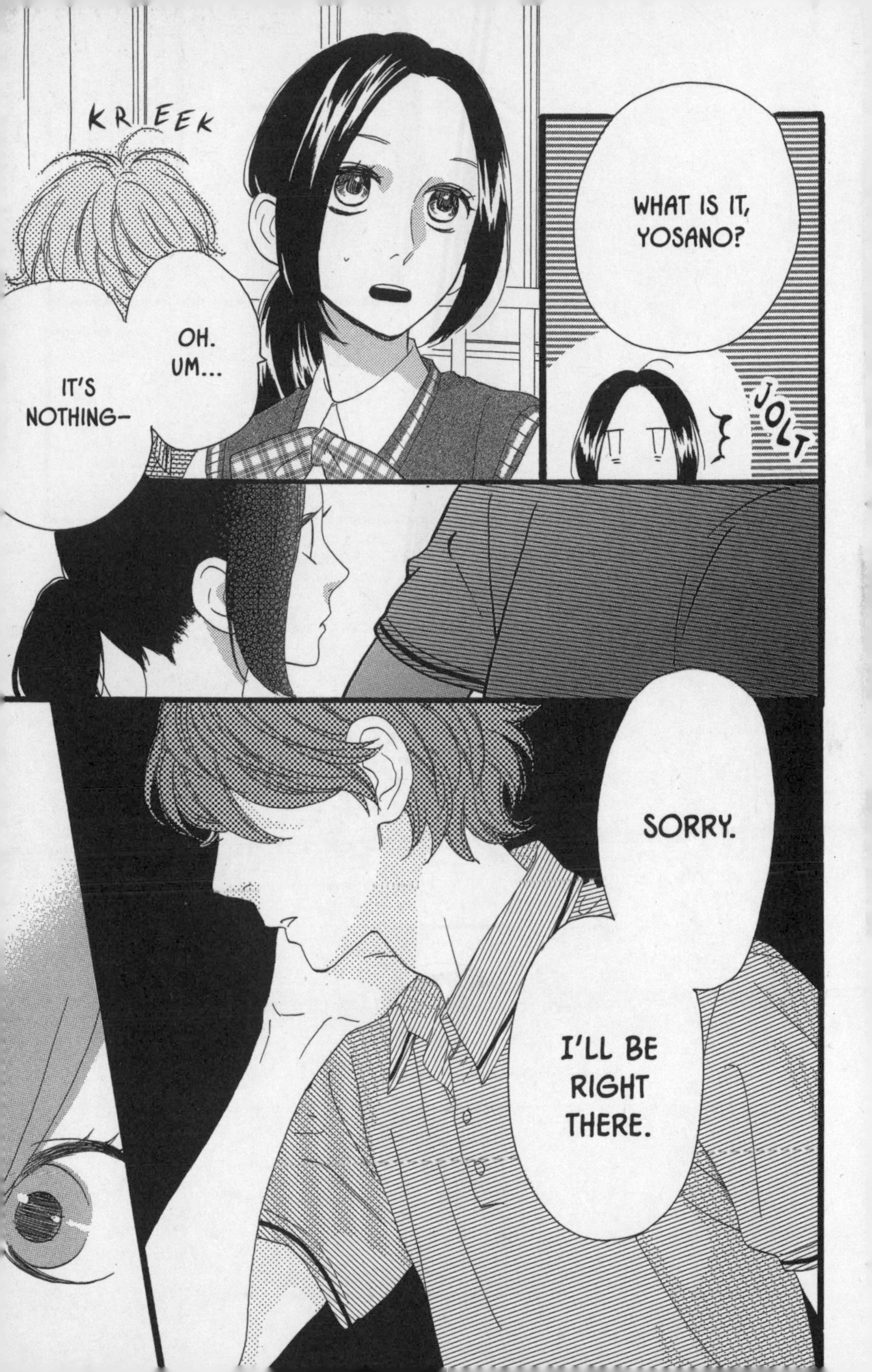
WHAT IS IT, YOSANO?
JOLT
KREEK
OH. UM...
IT'S NOTHING-
SORRY.
I'LL BE RIGHT THERE.

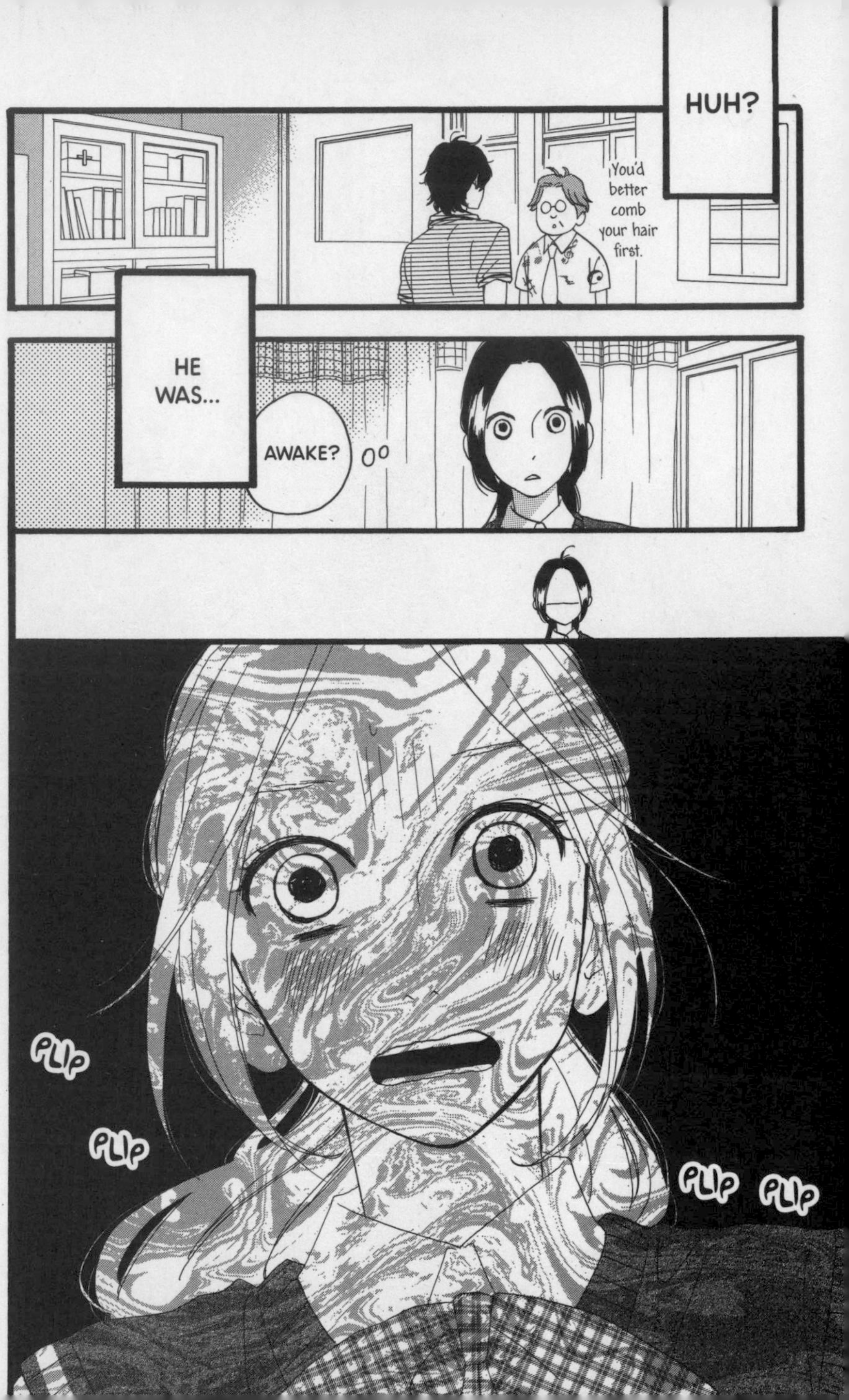
HUH?
You'd better comb your hair first.
HE WAS...
AWAKE?
Oo
PLIP
PLIP
PLIP
PLIP

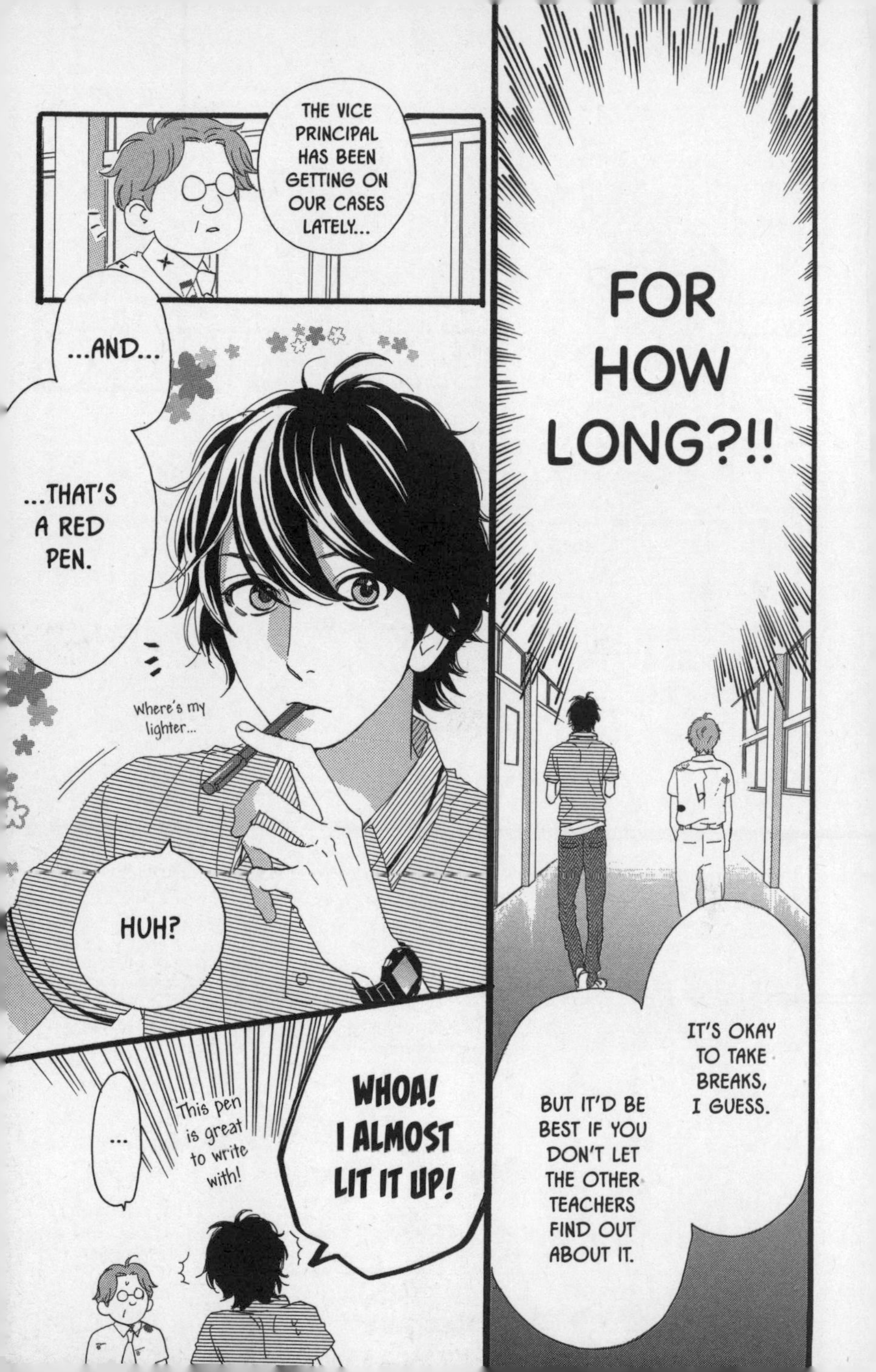

FOR HOW LONG?!!
IT'S OKAY TO TAKE BREAKS, I GUESS.
BUT IT'D BE BEST IF YOU DON'T LET THE OTHER TEACHERS FIND OUT ABOUT IT.
THE VICE PRINCIPAL HAS BEEN GETTING ON OUR CASES LATELY...
...AND...
...THAT'S A RED PEN.
Where's my lighter...
HUH?
WHOA! I ALMOST LIT IT UP!
This pen is great to write with!
...

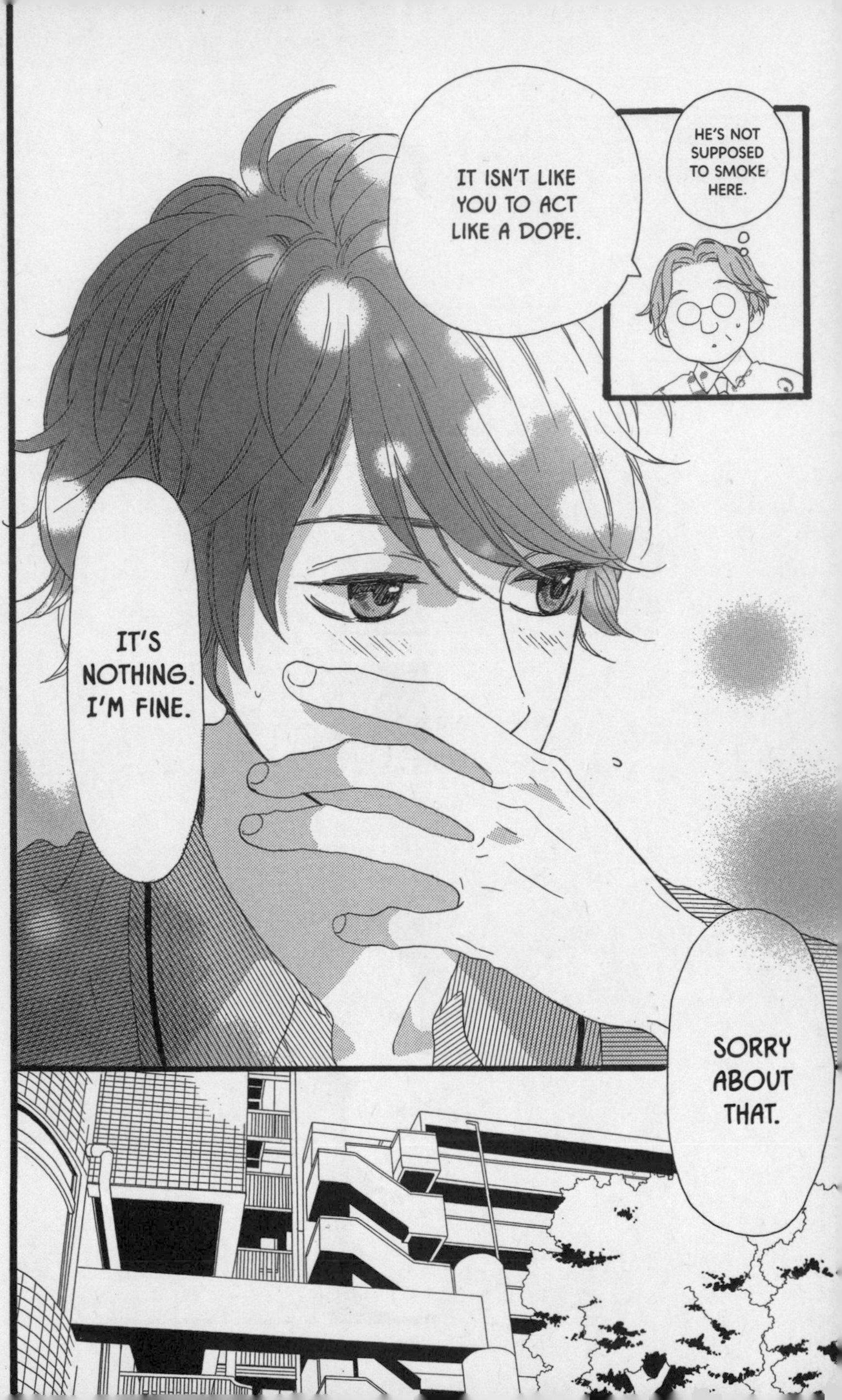
HE'S NOT SUPPOSED TO SMOKE HERE.
IT ISN'T LIKE YOU TO ACT LIKE A DOPE.
IT'S NOTHING. I'M FINE.
SORRY ABOUT THAT.

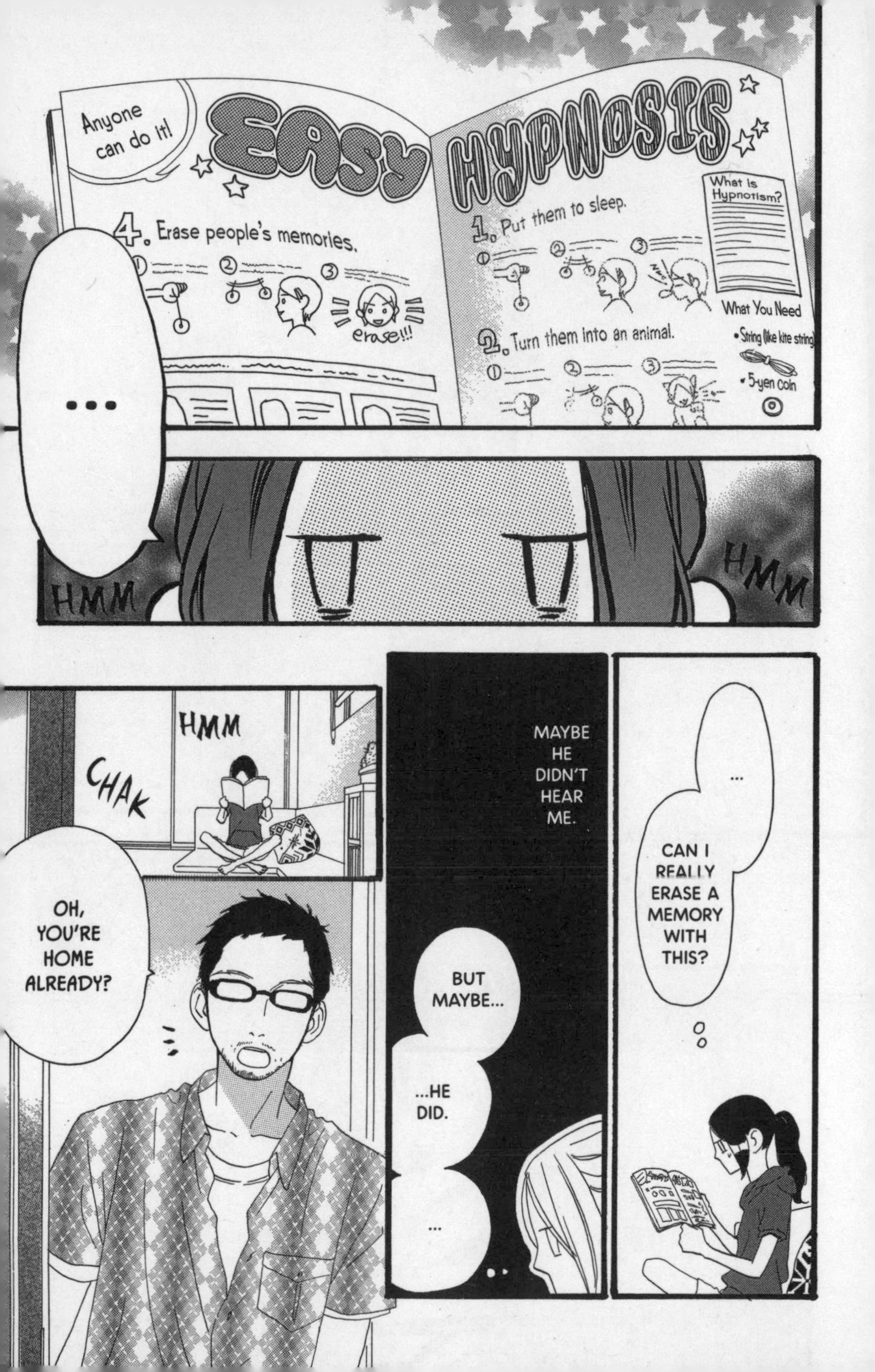
Anyone can do it!
EASY HYPNOSIS
What Is Hypnotism?
1. Put them to sleep.
2. Turn them into an animal.
What You Need
•String (like kite string)
•5-yen coin
4. Erase people's memories.
erase!!!
...
HMM
HMM
...
CAN I REALLY ERASE A MEMORY WITH THIS?
MAYBE HE DIDN'T HEAR ME.
BUT MAYBE...
...HE DID.
...
HMM
CHAK
OH, YOU'RE HOME ALREADY?

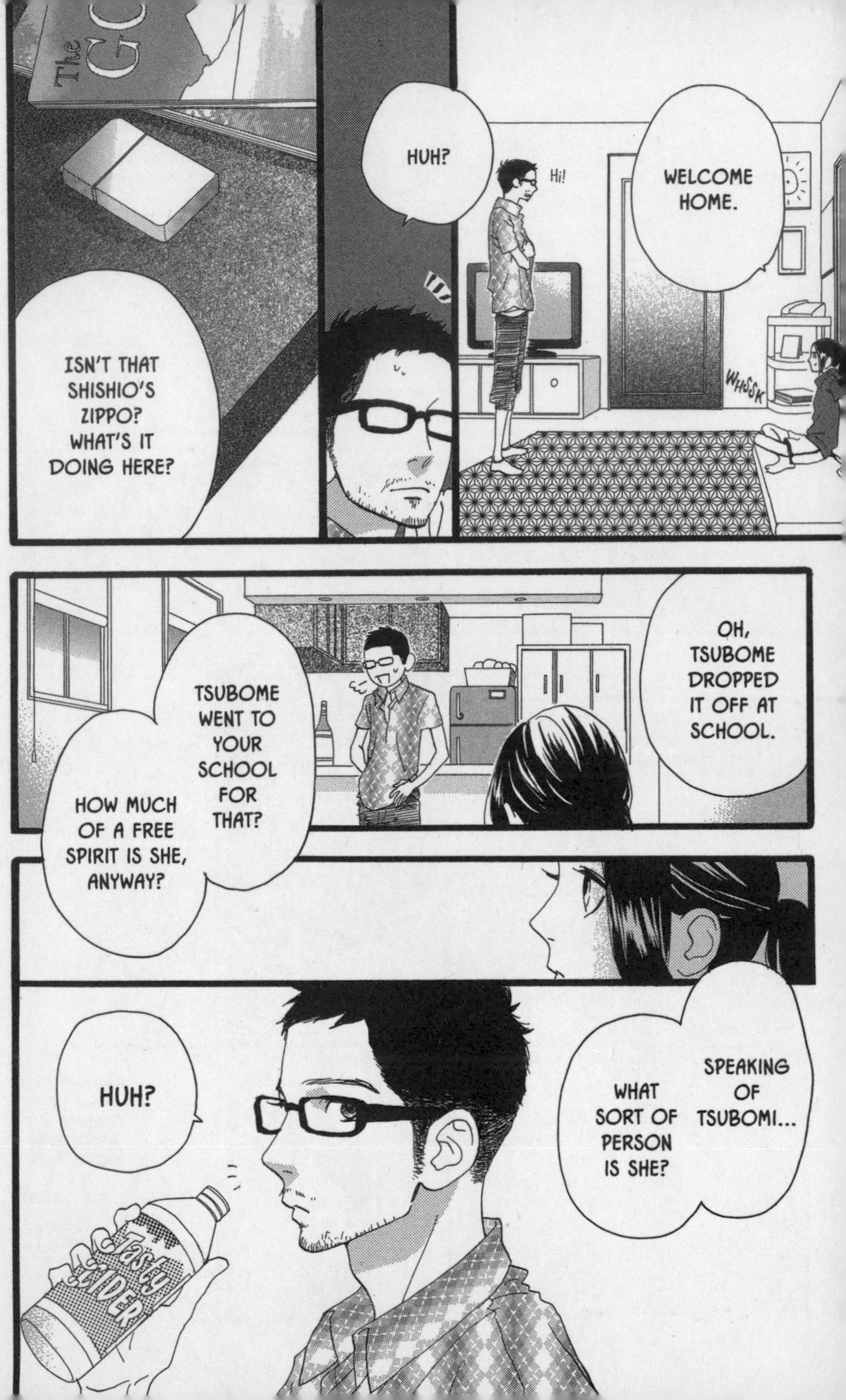
WELCOME HOME.
Hi!
WHSSK
HUH?
ISN'T THAT SHISHIO'S ZIPPO? WHAT'S IT DOING HERE?
OH, TSUBOME DROPPED IT OFF AT SCHOOL.
TSUBOME WENT TO YOUR SCHOOL FOR THAT?
HOW MUCH OF A FREE SPIRIT IS SHE, ANYWAY?
SPEAKING OF TSUBOMI...
WHAT SORT OF PERSON IS SHE?
HUH?
Tasty CIDER

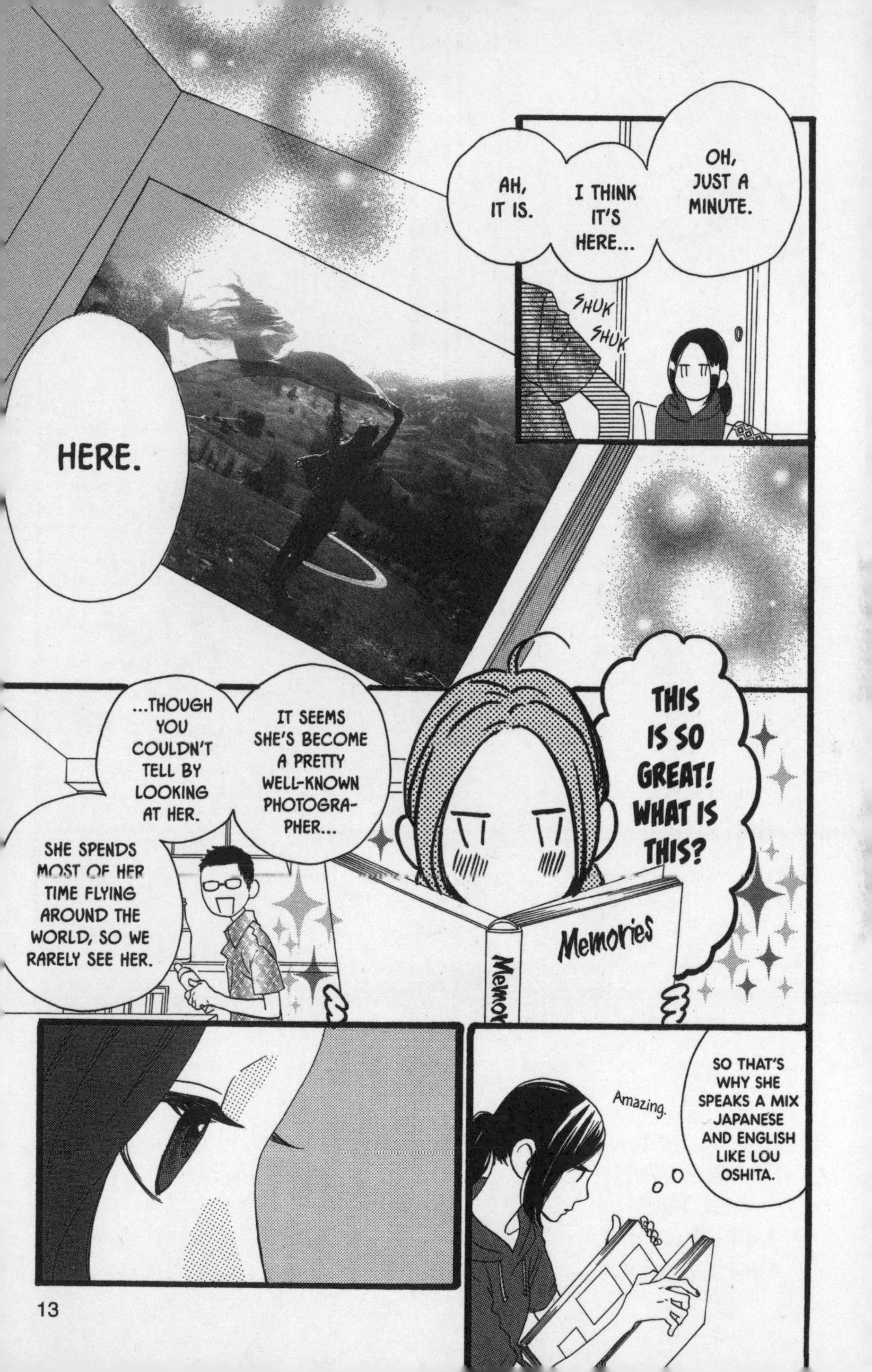
OH, JUST A MINUTE.
I THINK IT'S HERE...
AH, IT IS.
SHUK SHUK
HERE.
THIS IS SO GREAT! WHAT IS THIS?
Memories
Memor
IT SEEMS SHE'S BECOME A PRETTY WELL-KNOWN PHOTOGRAPHER...
...THOUGH YOU COULDN'T TELL BY LOOKING AT HER.
SHE SPENDS MOST OF HER TIME FLYING AROUND THE WORLD, SO WE RARELY SEE HER.
SO THAT'S WHY SHE SPEAKS A MIX JAPANESE AND ENGLISH LIKE LOU OSHITA.
Amazing.

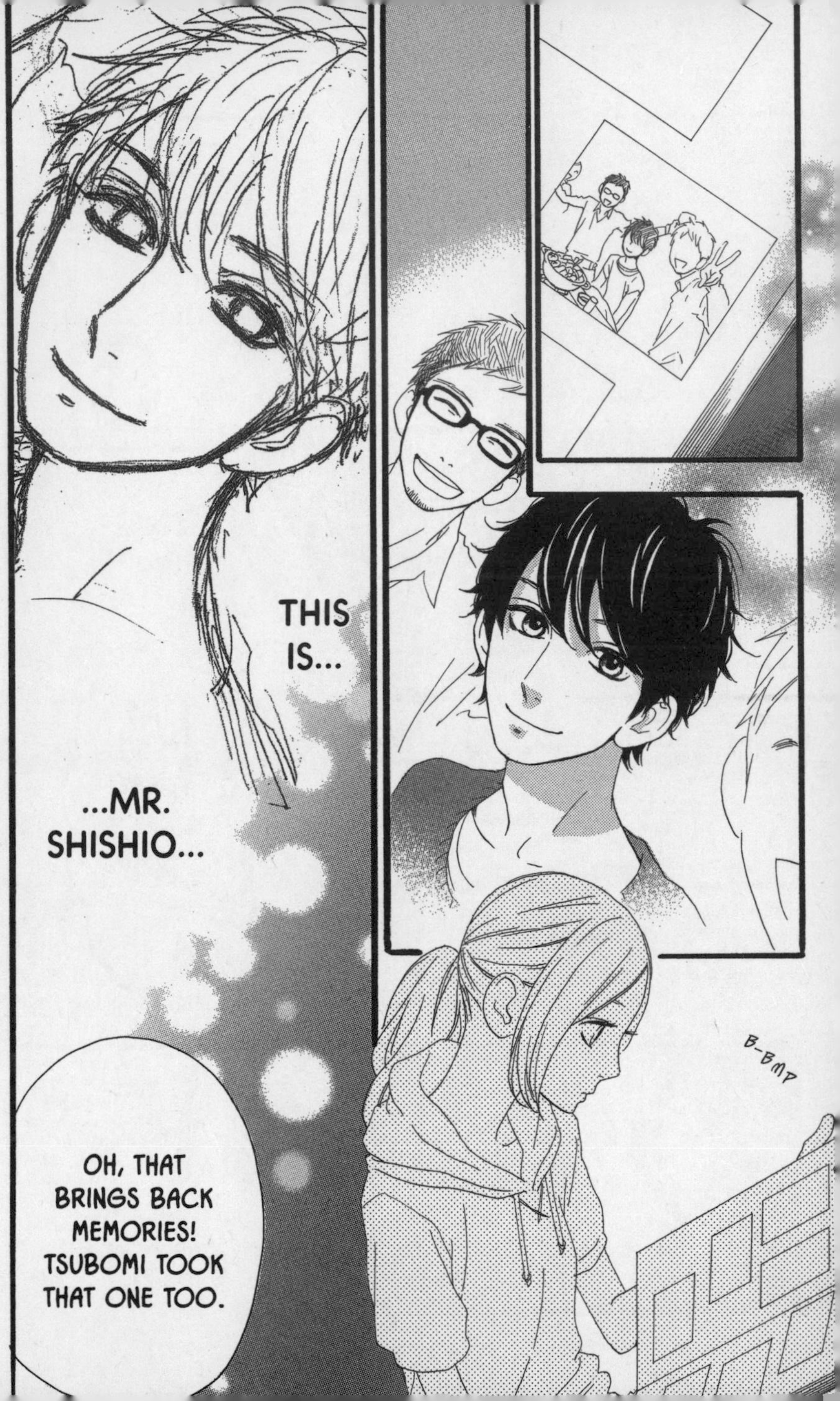
B-BMP
THIS IS...
...MR. SHISHIO...
OH, THAT BRINGS BACK MEMORIES! TSUBOMI TOOK THAT ONE TOO.

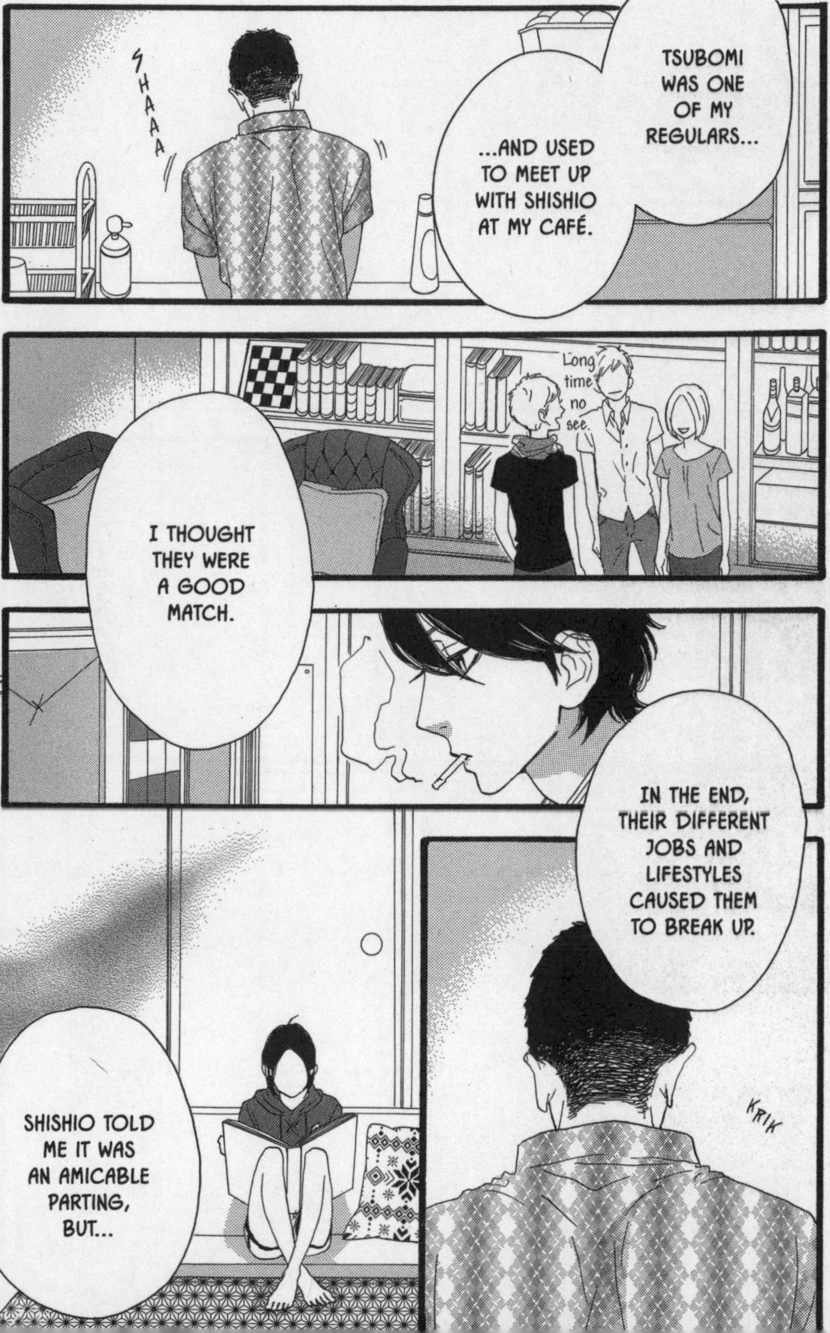
TSUBOMI WAS ONE OF MY REGULARS...
...AND USED TO MEET UP WITH SHISHIO AT MY CAFÉ.
SHAAAA
Long time no see.
I THOUGHT THEY WERE A GOOD MATCH.
IN THE END, THEIR DIFFERENT JOBS AND LIFESTYLES CAUSED THEM TO BREAK UP.
KRIK
SHISHIO TOLD ME IT WAS AN AMICABLE PARTING, BUT...

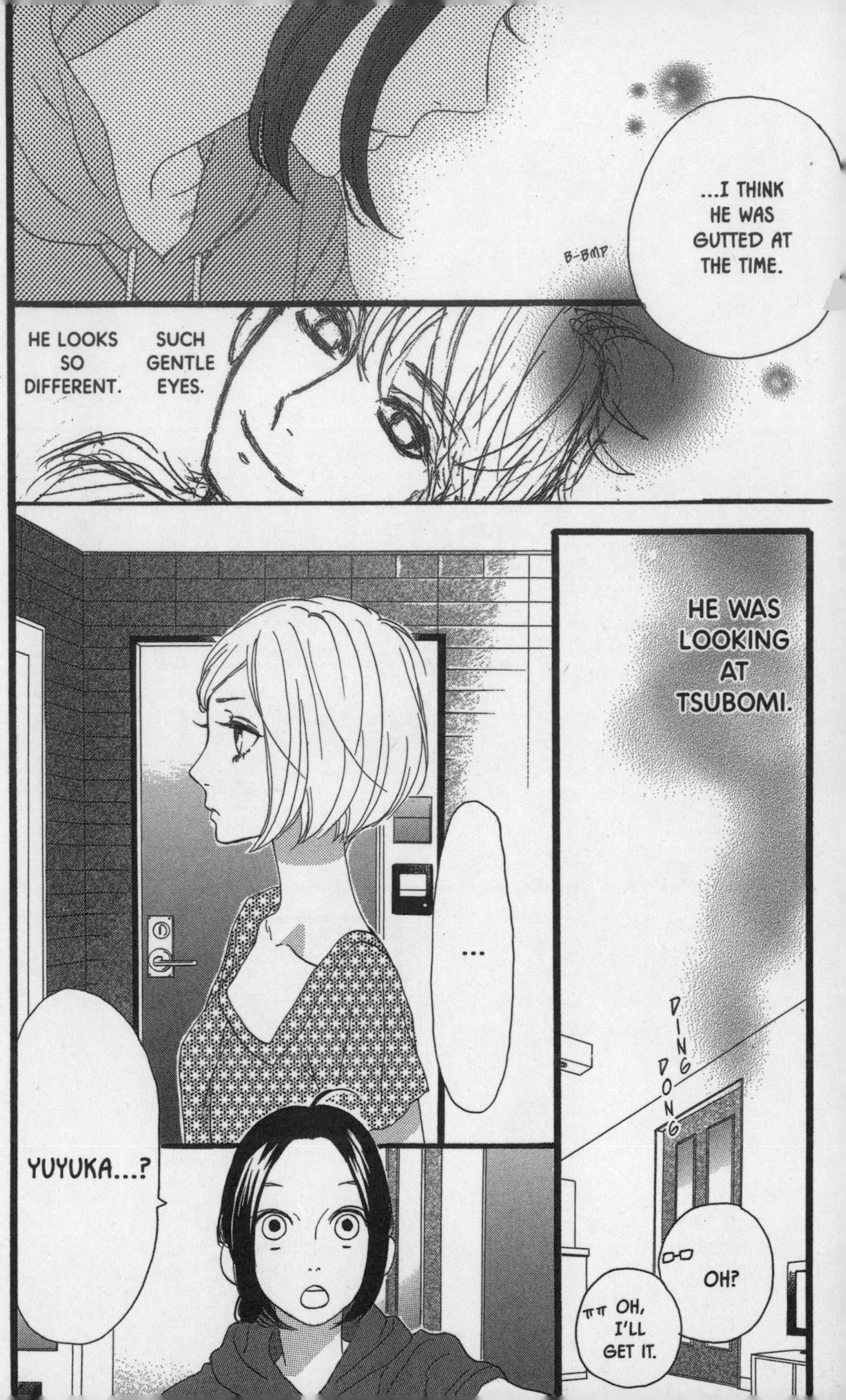
...I THINK HE WAS GUTTED AT THE TIME.
B-BMP
SUCH GENTLE EYES.
HE LOOKS SO DIFFERENT.
HE WAS LOOKING AT TSUBOMI.
DING DONG
OH?
OH, I'LL GET IT.
...
YUYUKA...?

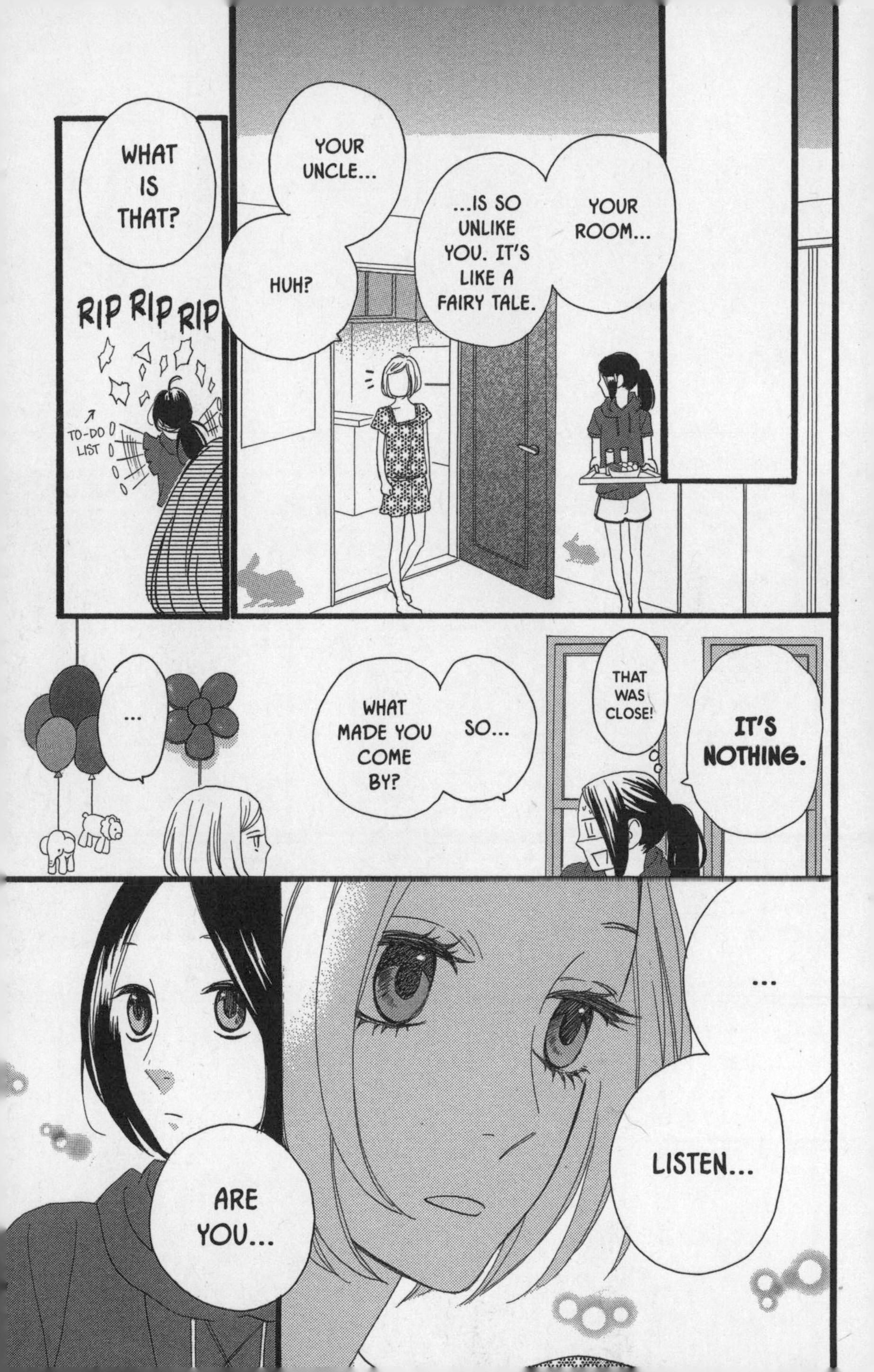
YOUR ROOM...
...IS SO UNLIKE YOU. IT'S LIKE A FAIRY TALE.
YOUR UNCLE...
HUH?
WHAT IS THAT?
RIP RIP RIP
TO-DO LIST
IT'S NOTHING.
THAT WAS CLOSE!
SO...
WHAT MADE YOU COME BY?
...
...
LISTEN...
ARE YOU...

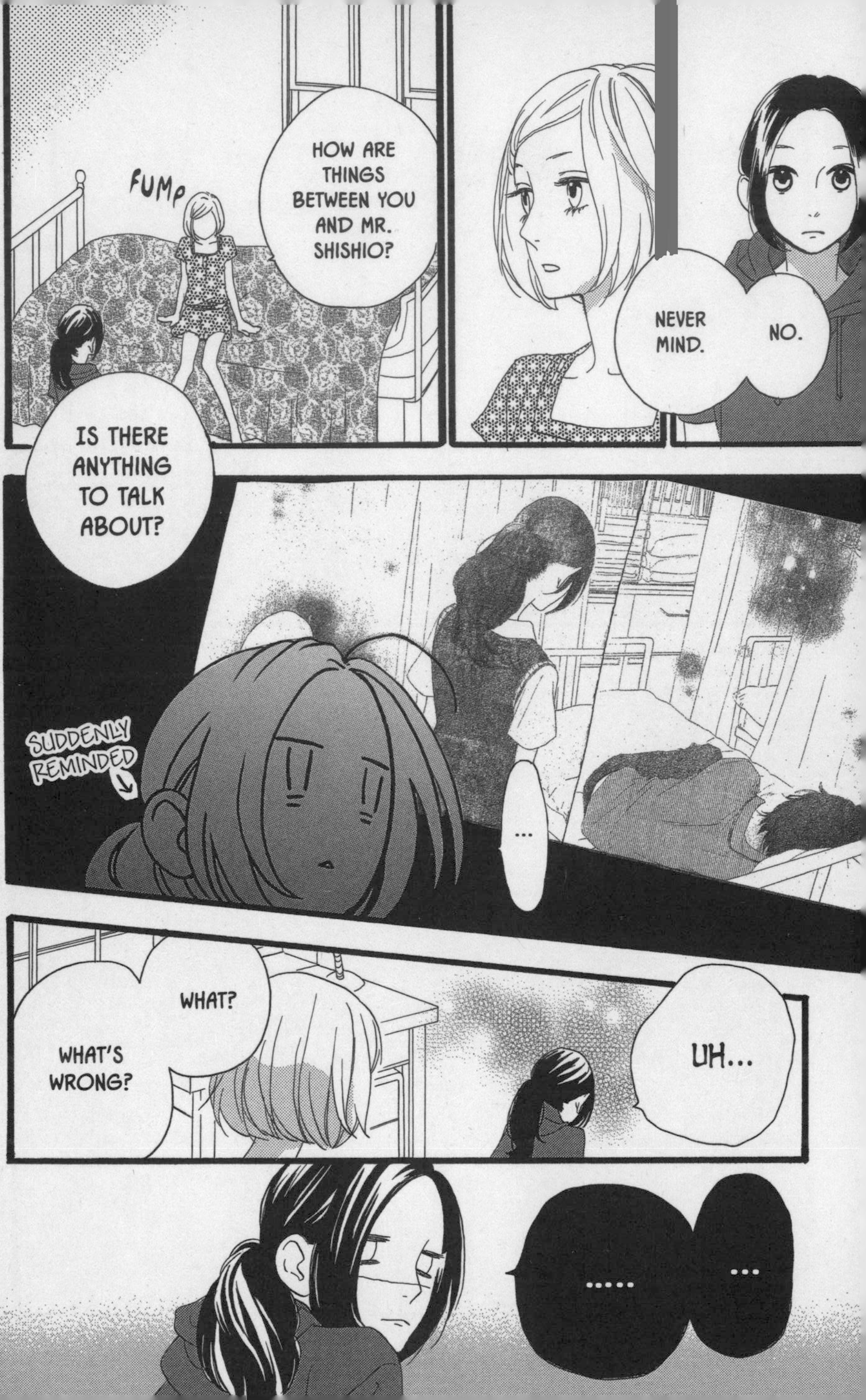
NO.
NEVER MIND.
FUMP
HOW ARE THINGS BETWEEN YOU AND MR. SHISHIO?
IS THERE ANYTHING TO TALK ABOUT?
SUDDENLY REMINDED
...
UH...
WHAT?
WHAT'S WRONG?
...
......

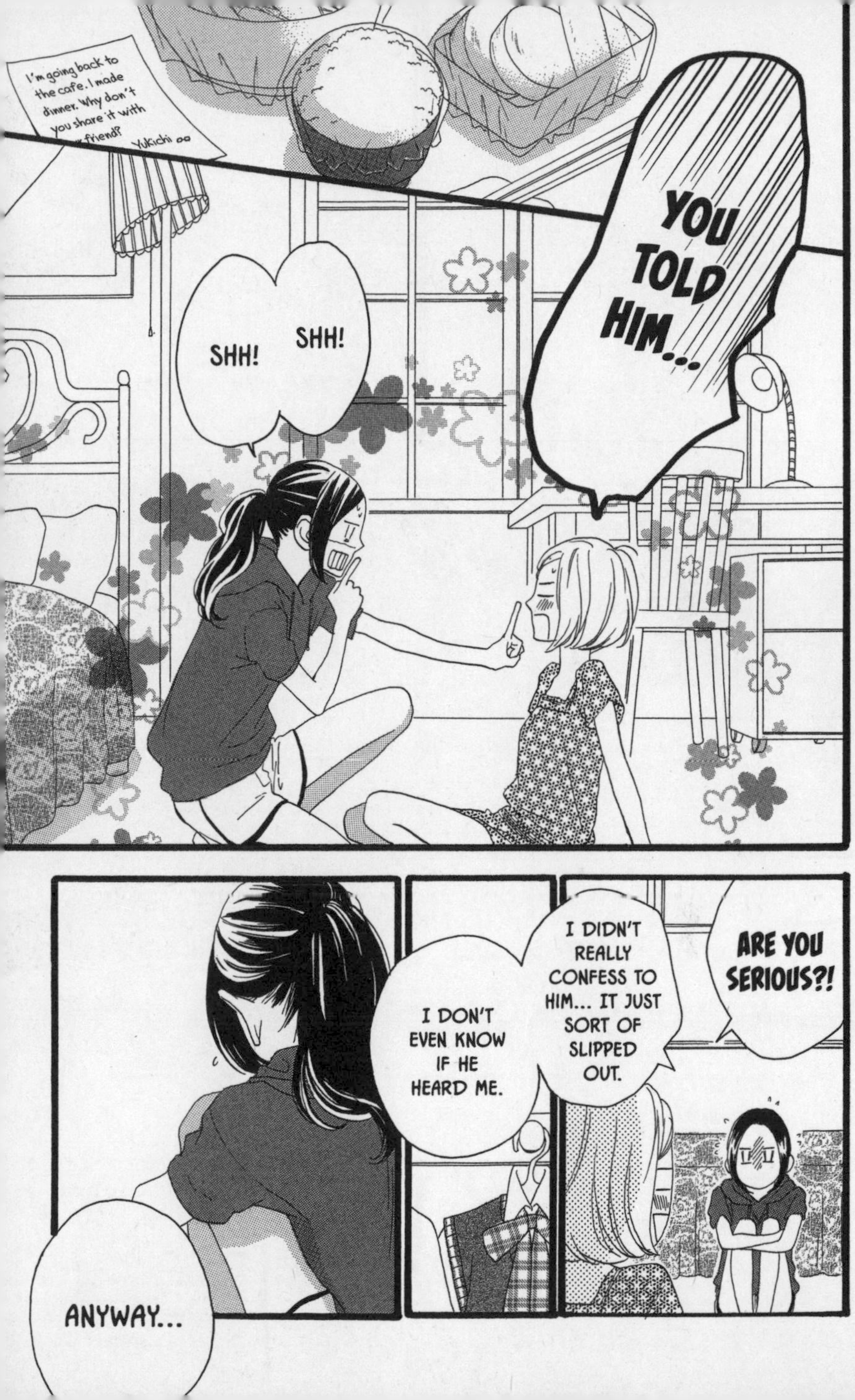
I'm going back to the cafe. I made dinner. Why don't you share it with
friend?
Yukichi
YOU TOLD HIM...
SHH!
SHH!
ARE YOU SERIOUS?!
I DIDN'T REALLY CONFESS TO HIM... IT JUST SORT OF SLIPPED OUT.
I DON'T EVEN KNOW IF HE HEARD ME.
ANYWAY...

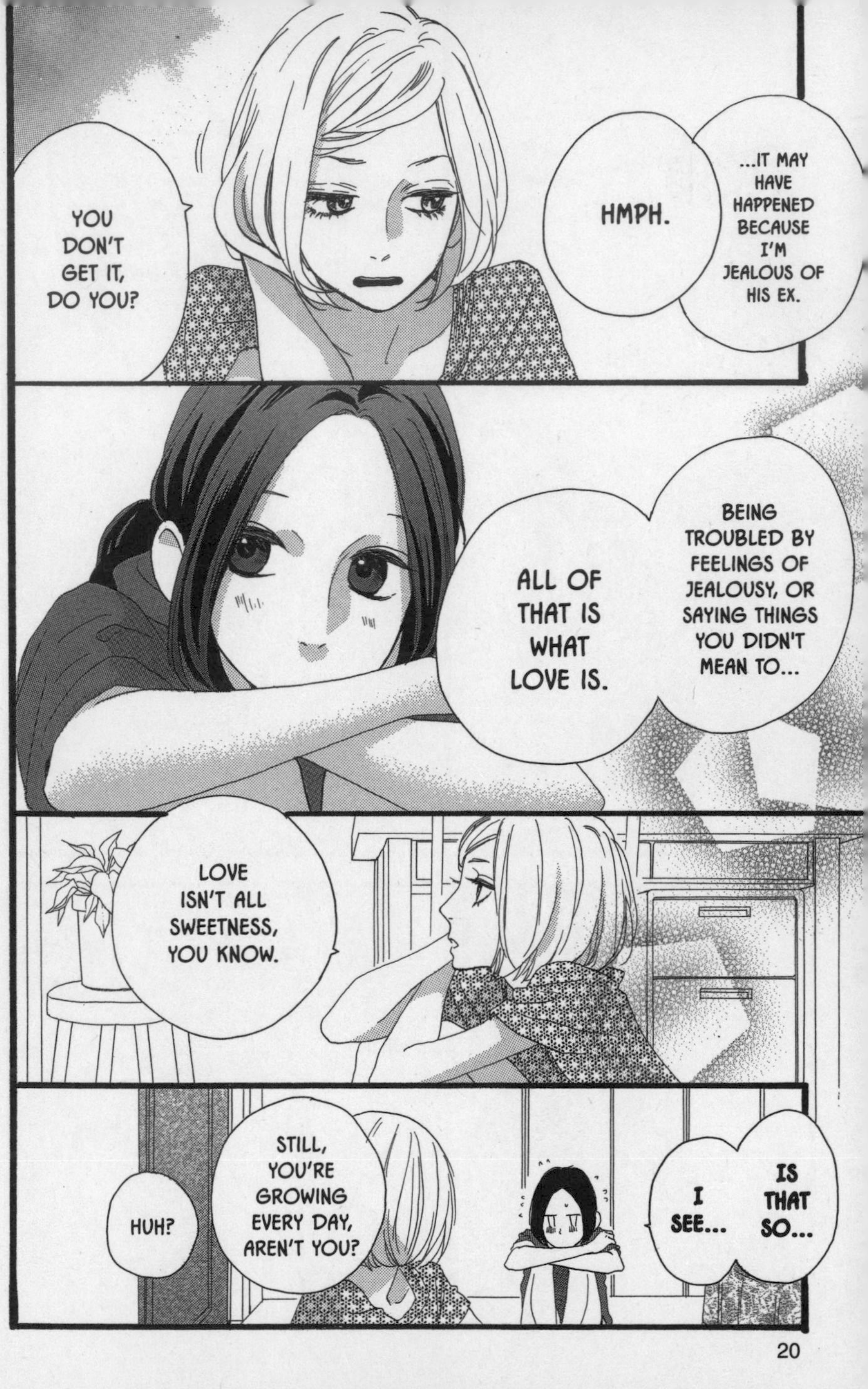
...IT MAY HAVE HAPPENED BECAUSE I'M JEALOUS OF HIS EX.
HMPH.
YOU DON'T GET IT, DO YOU?
BEING TROUBLED BY FEELINGS OF JEALOUSY, OR SAYING THINGS YOU DIDN'T MEAN TO...
ALL OF THAT IS WHAT LOVE IS.
LOVE ISN'T ALL SWEETNESS, YOU KNOW.
IS THAT SO...
I SEE...
STILL, YOU'RE GROWING EVERY DAY, AREN'T YOU?
HUH?

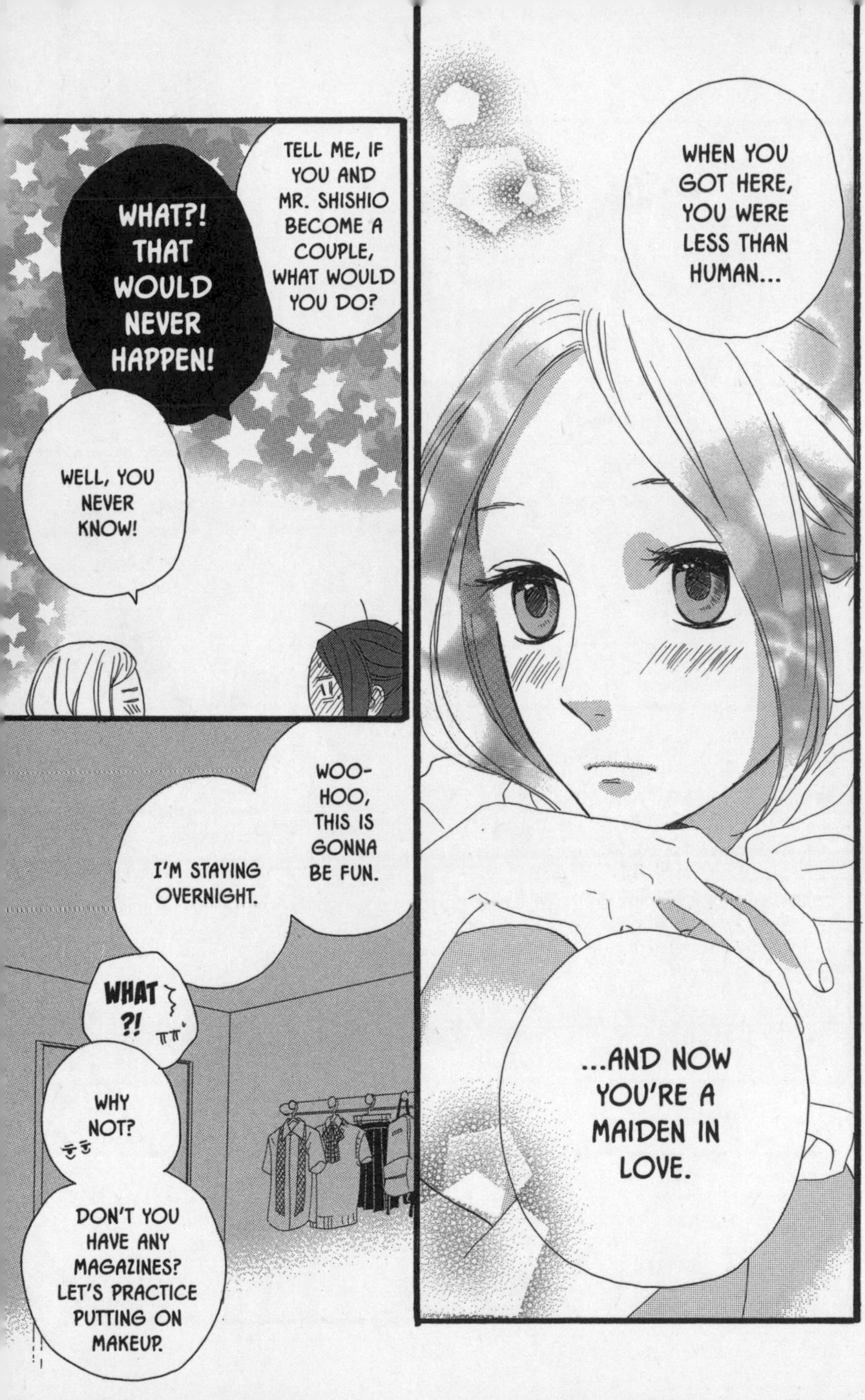
WHEN YOU GOT HERE, YOU WERE LESS THAN HUMAN...
...AND NOW YOU'RE A MAIDEN IN LOVE.
TELL ME, IF YOU AND MR. SHISHIO BECOME A COUPLE, WHAT WOULD YOU DO?
WHAT?! THAT WOULD NEVER HAPPEN!
WELL, YOU NEVER KNOW!
WOO-HOO, THIS IS GONNA BE FUN.
I'M STAYING OVERNIGHT.
WHAT?!
WHY NOT?
DON'T YOU HAVE ANY MAGAZINES? LET'S PRACTICE PUTTING ON MAKEUP.

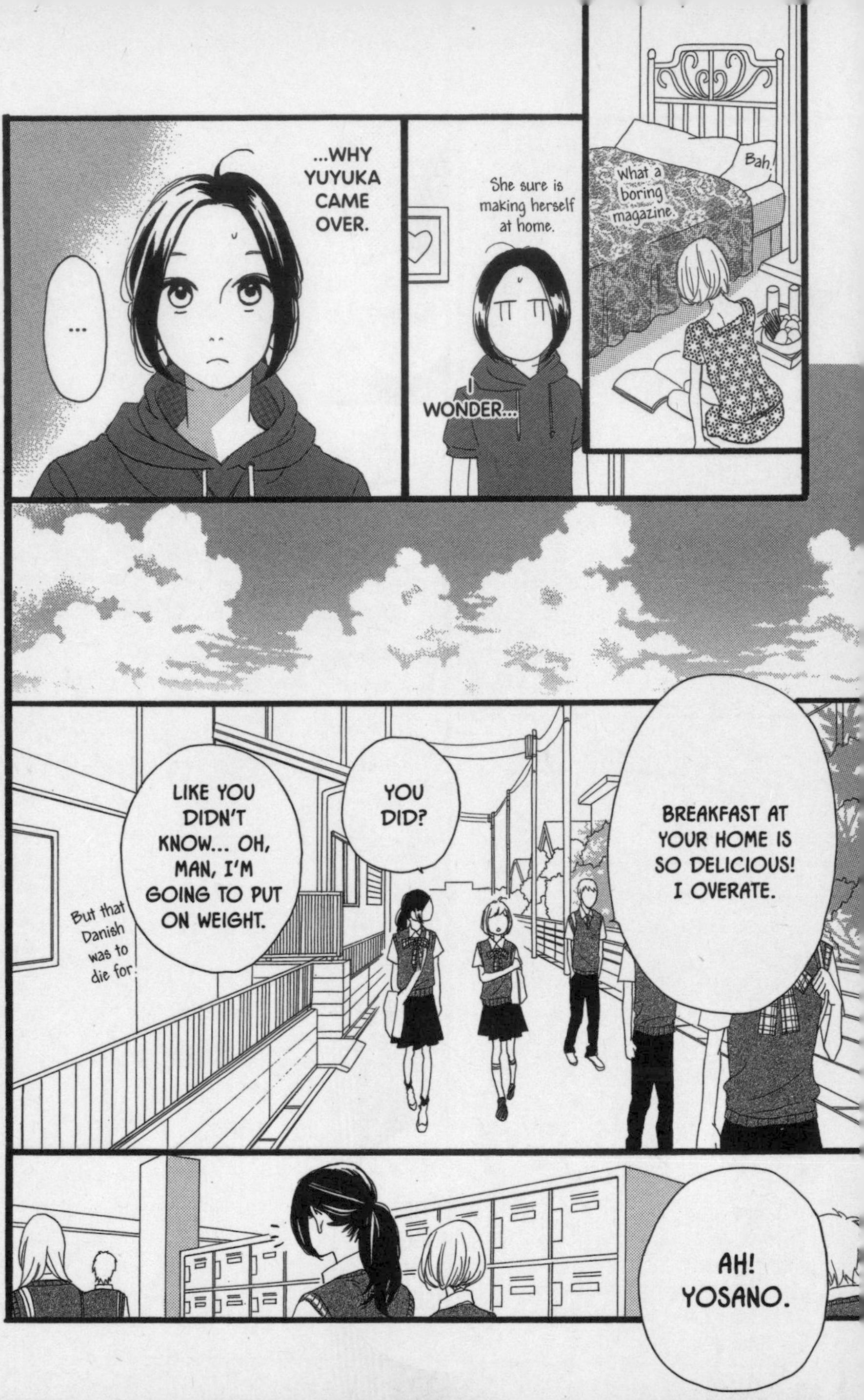
Bah.
What a boring magazine.
She sure is making herself at home.
I WONDER...
...WHY YUYUKA CAME OVER.
...
BREAKFAST AT YOUR HOME IS SO DELICIOUS! I OVERATE.
YOU DID?
LIKE YOU DIDN'T KNOW... OH, MAN, I'M GOING TO PUT ON WEIGHT.
But that Danish was to die for.
AH! YOSANO.

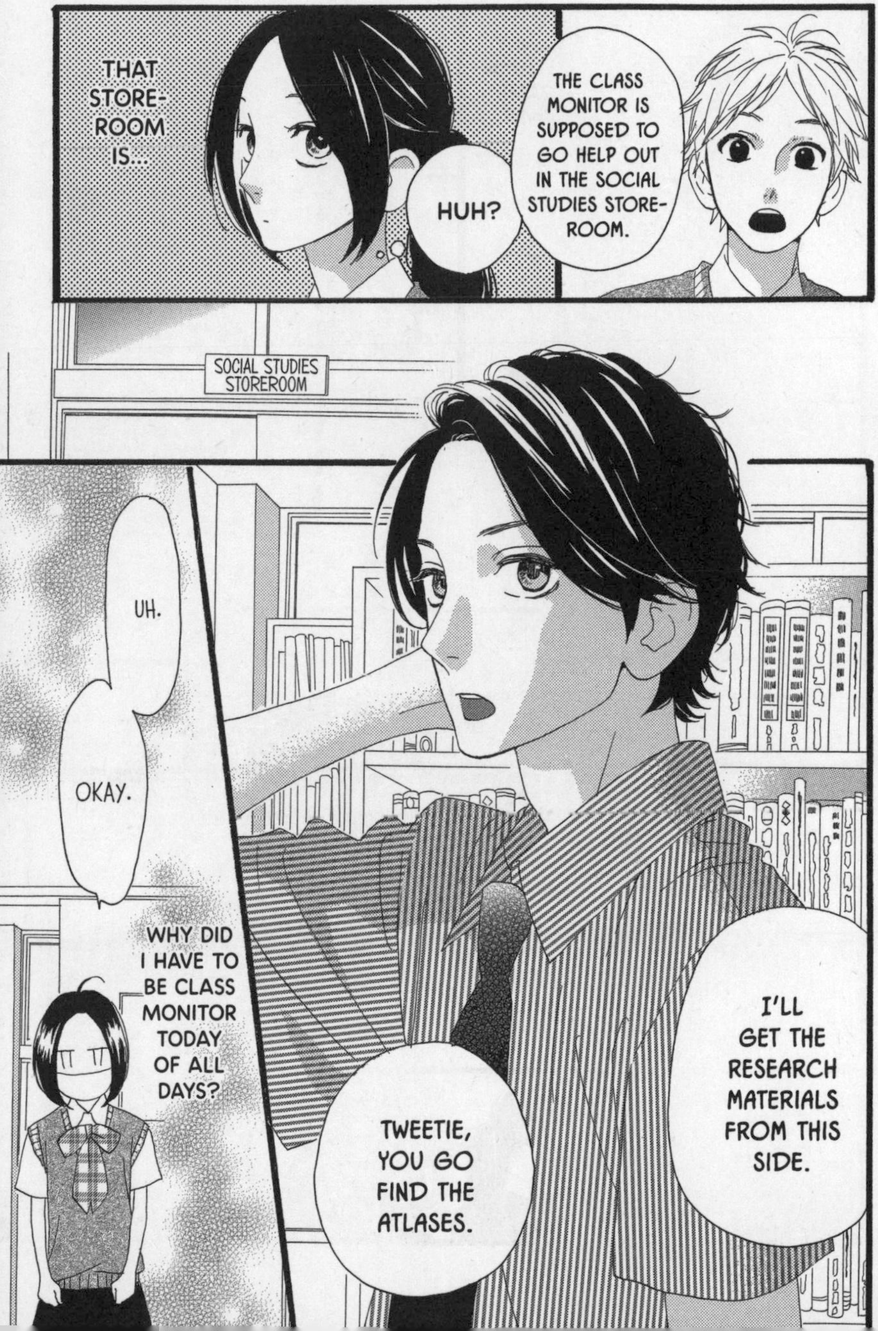
THE CLASS MONITOR IS SUPPOSED TO GO HELP OUT IN THE SOCIAL STUDIES STORE-ROOM.
HUH?
THAT STORE-ROOM IS...
SOCIAL STUDIES STOREROOM
I'LL GET THE RESEARCH MATERIALS FROM THIS SIDE.
TWEETIE, YOU GO FIND THE ATLASES.
UH.
OKAY.
WHY DID I HAVE TO BE CLASS MONITOR TODAY OF ALL DAYS?

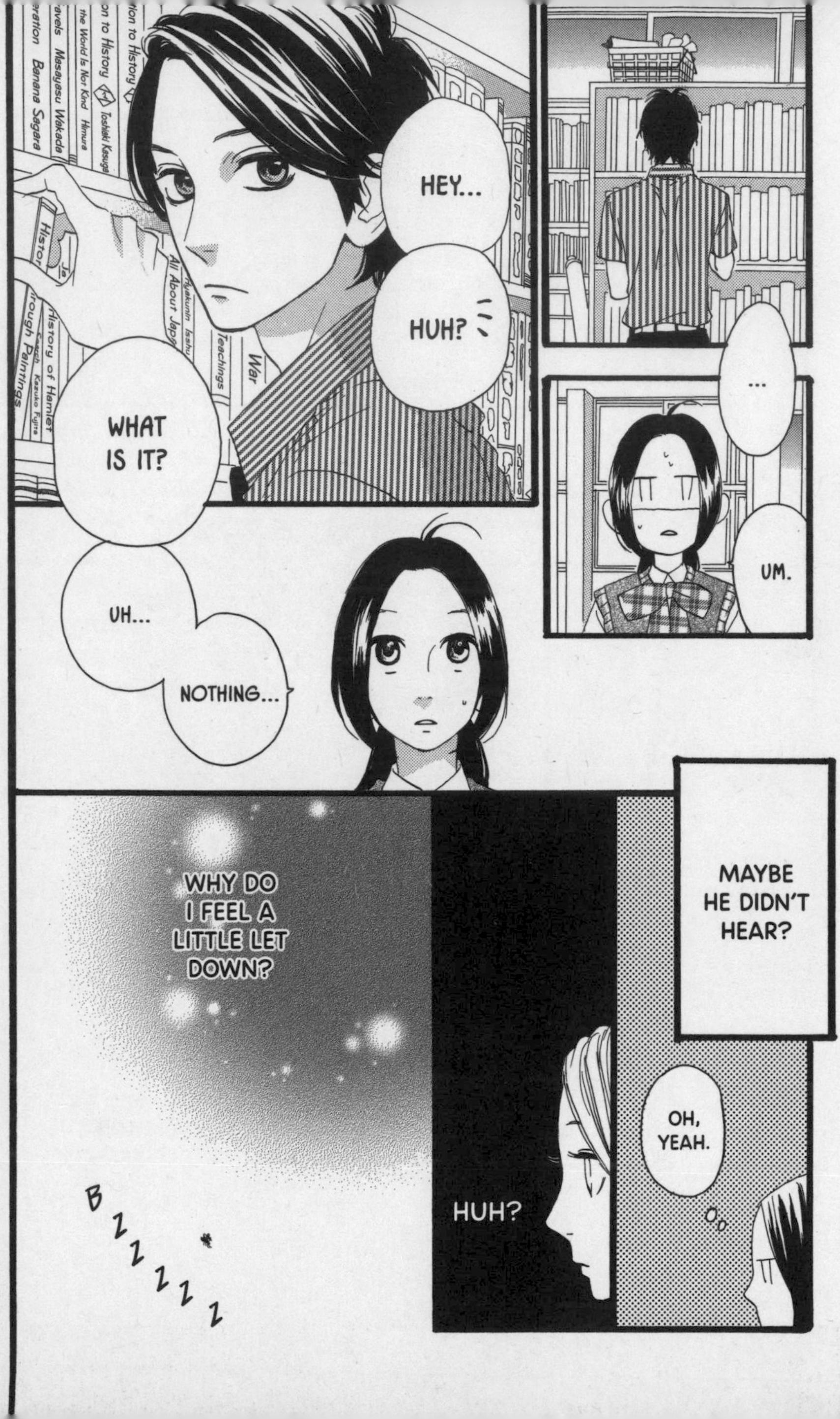
...
UM.
HEY...
HUH?
WHAT IS IT?
UH...
NOTHING...
MAYBE HE DIDN'T HEAR?
OH, YEAH.
HUH?
WHY DO I FEEL A LITTLE LET DOWN?
BZZZZZZ

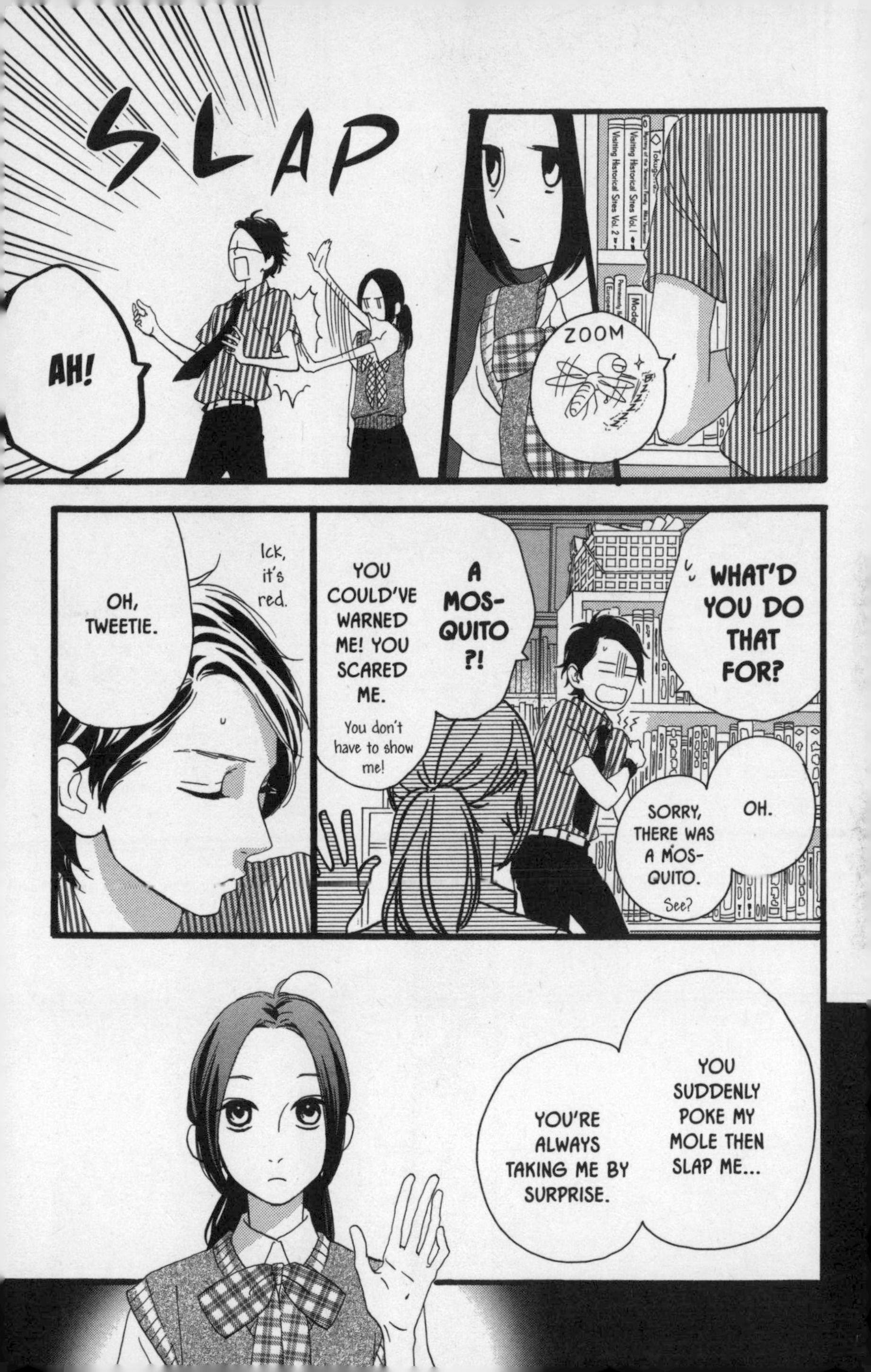
Visiting Historical Sites Vol. 1
Visiting Historical Sites Vol. 2
ZOOM
SLAP
AH!
WHAT'D YOU DO THAT FOR?
SORRY, THERE WAS A MOS-QUITO.
See?
OH.
A MOS-QUITO ?!
YOU COULD'VE WARNED ME! YOU SCARED ME.
You don't have to show me!
Ick, it's red.
OH, TWEETIE.
YOU SUDDENLY POKE MY MOLE THEN SLAP ME...
YOU'RE ALWAYS TAKING ME BY SURPRISE.

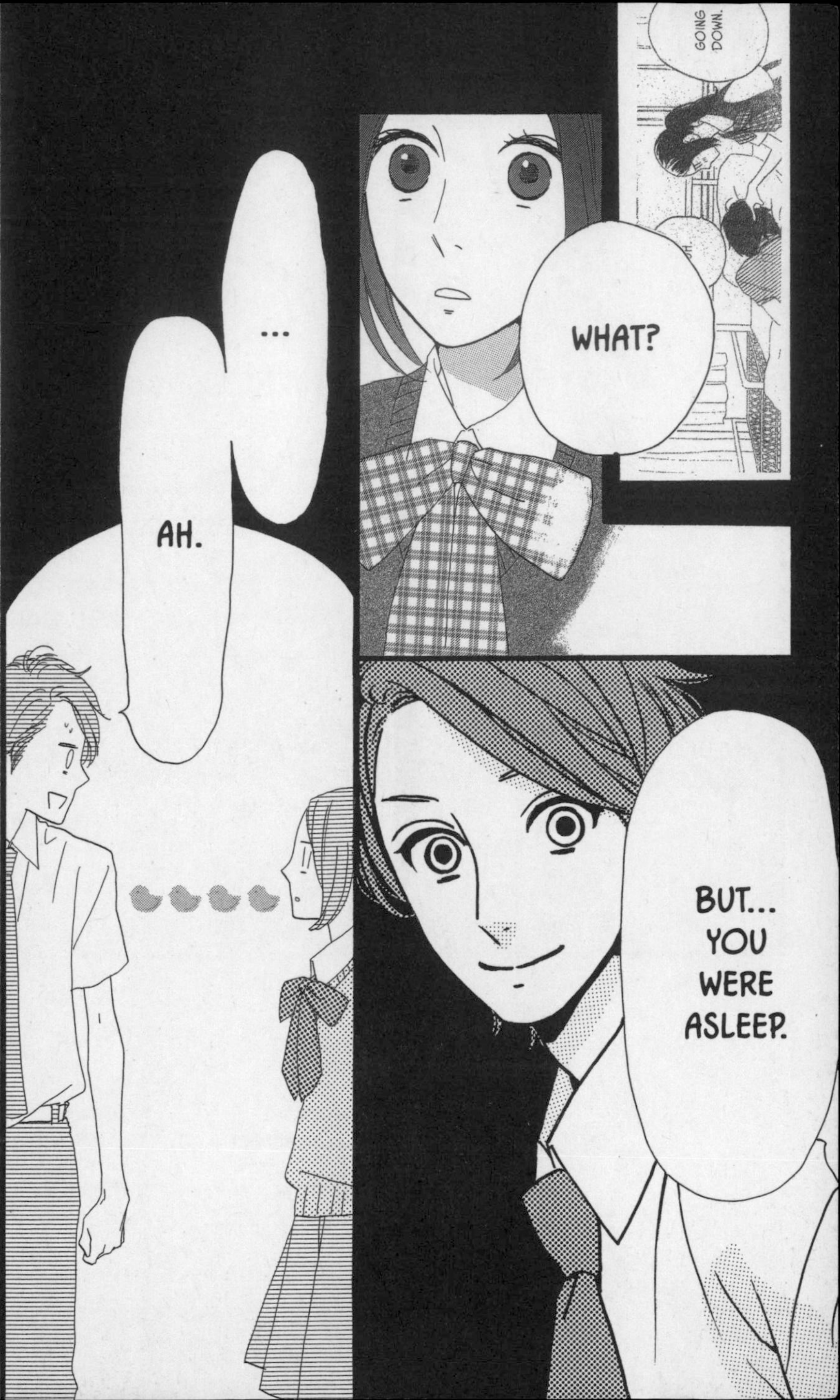
GOING DOWN.
WHAT?
BUT... YOU WERE ASLEEP.
...
AH.

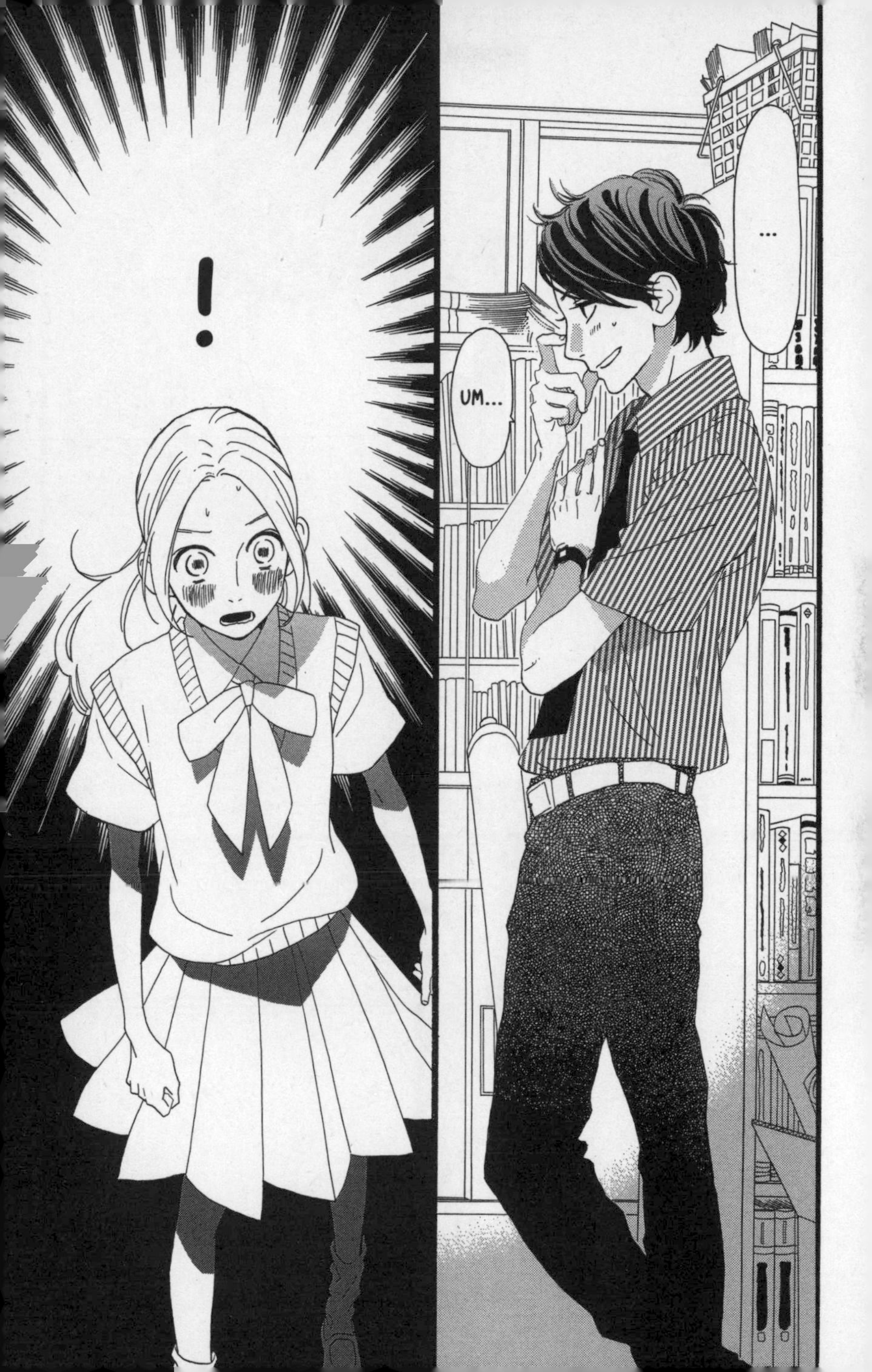
...
UM...
!

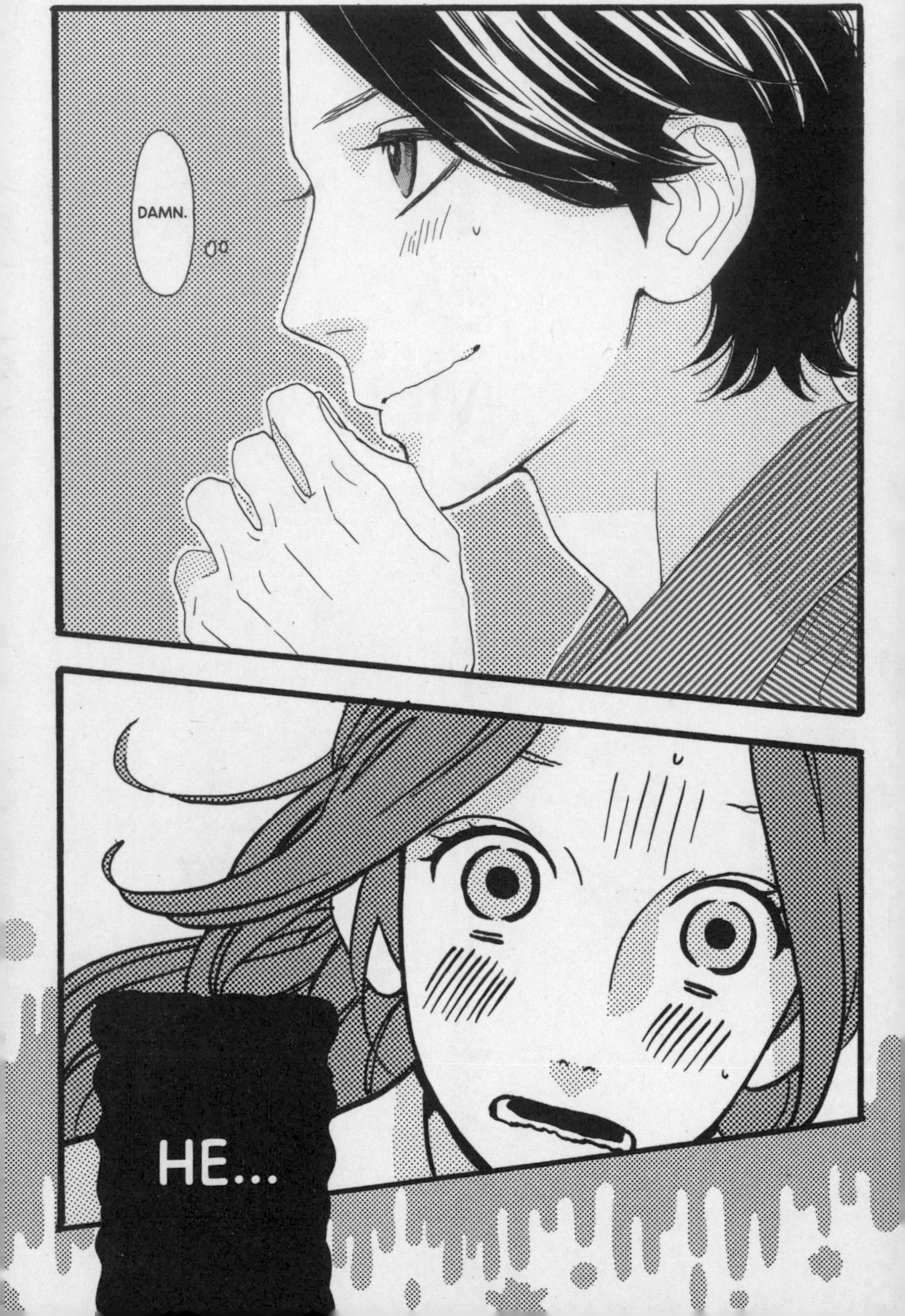
DAMN.
HE...

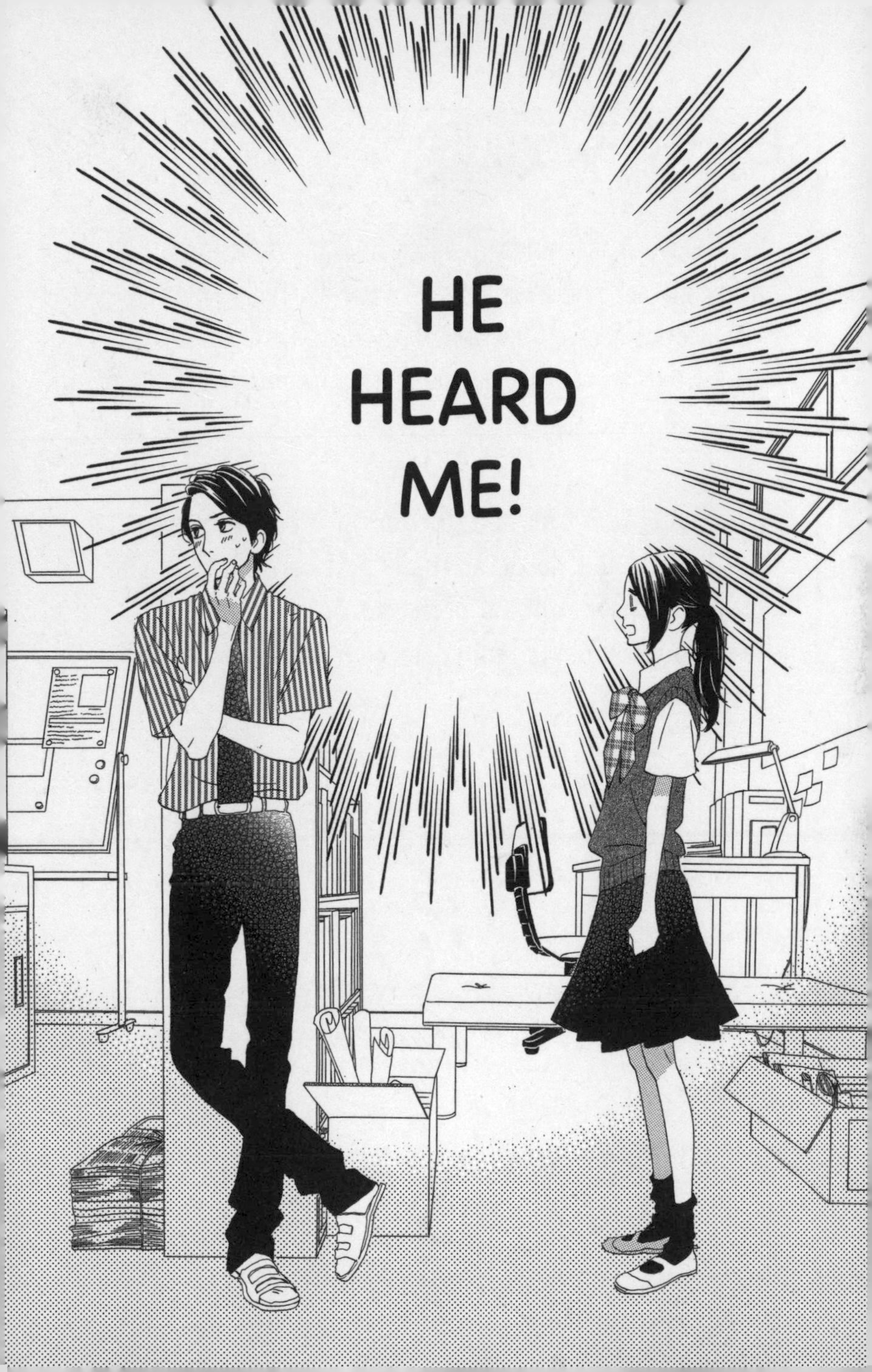
HE HEARD ME!

By the way...

I've run out of things to write in this space, so I think I'll ask for illustration requests. If there are any scenes from *Daytime Shooting Star* that you would like to see, please send in your requests.

I probably won't be able to draw all your requests, but I would like to do as many as I can. Please write me if you have nothing better to do. Also please keep your requests limited to *Daytime Shooting Star* characters.

You may ask me any questions you have too.

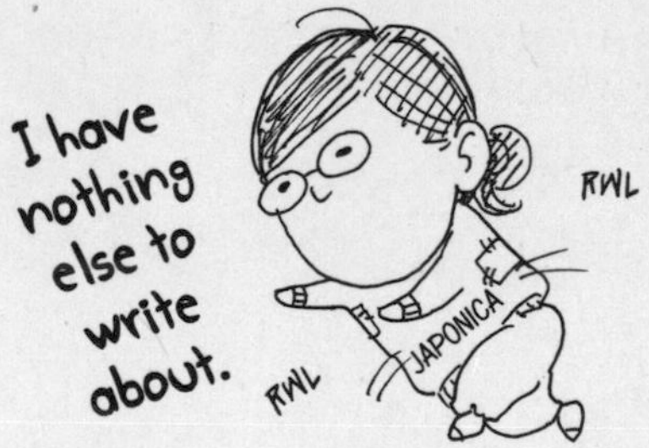
I have nothing else to write about.
RWL
RWL
JAPONICA

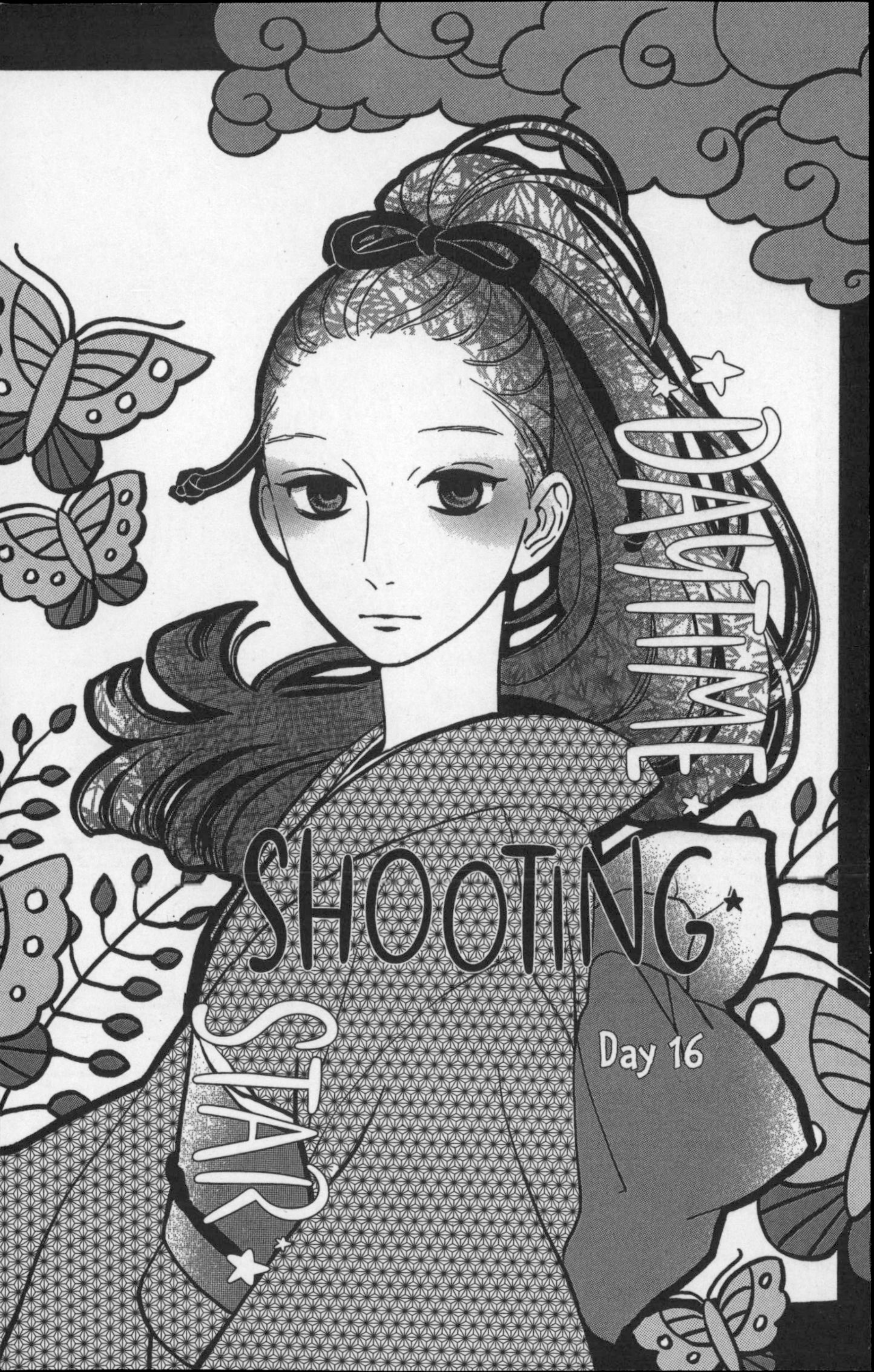
DAYTIME
SHOOTING
STAR
Day 16

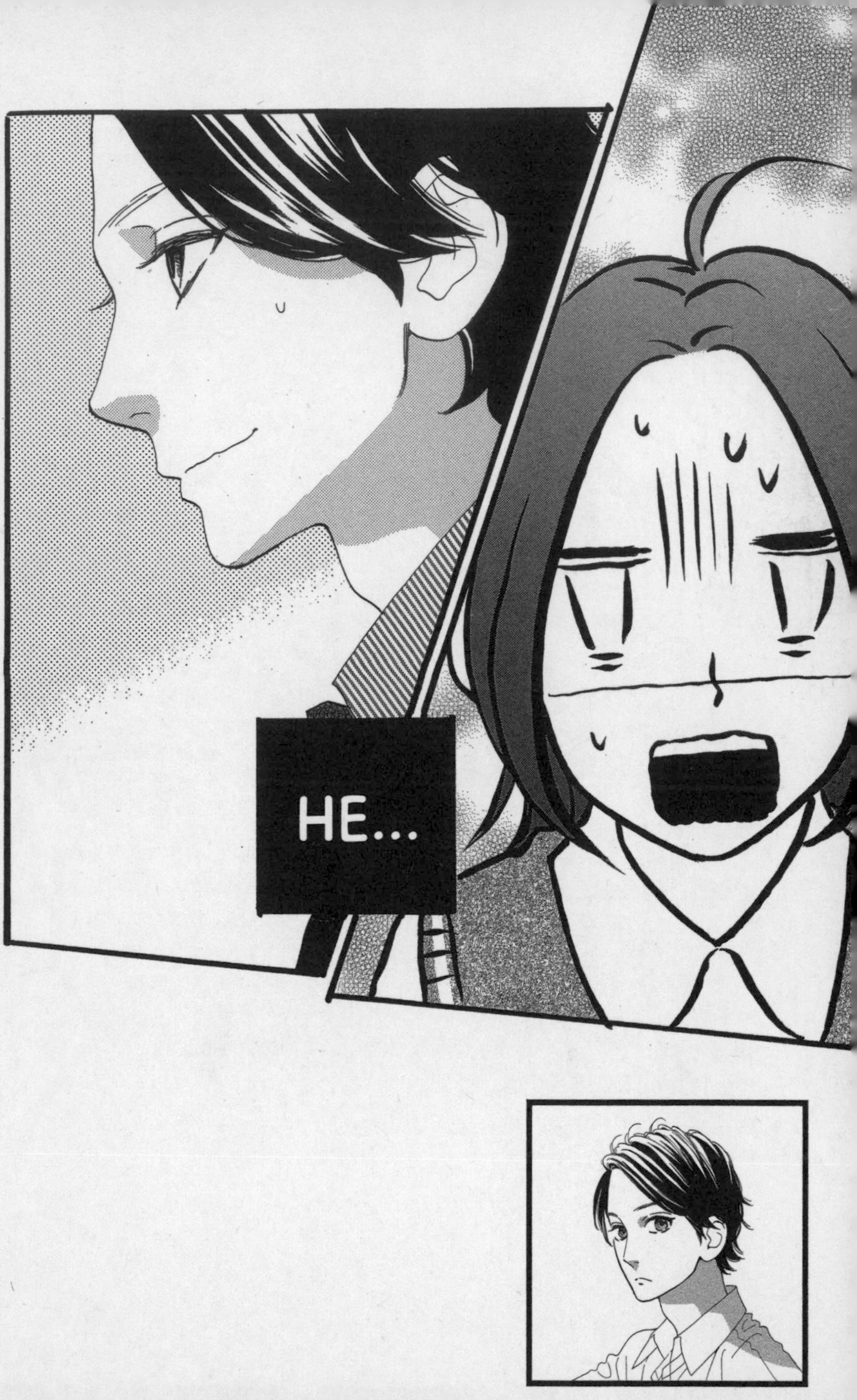
HE...

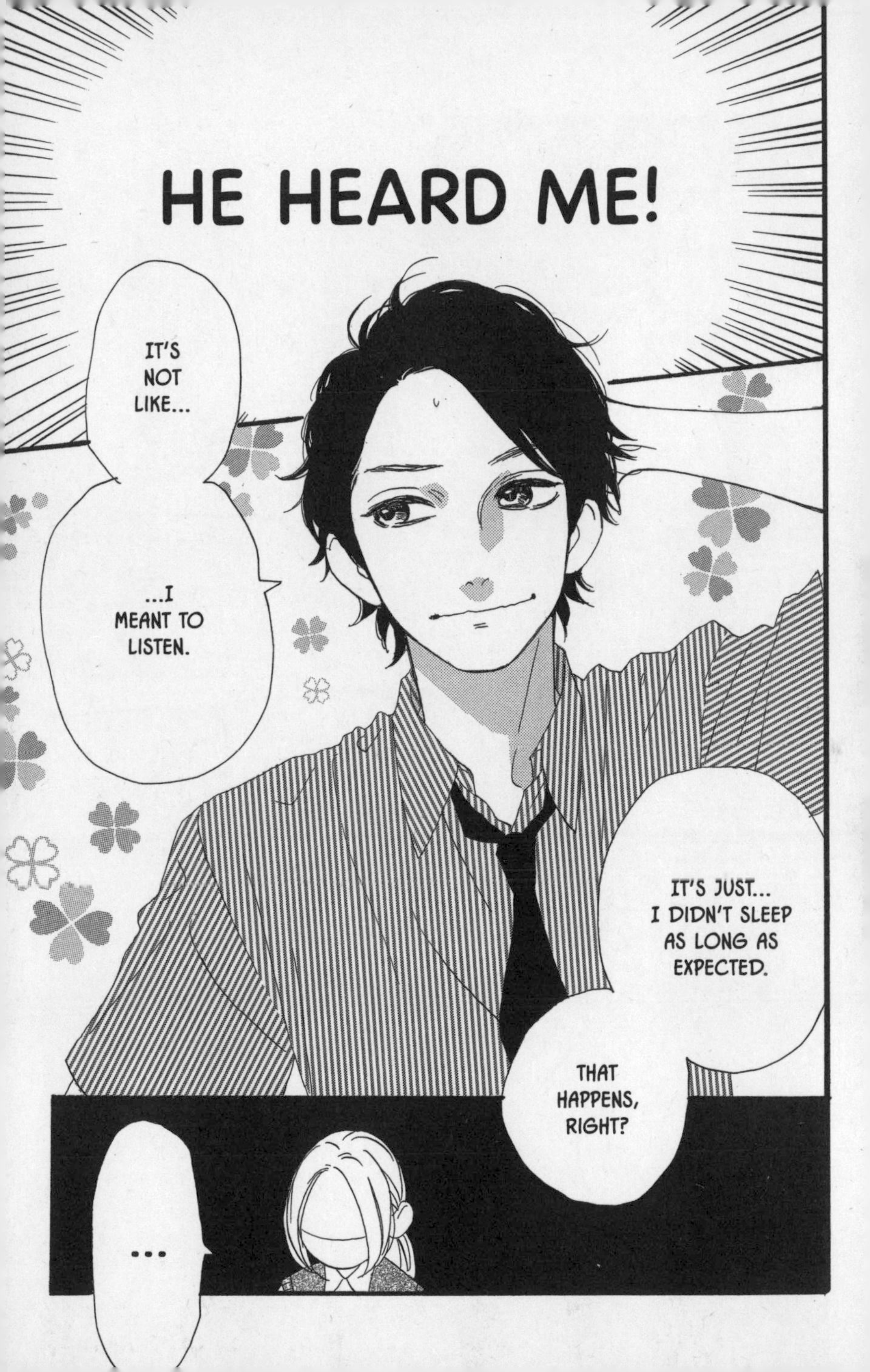
HE HEARD ME!
IT'S NOT LIKE...
...I MEANT TO LISTEN.
IT'S JUST... I DIDN'T SLEEP AS LONG AS EXPECTED.
THAT HAPPENS, RIGHT?
...

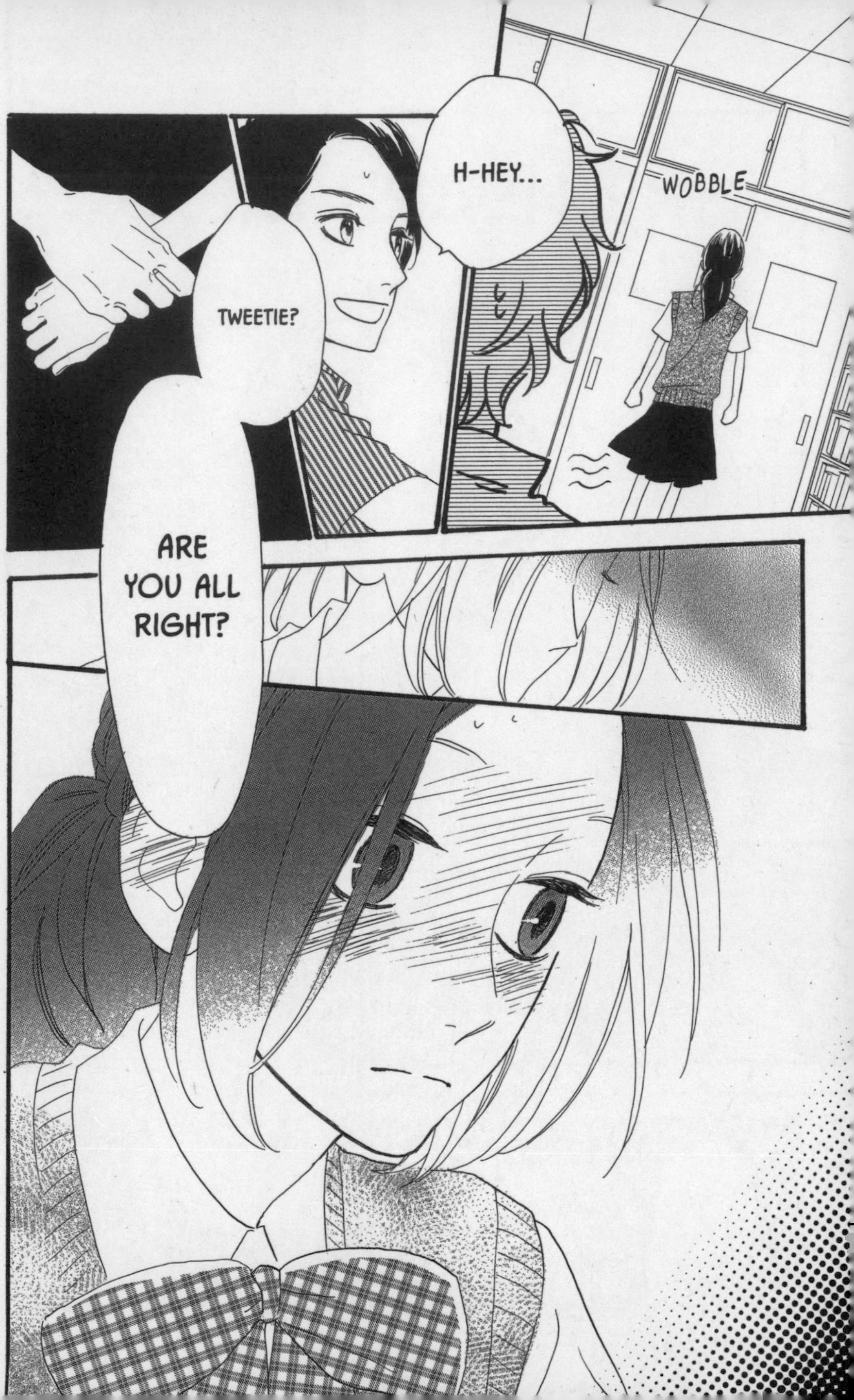

WOBBLE
H-HEY...
TWEETIE?
ARE YOU ALL RIGHT?

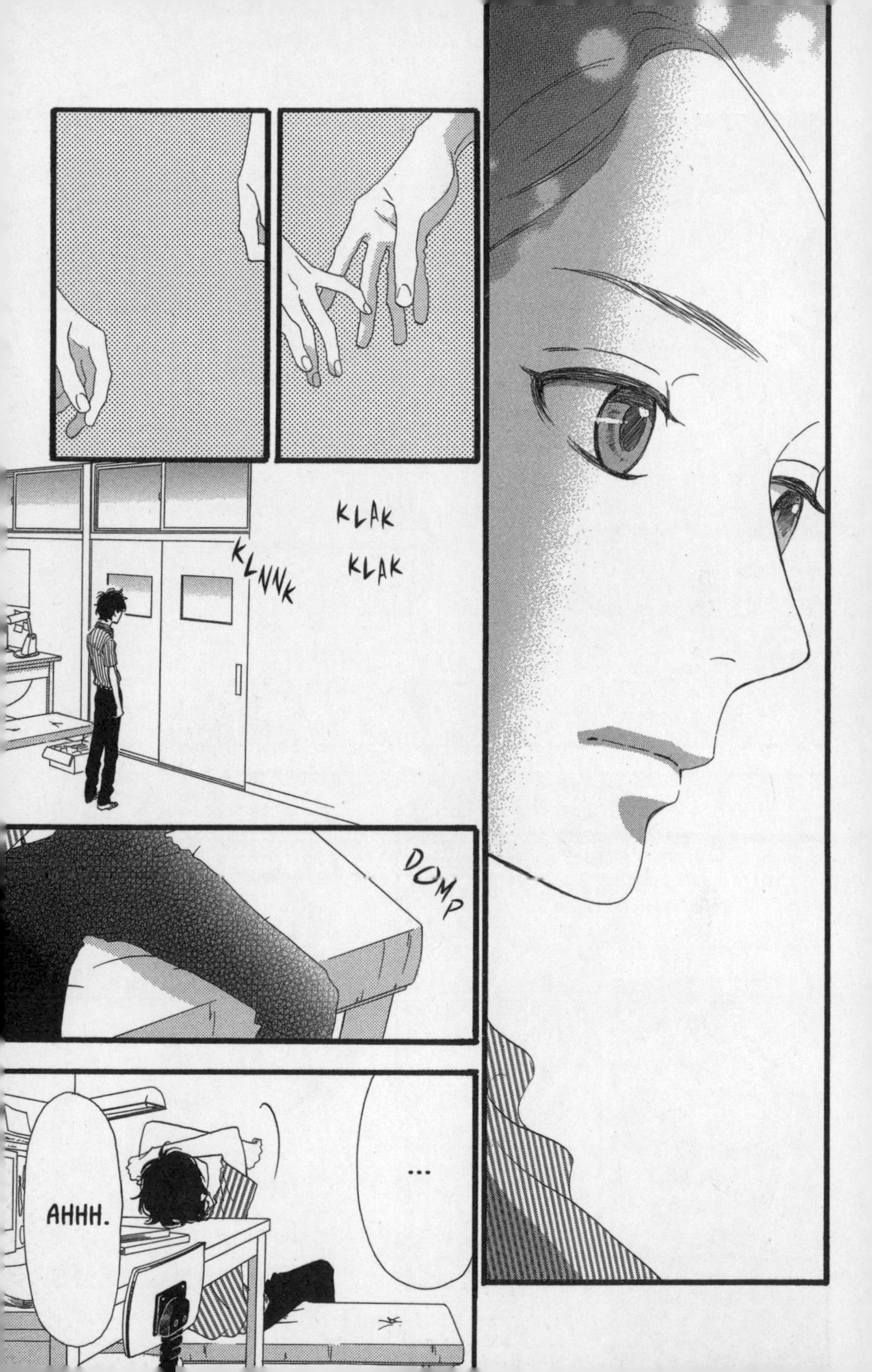
KLAK
KLAK
KLNNK
DOMP
...
AHHH.

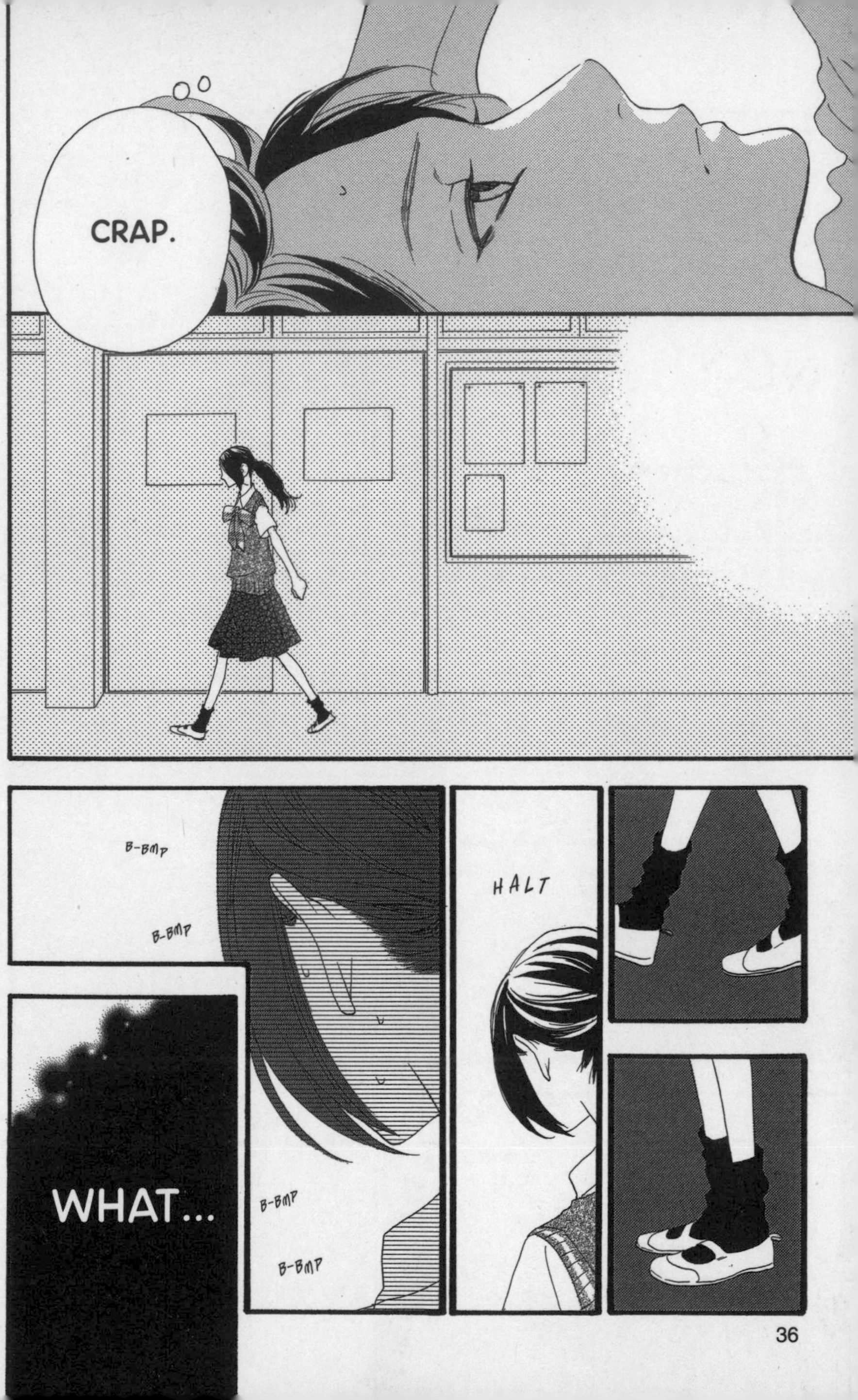
CRAP.
HALT
B-BMP
B-BMP
B-BMP
B-BMP
WHAT...

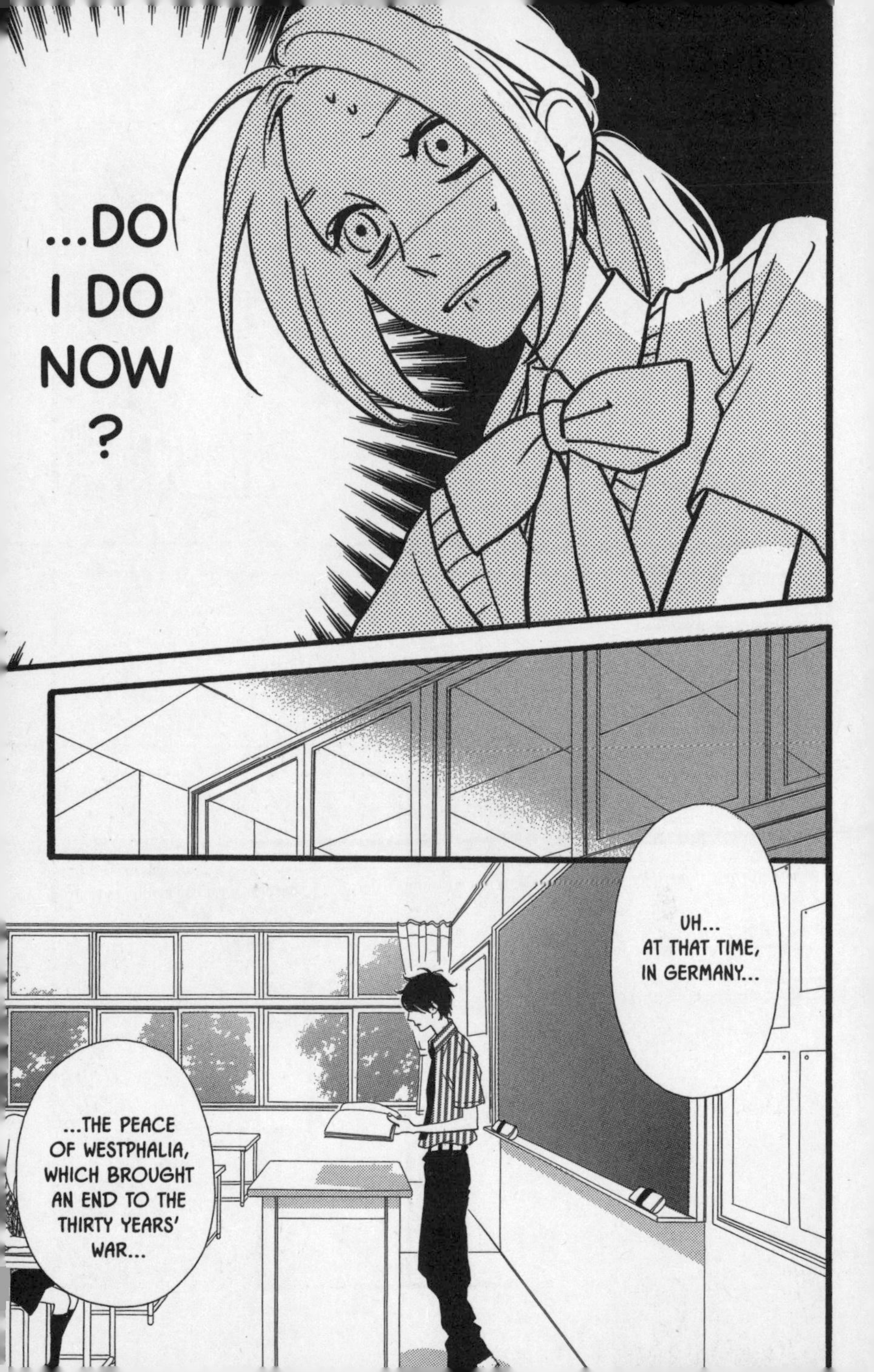
...DO I DO NOW ?
UH... AT THAT TIME, IN GERMANY...
...THE PEACE OF WESTPHALIA, WHICH BROUGHT AN END TO THE THIRTY YEARS' WAR...

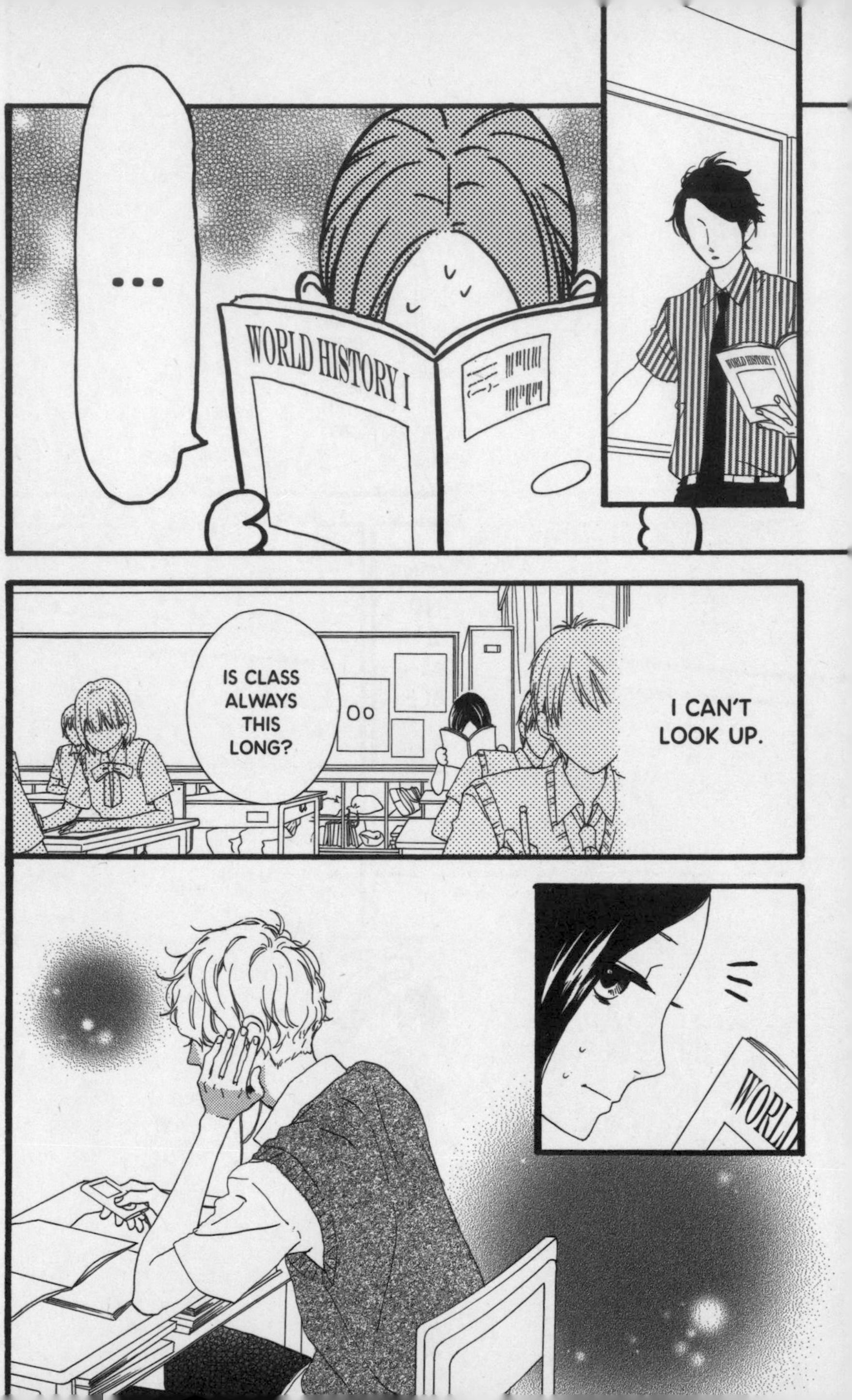
...
I CAN'T LOOK UP.
IS CLASS ALWAYS THIS LONG?
WORLD HISTORY I

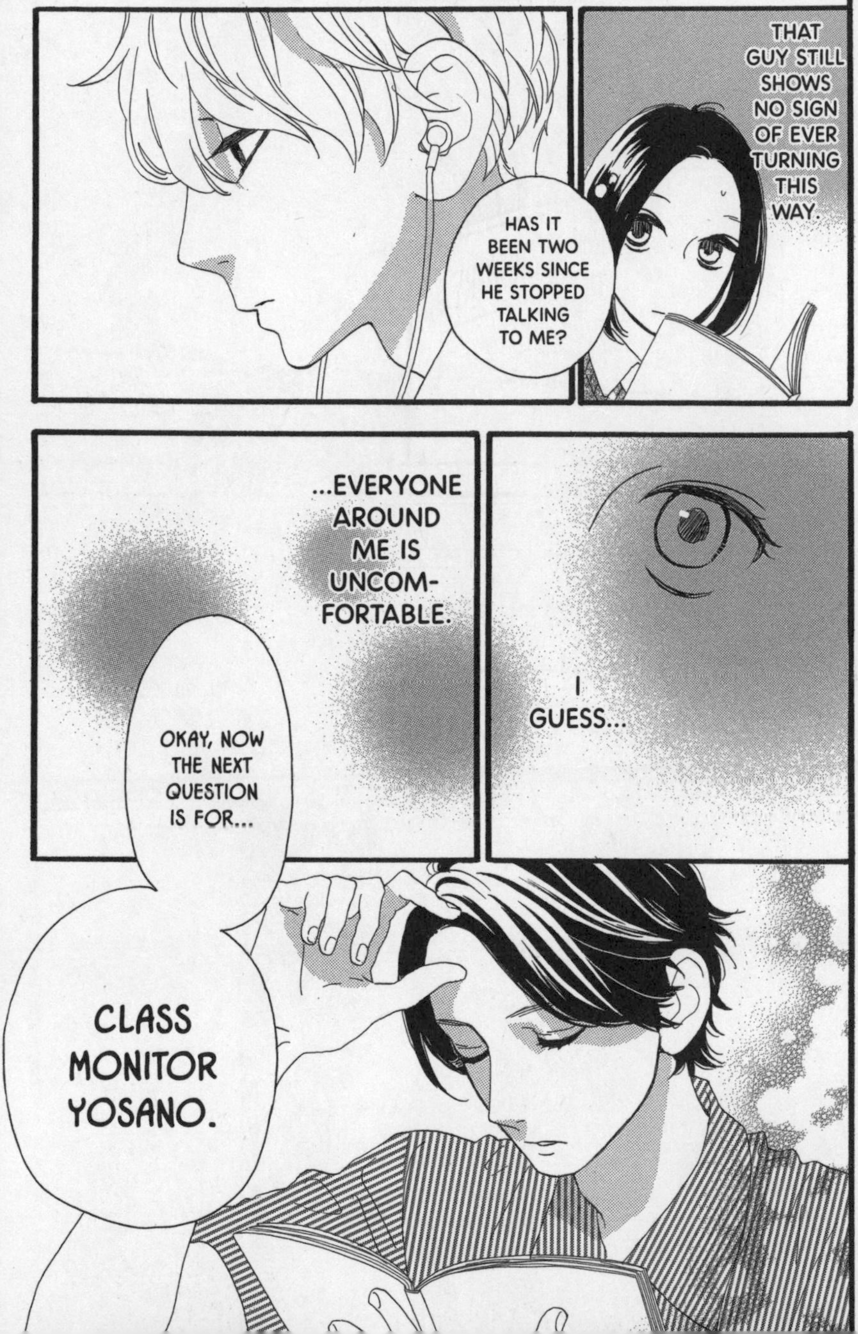
THAT GUY STILL SHOWS NO SIGN OF EVER TURNING THIS WAY.
HAS IT BEEN TWO WEEKS SINCE HE STOPPED TALKING TO ME?
I GUESS...
...EVERYONE AROUND ME IS UNCOM-FORTABLE.
OKAY, NOW THE NEXT QUESTION IS FOR...
CLASS MONITOR YOSANO.

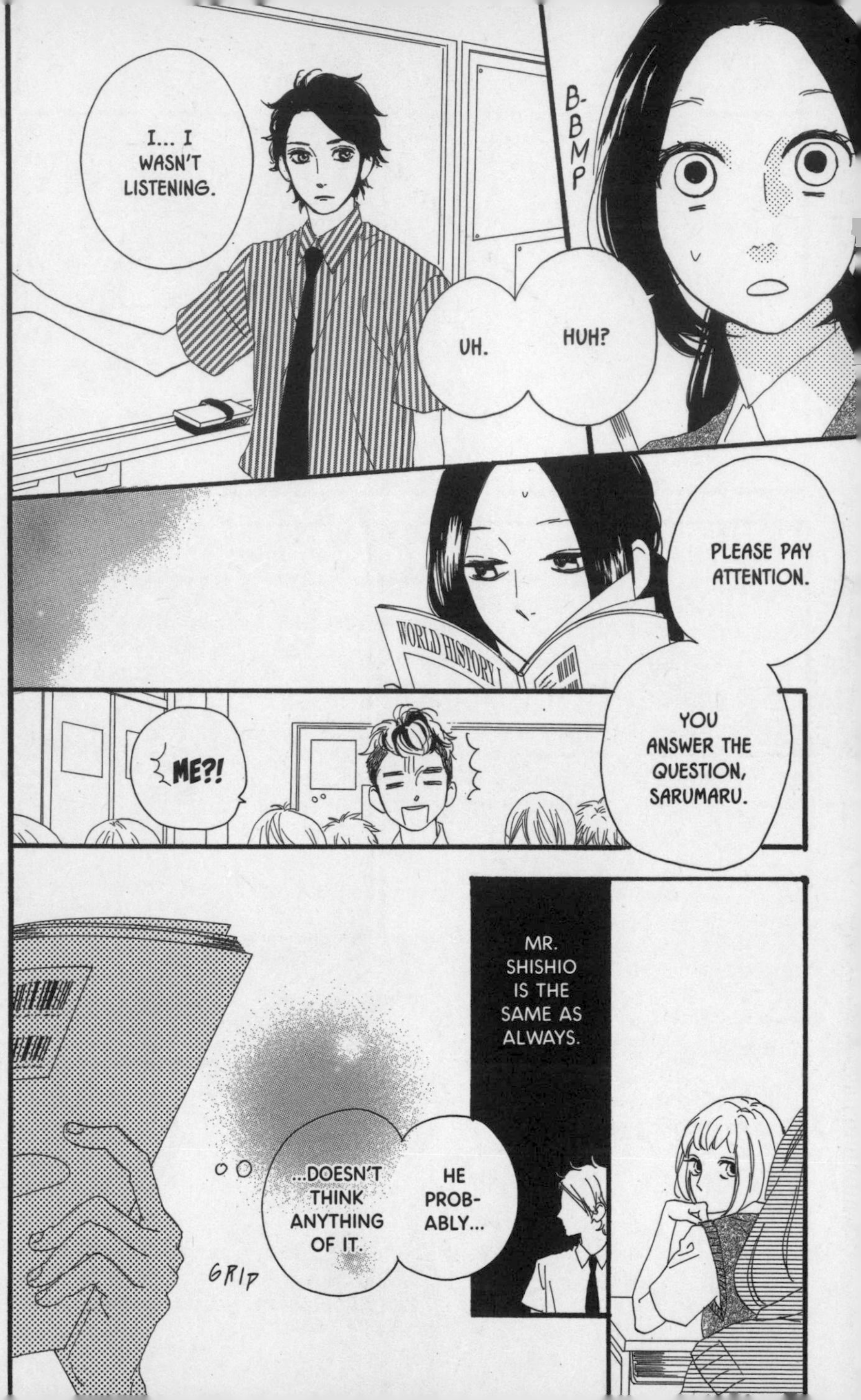
B-BBMP
UH. HUH?
I... I WASN'T LISTENING.
PLEASE PAY ATTENTION.
WORLD HISTORY I
YOU ANSWER THE QUESTION, SARUMARU.
ME?!
MR. SHISHIO IS THE SAME AS ALWAYS.
HE PROBABLY...
...DOESN'T THINK ANYTHING OF IT.
GRIP

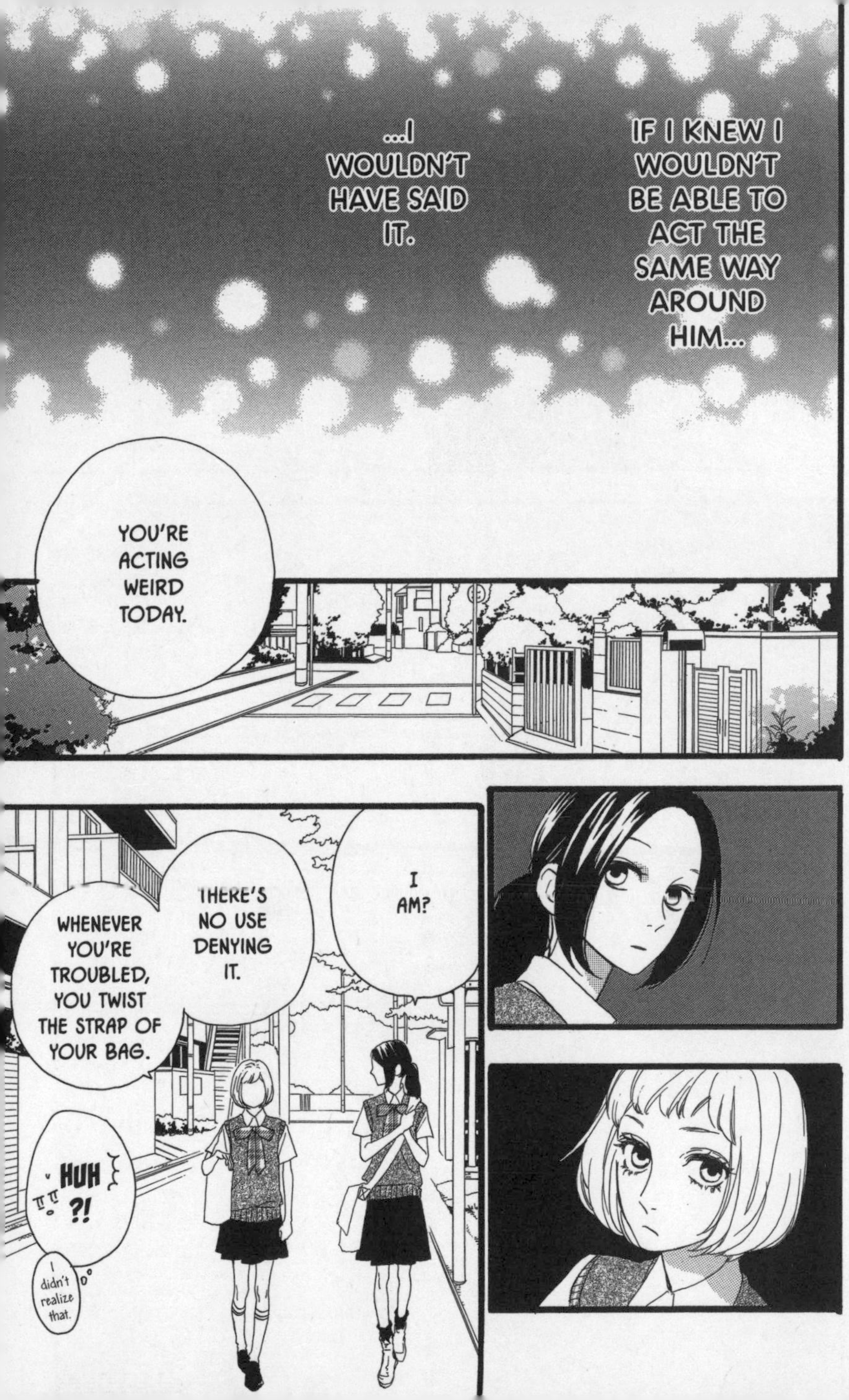
IF I KNEW I WOULDN'T BE ABLE TO ACT THE SAME WAY AROUND HIM...
...I WOULDN'T HAVE SAID IT.
YOU'RE ACTING WEIRD TODAY.
I AM?
THERE'S NO USE DENYING IT.
WHENEVER YOU'RE TROUBLED, YOU TWIST THE STRAP OF YOUR BAG.
HUH?!
I didn't realize that.

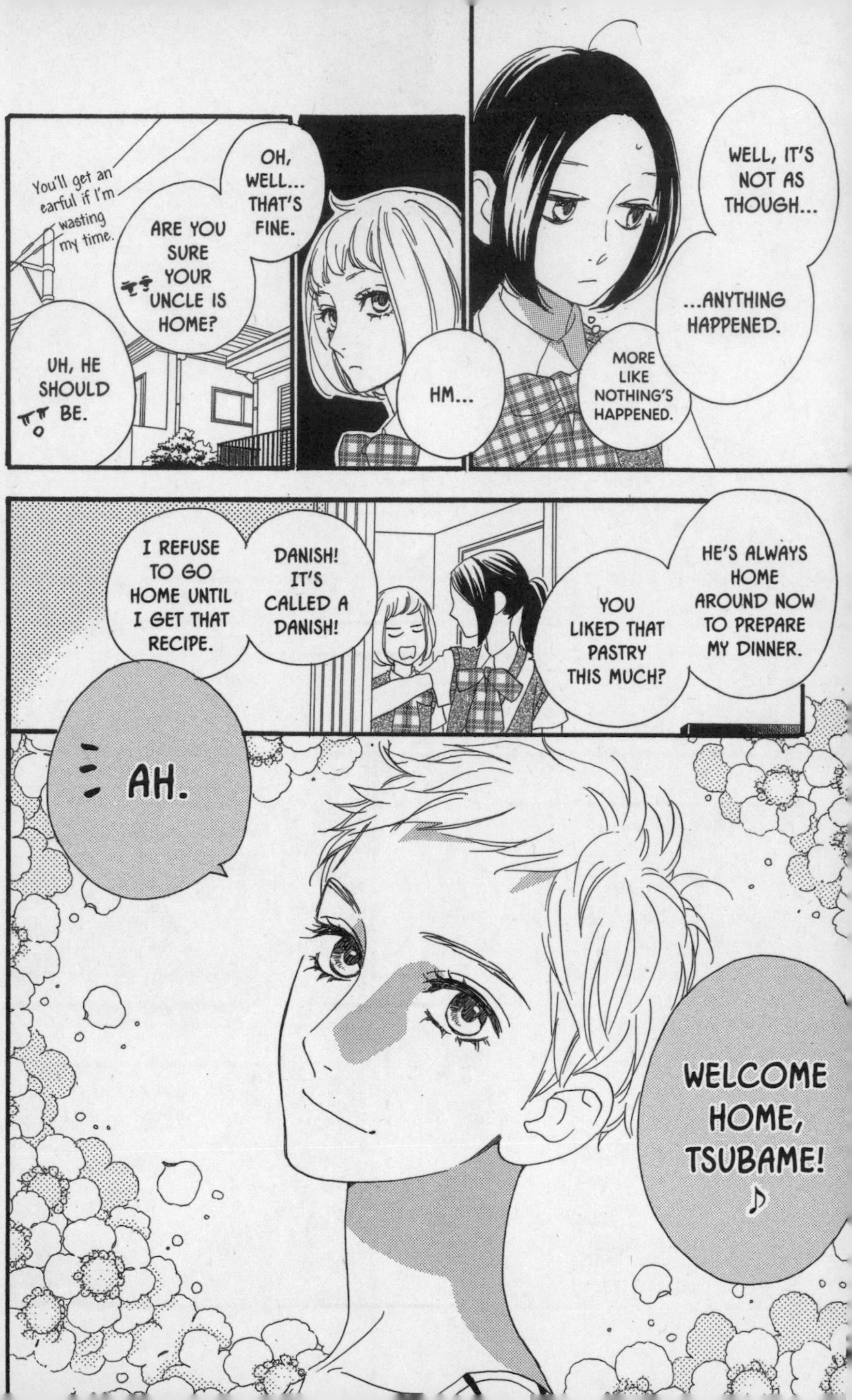
WELL, IT'S NOT AS THOUGH...
...ANYTHING HAPPENED.
MORE LIKE NOTHING'S HAPPENED.
HM...
OH, WELL... THAT'S FINE.
ARE YOU SURE YOUR UNCLE IS HOME?
You'll get an earful if I'm wasting my time.
UH, HE SHOULD BE.
HE'S ALWAYS HOME AROUND NOW TO PREPARE MY DINNER.
YOU LIKED THAT PASTRY THIS MUCH?
DANISH! IT'S CALLED A DANISH!
I REFUSE TO GO HOME UNTIL I GET THAT RECIPE.
AH.
WELCOME HOME, TSUBAME! ♪

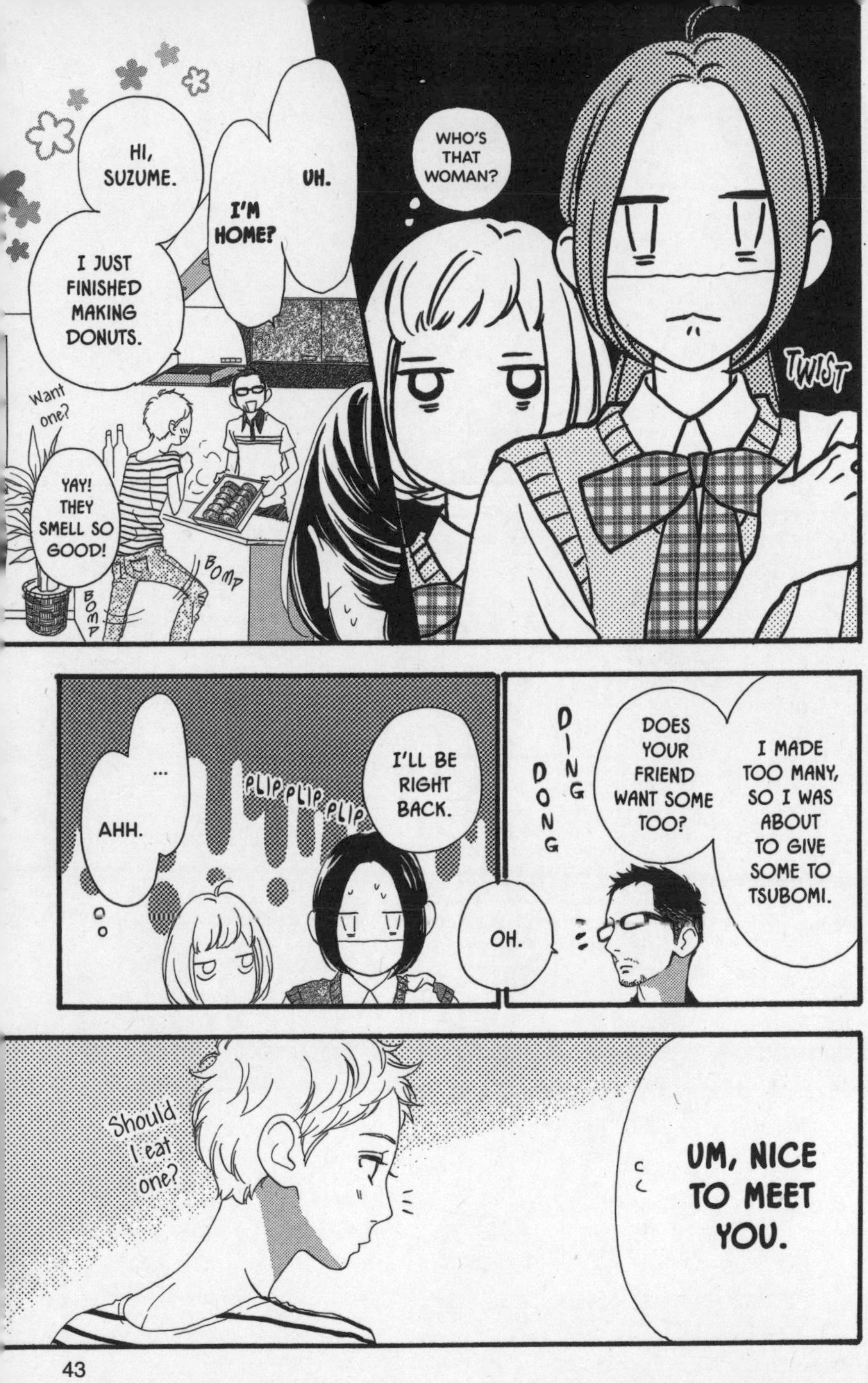
WHO'S THAT WOMAN?
TWIST
UH. I'M HOME?
HI, SUZUME.
I JUST FINISHED MAKING DONUTS.
Want one?
YAY! THEY SMELL SO GOOD!
BOMP
BOMP
I MADE TOO MANY, SO I WAS ABOUT TO GIVE SOME TO TSUBOMI.
DOES YOUR FRIEND WANT SOME TOO?
DING
DONG
OH.
I'LL BE RIGHT BACK.
PLIP PLIP PLIP
... AHH.
UM, NICE TO MEET YOU.
Should I eat one?

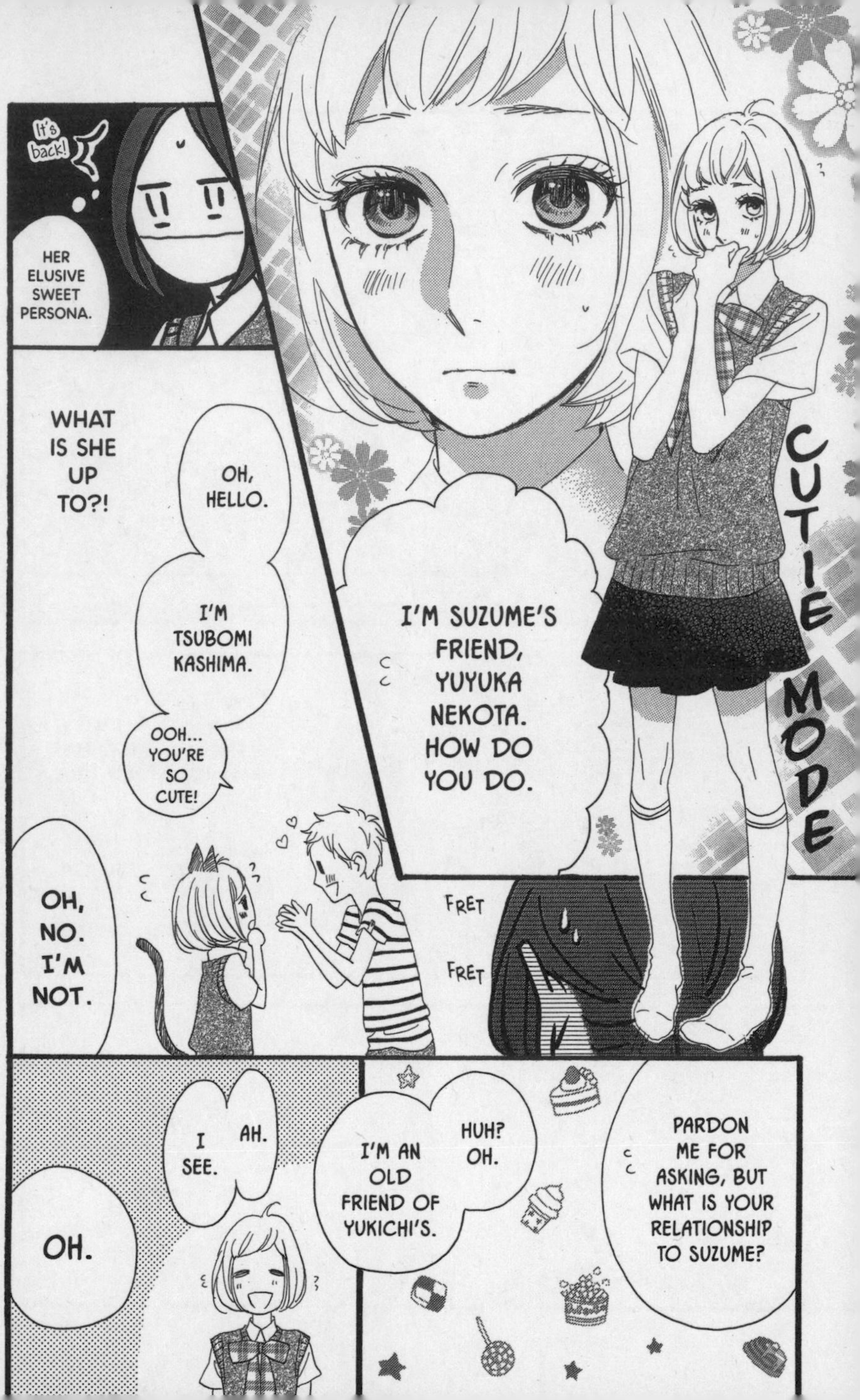
CUTIE MODE
I'M SUZUME'S FRIEND, YUYUKA NEKOTA. HOW DO YOU DO.
FRET
FRET
It's back!
HER ELUSIVE SWEET PERSONA.
OH, HELLO.
I'M TSUBOMI KASHIMA.
WHAT IS SHE UP TO?!
OOH... YOU'RE SO CUTE!
OH, NO. I'M NOT.
PARDON ME FOR ASKING, BUT WHAT IS YOUR RELATIONSHIP TO SUZUME?
HUH? OH.
I'M AN OLD FRIEND OF YUKICHI'S.
AH.
I SEE.
OH.

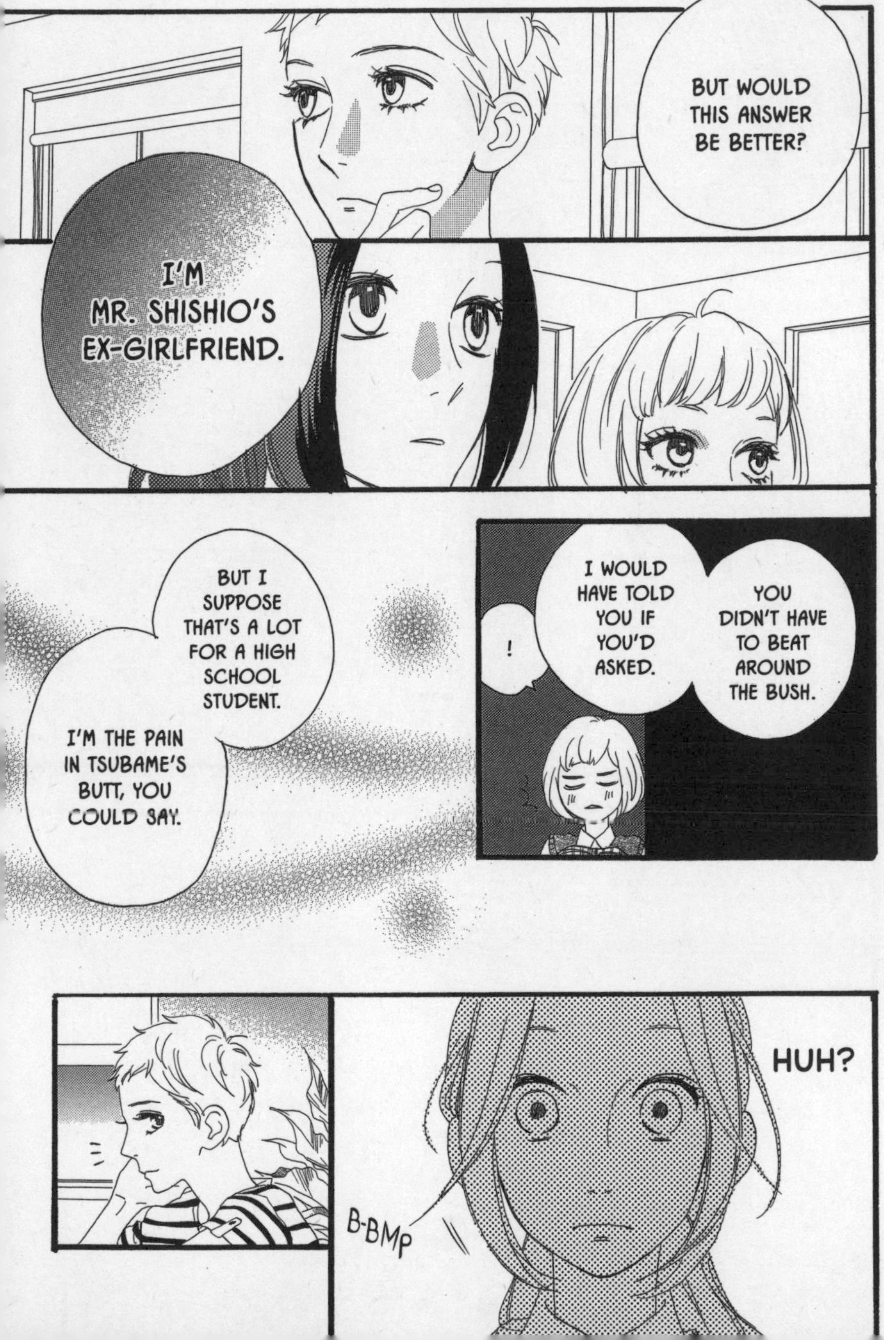
BUT WOULD THIS ANSWER BE BETTER?
I'M MR. SHISHIO'S EX-GIRLFRIEND.
YOU DIDN'T HAVE TO BEAT AROUND THE BUSH.
I WOULD HAVE TOLD YOU IF YOU'D ASKED.
!
BUT I SUPPOSE THAT'S A LOT FOR A HIGH SCHOOL STUDENT.
I'M THE PAIN IN TSUBAME'S BUTT, YOU COULD SAY.
HUH?
B-BMP

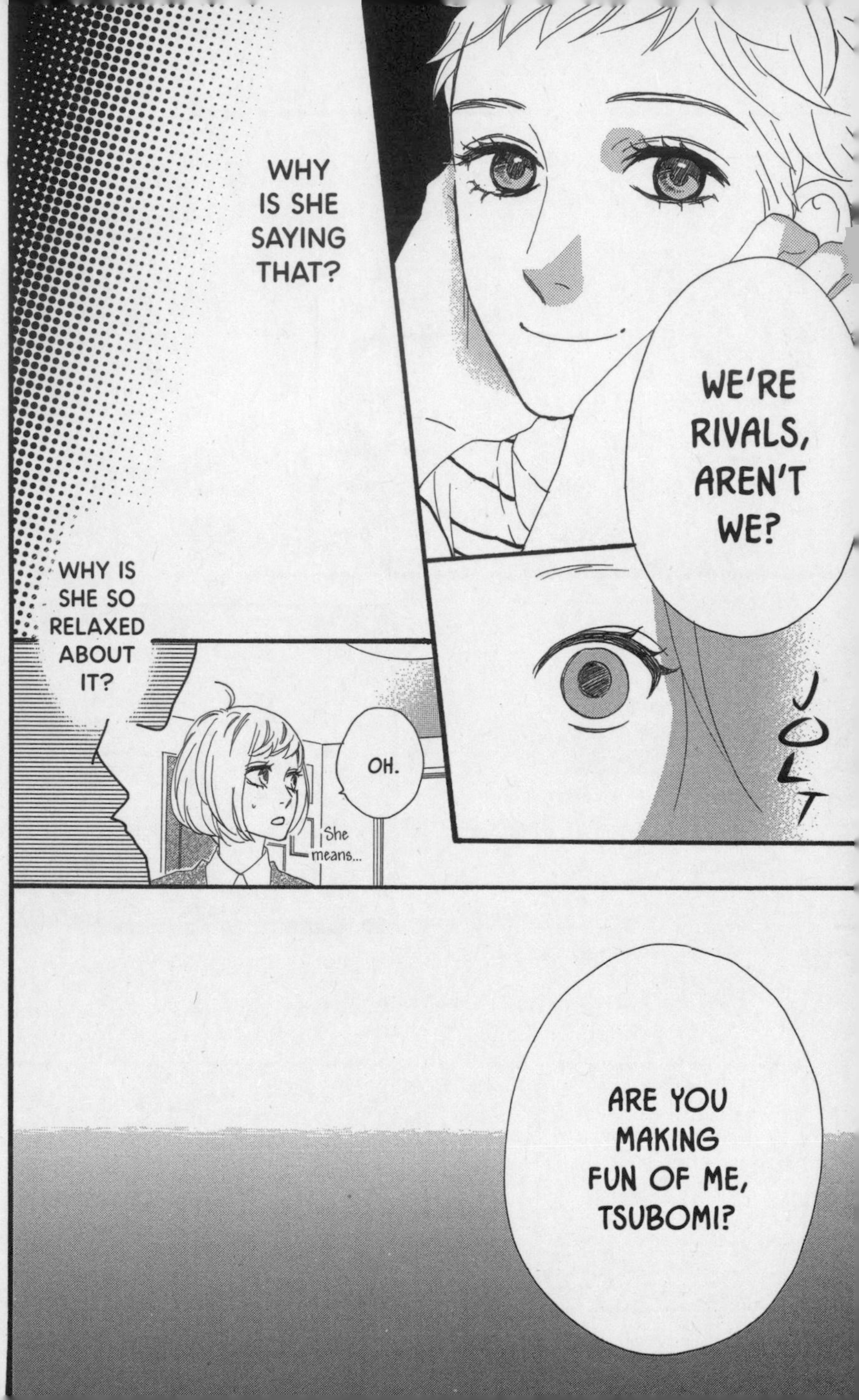
WE'RE RIVALS, AREN'T WE?
JOLT
WHY IS SHE SAYING THAT?
WHY IS SHE SO RELAXED ABOUT IT?
OH.
She means...
ARE YOU MAKING FUN OF ME, TSUBOMI?

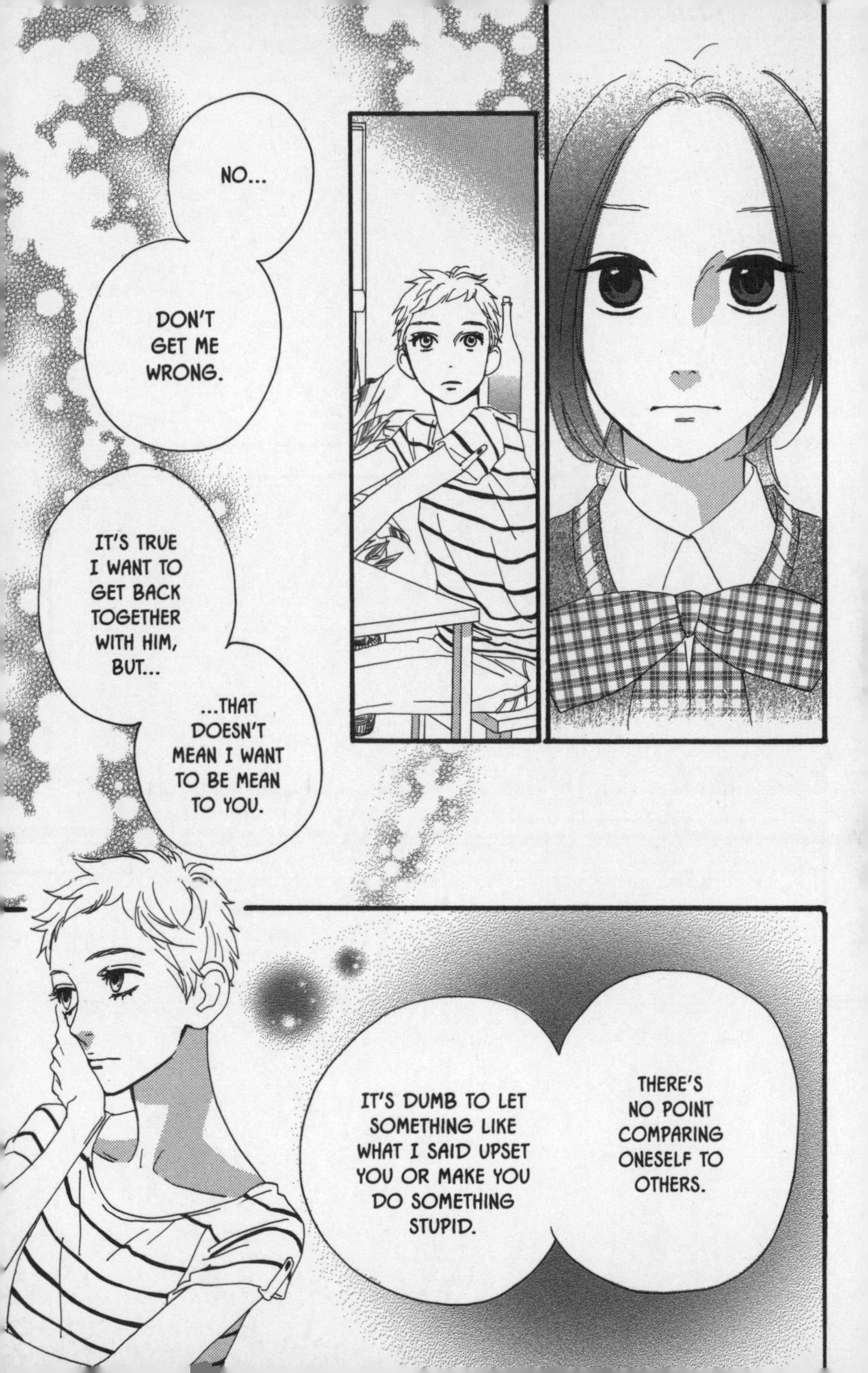
NO...
DON'T GET ME WRONG.
IT'S TRUE I WANT TO GET BACK TOGETHER WITH HIM, BUT...
...THAT DOESN'T MEAN I WANT TO BE MEAN TO YOU.
THERE'S NO POINT COMPARING ONESELF TO OTHERS.
IT'S DUMB TO LET SOMETHING LIKE WHAT I SAID UPSET YOU OR MAKE YOU DO SOMETHING STUPID.

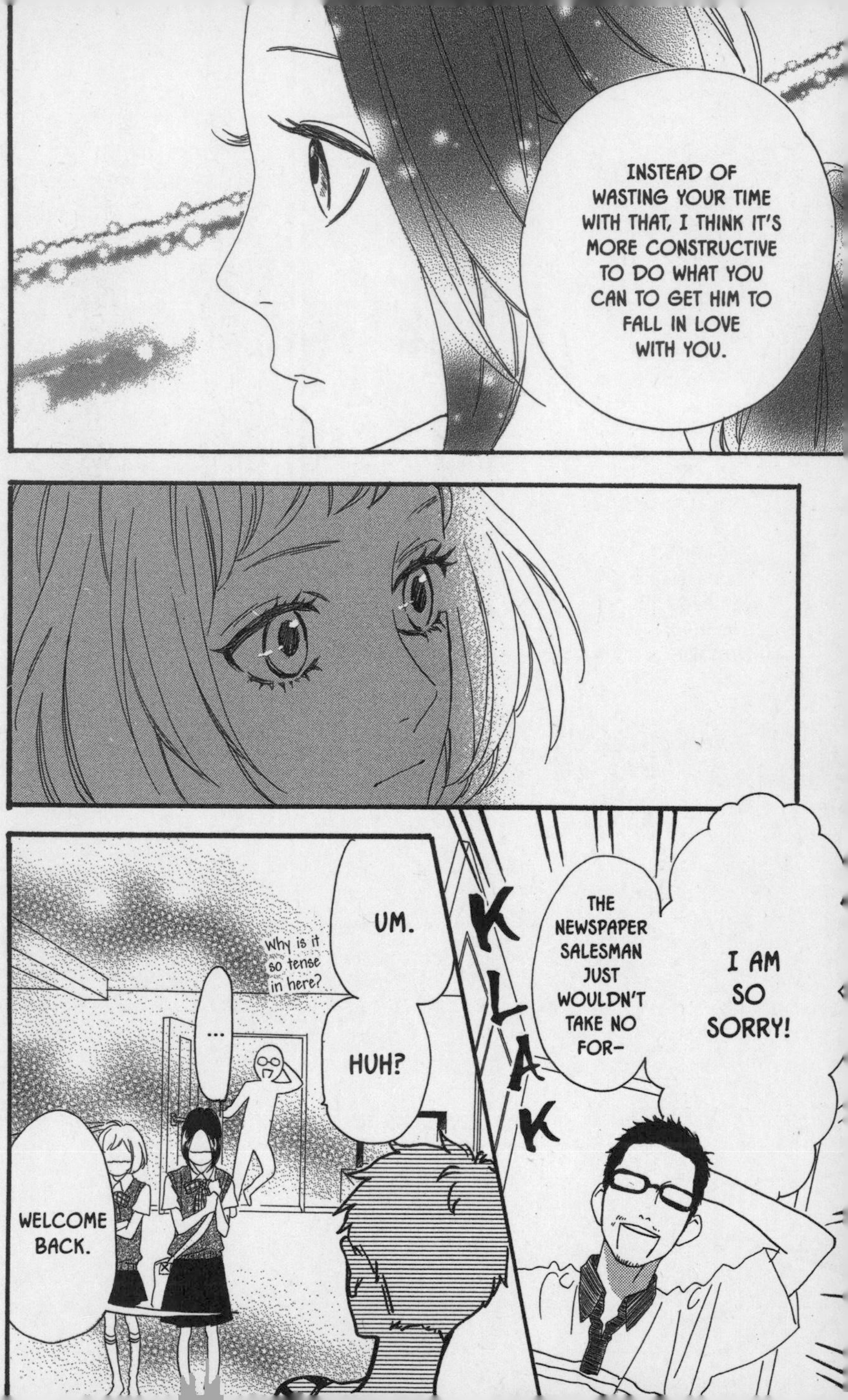
INSTEAD OF WASTING YOUR TIME WITH THAT, I THINK IT'S MORE CONSTRUCTIVE TO DO WHAT YOU CAN TO GET HIM TO FALL IN LOVE WITH YOU.
I AM SO SORRY!
THE NEWSPAPER SALESMAN JUST WOULDN'T TAKE NO FOR–
KLAK
UM.
HUH?
Why is it so tense in here?
...
WELCOME BACK.

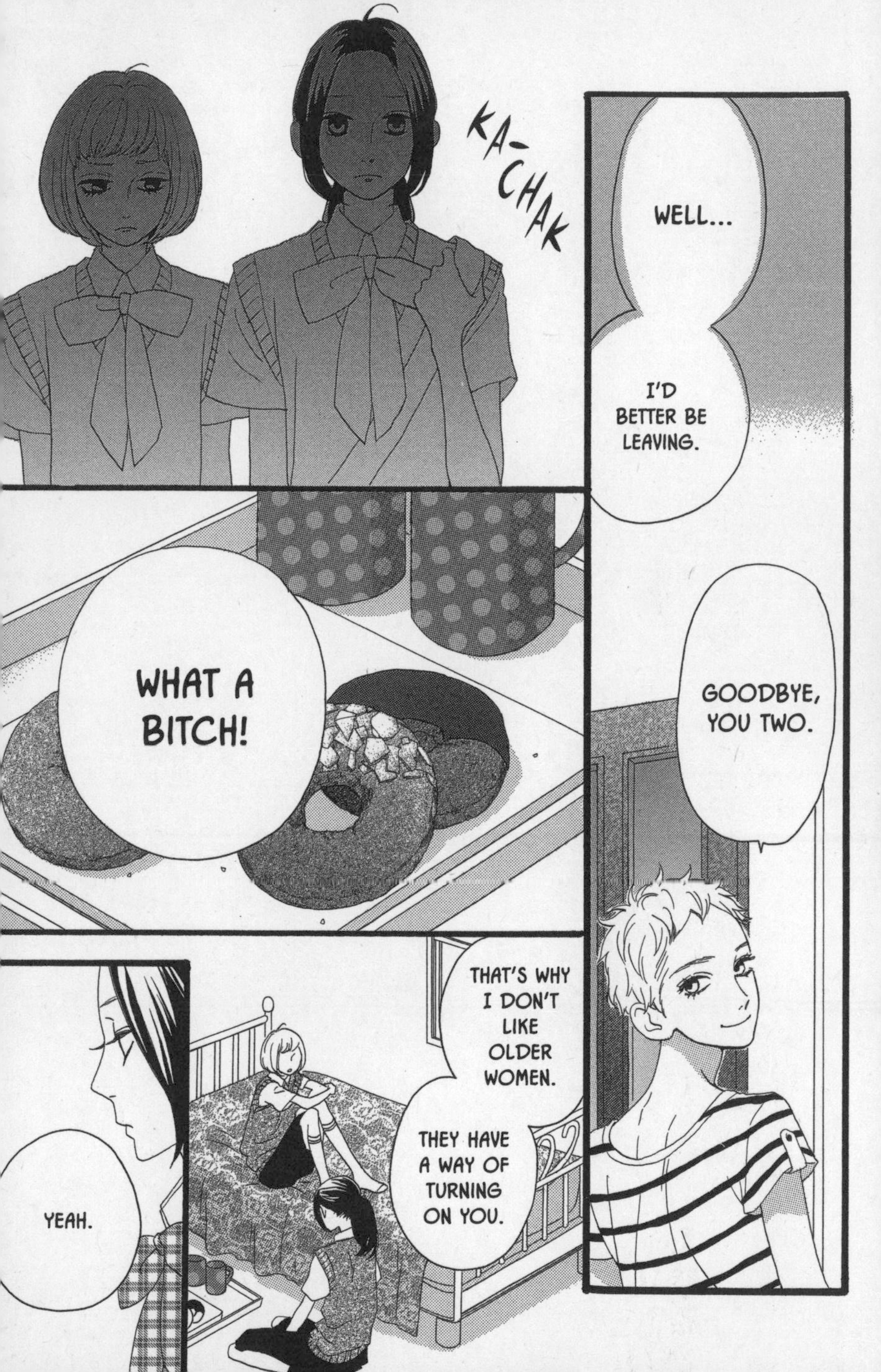
WELL...
I'D BETTER BE LEAVING.
GOODBYE, YOU TWO.
KA-CHAK
WHAT A BITCH!
THAT'S WHY I DON'T LIKE OLDER WOMEN.
THEY HAVE A WAY OF TURNING ON YOU.
YEAH.

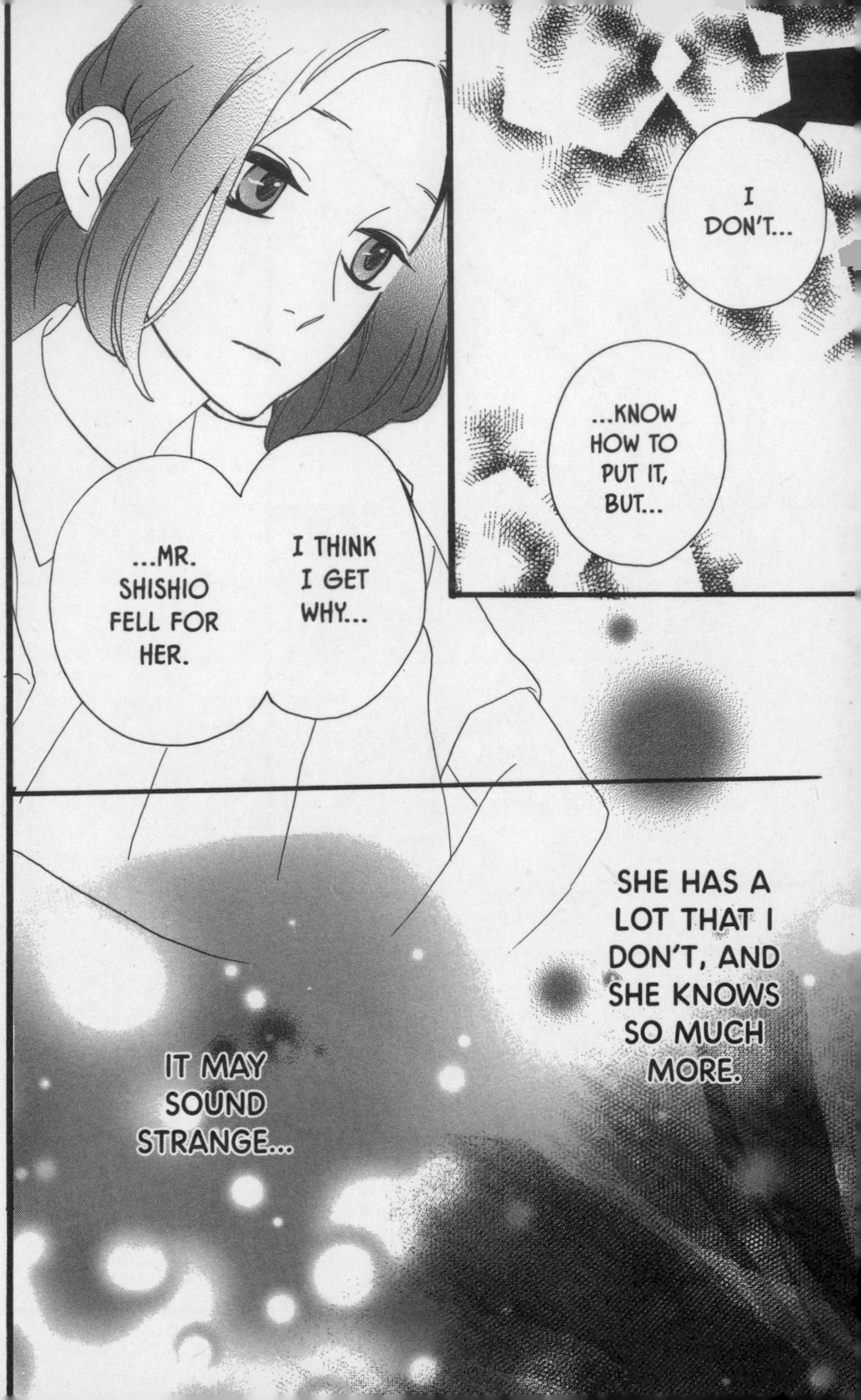
I DON'T...
...KNOW HOW TO PUT IT, BUT...
I THINK I GET WHY...
...MR. SHISHIO FELL FOR HER.
SHE HAS A LOT THAT I DON'T, AND SHE KNOWS SO MUCH MORE.
IT MAY SOUND STRANGE...

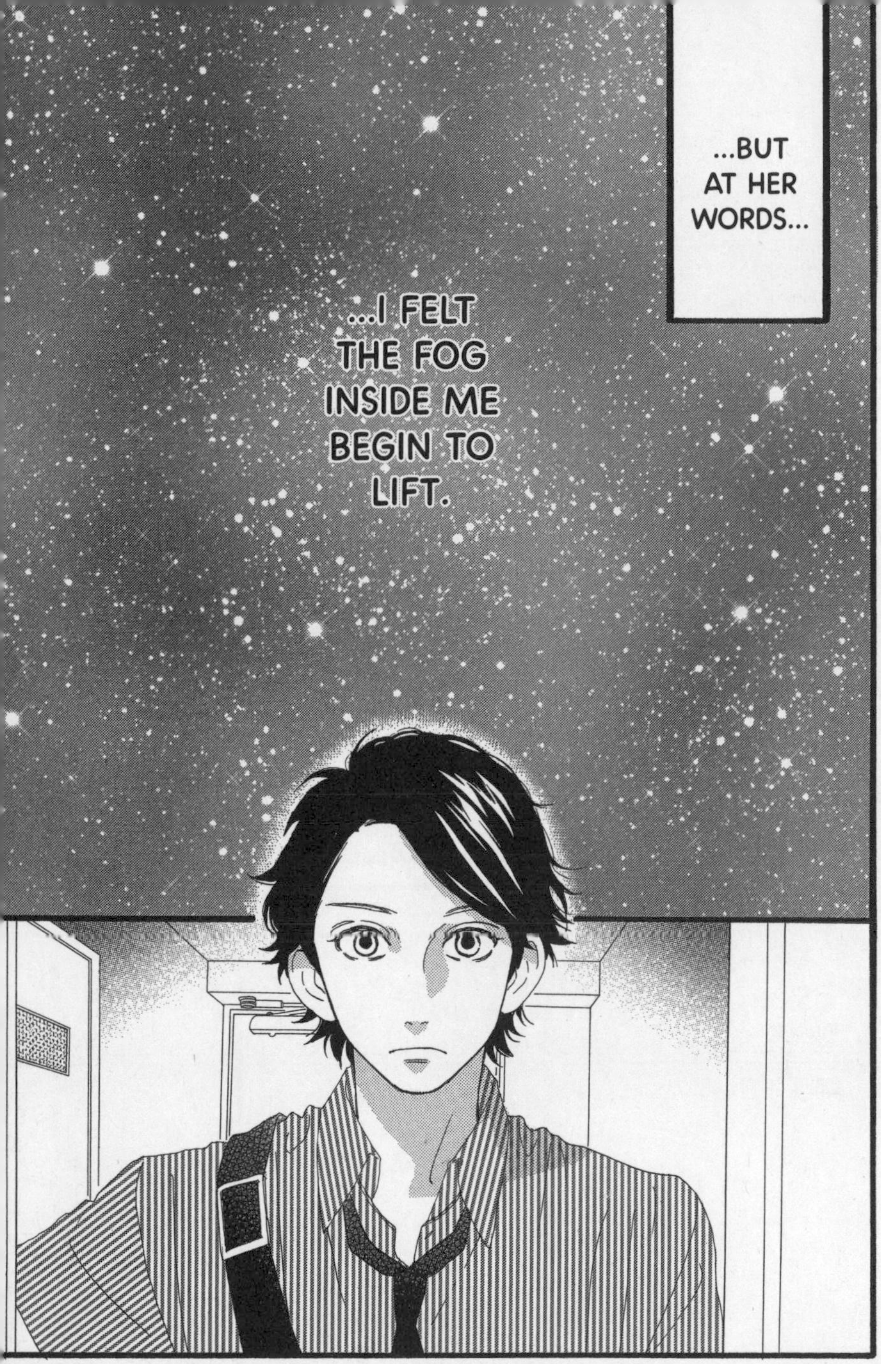
...BUT AT HER WORDS...
...I FELT THE FOG INSIDE ME BEGIN TO LIFT.

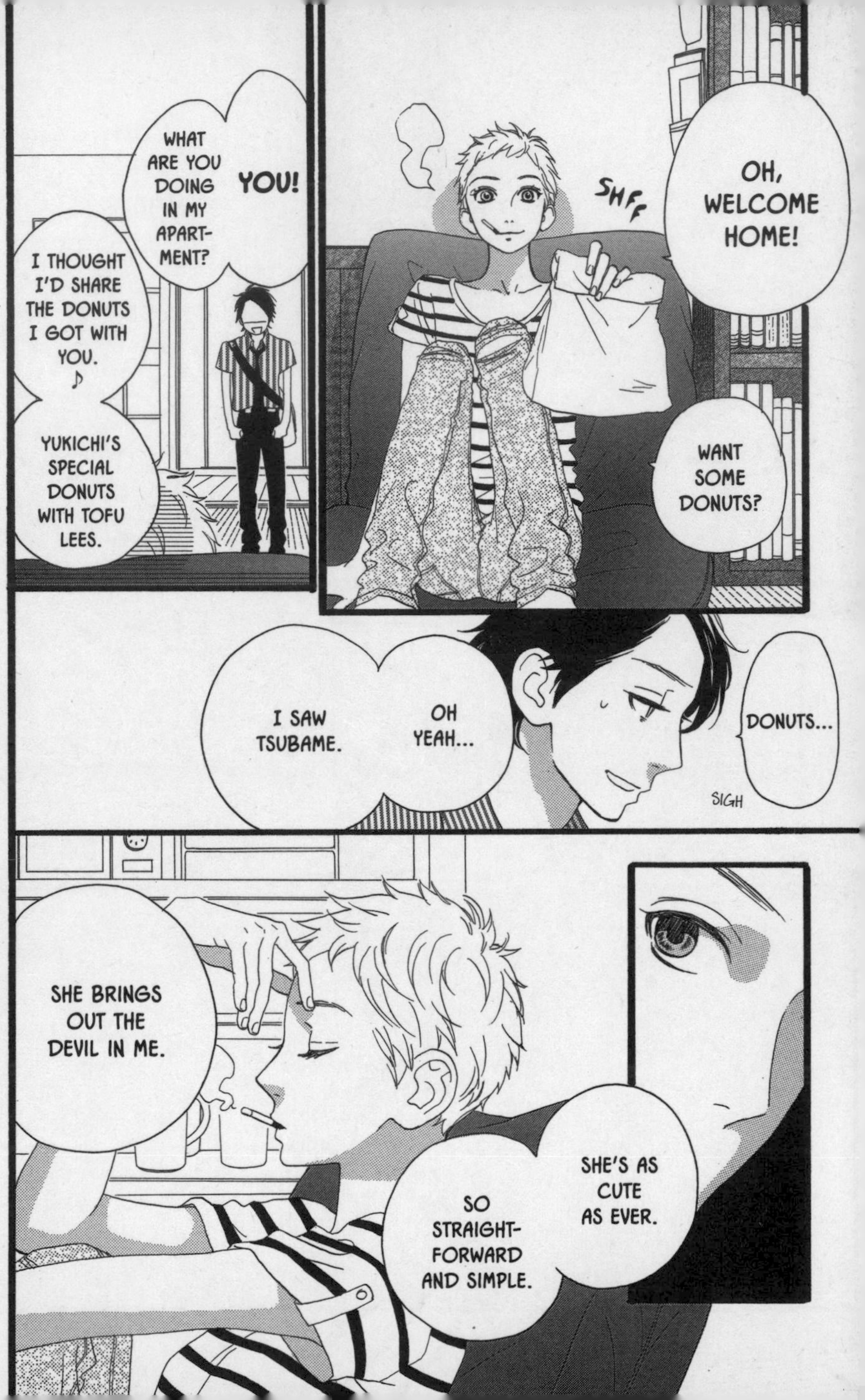

OH, WELCOME HOME!
SHFF
WANT SOME DONUTS?
WHAT ARE YOU DOING IN MY APARTMENT? YOU!
I THOUGHT I'D SHARE THE DONUTS I GOT WITH YOU. ♪
YUKICHI'S SPECIAL DONUTS WITH TOFU LEES.
DONUTS...
SIGH
OH YEAH...
I SAW TSUBAME.
SHE'S AS CUTE AS EVER.
SO STRAIGHT-FORWARD AND SIMPLE.
SHE BRINGS OUT THE DEVIL IN ME.

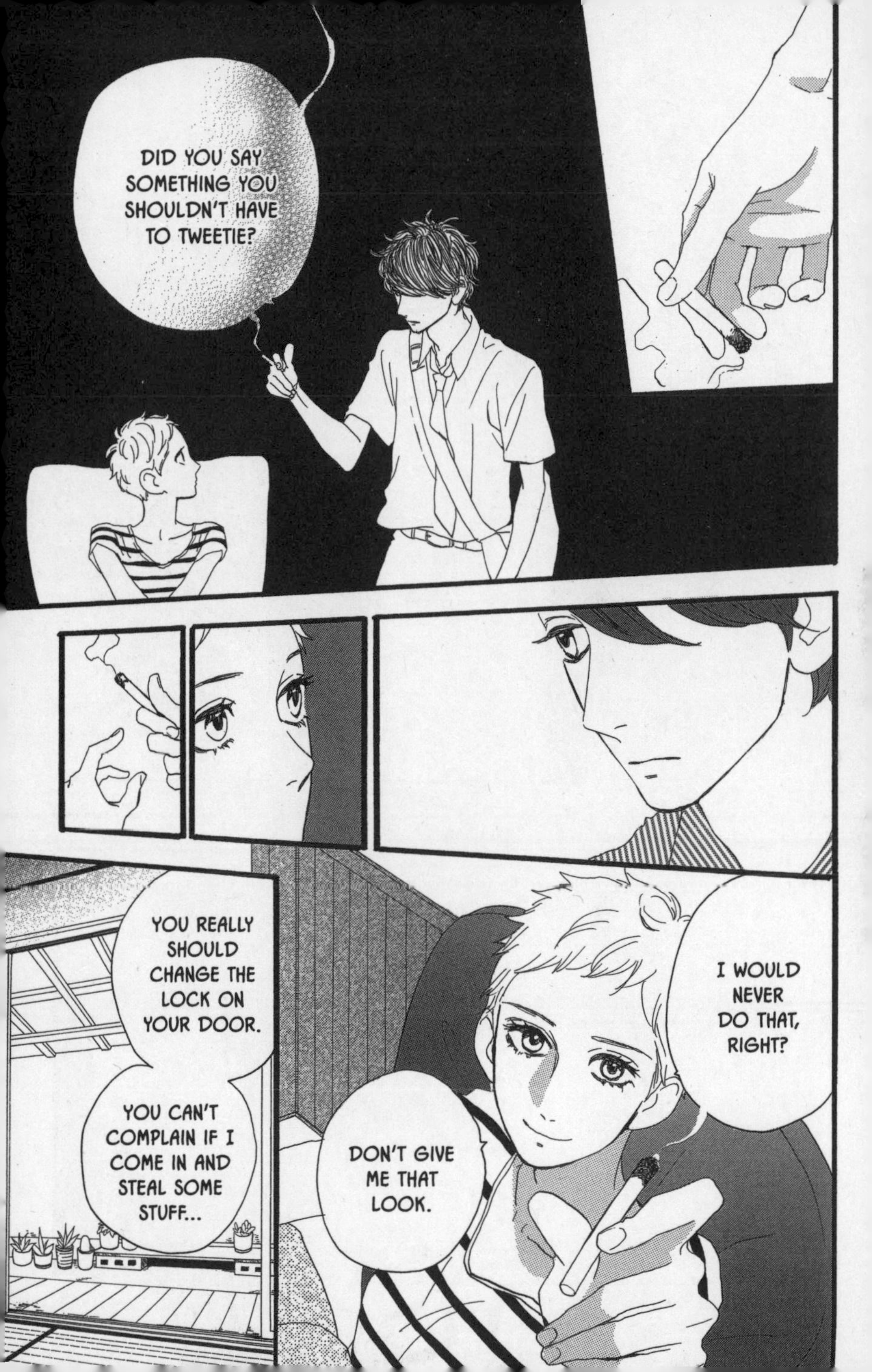
DID YOU SAY SOMETHING YOU SHOULDN'T HAVE TO TWEETIE?
I WOULD NEVER DO THAT, RIGHT?
YOU REALLY SHOULD CHANGE THE LOCK ON YOUR DOOR.
YOU CAN'T COMPLAIN IF I COME IN AND STEAL SOME STUFF...
DON'T GIVE ME THAT LOOK.

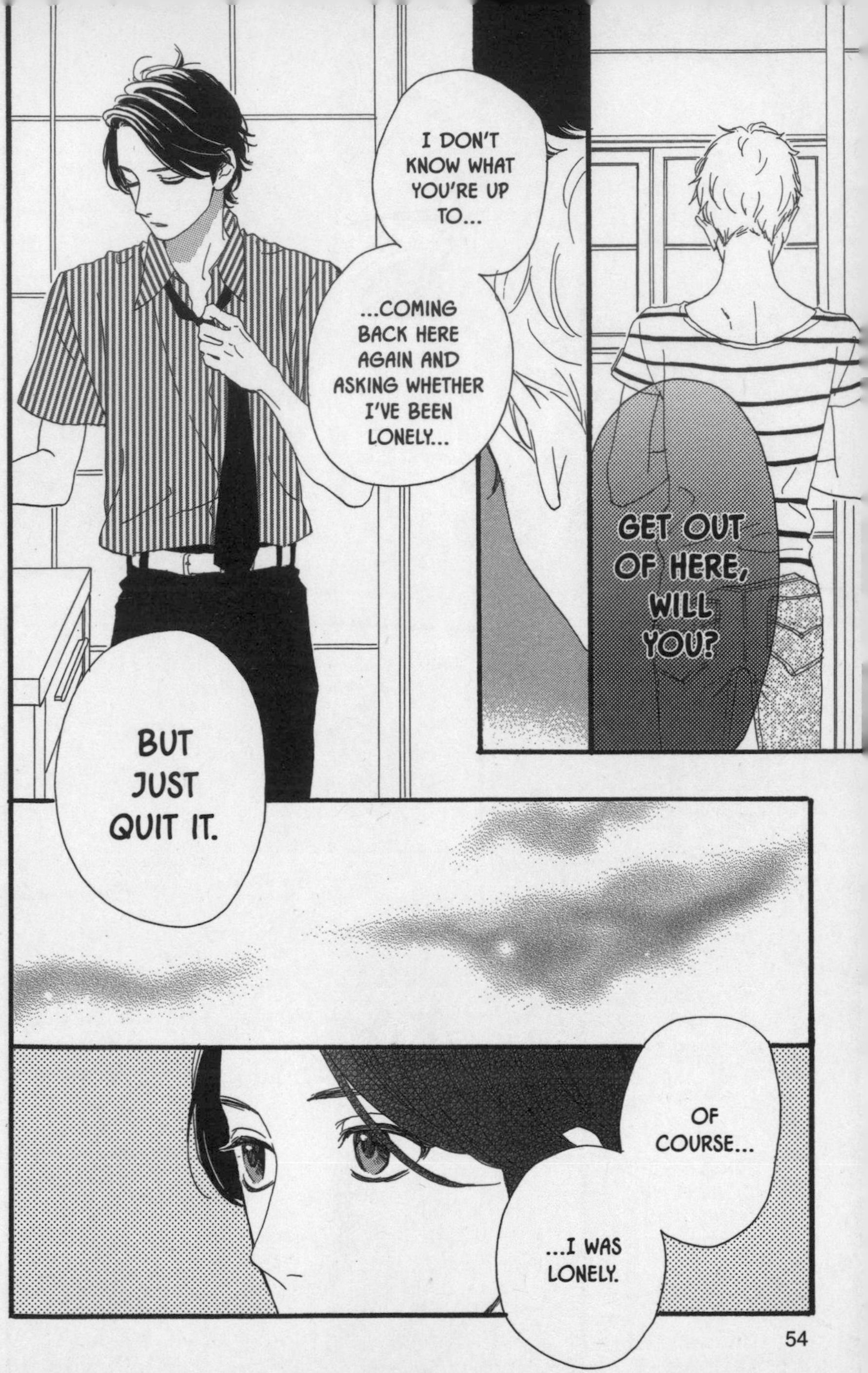
GET OUT OF HERE, WILL YOU?
I DON'T KNOW WHAT YOU'RE UP TO...
...COMING BACK HERE AGAIN AND ASKING WHETHER I'VE BEEN LONELY...
BUT JUST QUIT IT.
OF COURSE...
...I WAS LONELY.

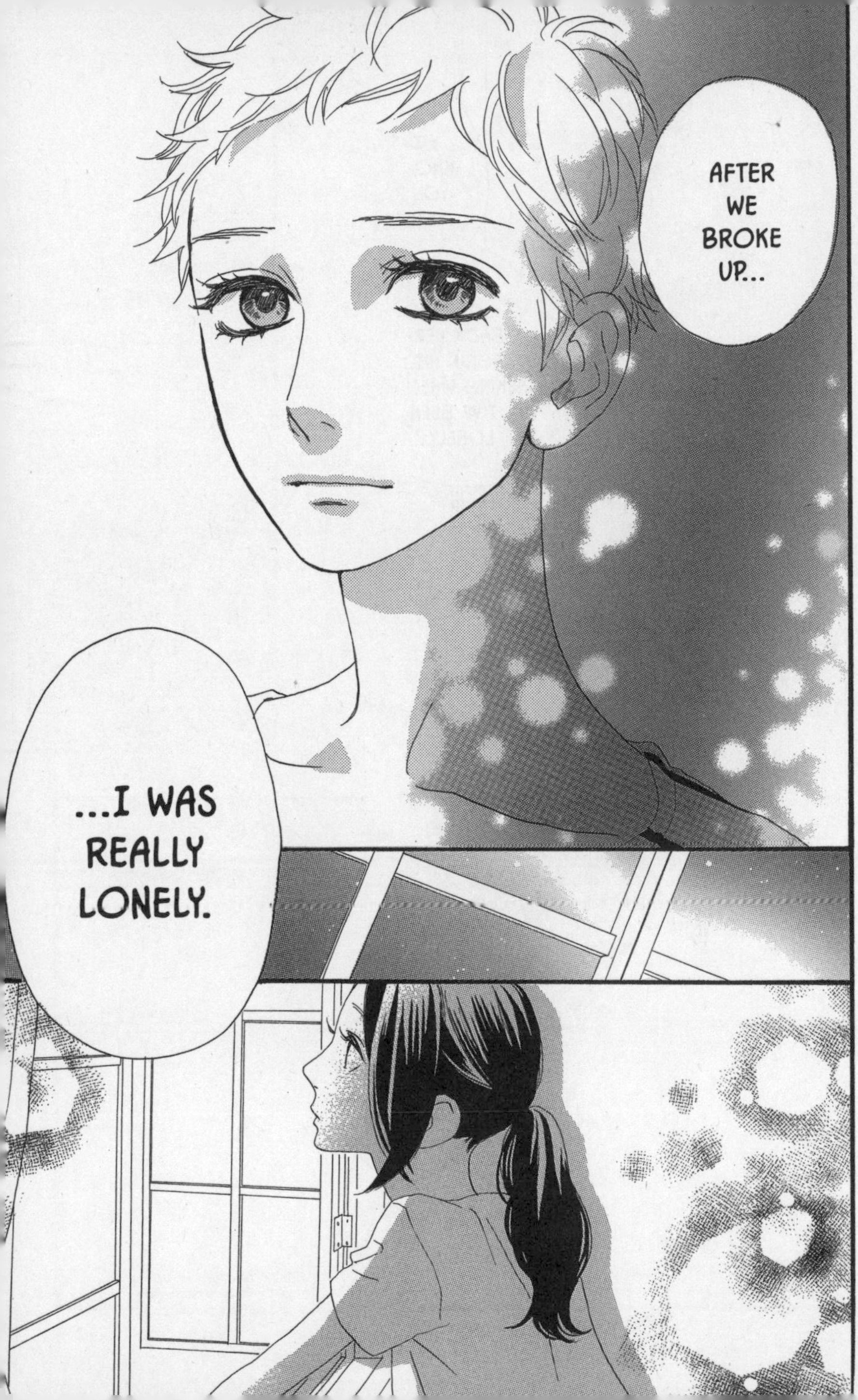
AFTER WE BROKE UP...
...I WAS REALLY LONELY.

Lately~

The background music in our workplace has been leaning toward movie soundtracks. The most often played is *Sherlock Holmes*. We also play *Madagascar 2*, *Kung Fu Panda*, and *Snatch* among others. The other week when we were working in a frenzy, it was a little surreal to listen to "Copacabana" on full blast.

It seems my editor K, who was waiting in the next room, found it a little funny.

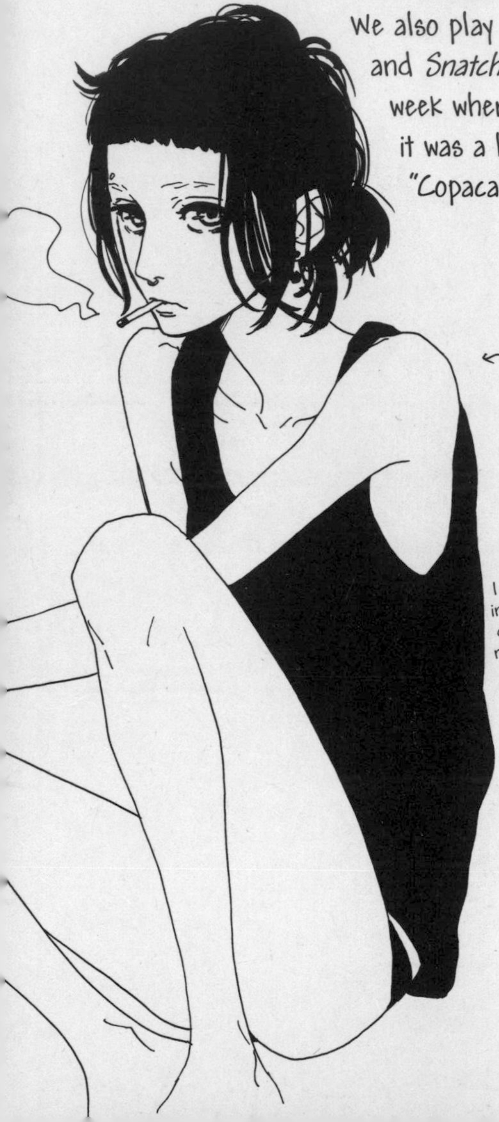

← The Girl with the Dragon Tattoo

Lisbeth was cute.
She was cute.

(That story stayed in my head for a good three days.)

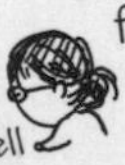

I fell into a dark mood.

I don't care for those sorts of stories much. Heh heh.

But, Lisbeth was cute.

I think she's the epitome of a *yandere* character.

**Yandere* characters are violent and deranged with a strong romantic affection.

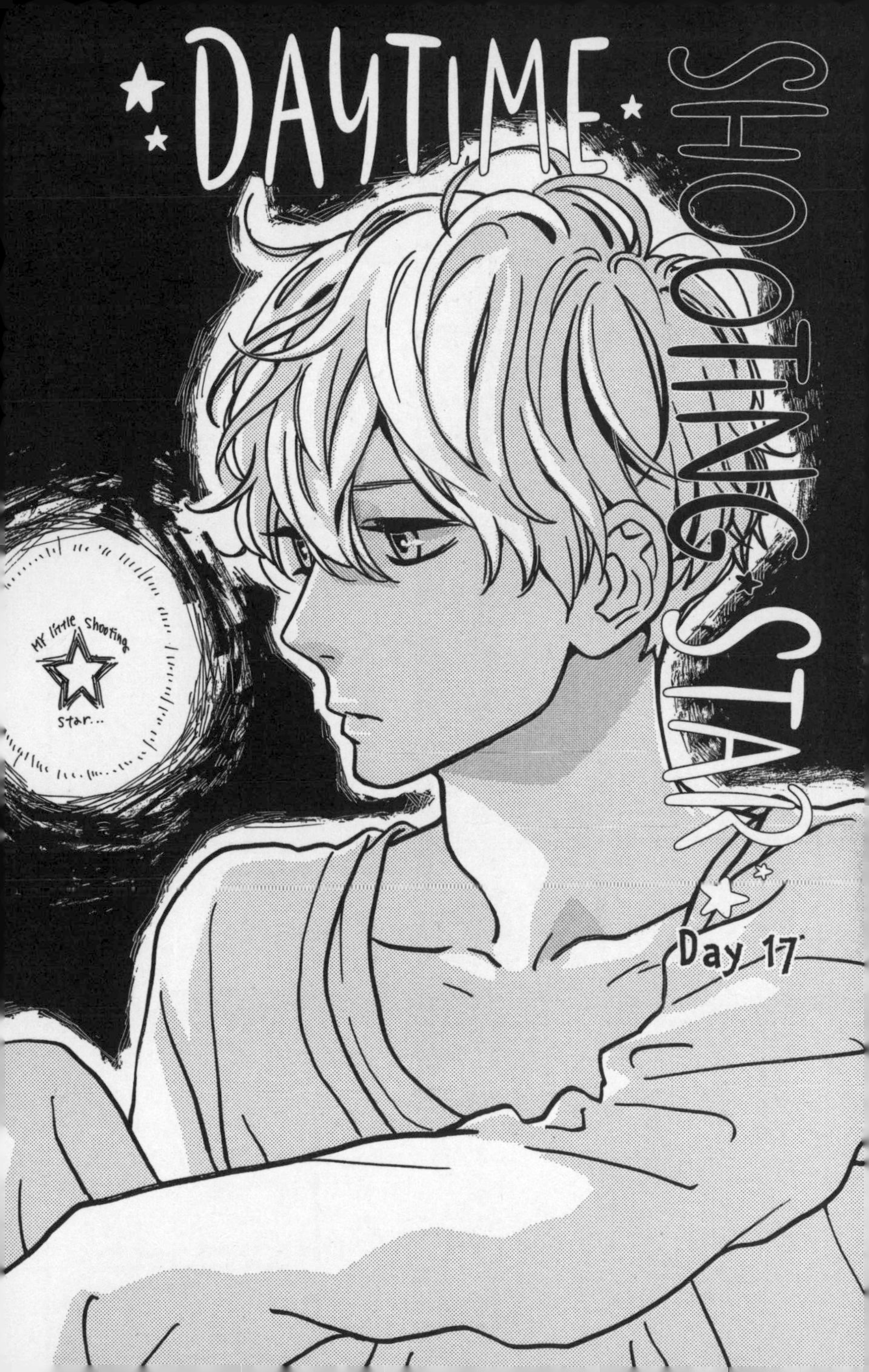
DAYTIME
SHOOTING STAR
Day 17
My little shooting star...

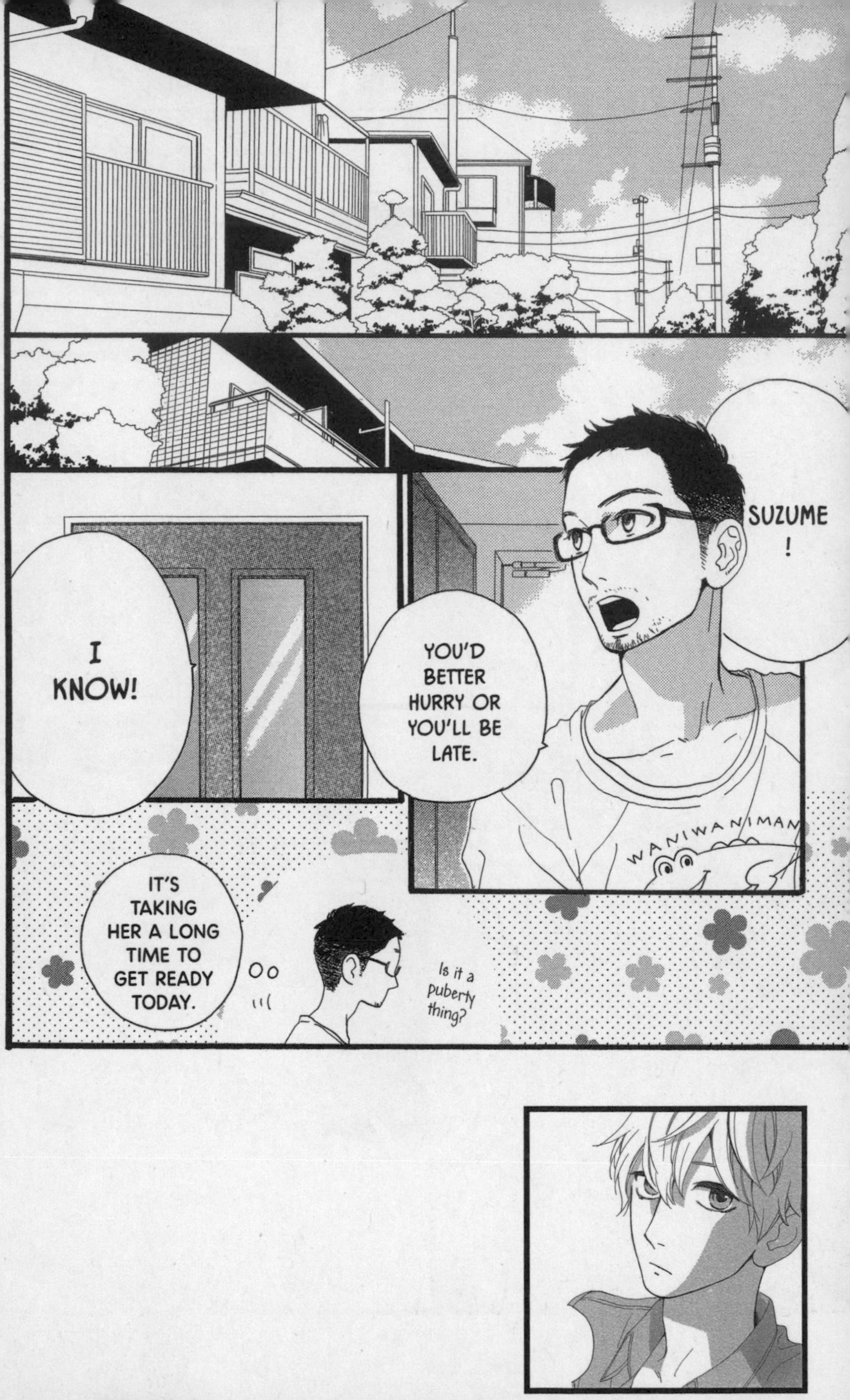
SUZUME!
YOU'D BETTER HURRY OR YOU'LL BE LATE.
WANIWANIMAN
I KNOW!
IT'S TAKING HER A LONG TIME TO GET READY TODAY.
Is it a puberty thing?

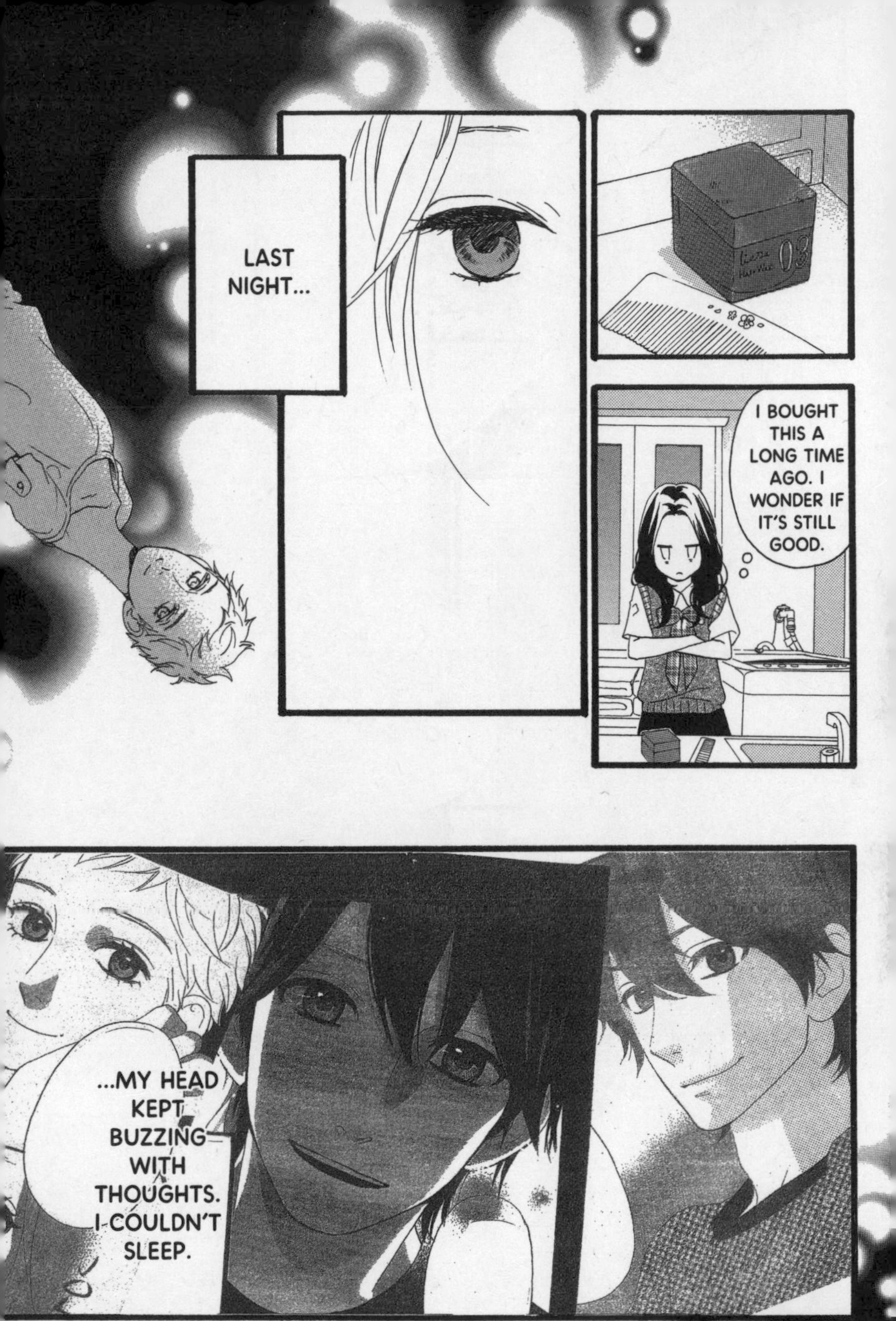
I BOUGHT THIS A LONG TIME AGO. I WONDER IF IT'S STILL GOOD.
LAST NIGHT...
...MY HEAD KEPT BUZZING WITH THOUGHTS. I COULDN'T SLEEP.

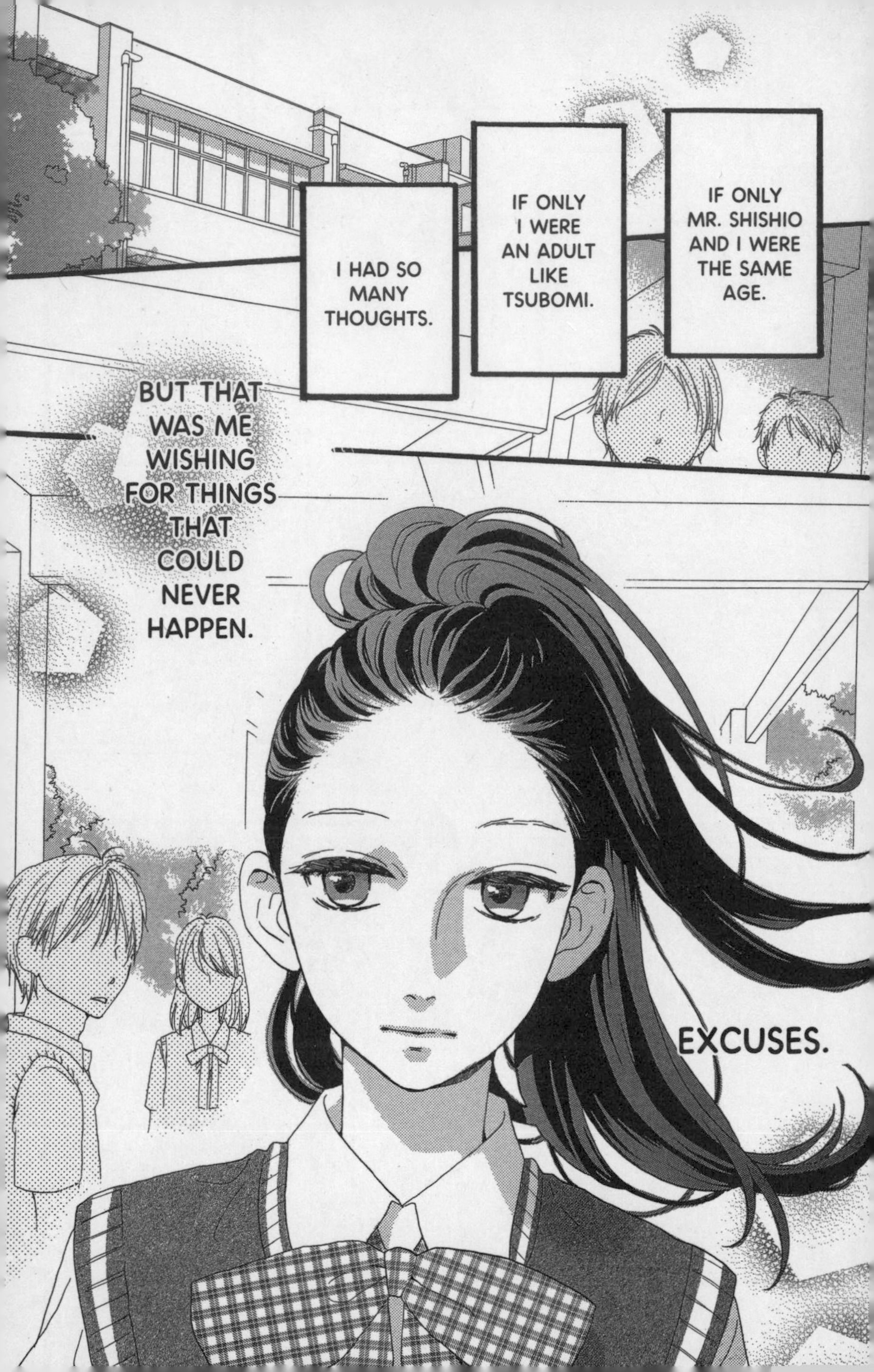
IF ONLY MR. SHISHIO AND I WERE THE SAME AGE.
IF ONLY I WERE AN ADULT LIKE TSUBOMI.
I HAD SO MANY THOUGHTS.
BUT THAT WAS ME WISHING FOR THINGS THAT COULD NEVER HAPPEN.
EXCUSES.

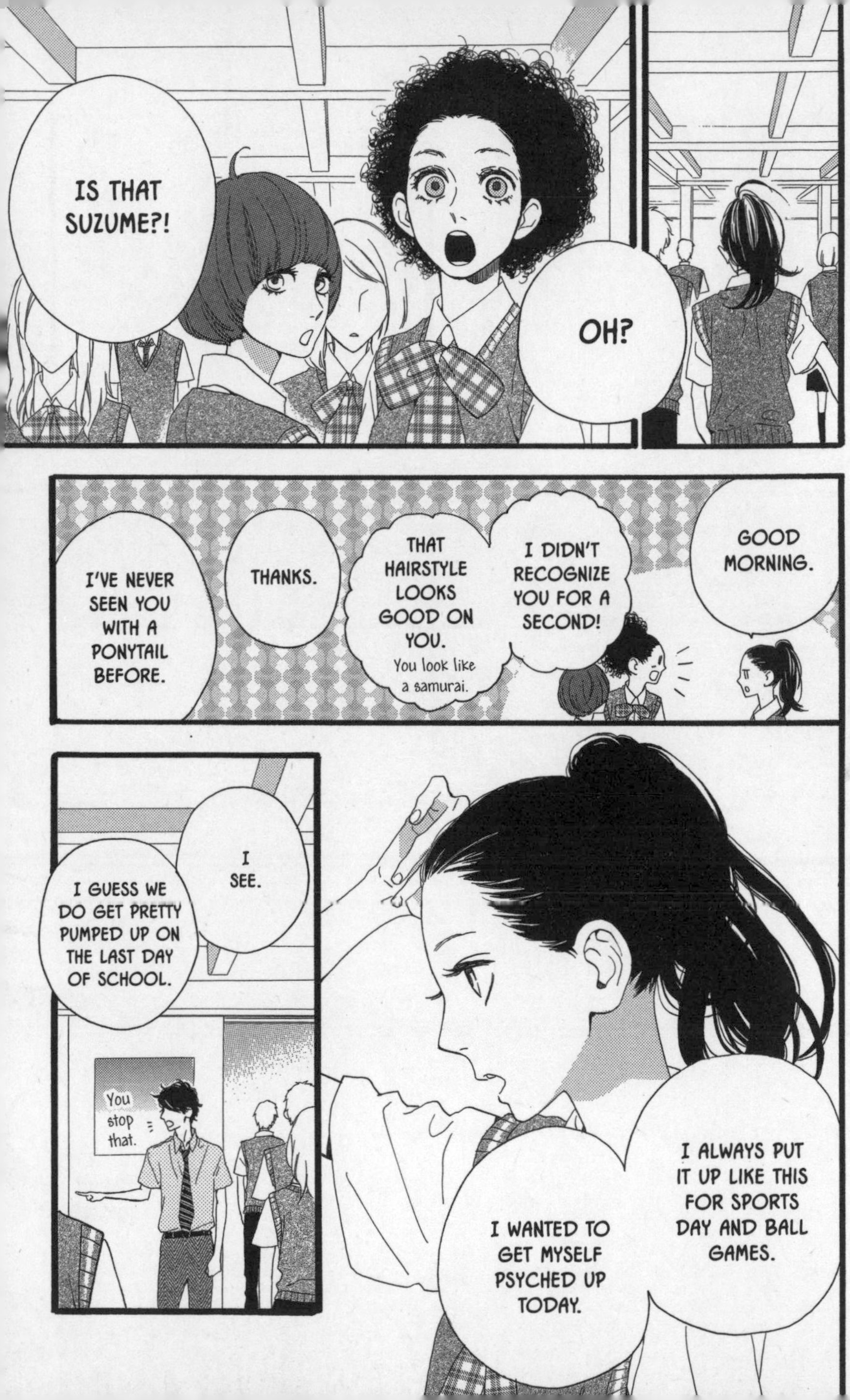
OH?
IS THAT SUZUME?!
GOOD MORNING.
I DIDN'T RECOGNIZE YOU FOR A SECOND!
THAT HAIRSTYLE LOOKS GOOD ON YOU.
You look like a samurai.
THANKS.
I'VE NEVER SEEN YOU WITH A PONYTAIL BEFORE.
I ALWAYS PUT IT UP LIKE THIS FOR SPORTS DAY AND BALL GAMES.
I WANTED TO GET MYSELF PSYCHED UP TODAY.
I SEE.
I GUESS WE DO GET PRETTY PUMPED UP ON THE LAST DAY OF SCHOOL.
You stop that.

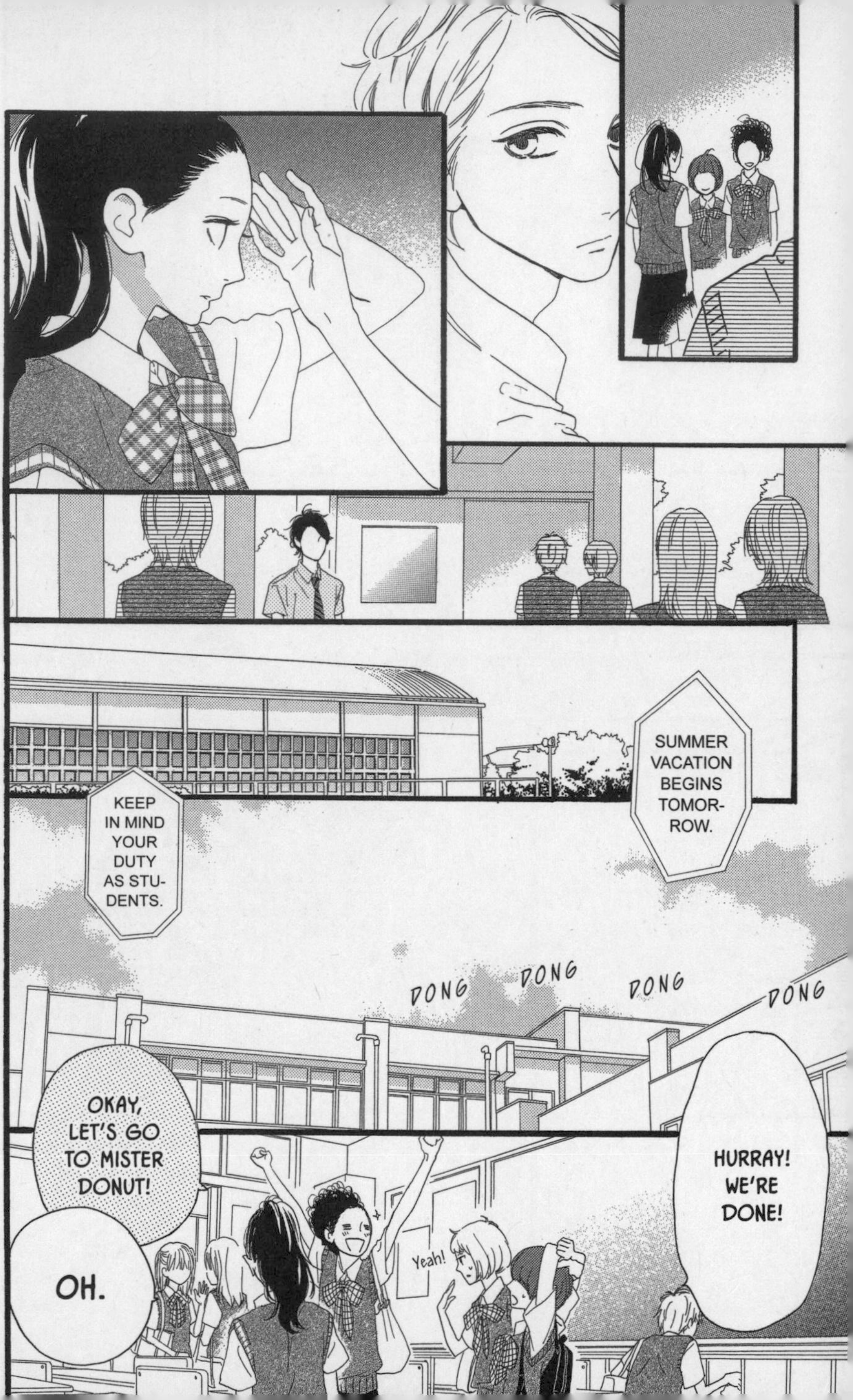
SUMMER VACATION BEGINS TOMORROW.
KEEP IN MIND YOUR DUTY AS STUDENTS.
DONG
DONG
DONG
DONG
HURRAY! WE'RE DONE!
Yeah!
OKAY, LET'S GO TO MISTER DONUT!
OH.

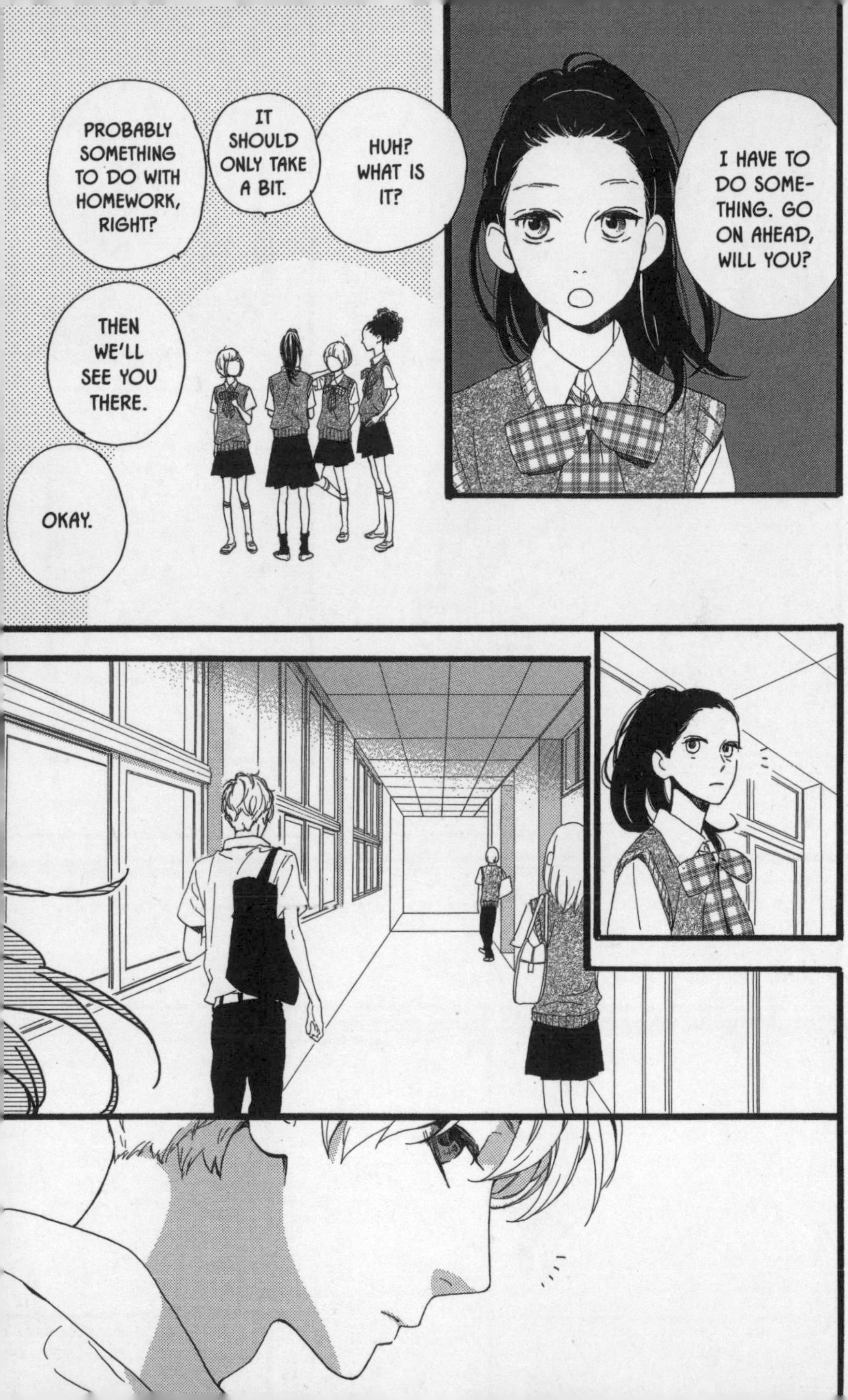
I HAVE TO DO SOME-THING. GO ON AHEAD, WILL YOU?
HUH? WHAT IS IT?
IT SHOULD ONLY TAKE A BIT.
PROBABLY SOMETHING TO DO WITH HOMEWORK, RIGHT?
THEN WE'LL SEE YOU THERE.
OKAY.

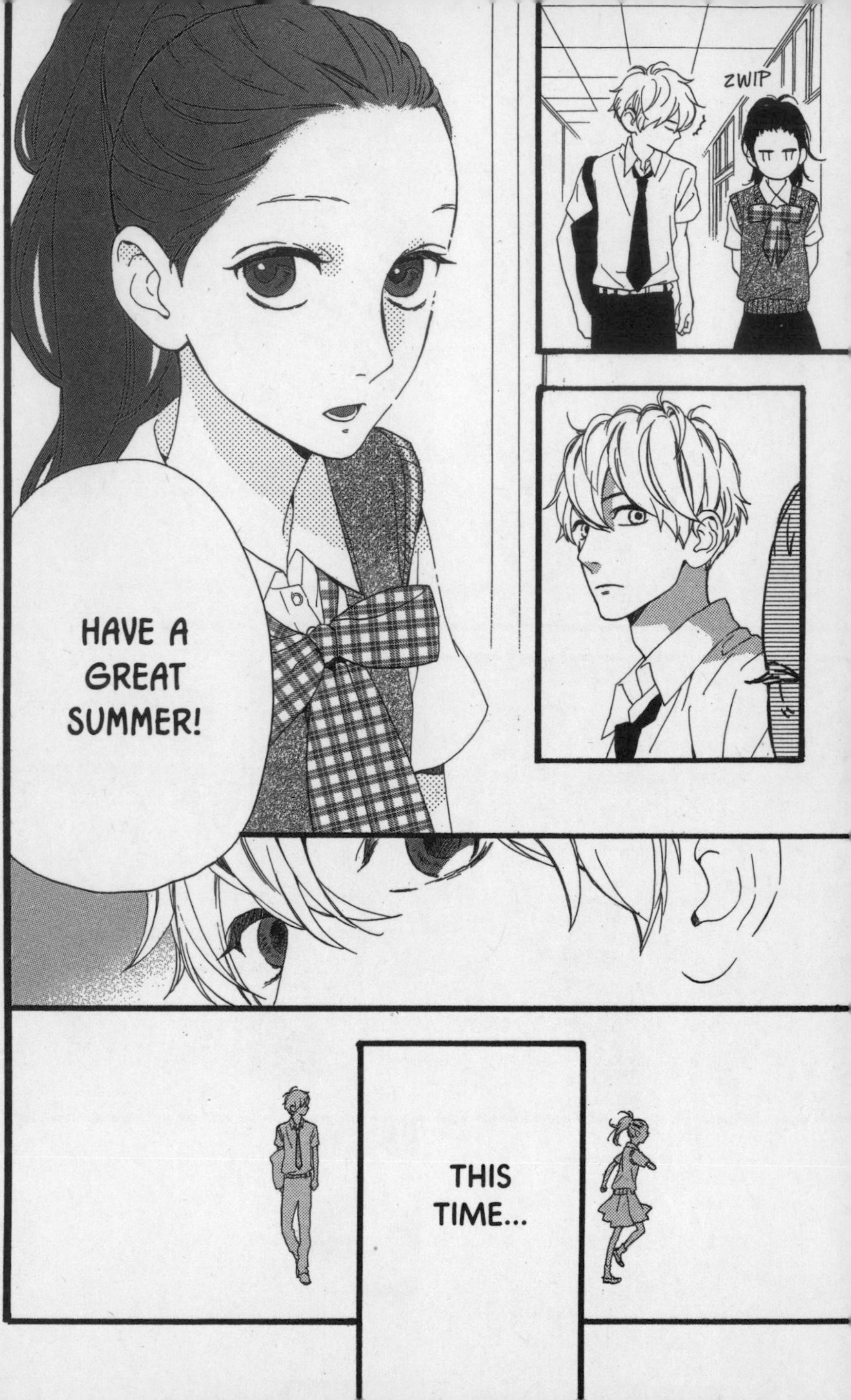
ZWIP
HAVE A GREAT SUMMER!
THIS TIME...

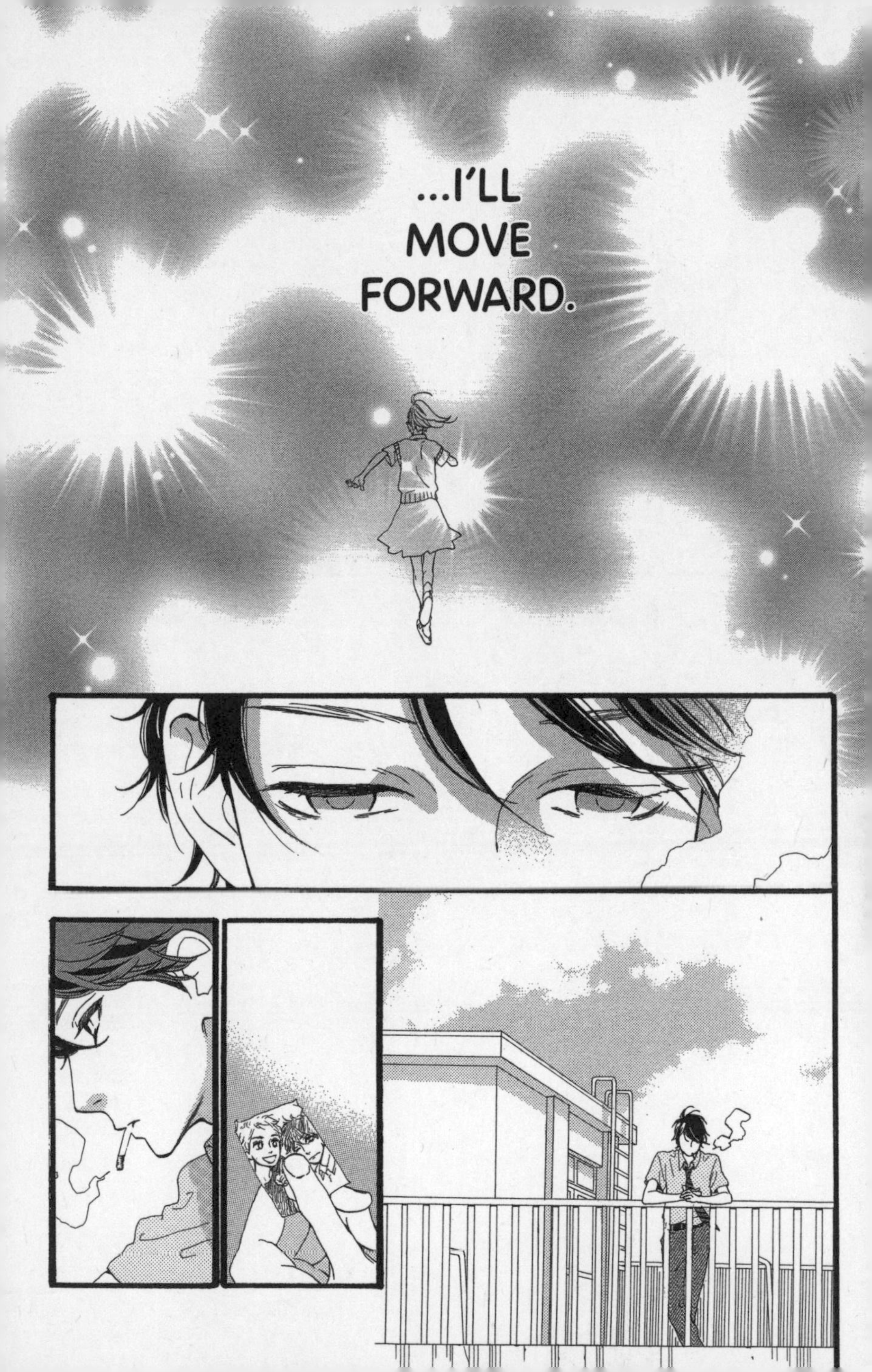
...I'LL MOVE FORWARD.

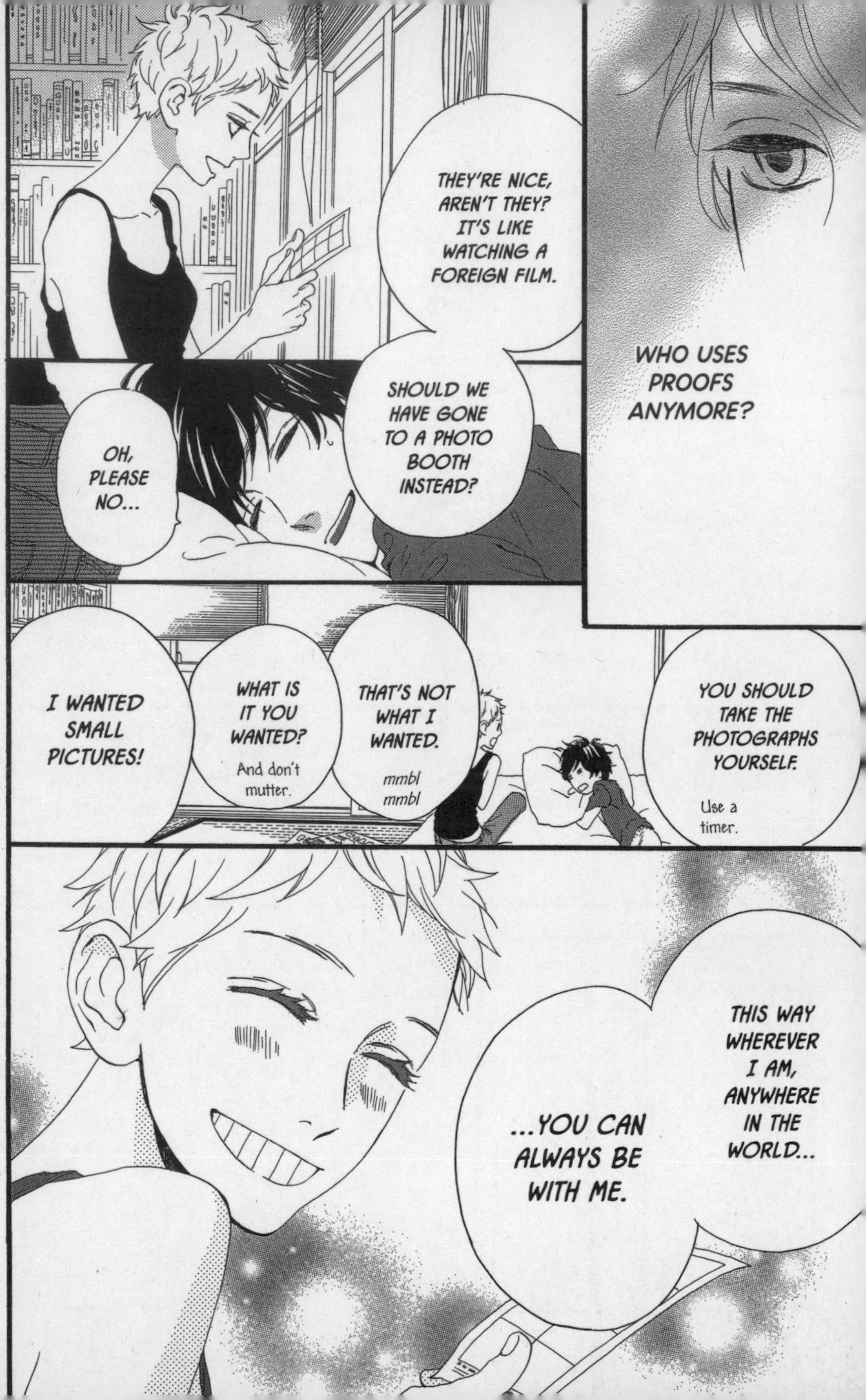
WHO USES PROOFS ANYMORE?
THEY'RE NICE, AREN'T THEY? IT'S LIKE WATCHING A FOREIGN FILM.
SHOULD WE HAVE GONE TO A PHOTO BOOTH INSTEAD?
OH, PLEASE NO...
YOU SHOULD TAKE THE PHOTOGRAPHS YOURSELF.
Use a timer.
THAT'S NOT WHAT I WANTED.
mmbl mmbl
WHAT IS IT YOU WANTED?
And don't mutter.
I WANTED SMALL PICTURES!
THIS WAY WHEREVER I AM, ANYWHERE IN THE WORLD...
...YOU CAN ALWAYS BE WITH ME.

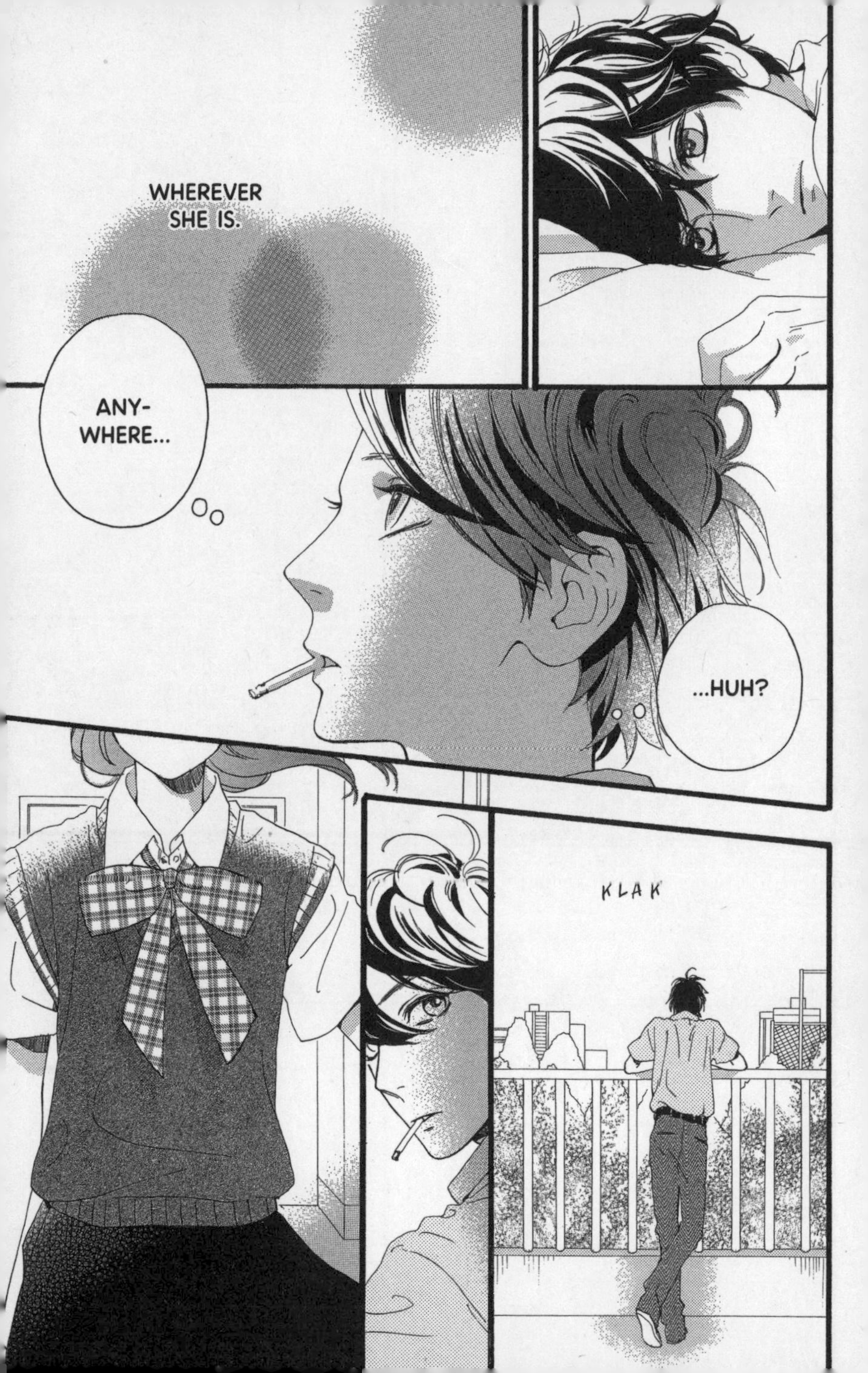
WHEREVER SHE IS.
ANY-WHERE...
...HUH?
KLAK

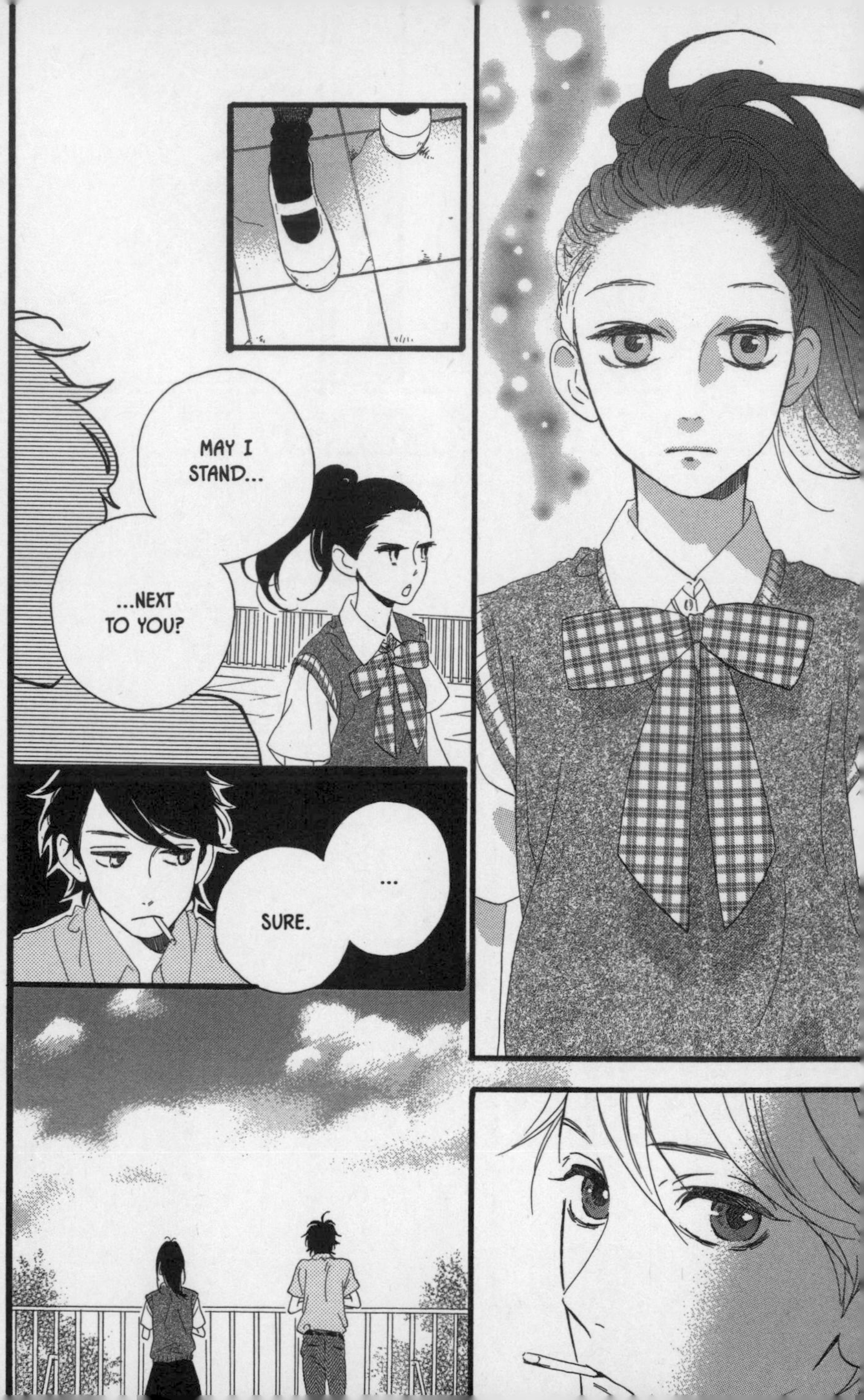
MAY I STAND...
...NEXT TO YOU?
...
SURE.

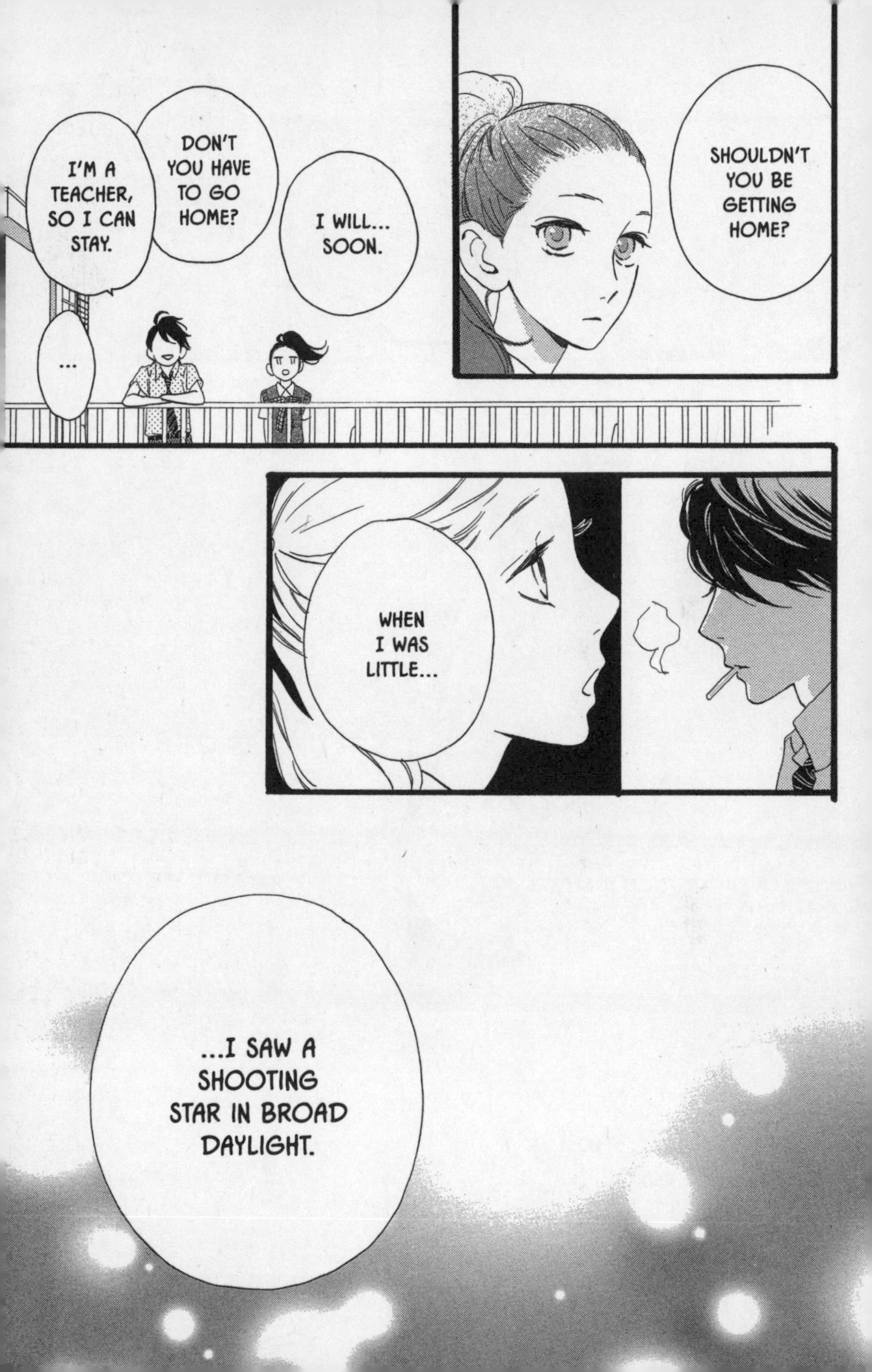
SHOULDN'T YOU BE GETTING HOME?
I WILL... SOON.
DON'T YOU HAVE TO GO HOME?
I'M A TEACHER, SO I CAN STAY.
...
WHEN I WAS LITTLE...
...I SAW A SHOOTING STAR IN BROAD DAYLIGHT.

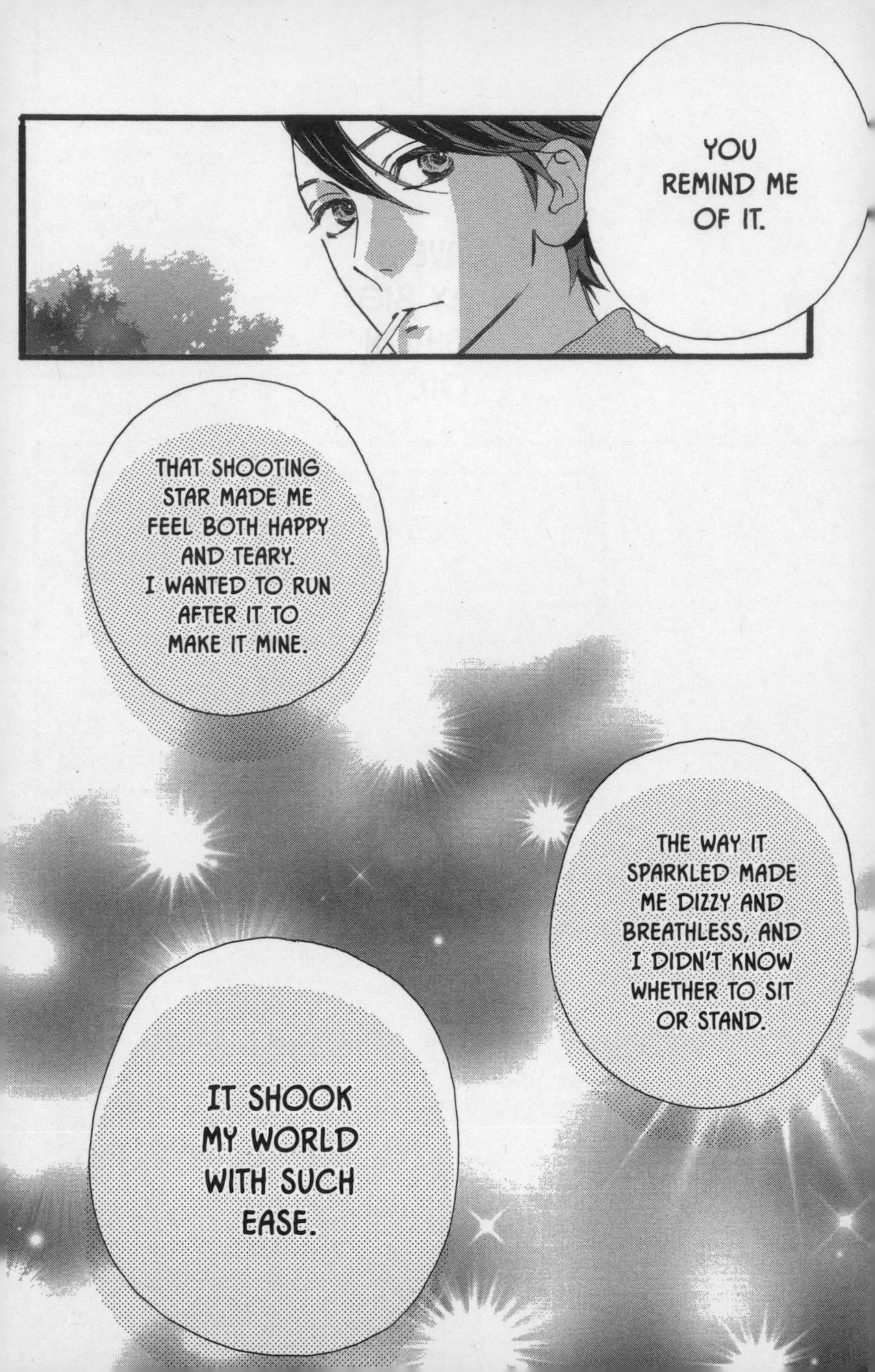
YOU REMIND ME OF IT.
THAT SHOOTING STAR MADE ME FEEL BOTH HAPPY AND TEARY. I WANTED TO RUN AFTER IT TO MAKE IT MINE.
THE WAY IT SPARKLED MADE ME DIZZY AND BREATHLESS, AND I DIDN'T KNOW WHETHER TO SIT OR STAND.
IT SHOOK MY WORLD WITH SUCH EASE.

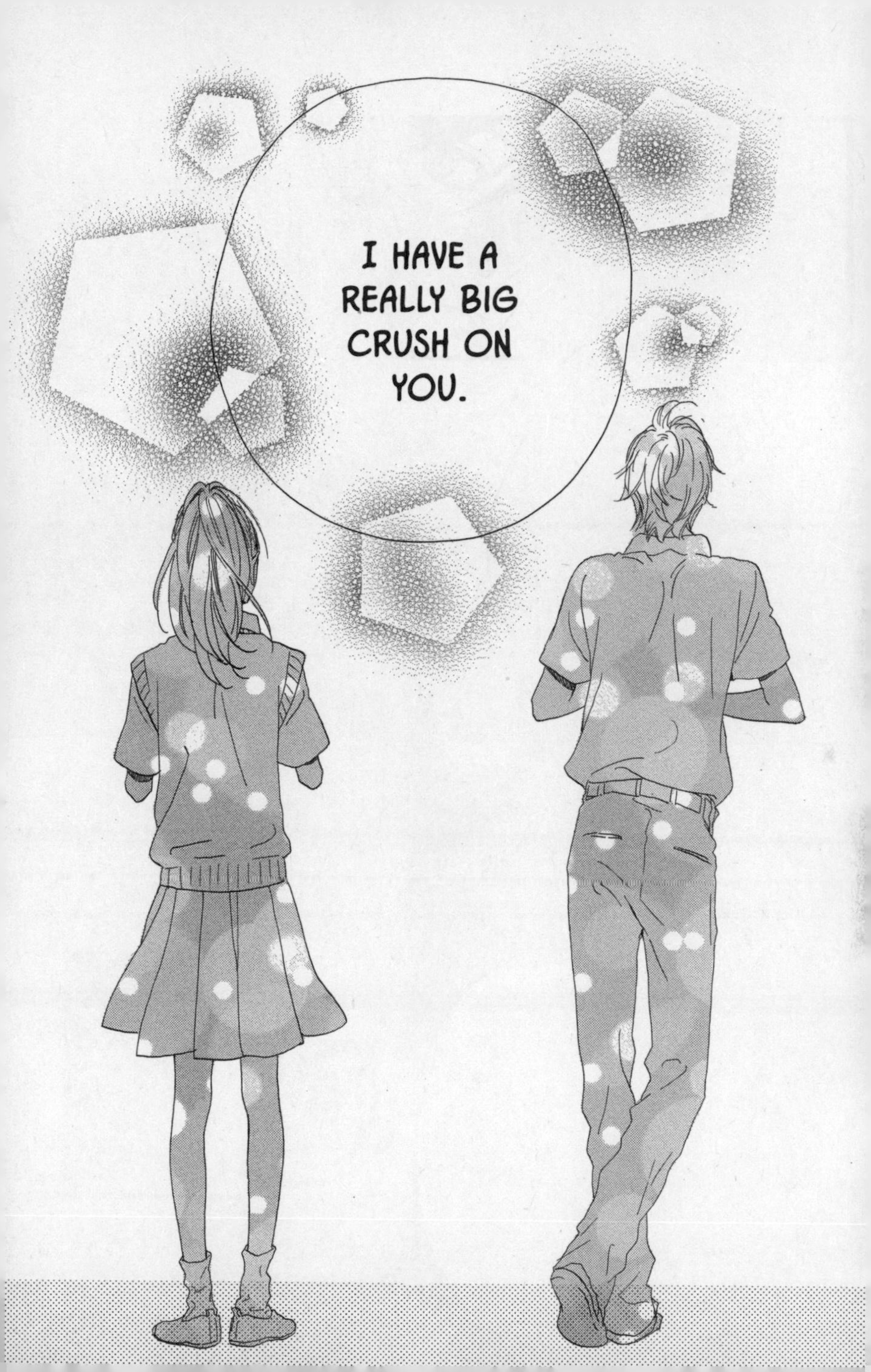
I HAVE A REALLY BIG CRUSH ON YOU.

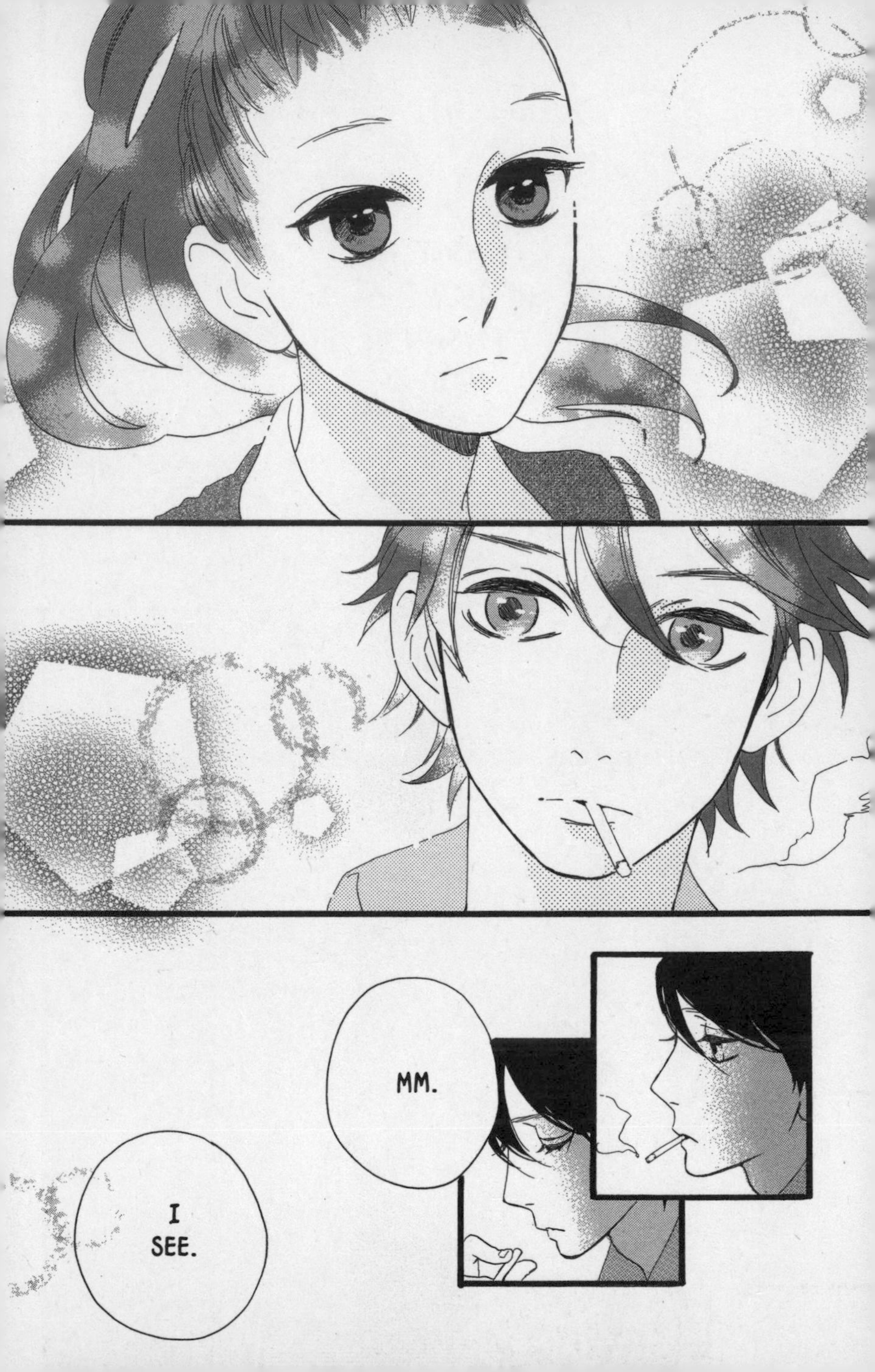
MM.
I SEE.

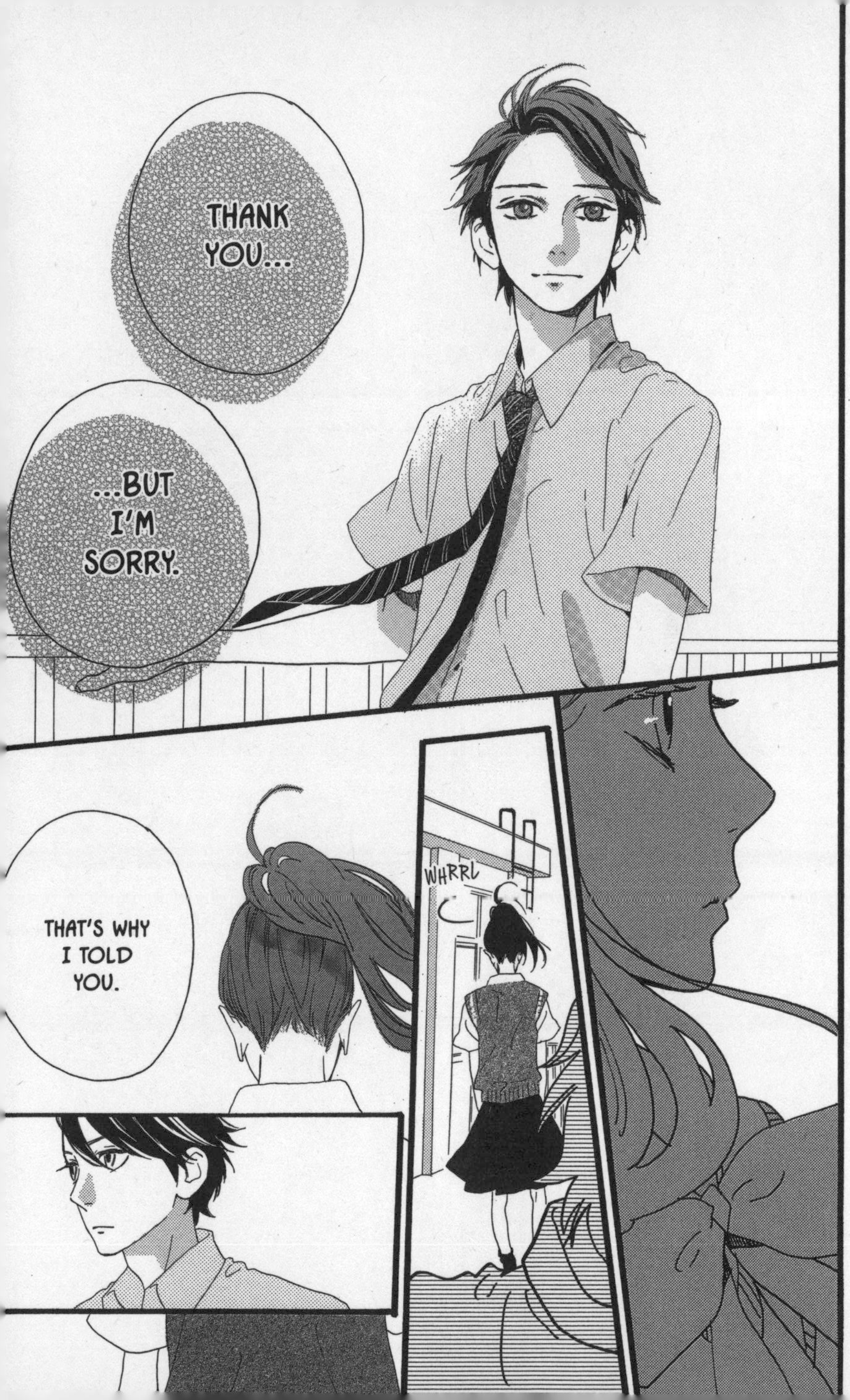
THANK YOU...
...BUT I'M SORRY.
WHRRL
THAT'S WHY I TOLD YOU.

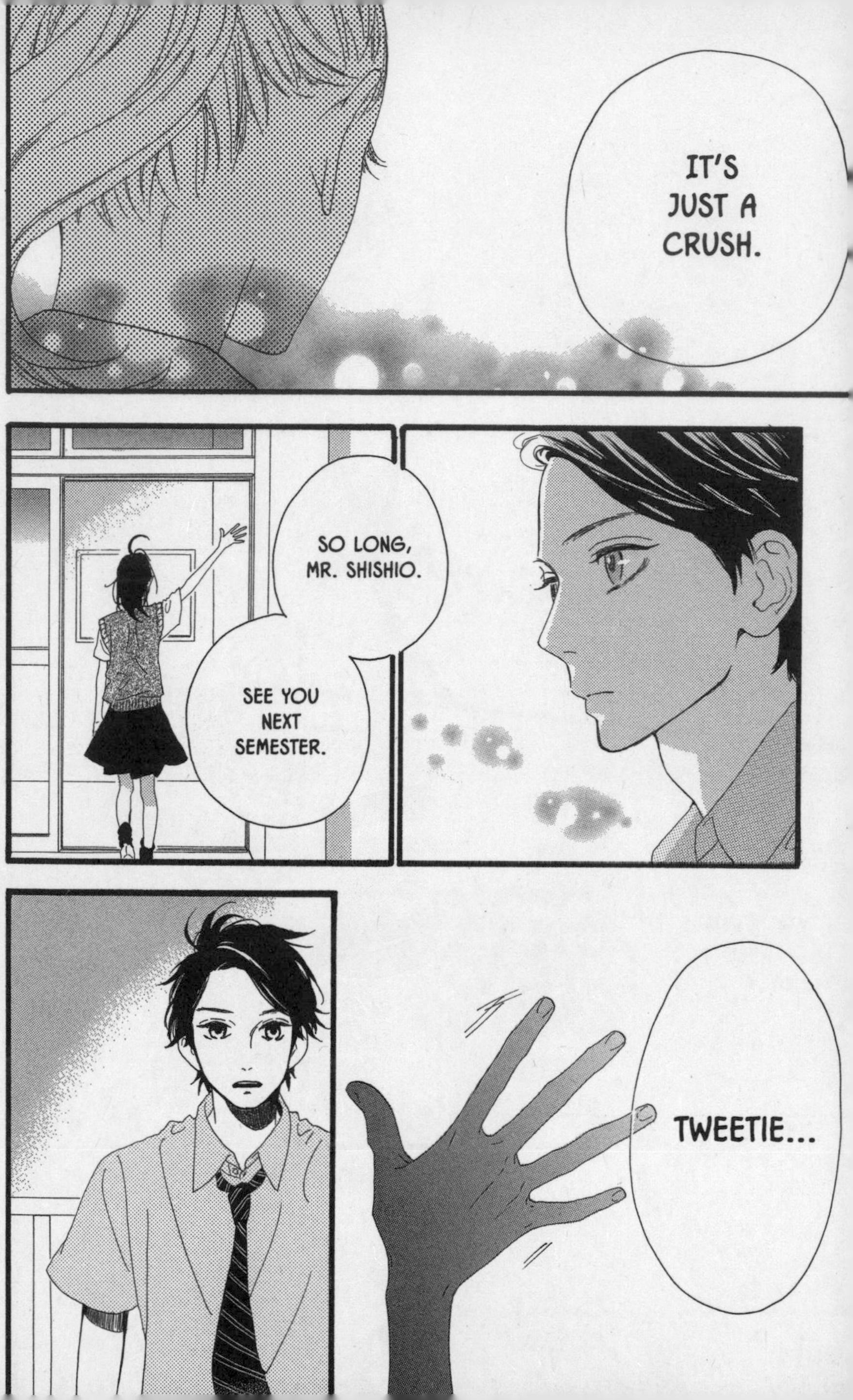
IT'S JUST A CRUSH.
SO LONG, MR. SHISHIO.
SEE YOU NEXT SEMESTER.
TWEETIE...

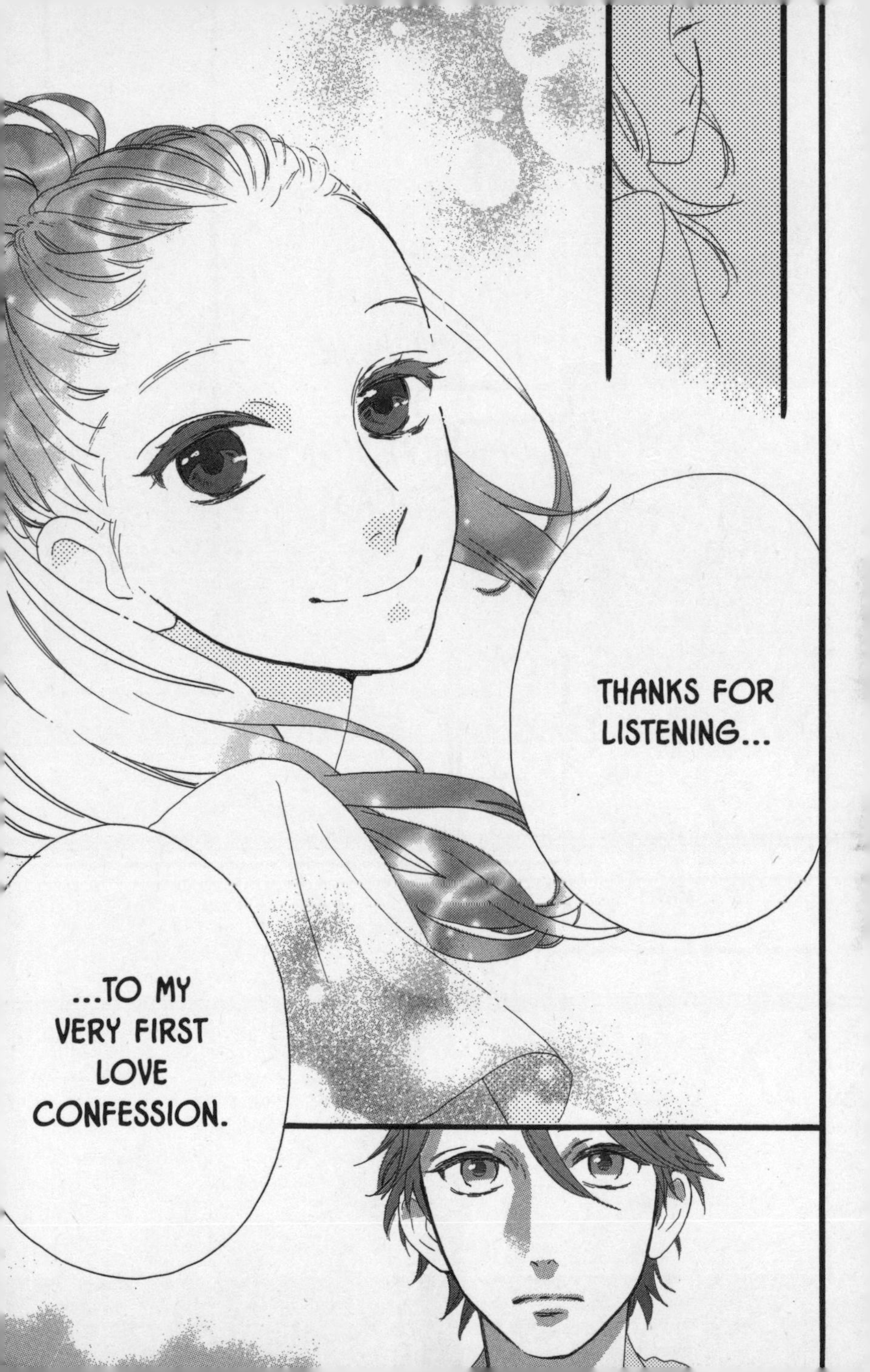
THANKS FOR LISTENING...
...TO MY VERY FIRST LOVE CONFESSION.

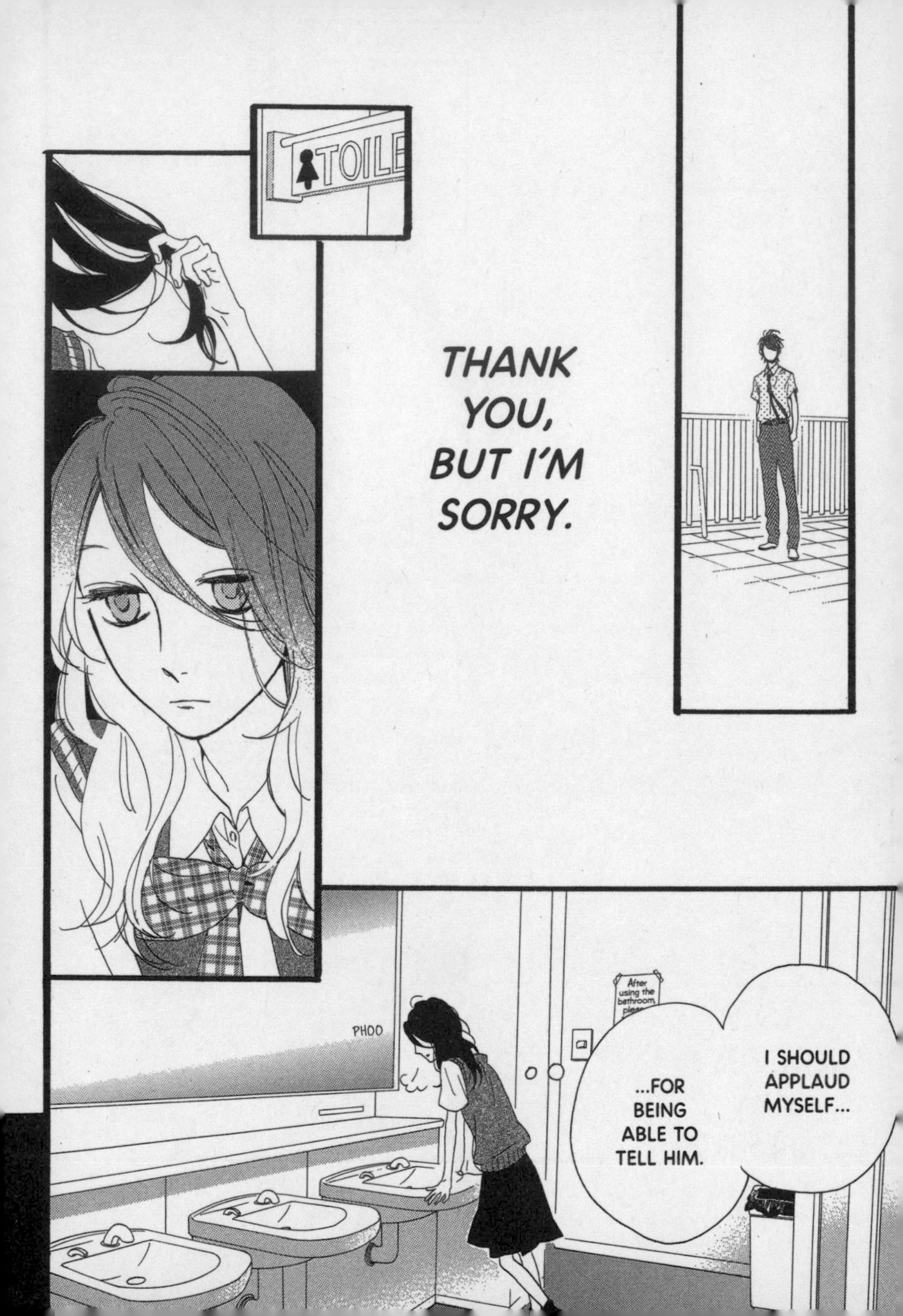
THANK YOU, BUT I'M SORRY.
TOILE
I SHOULD APPLAUD MYSELF...
...FOR BEING ABLE TO TELL HIM.
After using the bathroom,
PHOO

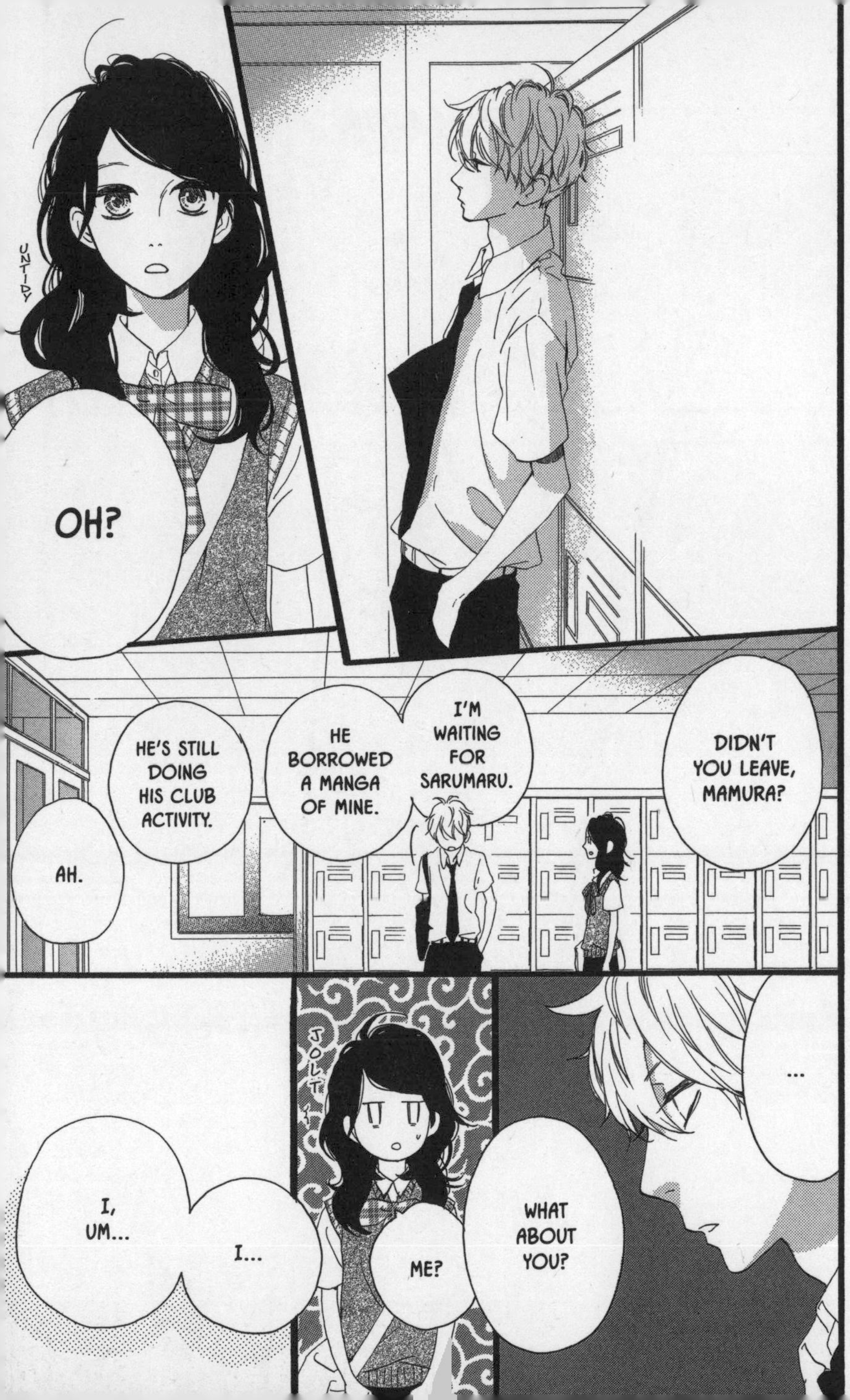
UNTIDY
OH?
DIDN'T YOU LEAVE, MAMURA?
I'M WAITING FOR SARUMARU.
HE BORROWED A MANGA OF MINE.
HE'S STILL DOING HIS CLUB ACTIVITY.
AH.
...
WHAT ABOUT YOU?
JOLT
ME?
I, UM...
I...

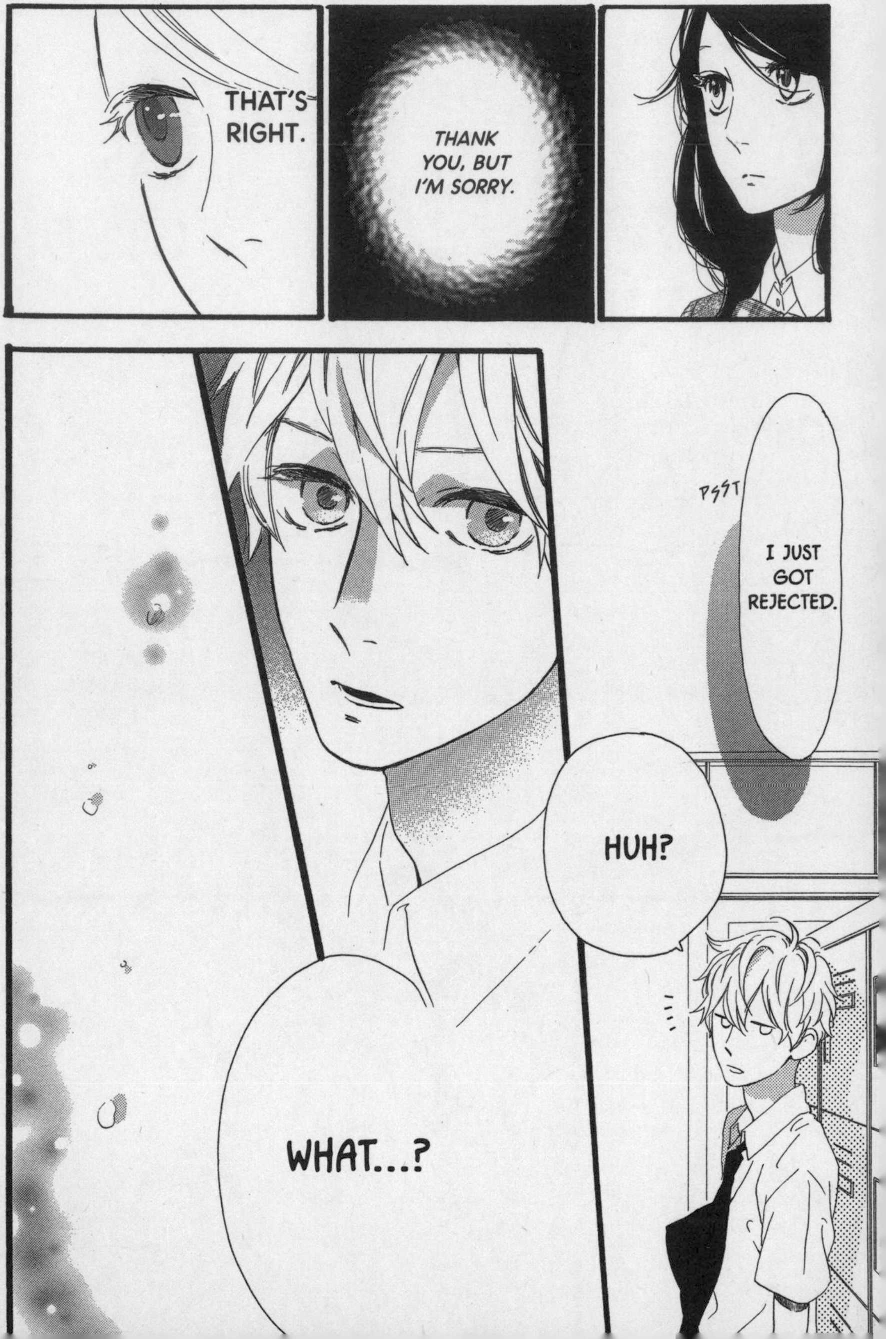
THANK YOU, BUT I'M SORRY.
THAT'S RIGHT.
PSST
I JUST GOT REJECTED.
HUH?
WHAT...?

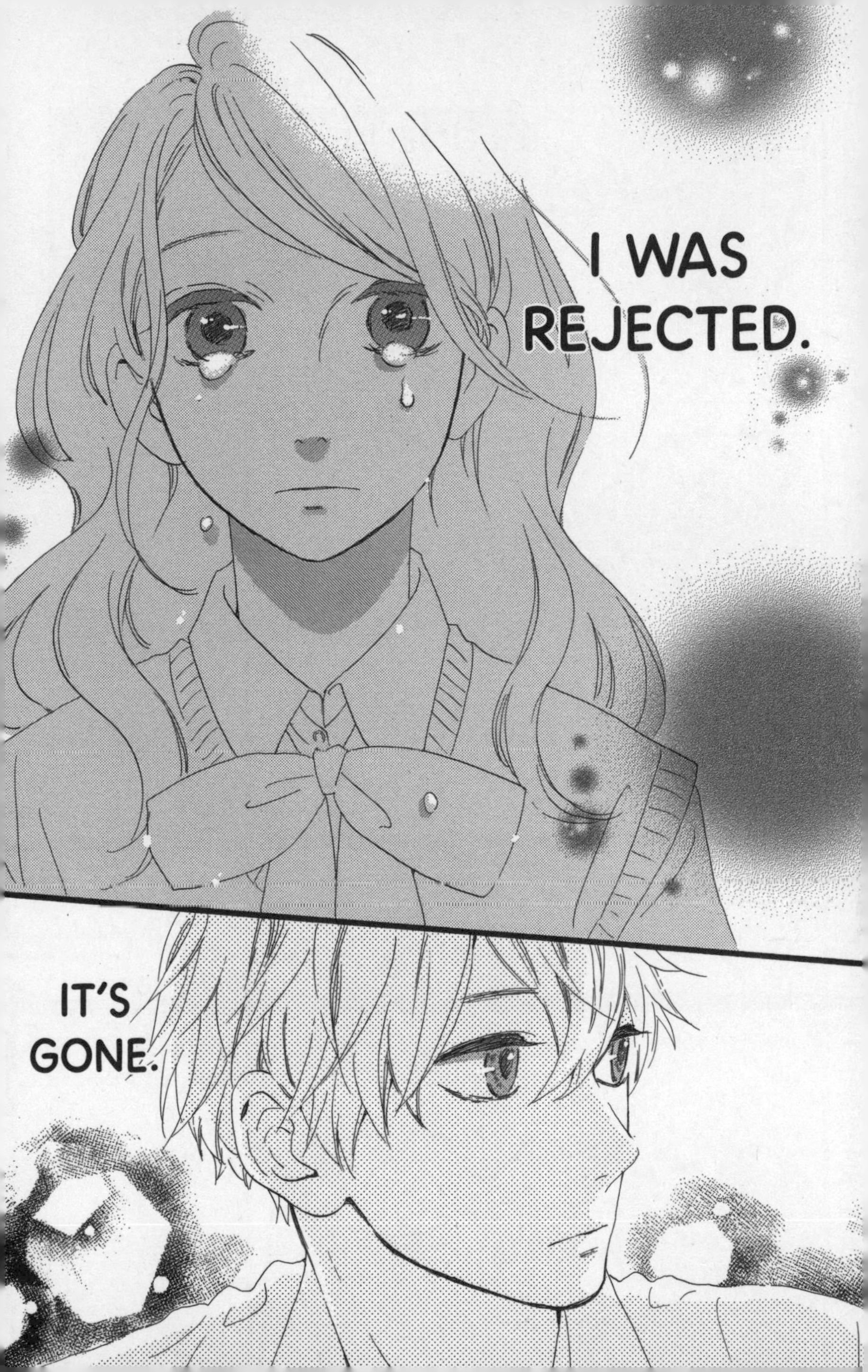
I WAS REJECTED.
IT'S GONE.

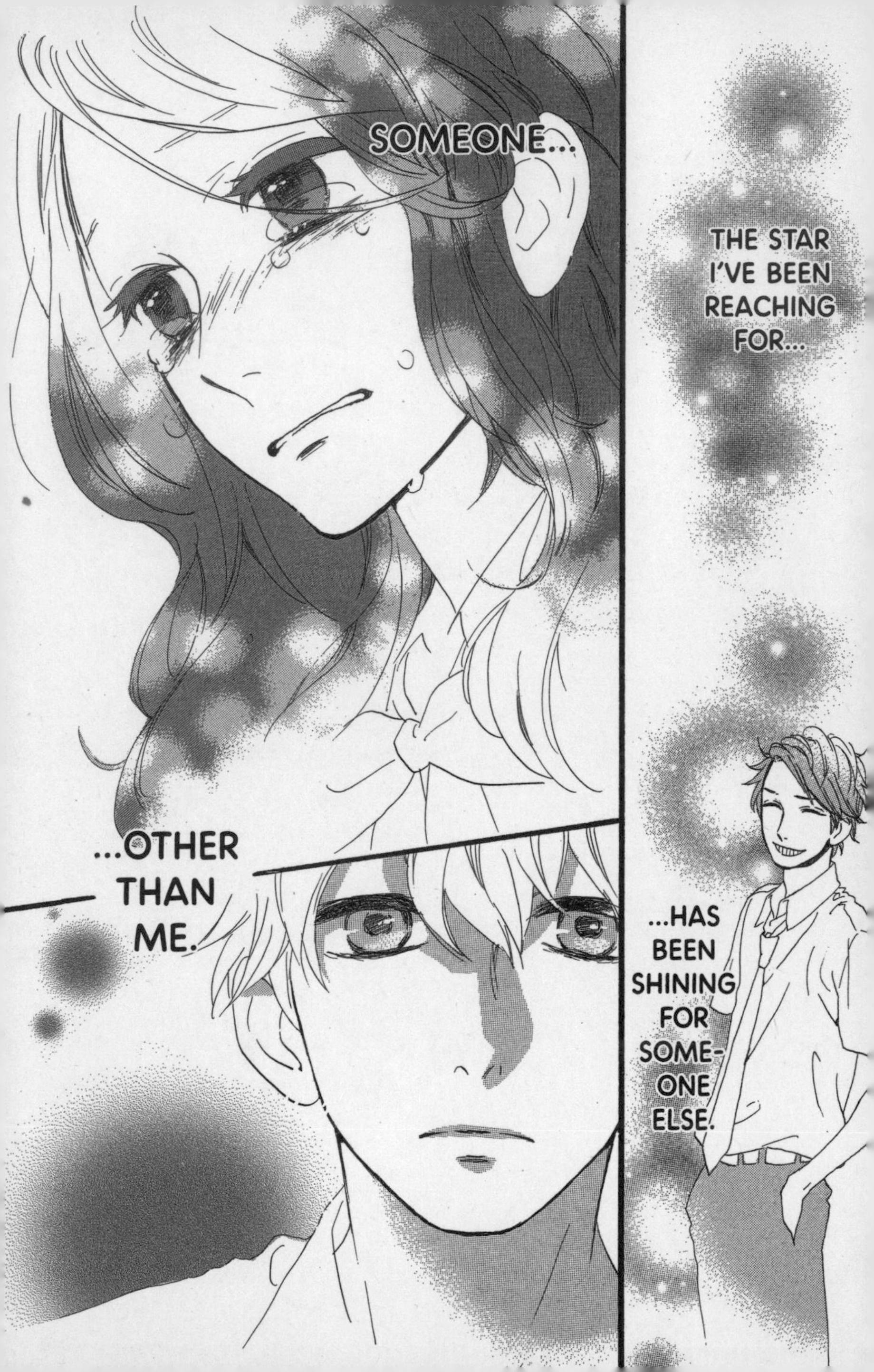
THE STAR I'VE BEEN REACHING FOR...
...HAS BEEN SHINING FOR SOME-ONE ELSE.
SOMEONE...
...OTHER THAN ME.

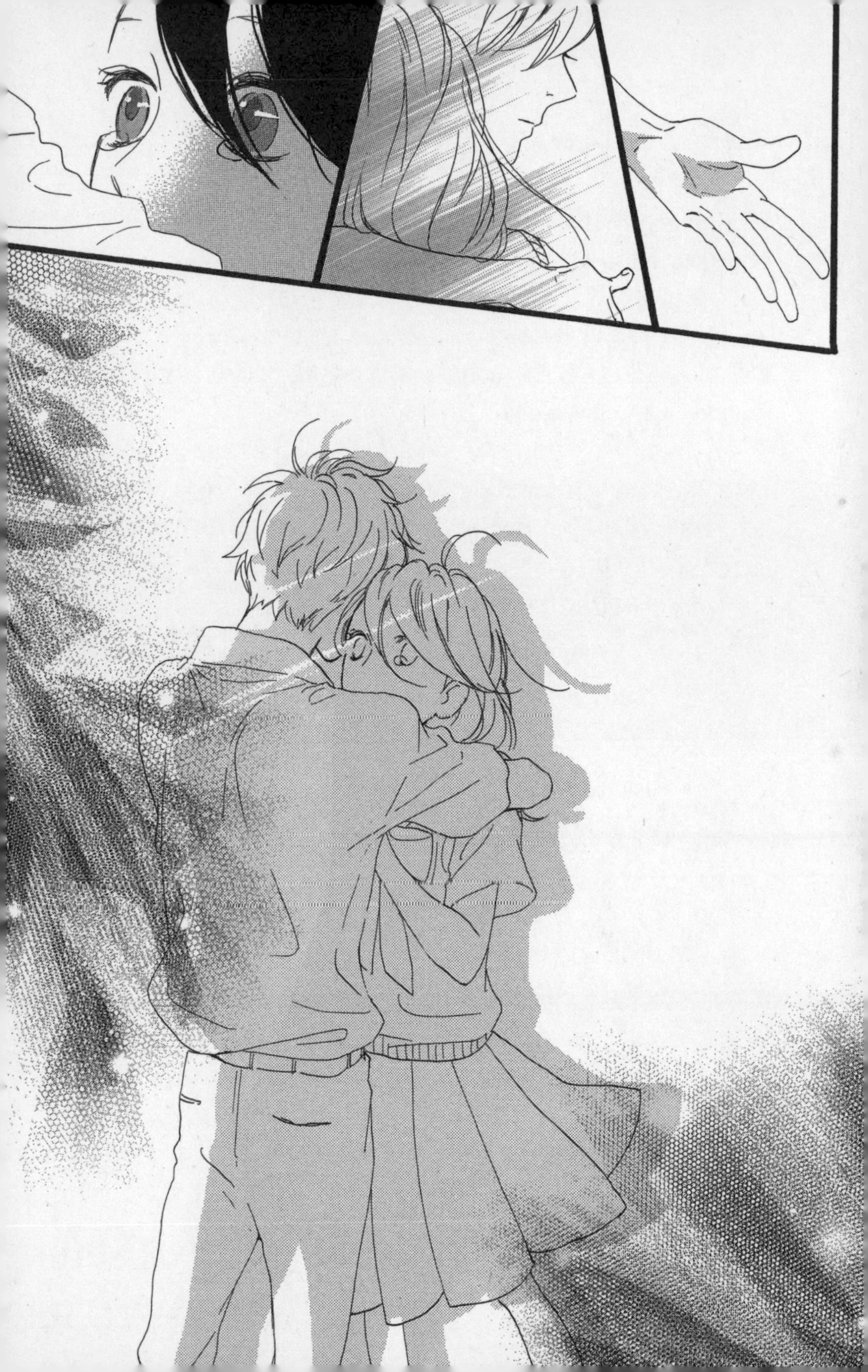

By the way...

I had Momoko Koda from *Bessatsu Margaret* do illustrations of Mamura and Shishio of *Daytime Shooting Star*.

Volume 7 of *Heroine Shikkaku* has also gone on sale! Please buy it! My illustrations of Rita and Hiromitsu are in that volume. Thank you, Koda! ☺

Koda and I are the same age and have the same blood type and zodiac sign. This year we went on an overnighter at D●sney Resort. (*laugh*)

(I saw the infamous Koda in action, and thought I would die laughing.)

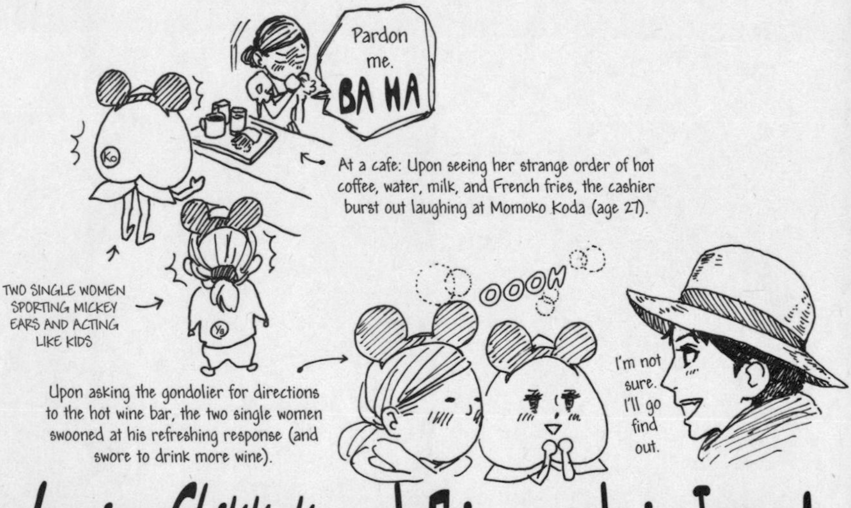
Pardon me.
BA HA
At a cafe: Upon seeing her strange order of hot coffee, water, milk, and French fries, the cashier burst out laughing at Momoko Koda (age 27).
TWO SINGLE WOMEN SPORTING MICKEY EARS AND ACTING LIKE KIDS
I'm not sure. I'll go find out.
OOOOH
Upon asking the gondolier for directions to the hot wine bar, the two single women swooned at his refreshing response (and swore to drink more wine).

Heroine Shikkaku vol. 7 is on sale in Japan!

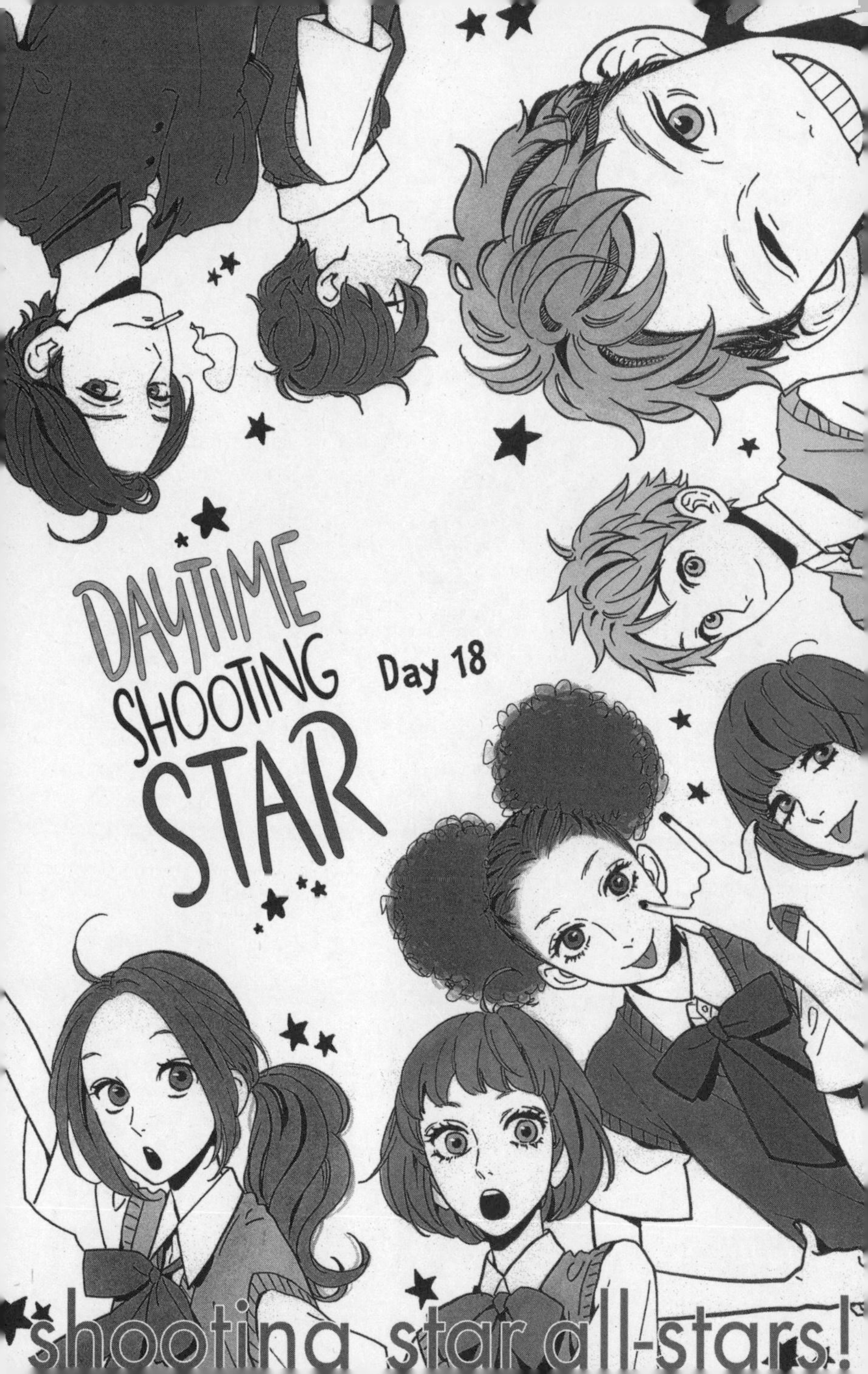
DAYTIME SHOOTING STAR
Day 18
shooting star all-stars!

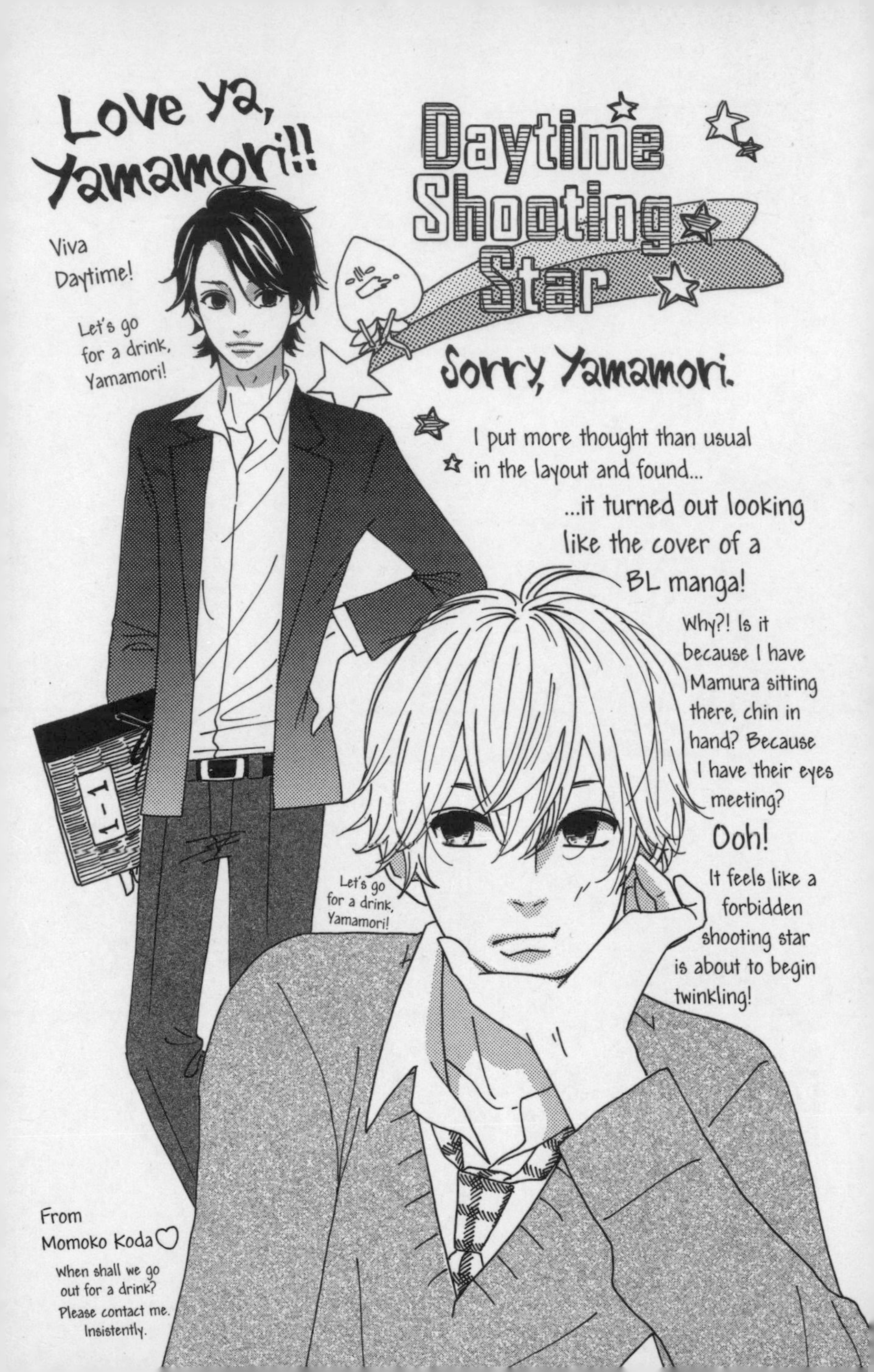
Daytime Shooting Star
Sorry, Yamamori.
I put more thought than usual in the layout and found...
...it turned out looking like the cover of a BL manga!
Why?! Is it because I have Mamura sitting there, chin in hand? Because I have their eyes meeting?
Ooh!
It feels like a forbidden shooting star is about to begin twinkling!
Let's go for a drink, Yamamori!
Love ya, Yamamori!!
Viva Daytime!
Let's go for a drink, Yamamori!
1-1
From Momoko Koda♡
When shall we go out for a drink? Please contact me. Insistently.

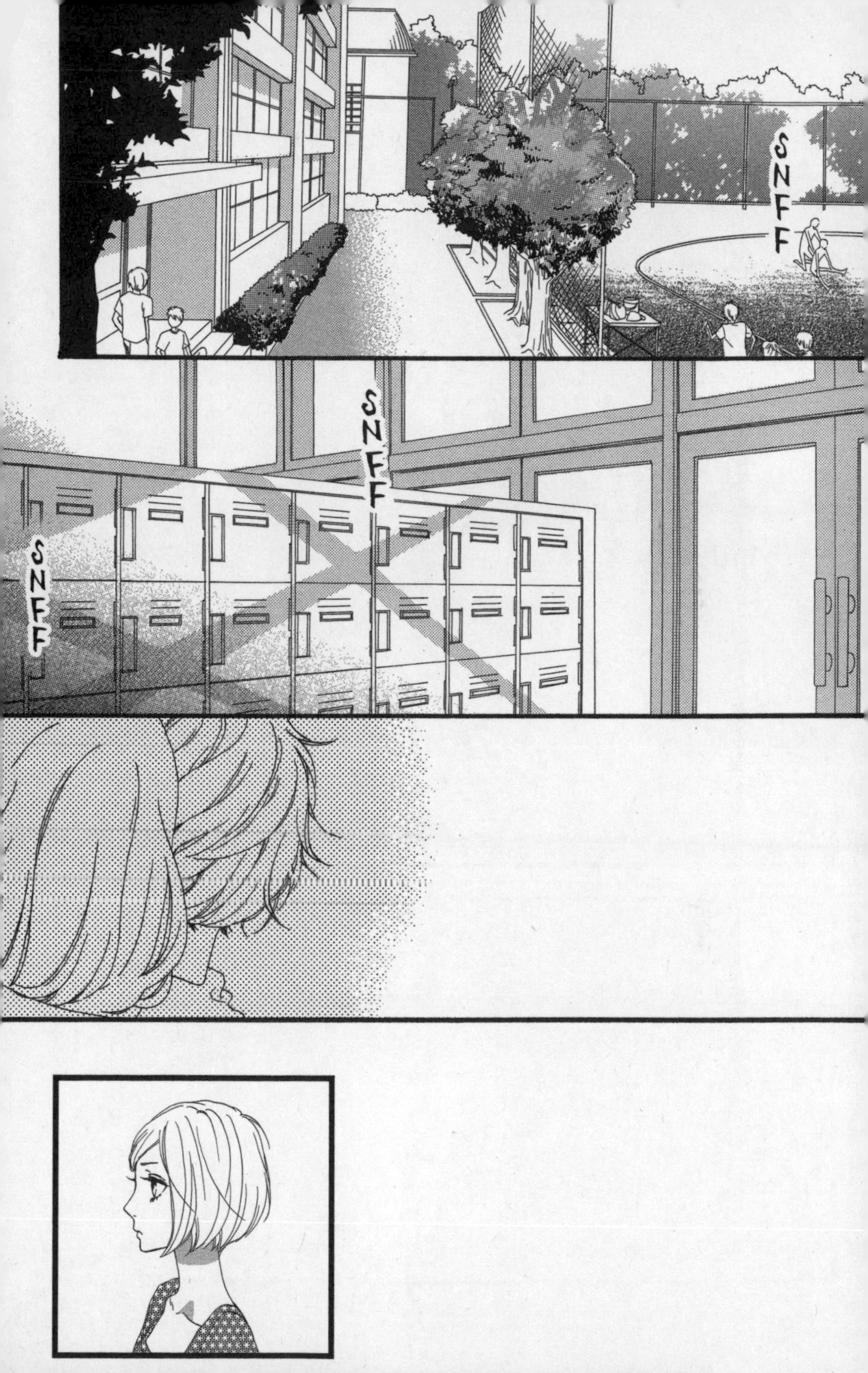
SNFF
SNFF
SNFF

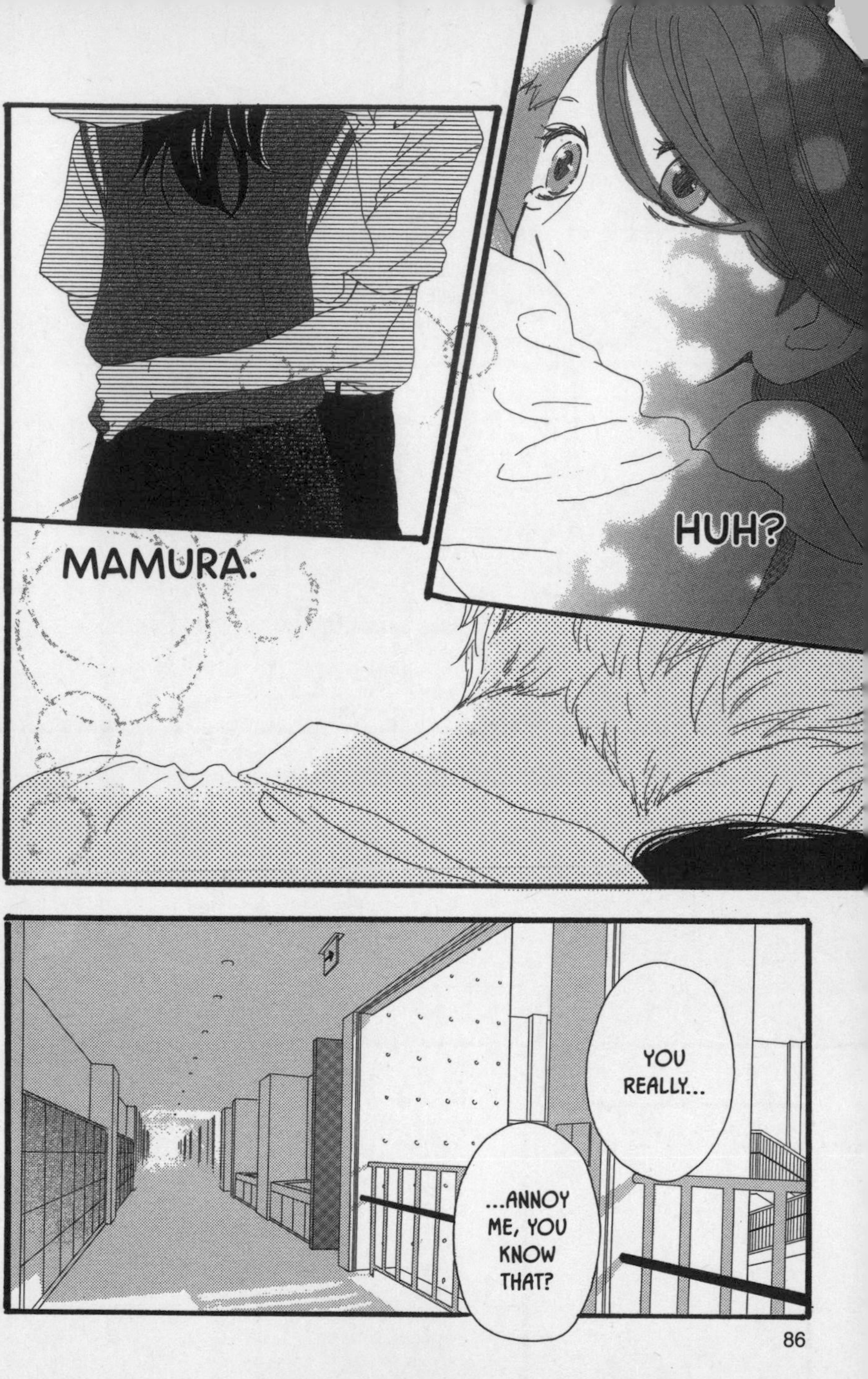
HUH?
MAMURA.
YOU REALLY...
...ANNOY ME, YOU KNOW THAT?

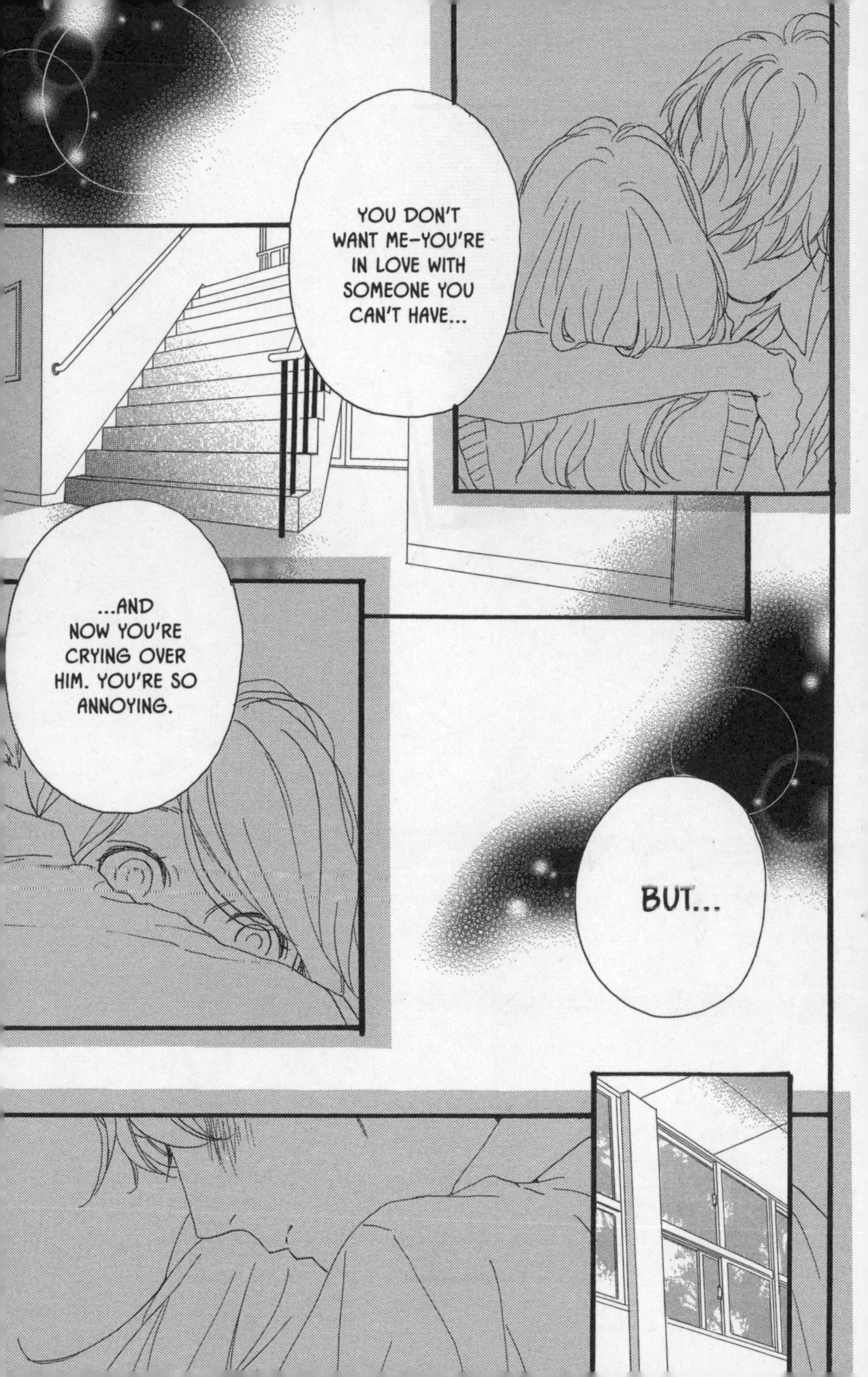
YOU DON'T WANT ME—YOU'RE IN LOVE WITH SOMEONE YOU CAN'T HAVE...
...AND NOW YOU'RE CRYING OVER HIM. YOU'RE SO ANNOYING.
BUT...

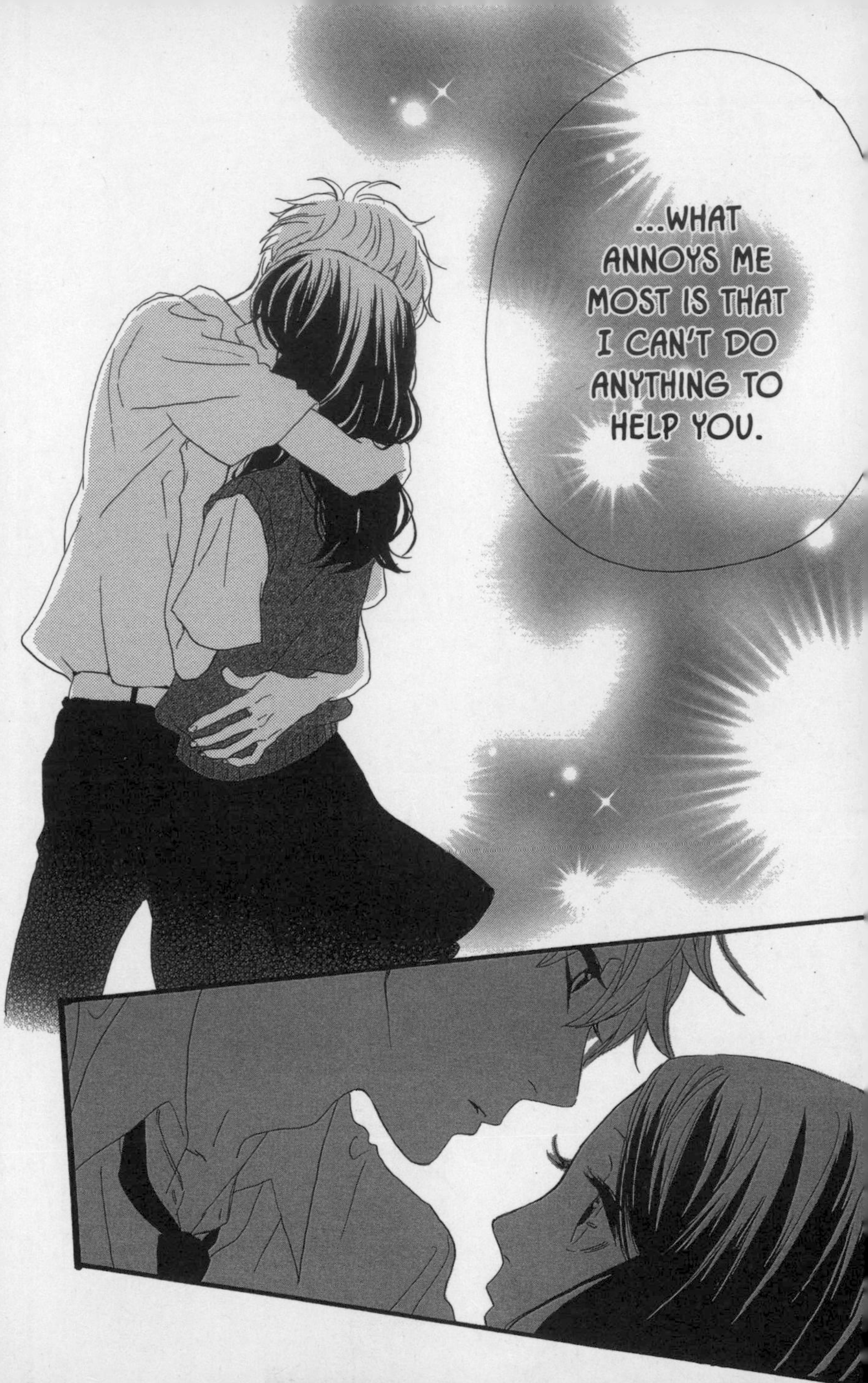
...WHAT ANNOYS ME MOST IS THAT I CAN'T DO ANYTHING TO HELP YOU.

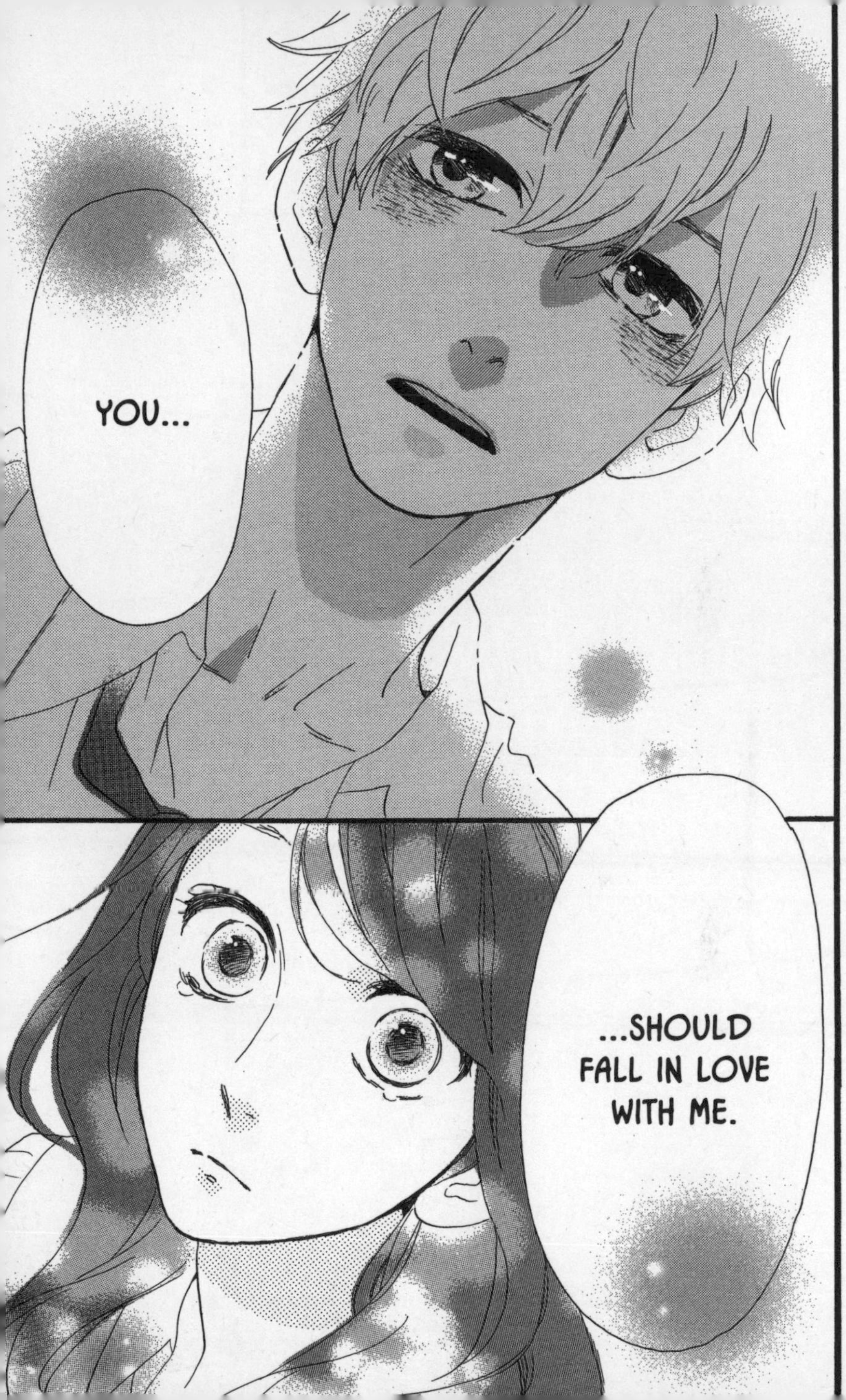
YOU...
...SHOULD FALL IN LOVE WITH ME.

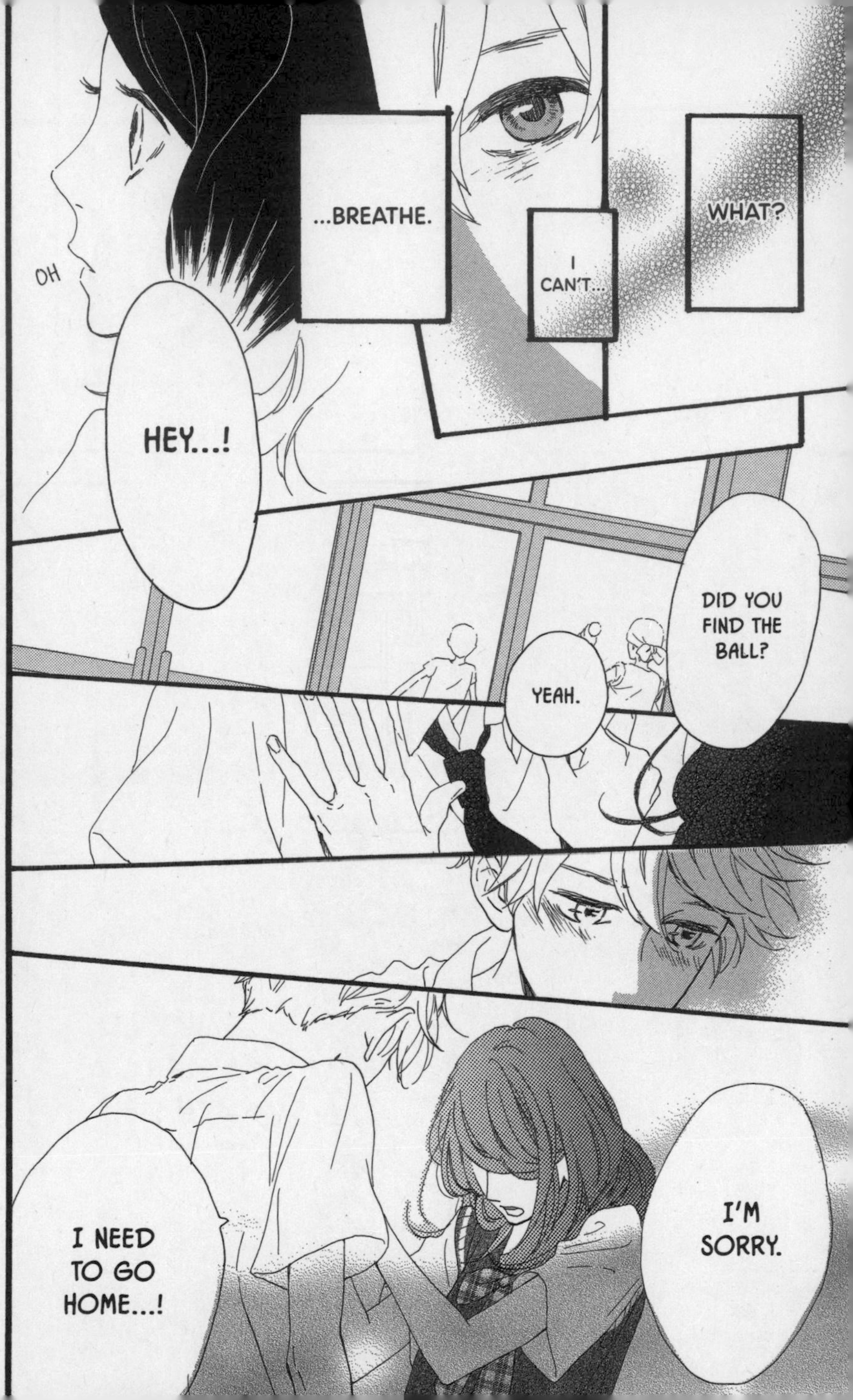
WHAT?
I CAN'T...
...BREATHE.
OH
HEY...!
DID YOU FIND THE BALL?
YEAH.
I'M SORRY.
I NEED TO GO HOME...!

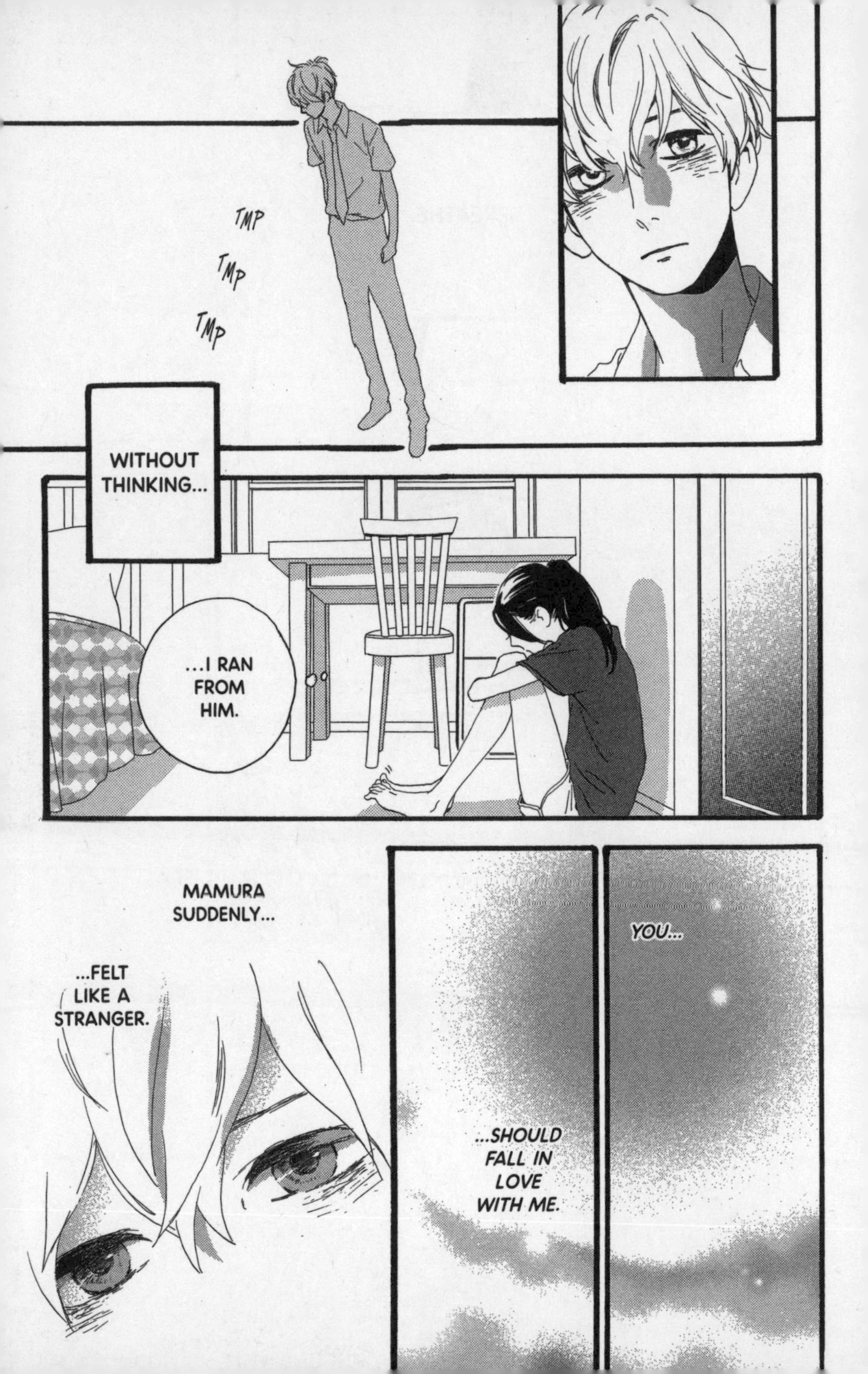
TMP
TMP
TMP
WITHOUT THINKING...
...I RAN FROM HIM.
YOU...
...SHOULD FALL IN LOVE WITH ME.
MAMURA SUDDENLY...
...FELT LIKE A STRANGER.

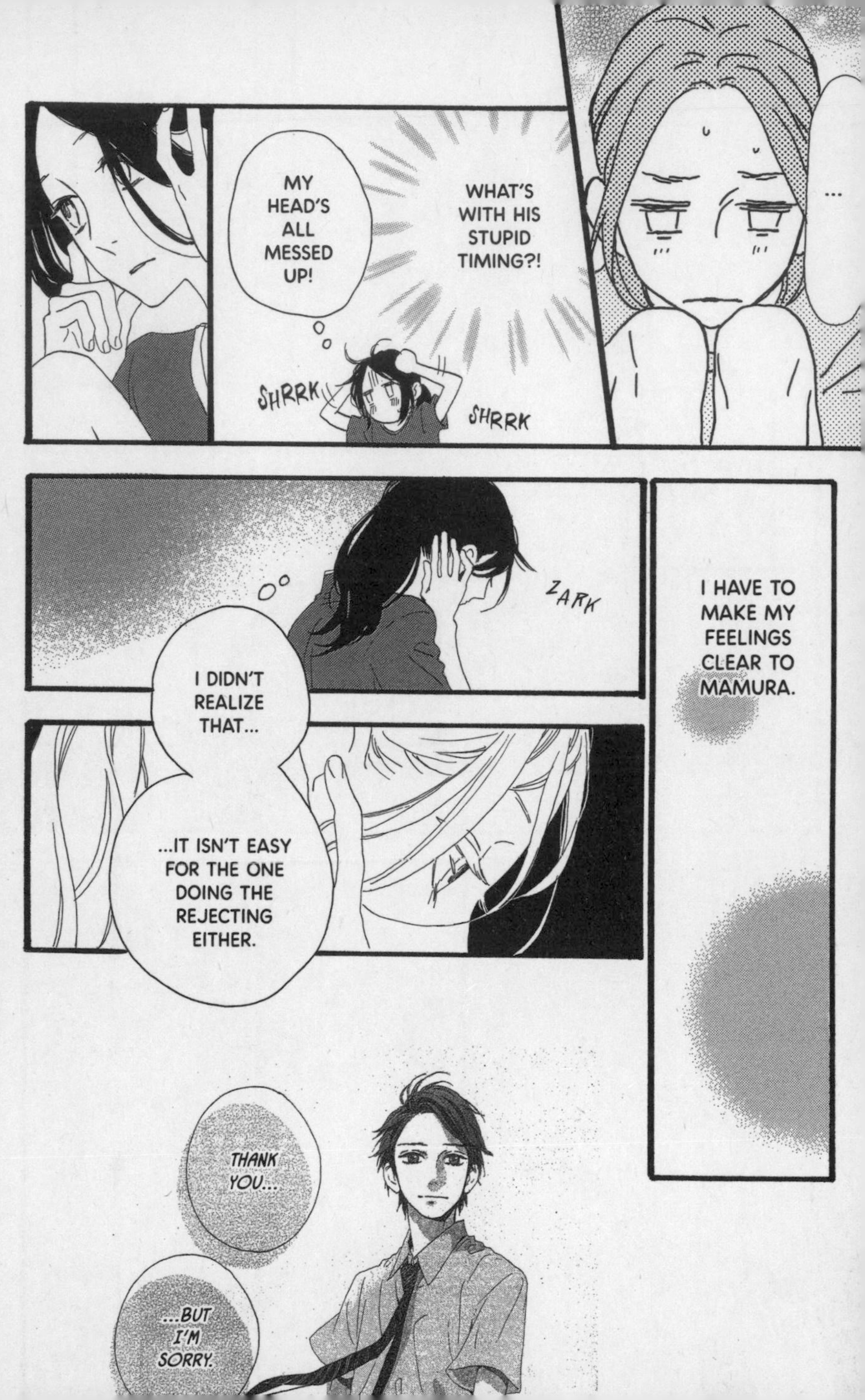
...
WHAT'S WITH HIS STUPID TIMING?!
MY HEAD'S ALL MESSED UP!
SHRRK
SHRRK
I HAVE TO MAKE MY FEELINGS CLEAR TO MAMURA.
ZARK
I DIDN'T REALIZE THAT...
...IT ISN'T EASY FOR THE ONE DOING THE REJECTING EITHER.
THANK YOU...
...BUT I'M SORRY.

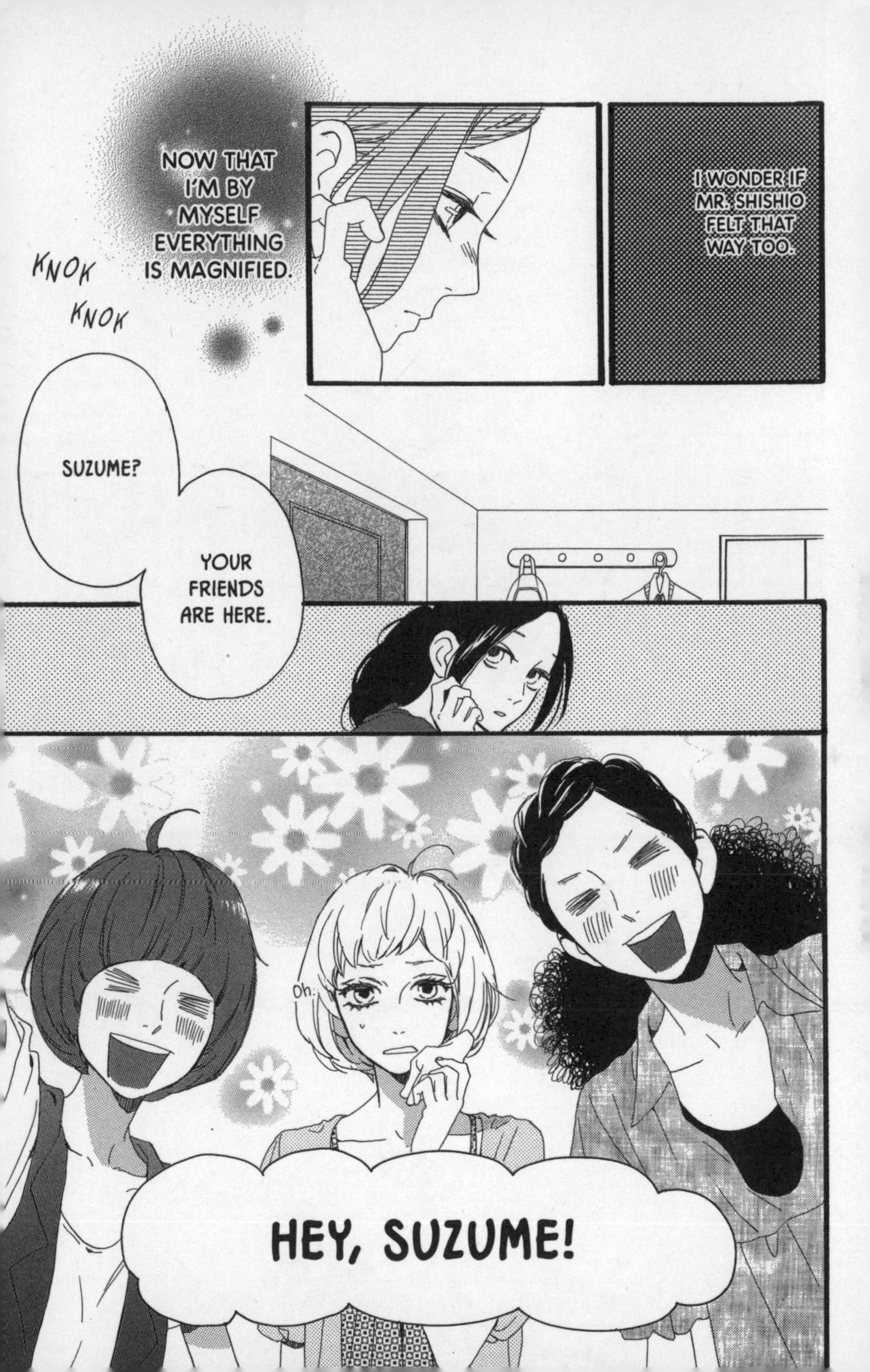
I WONDER IF MR. SHISHIO FELT THAT WAY TOO.
NOW THAT I'M BY MYSELF EVERYTHING IS MAGNIFIED.
KNOK
KNOK
SUZUME?
YOUR FRIENDS ARE HERE.
Oh...
HEY, SUZUME!

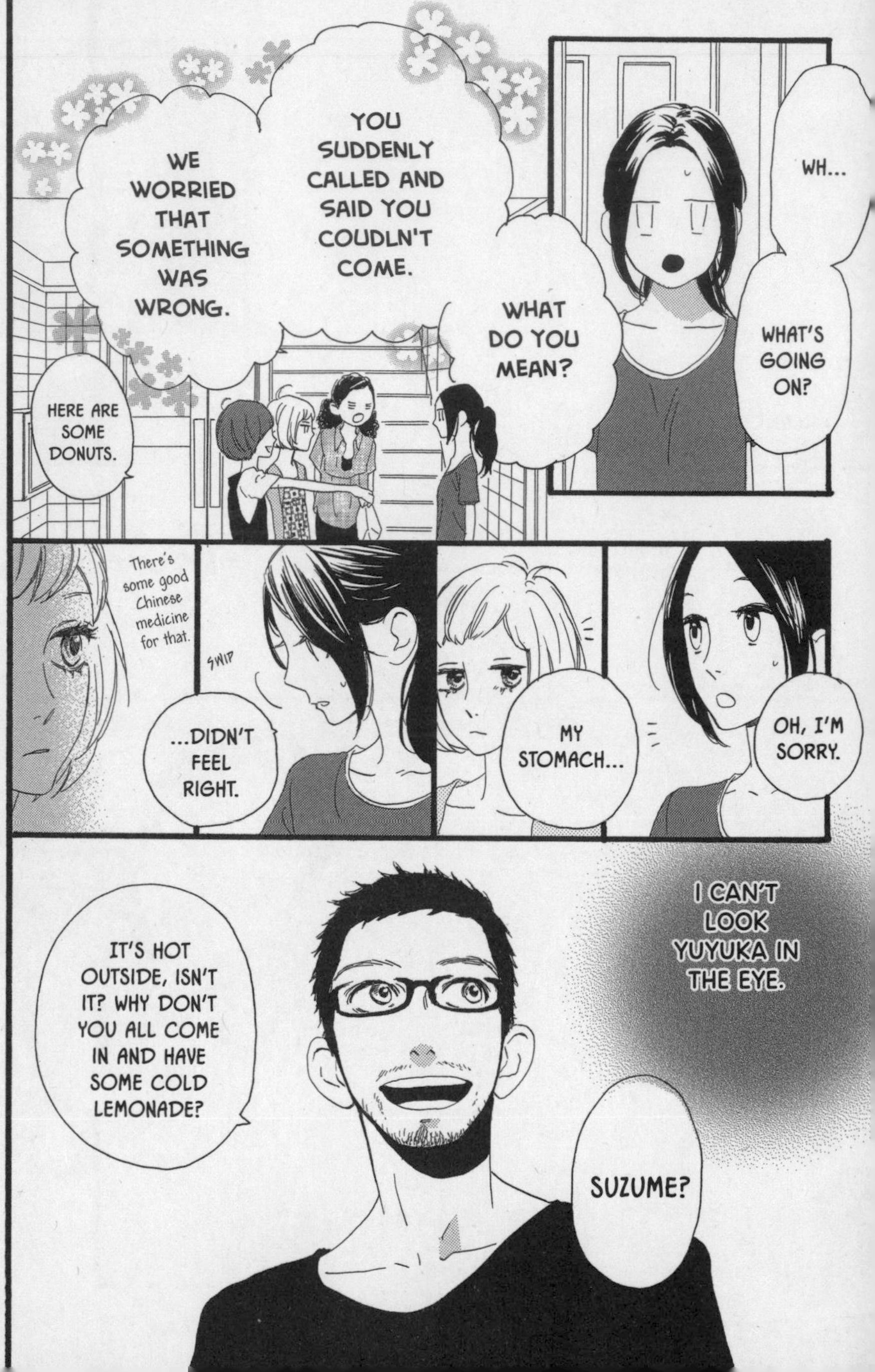
WH...
WHAT'S GOING ON?
YOU SUDDENLY CALLED AND SAID YOU COUDLN'T COME.
WE WORRIED THAT SOMETHING WAS WRONG.
WHAT DO YOU MEAN?
HERE ARE SOME DONUTS.
OH, I'M SORRY.
MY STOMACH...
...DIDN'T FEEL RIGHT.
SWIP
There's some good Chinese medicine for that.
I CAN'T LOOK YUYUKA IN THE EYE.
SUZUME?
IT'S HOT OUTSIDE, ISN'T IT? WHY DON'T YOU ALL COME IN AND HAVE SOME COLD LEMONADE?

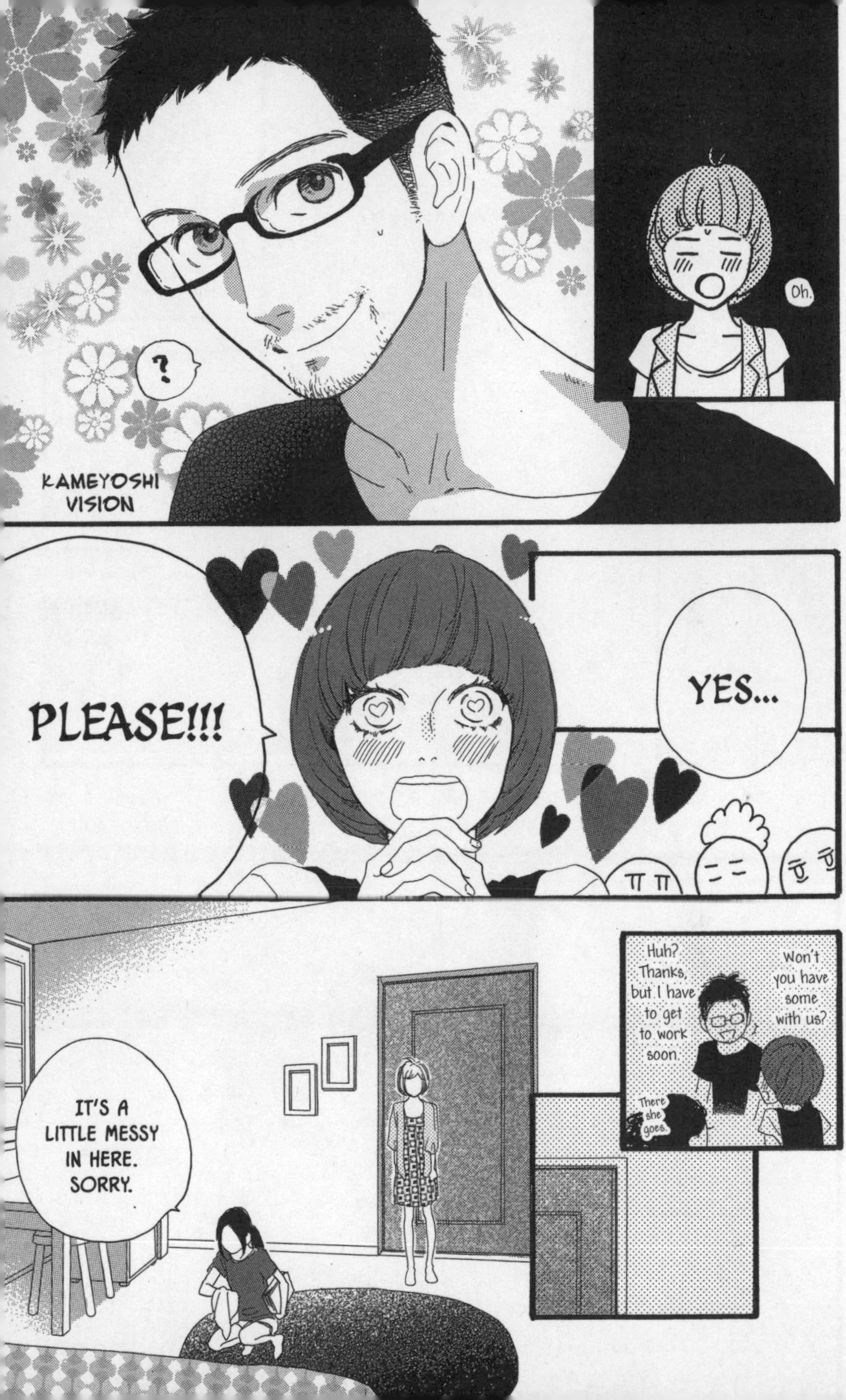
Oh.
?
KAMEYOSHI VISION
YES...
PLEASE!!!
Won't you have some with us?
Huh? Thanks, but I have to get to work soon.
There she goes.
IT'S A LITTLE MESSY IN HERE. SORRY.

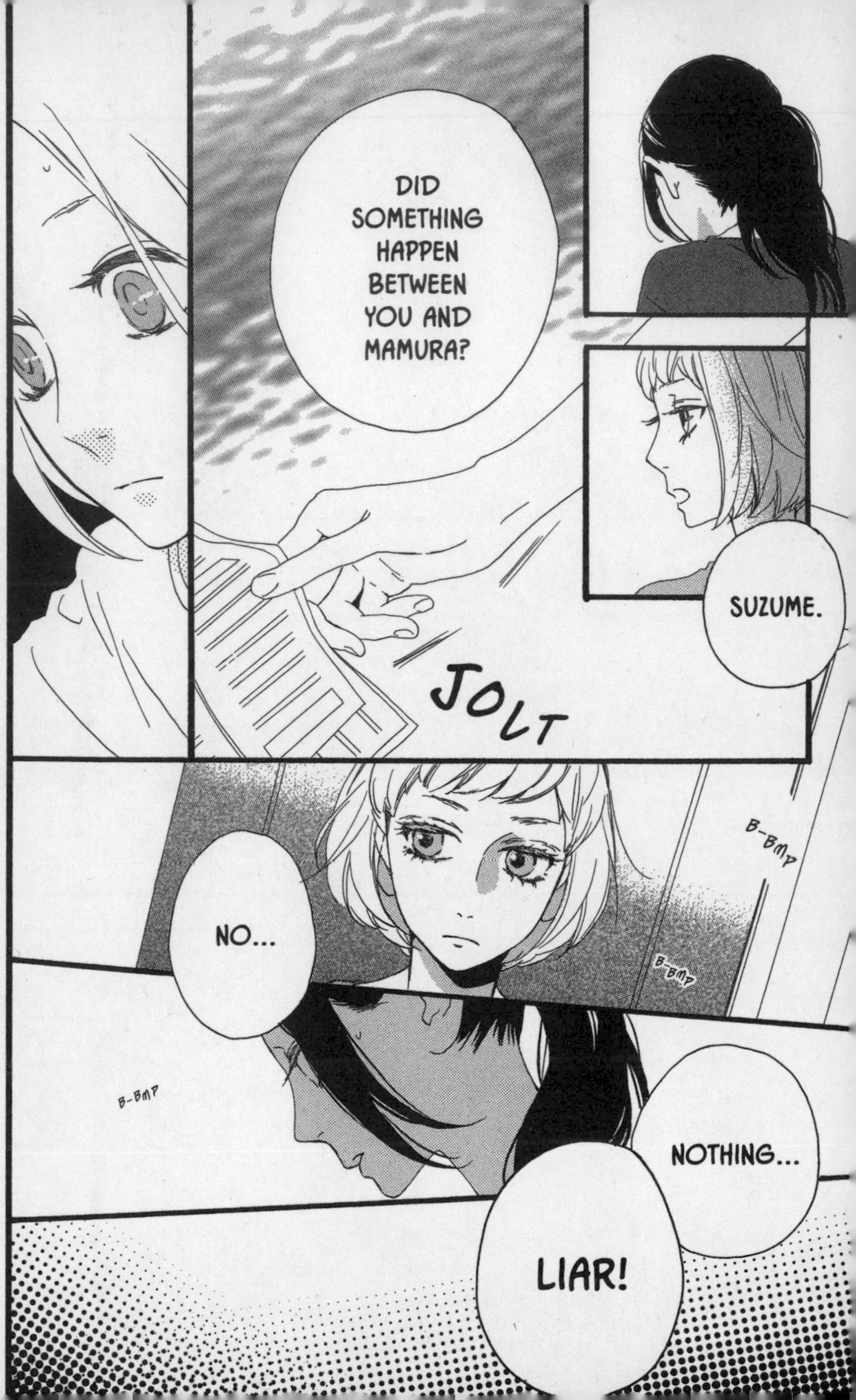
SUZUME.
DID SOMETHING HAPPEN BETWEEN YOU AND MAMURA?
JOLT
B-BMP
B-BMP
NO...
NOTHING...
B-BMP
LIAR!

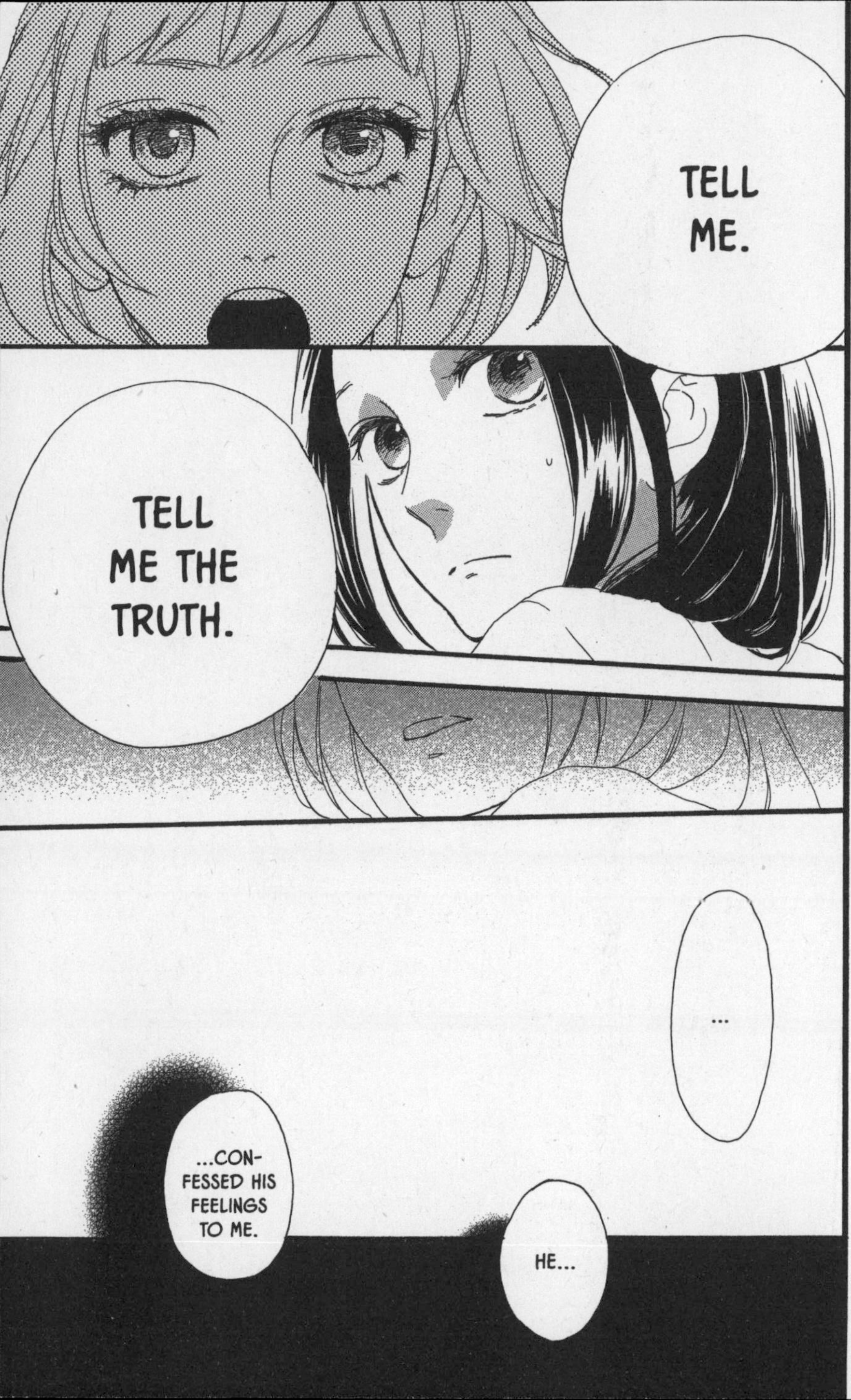
TELL ME.
TELL ME THE TRUTH.
...
HE...
...CON-FESSED HIS FEELINGS TO ME.

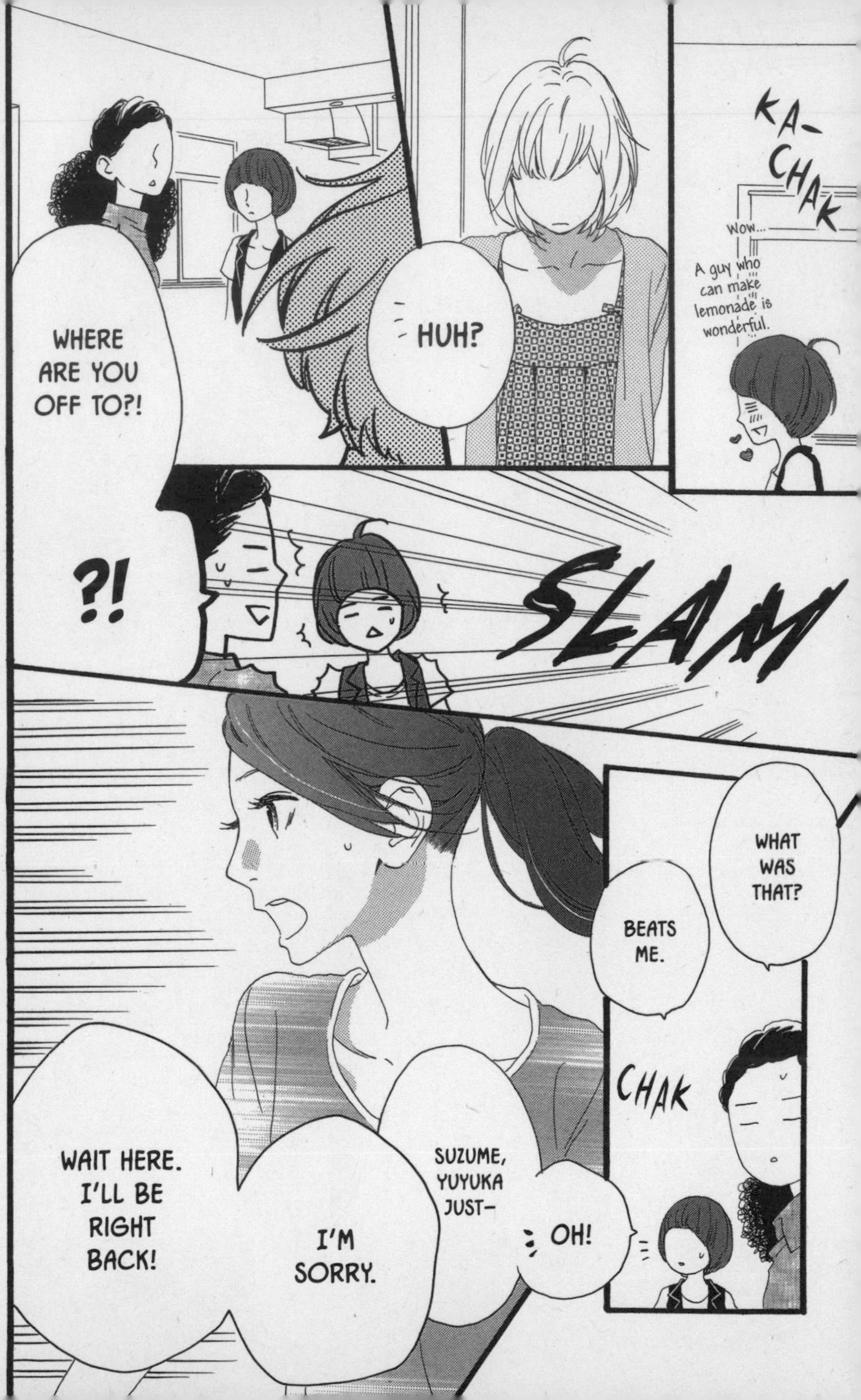
KA-CHAK
Wow...
A guy who can make lemonade is wonderful.
HUH?
WHERE ARE YOU OFF TO?!
SLAM
?!
WHAT WAS THAT?
BEATS ME.
CHAK
SUZUME, YUYUKA JUST—
OH!
I'M SORRY.
WAIT HERE. I'LL BE RIGHT BACK!

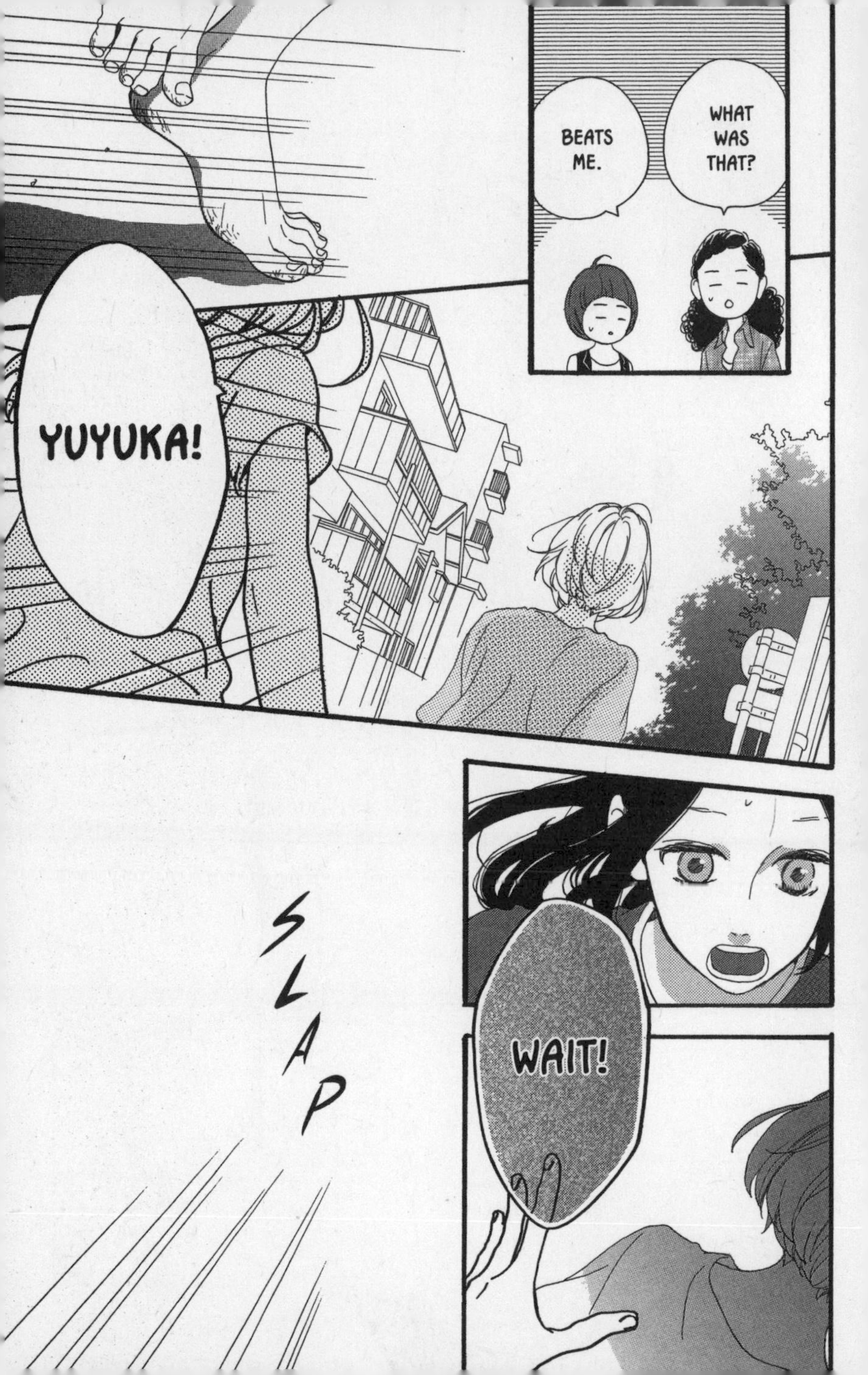
WHAT WAS THAT?
BEATS ME.
YUYUKA!
WAIT!
SLAP

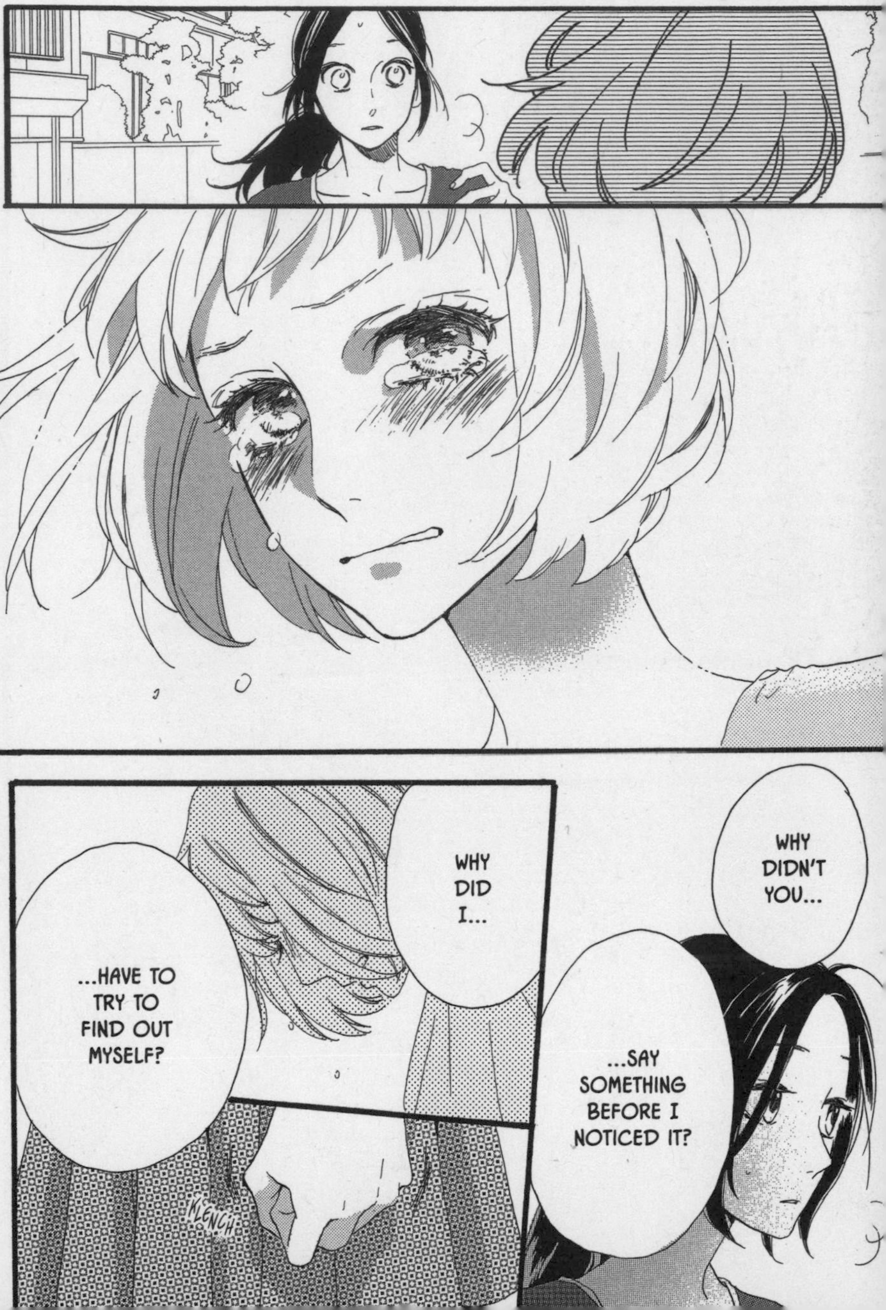
WHY DIDN'T YOU...
...SAY SOMETHING BEFORE I NOTICED IT?
WHY DID I...
...HAVE TO TRY TO FIND OUT MYSELF?
KLENCH

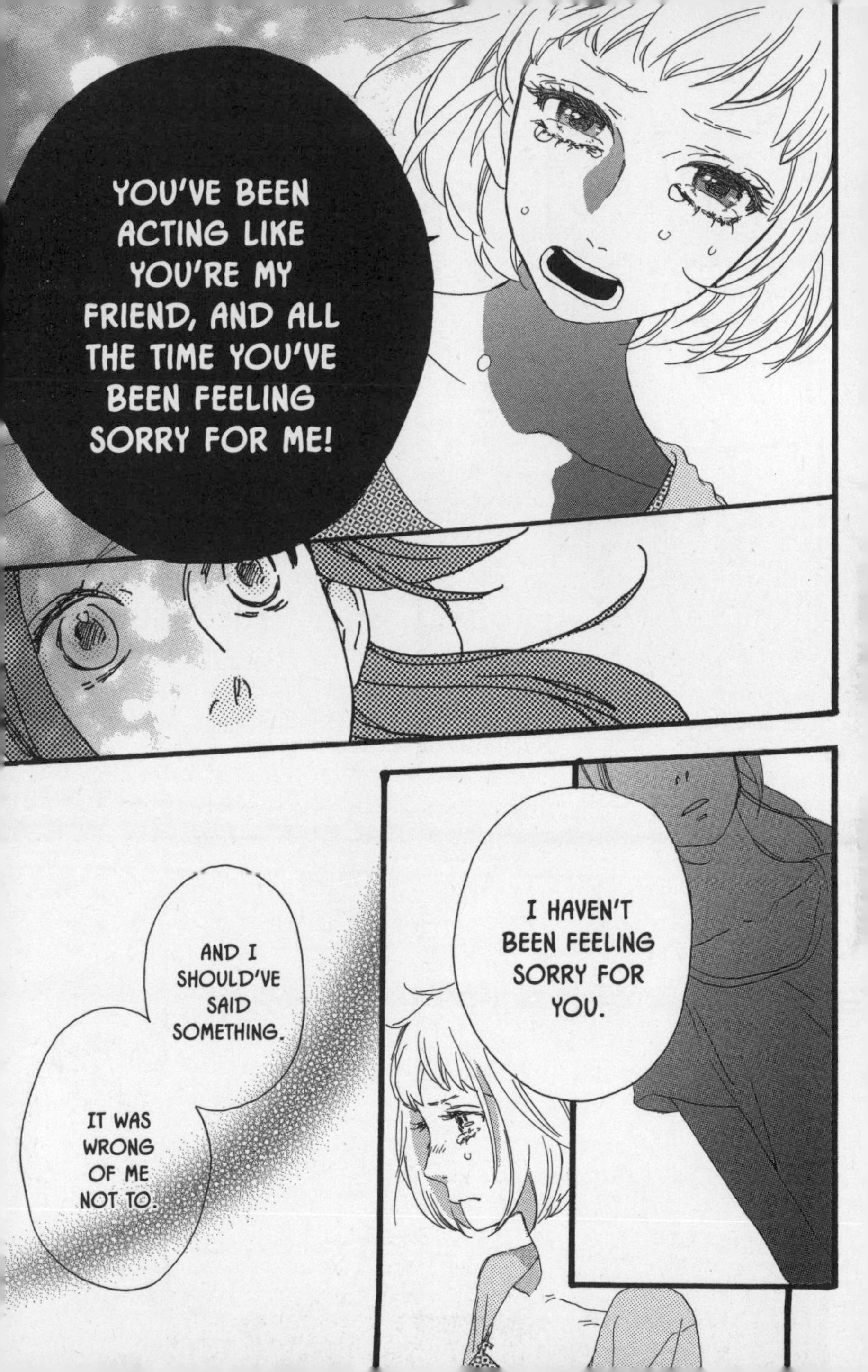
YOU'VE BEEN ACTING LIKE YOU'RE MY FRIEND, AND ALL THE TIME YOU'VE BEEN FEELING SORRY FOR ME!
I HAVEN'T BEEN FEELING SORRY FOR YOU.
AND I SHOULD'VE SAID SOMETHING.
IT WAS WRONG OF ME NOT TO.

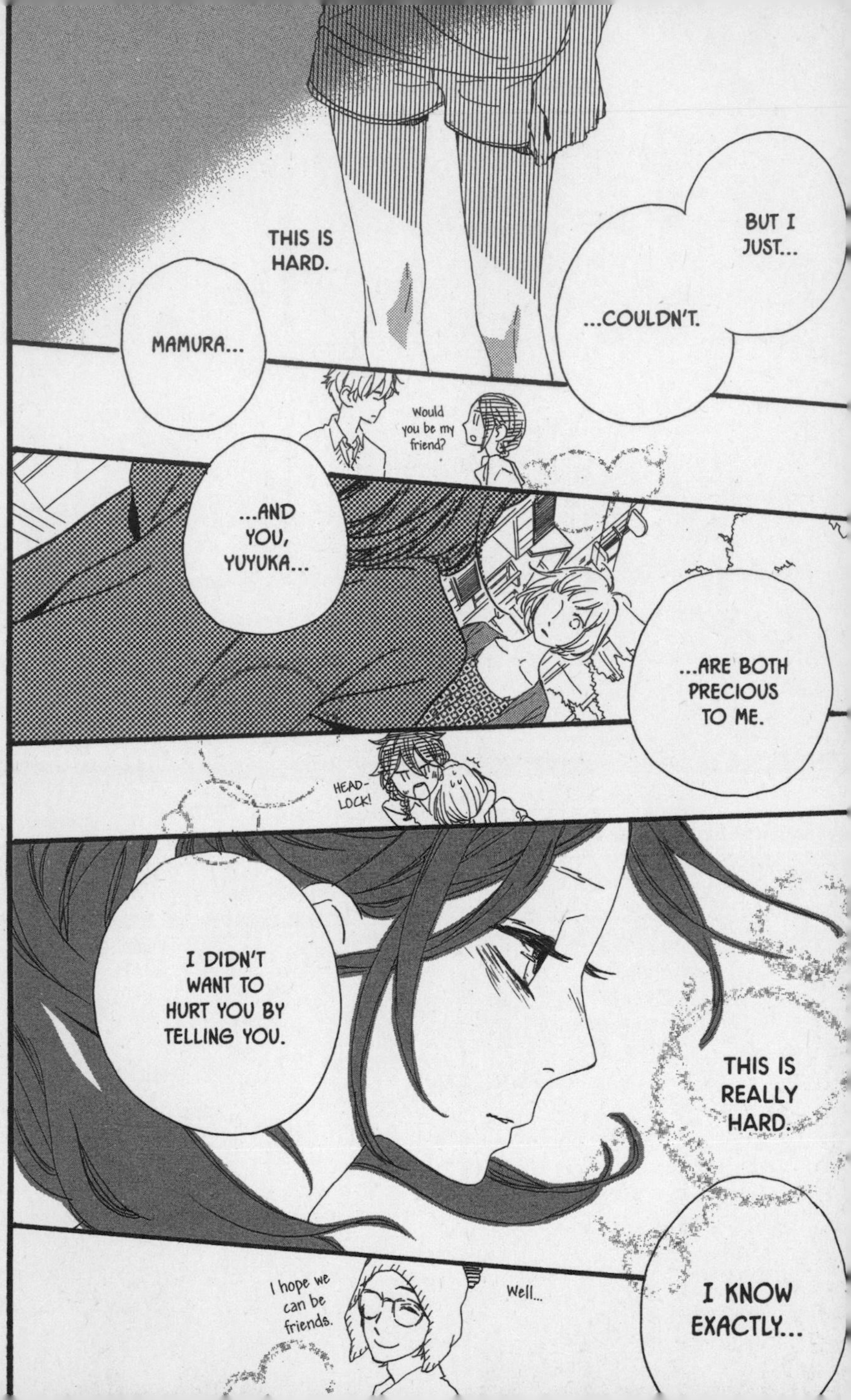
BUT I JUST...
...COULDN'T.
THIS IS HARD.
MAMURA...
Would you be my friend?
...AND YOU, YUYUKA...
...ARE BOTH PRECIOUS TO ME.
HEAD-LOCK!
THIS IS REALLY HARD.
I DIDN'T WANT TO HURT YOU BY TELLING YOU.
I KNOW EXACTLY...
Well...
I hope we can be friends.

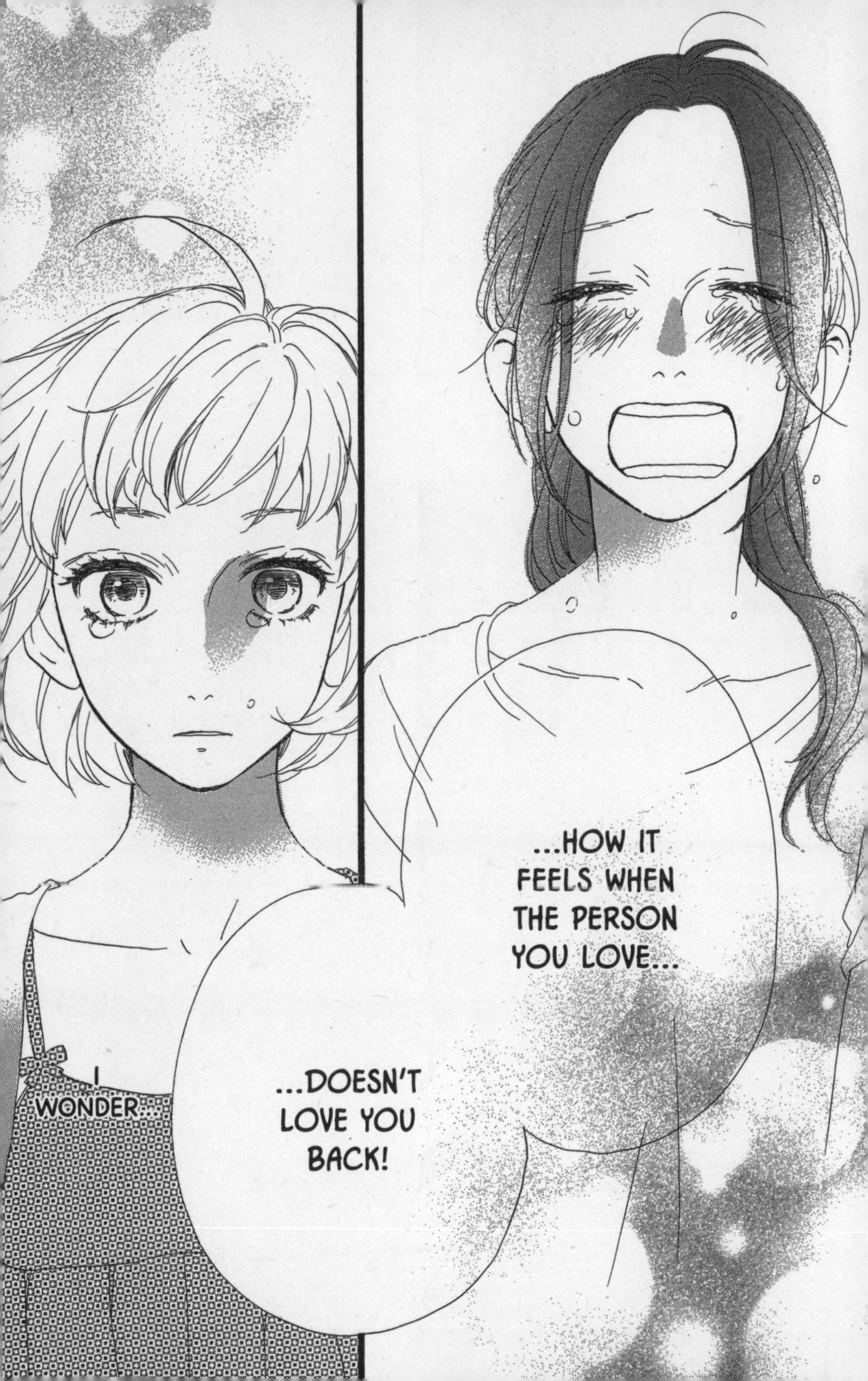
...HOW IT FEELS WHEN THE PERSON YOU LOVE...
...DOESN'T LOVE YOU BACK!
I WONDER...

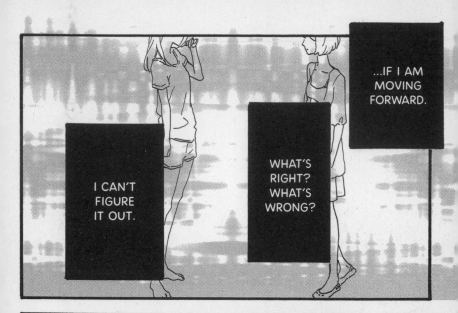

...IF I AM MOVING FORWARD.

WHAT'S RIGHT? WHAT'S WRONG?

I CAN'T FIGURE IT OUT.

INSTEAD I JUST FEEL LIKE CRYING.

BY THE WAY, SHOULD WE MAKE PLANS FOR THE SUMMER FESTIVAL?

GOMP

OH. IS IT THAT TIME OF YEAR ALREADY?

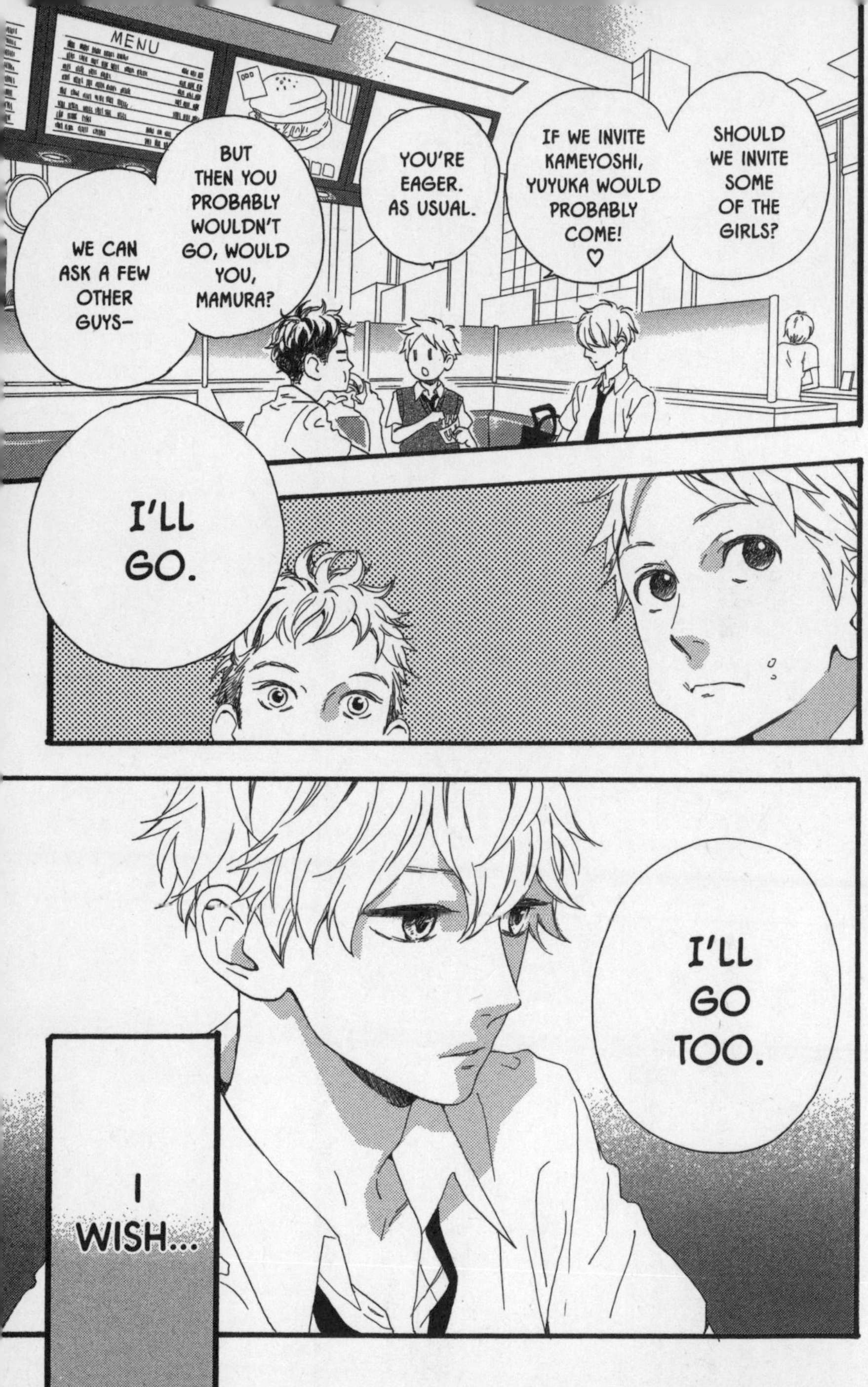
MENU
SHOULD WE INVITE SOME OF THE GIRLS?
IF WE INVITE KAMEYOSHI, YUYUKA WOULD PROBABLY COME! ♡
YOU'RE EAGER. AS USUAL.
BUT THEN YOU PROBABLY WOULDN'T GO, WOULD YOU, MAMURA?
WE CAN ASK A FEW OTHER GUYS-
I'LL GO.
I'LL GO TOO.
I WISH...

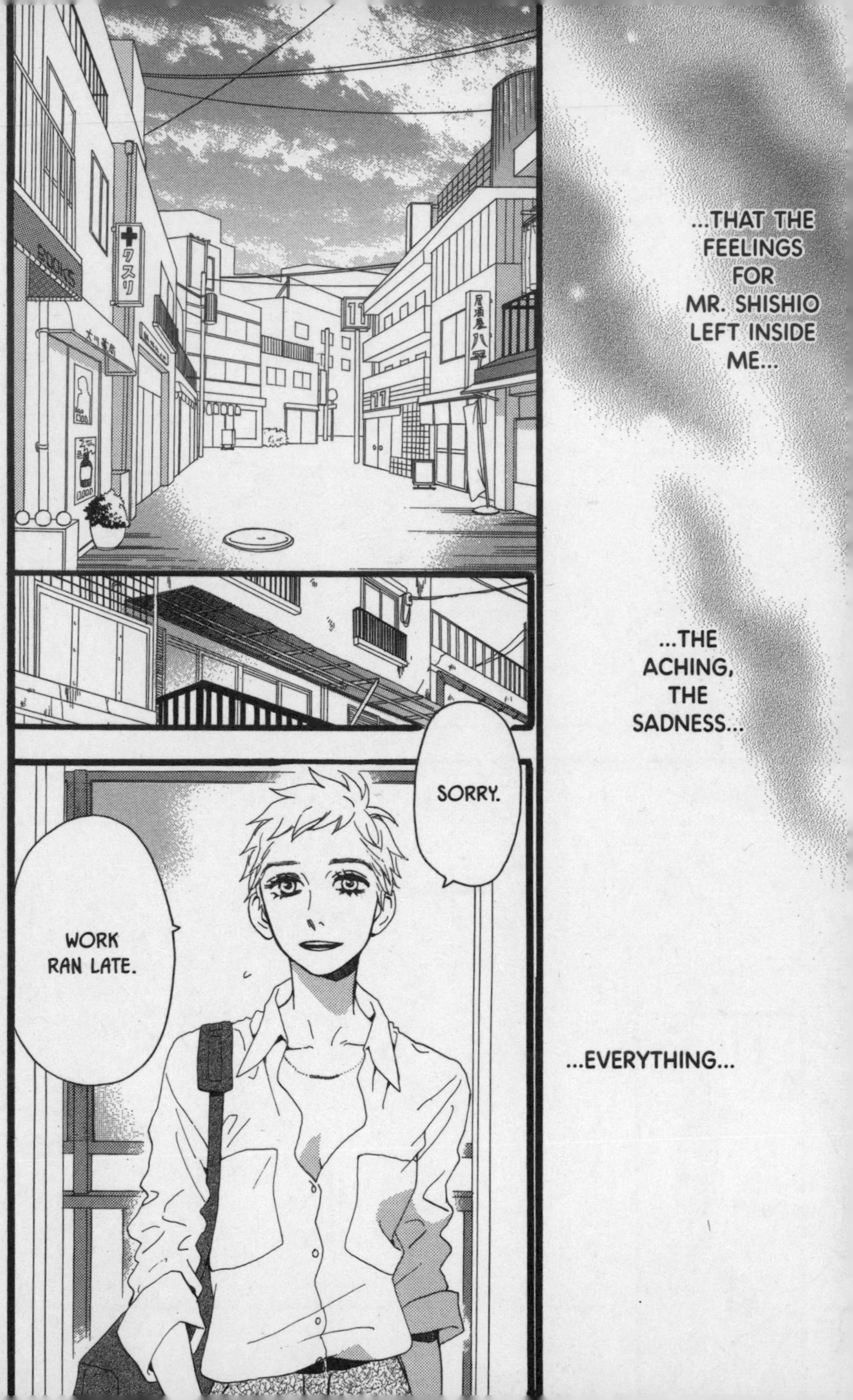
...THAT THE FEELINGS FOR MR. SHISHIO LEFT INSIDE ME...
...THE ACHING, THE SADNESS...
...EVERYTHING...
SORRY.
WORK RAN LATE.

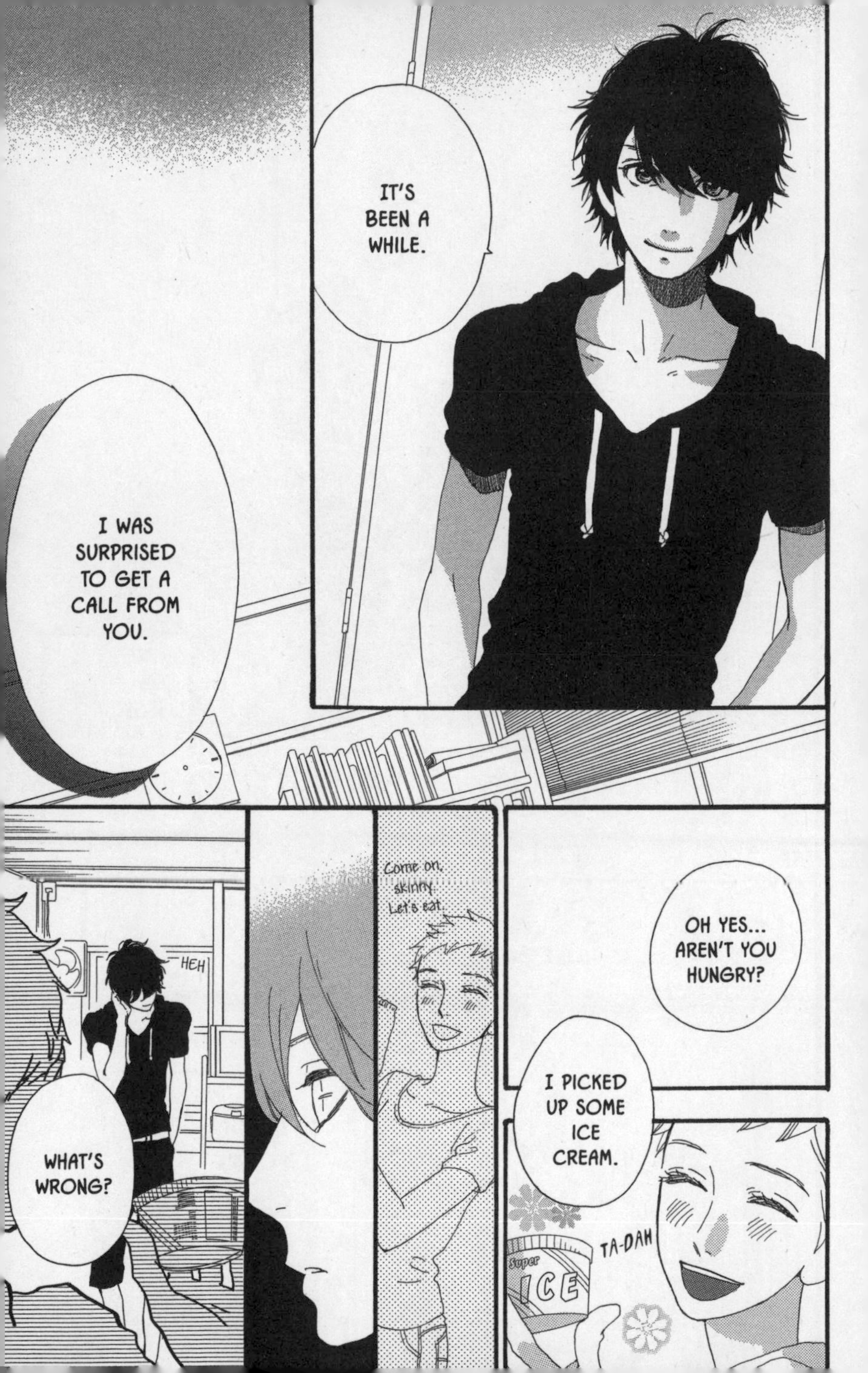
IT'S BEEN A WHILE.
I WAS SURPRISED TO GET A CALL FROM YOU.
OH YES... AREN'T YOU HUNGRY?
I PICKED UP SOME ICE CREAM.
TA-DAH
Super ICE
Come on, skinny. Let's eat.
HEH
WHAT'S WRONG?

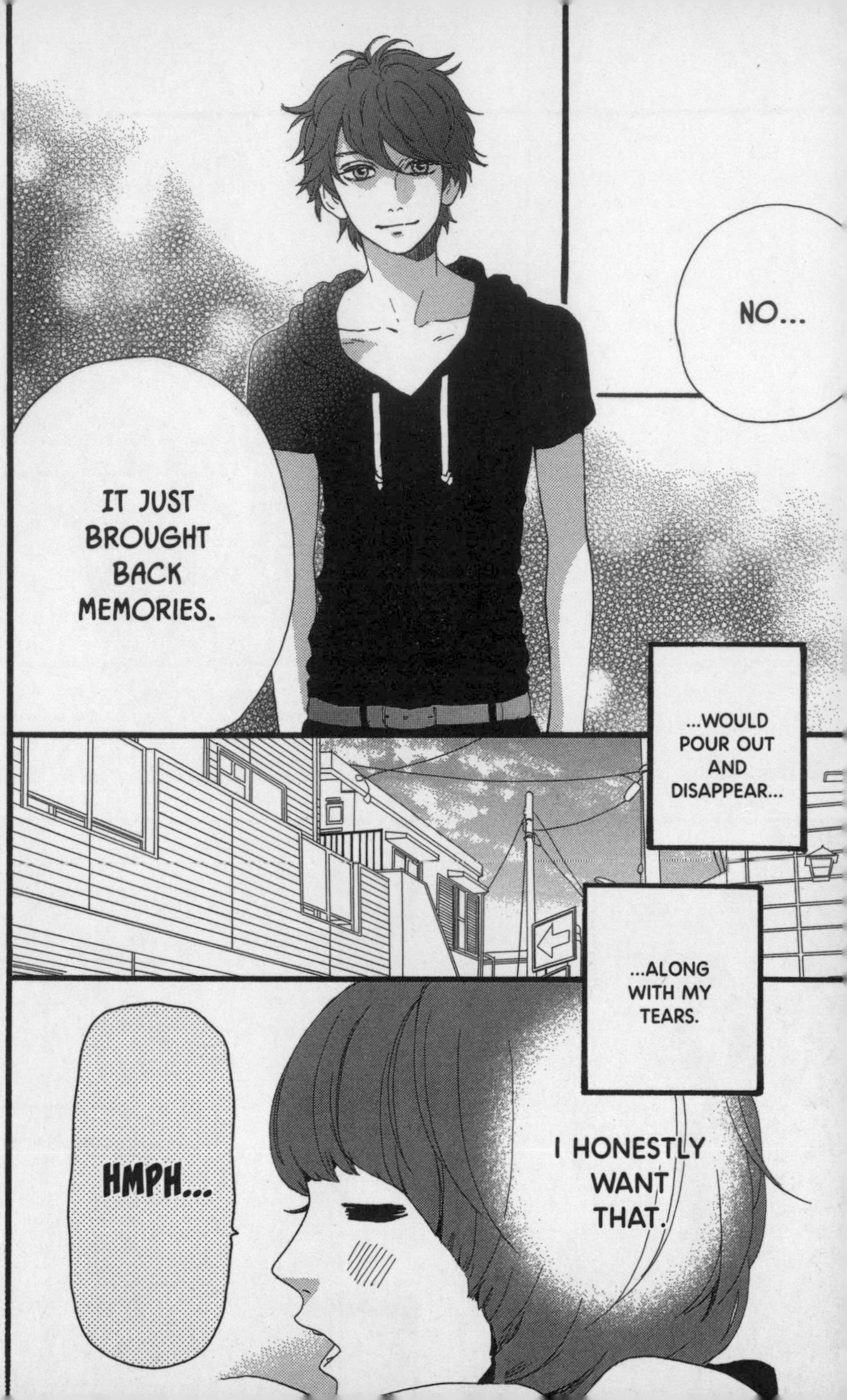
NO...
IT JUST BROUGHT BACK MEMORIES.
...WOULD POUR OUT AND DISAPPEAR...
...ALONG WITH MY TEARS.
I HONESTLY WANT THAT.
HMPH...

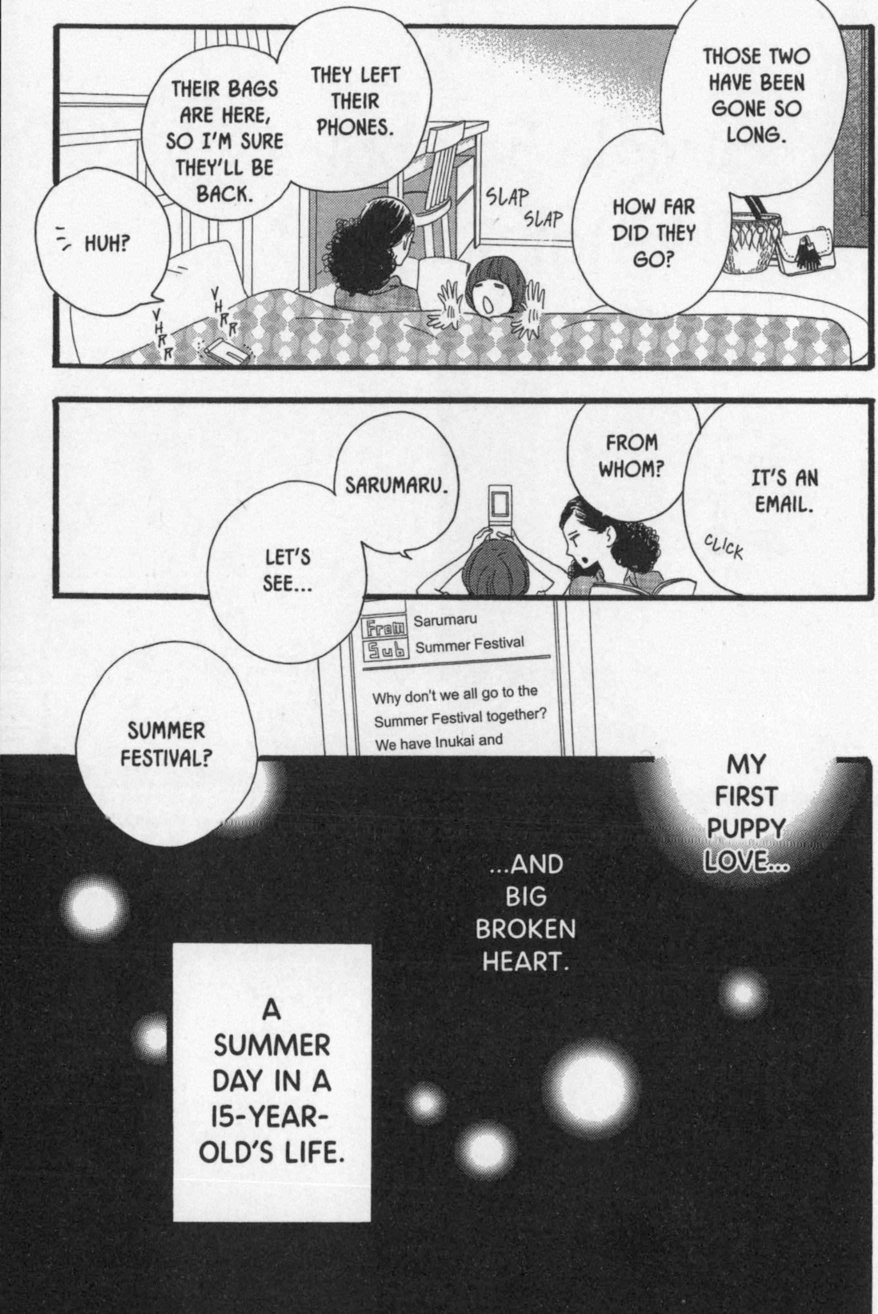
THOSE TWO HAVE BEEN GONE SO LONG.
HOW FAR DID THEY GO?
SLAP SLAP
THEY LEFT THEIR PHONES.
THEIR BAGS ARE HERE, SO I'M SURE THEY'LL BE BACK.
VHRR VHRR
HUH?
IT'S AN EMAIL.
CLICK
FROM WHOM?
SARUMARU.
LET'S SEE...
From Sarumaru
Sub Summer Festival
Why don't we all go to the Summer Festival together? We have Inukai and
SUMMER FESTIVAL?
MY FIRST PUPPY LOVE...
...AND BIG BROKEN HEART.
A SUMMER DAY IN A 15-YEAR-OLD'S LIFE.

Simple Scribbles "Nostalgic Trio"

I posted this on my blog and on Twitter, but since I don't have anything new, I will reuse it here!

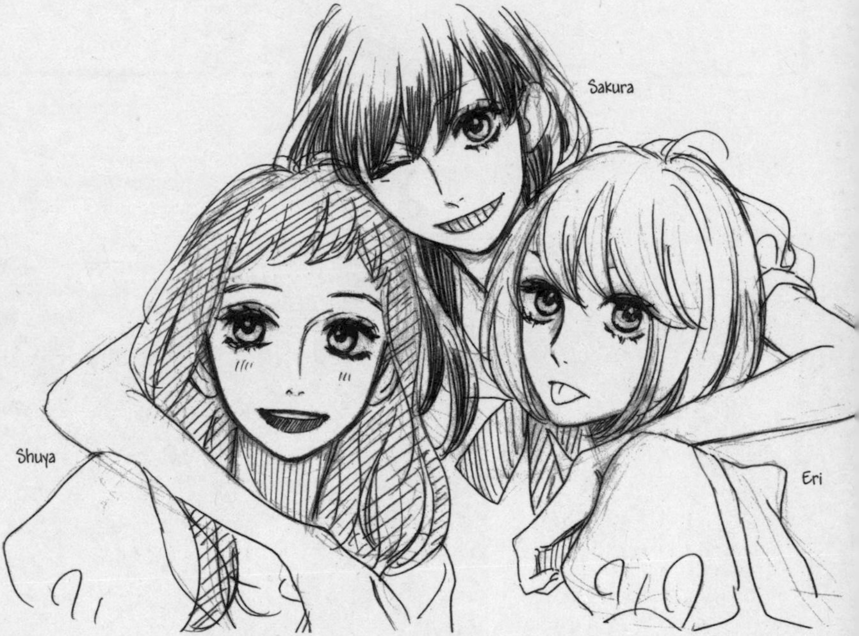
Sakura
Shuya
Eri

My apologies to those who don't know *Sugars*.

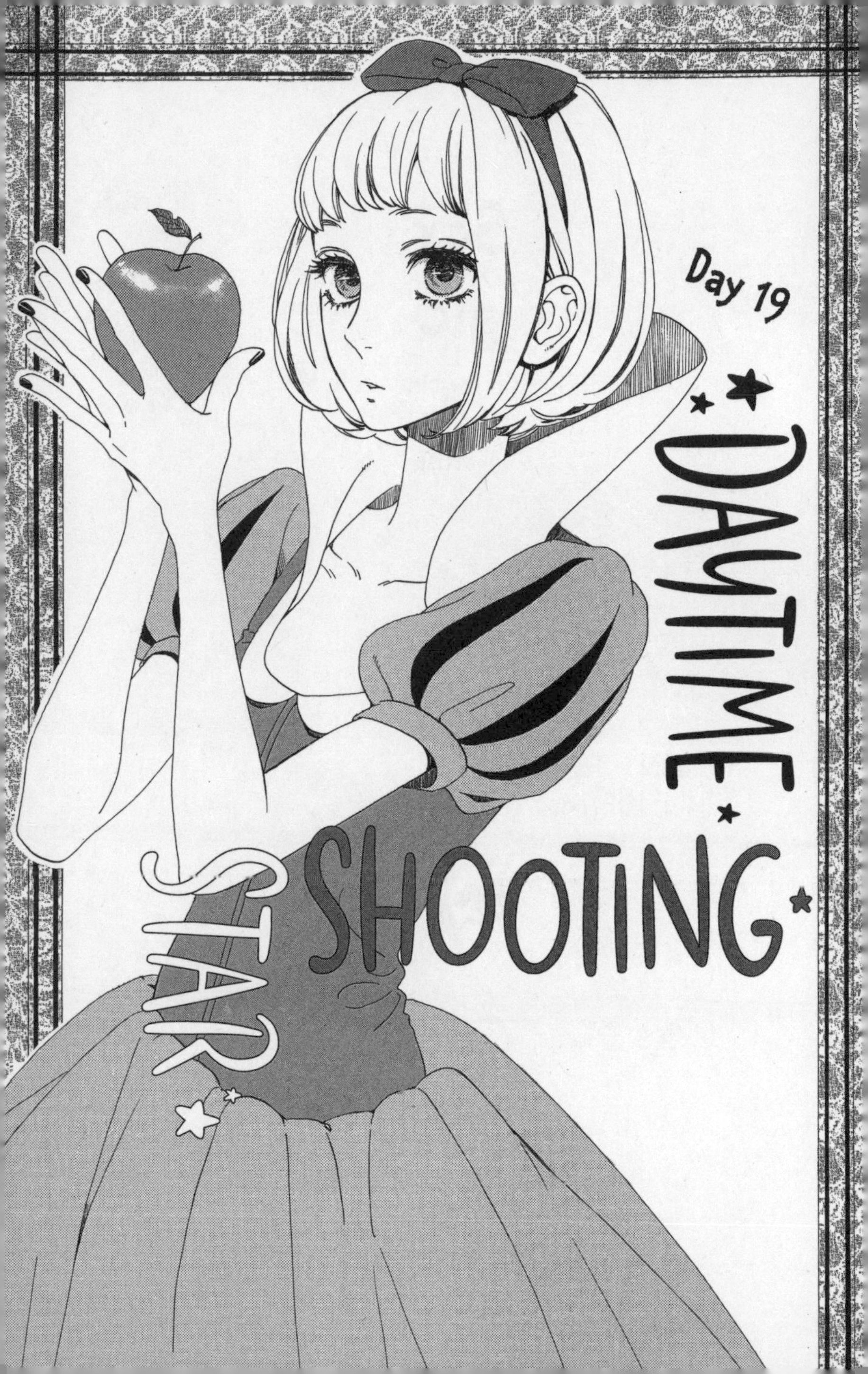
Day 19
DAYTIME
SHOOTING
STAR

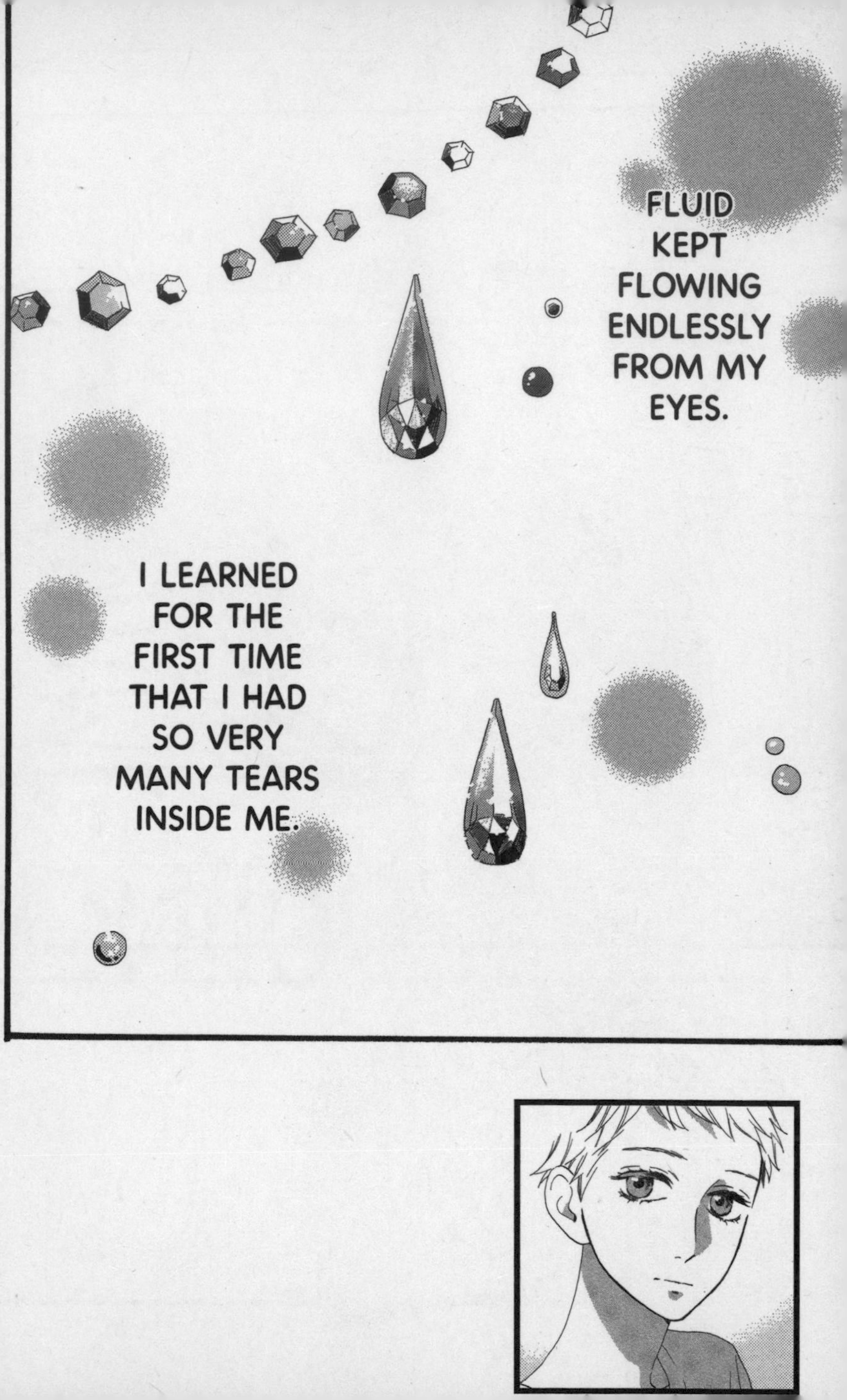
FLUID KEPT FLOWING ENDLESSLY FROM MY EYES.
I LEARNED FOR THE FIRST TIME THAT I HAD SO VERY MANY TEARS INSIDE ME.

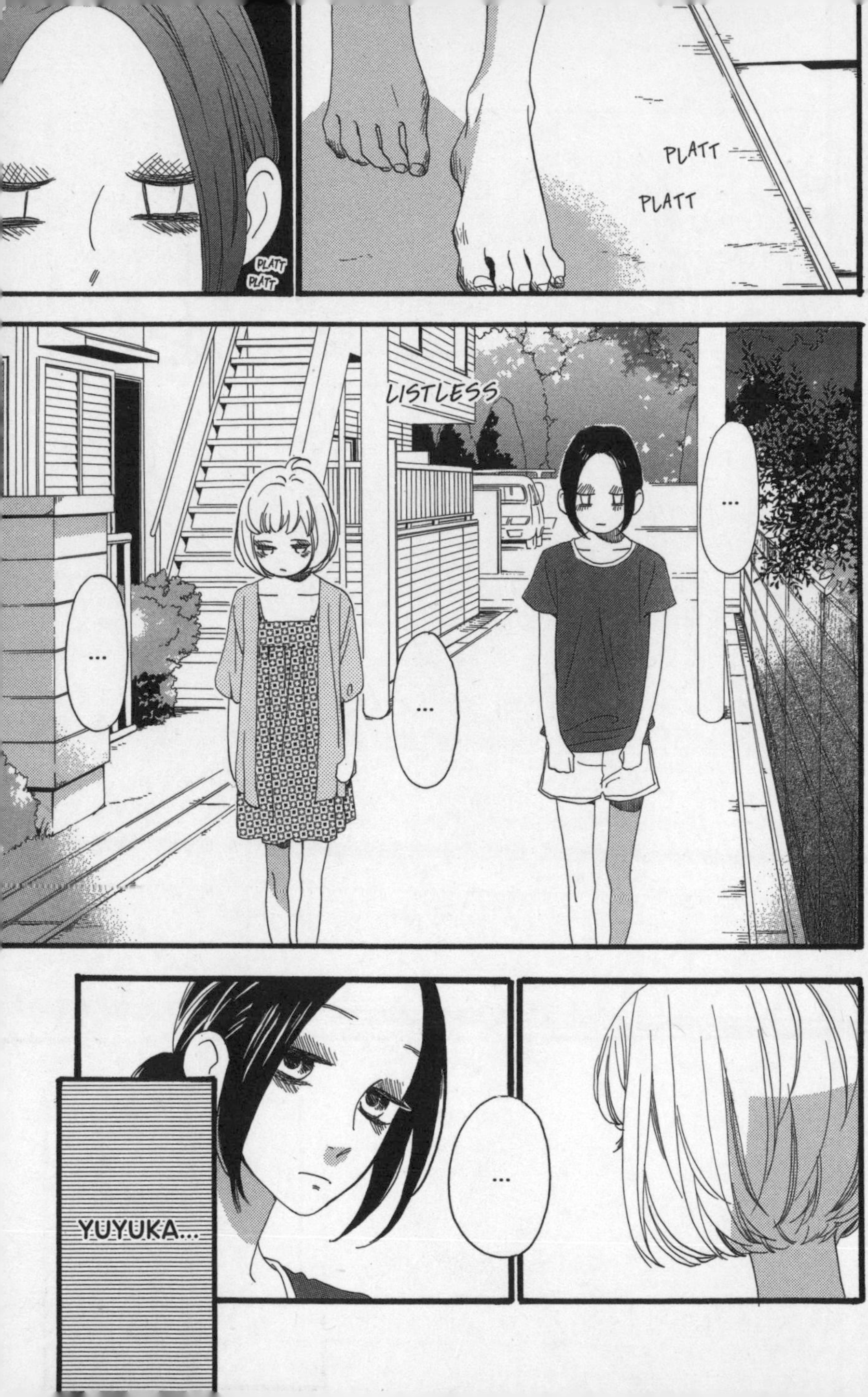
PLATT
PLATT
PLATT
PLATT
LISTLESS
...
...
...
...
YUYUKA...

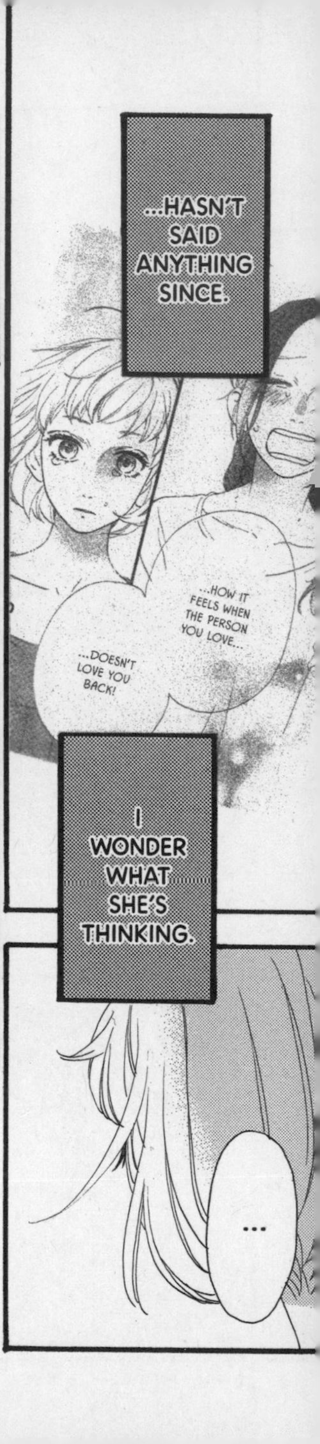
...HASN'T SAID ANYTHING SINCE.
...HOW IT FEELS WHEN THE PERSON YOU LOVE...
...DOESN'T LOVE YOU BACK!
I WONDER WHAT SHE'S THINKING.
...

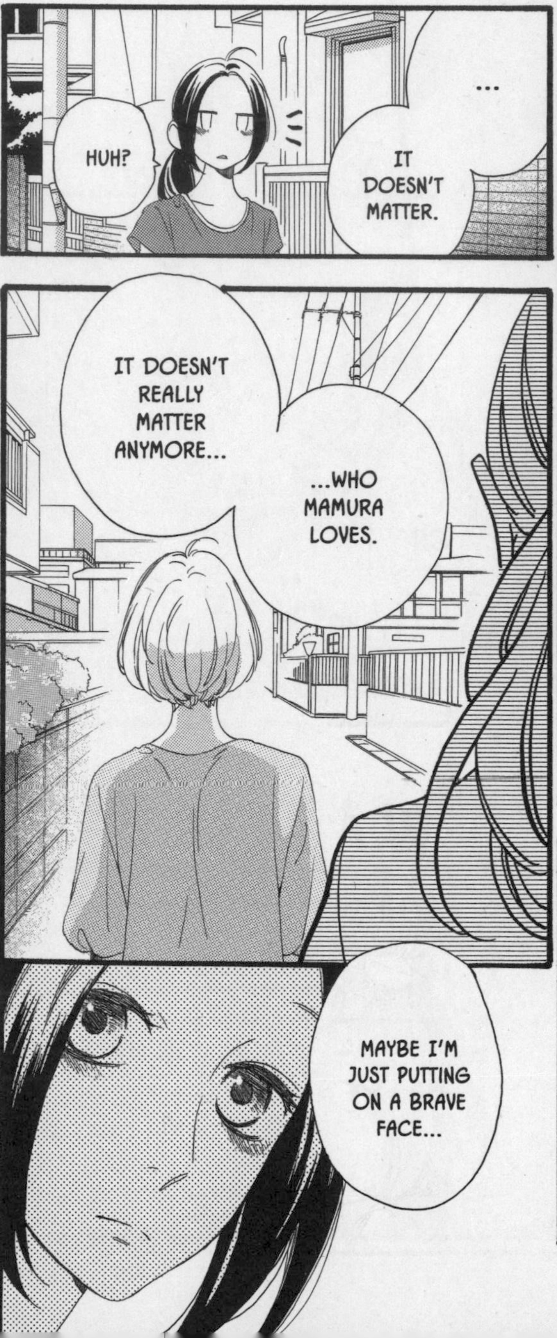
...
IT DOESN'T MATTER.
HUH?
IT DOESN'T REALLY MATTER ANYMORE...
...WHO MAMURA LOVES.
MAYBE I'M JUST PUTTING ON A BRAVE FACE...

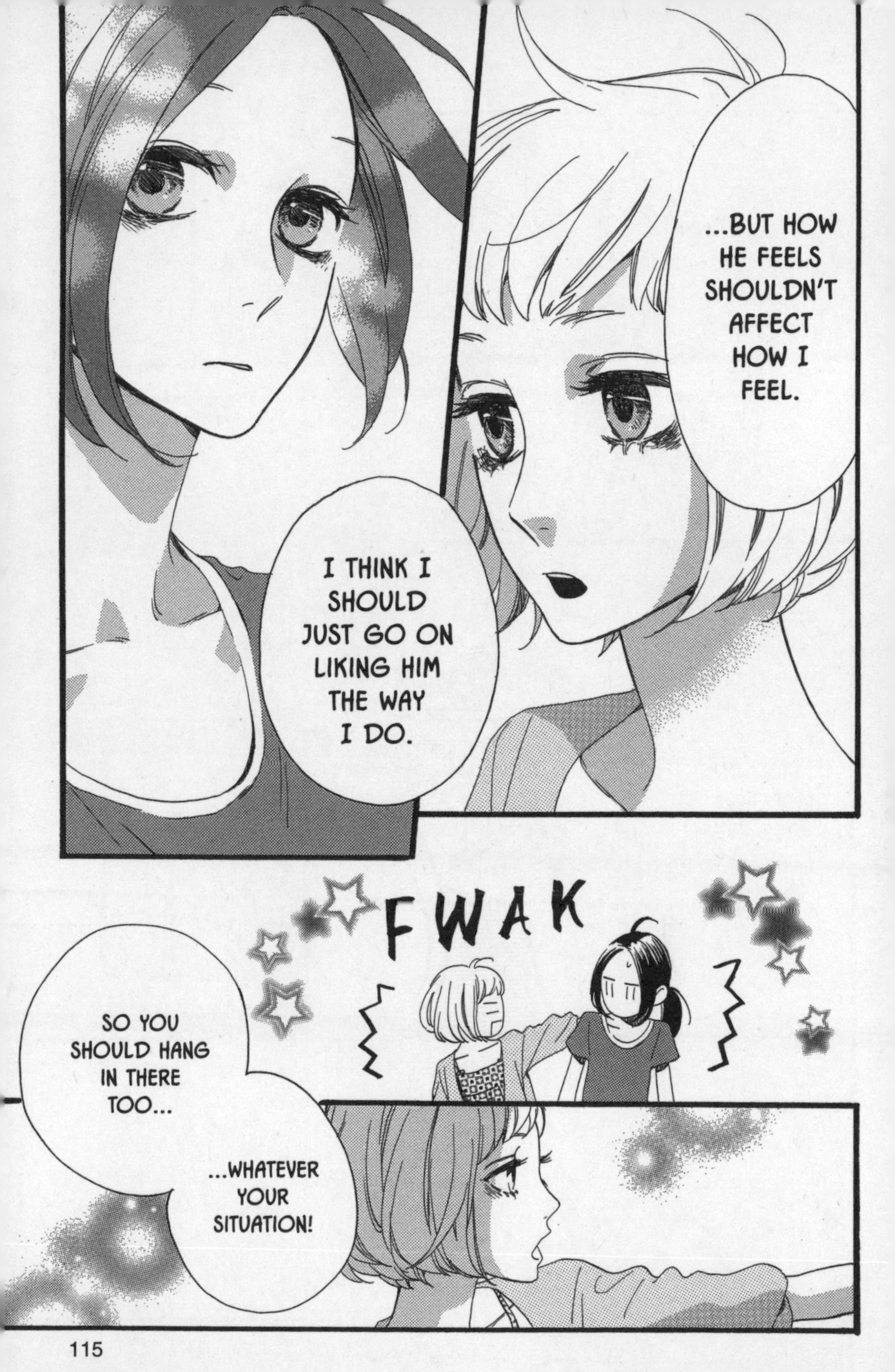
...BUT HOW HE FEELS SHOULDN'T AFFECT HOW I FEEL.
I THINK I SHOULD JUST GO ON LIKING HIM THE WAY I DO.
FWAK
SO YOU SHOULD HANG IN THERE TOO...
...WHATEVER YOUR SITUATION!

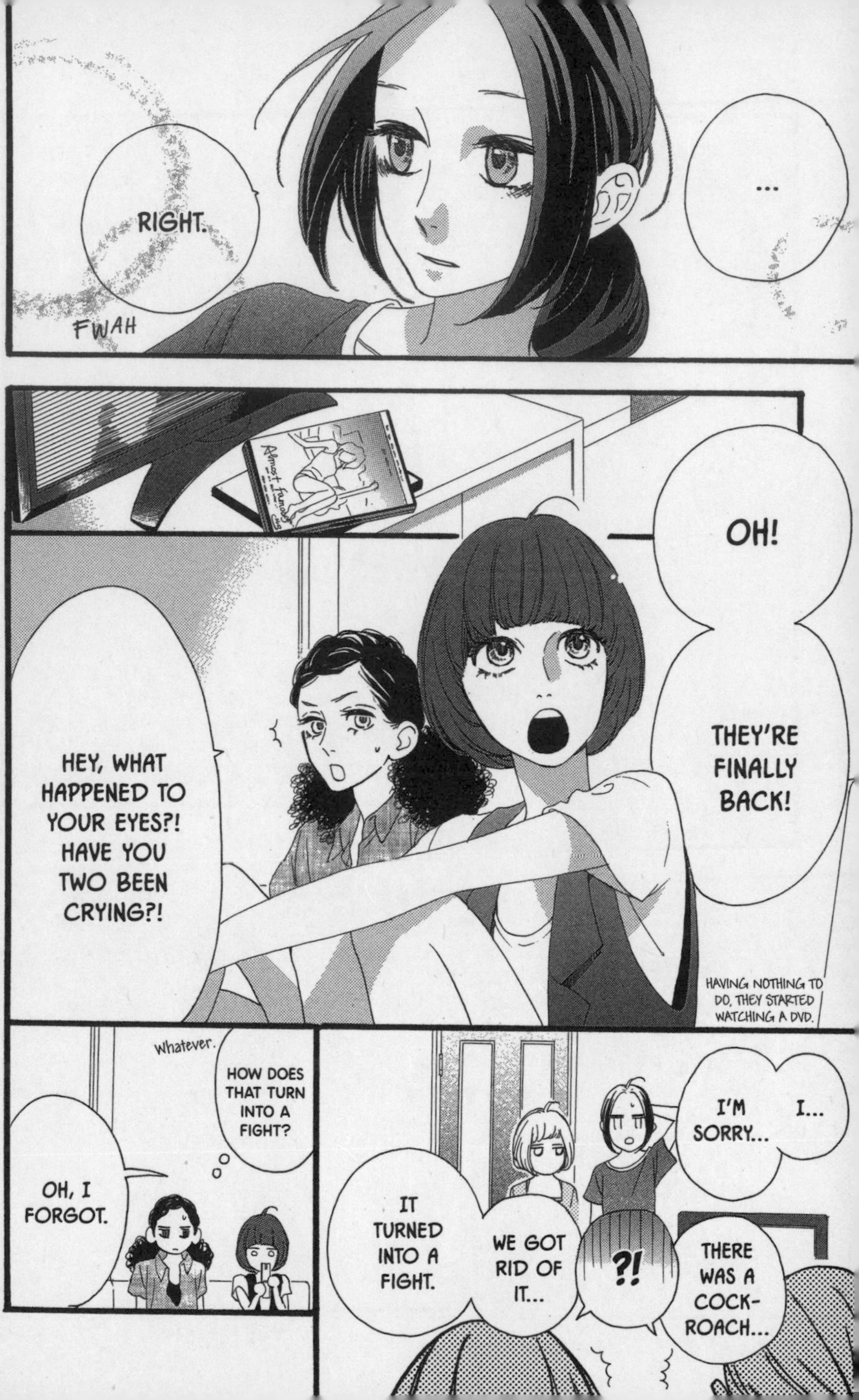
...
RIGHT.
FWAH
OH!
THEY'RE FINALLY BACK!
HEY, WHAT HAPPENED TO YOUR EYES?! HAVE YOU TWO BEEN CRYING?!
HAVING NOTHING TO DO, THEY STARTED WATCHING A DVD.
I...
I'M SORRY...
THERE WAS A COCK-ROACH...
?!
WE GOT RID OF IT...
IT TURNED INTO A FIGHT.
HOW DOES THAT TURN INTO A FIGHT?
Whatever.
OH, I FORGOT.

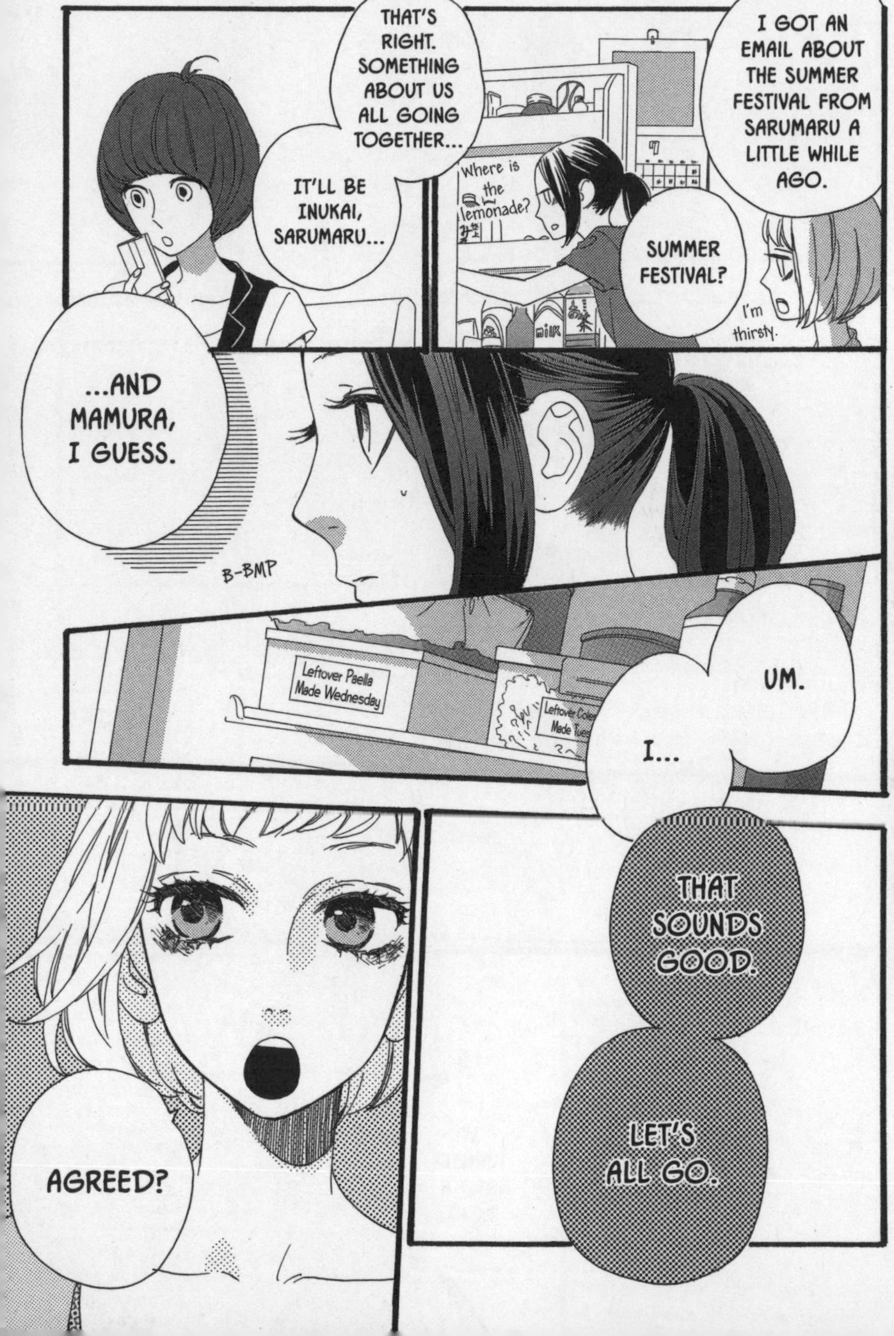
I GOT AN EMAIL ABOUT THE SUMMER FESTIVAL FROM SARUMARU A LITTLE WHILE AGO.
SUMMER FESTIVAL?
I'm thirsty.
Where is the lemonade?
THAT'S RIGHT. SOMETHING ABOUT US ALL GOING TOGETHER...
IT'LL BE INUKAI, SARUMARU...
...AND MAMURA, I GUESS.
B-BMP
UM.
I...
Leftover Paella Made Wednesday
THAT SOUNDS GOOD.
LET'S ALL GO.
AGREED?

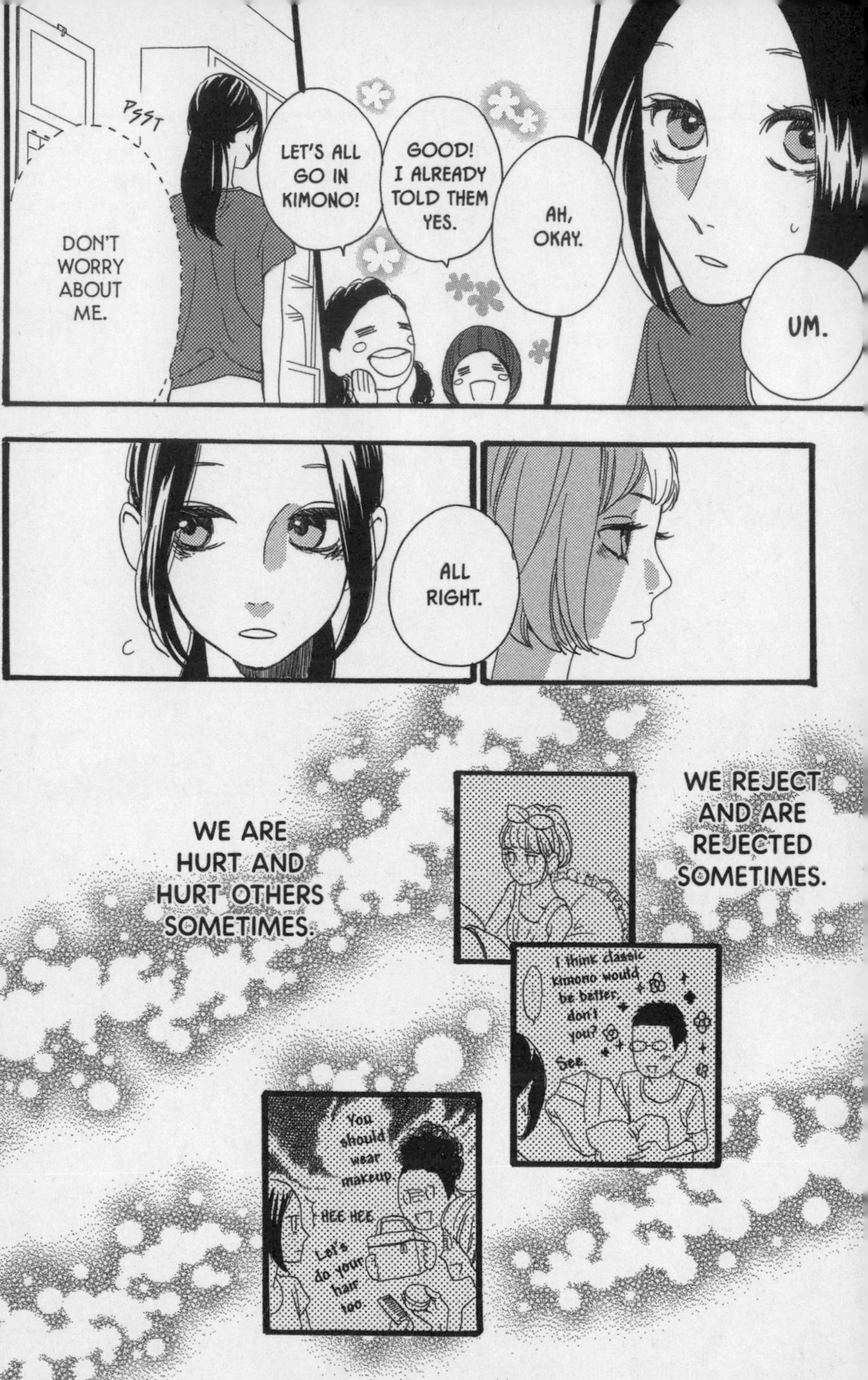
UM.
AH, OKAY.
GOOD! I ALREADY TOLD THEM YES.
LET'S ALL GO IN KIMONO!
PSST
DON'T WORRY ABOUT ME.
ALL RIGHT.
WE REJECT AND ARE REJECTED SOMETIMES.
WE ARE HURT AND HURT OTHERS SOMETIMES.
I think classic kimono would be better, don't you?
See.
You should wear makeup.
HEE HEE
Let's do your hair too.

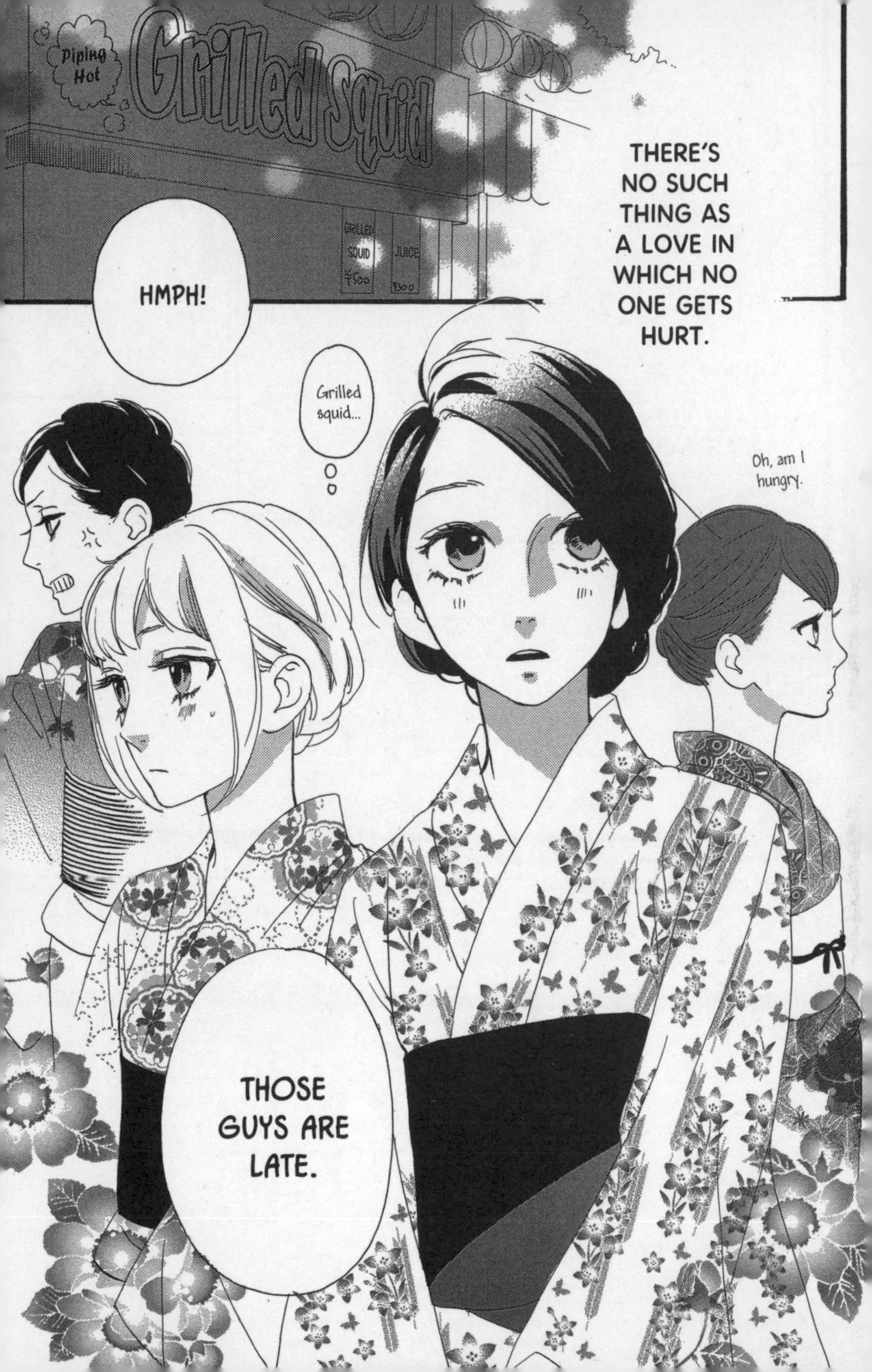
THERE'S NO SUCH THING AS A LOVE IN WHICH NO ONE GETS HURT.
Piping Hot
Grilled squid
GRILLED SQUID
JUICE
HMPH!
Oh, am I hungry.
Grilled squid...
THOSE GUYS ARE LATE.

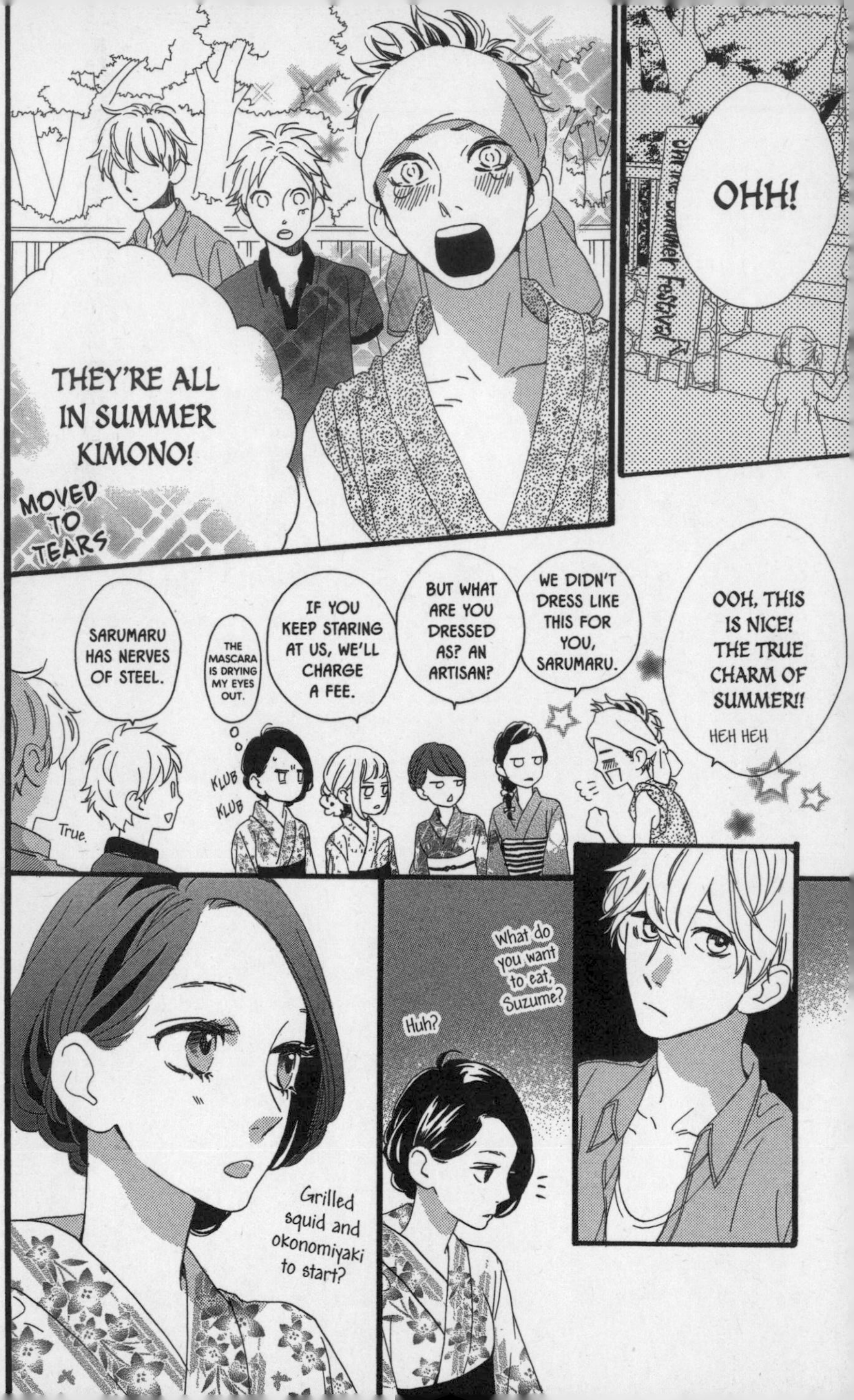
OHH!
Summer Festival
THEY'RE ALL IN SUMMER KIMONO!
MOVED TO TEARS
OOH, THIS IS NICE! THE TRUE CHARM OF SUMMER!!
HEH HEH
WE DIDN'T DRESS LIKE THIS FOR YOU, SARUMARU.
BUT WHAT ARE YOU DRESSED AS? AN ARTISAN?
IF YOU KEEP STARING AT US, WE'LL CHARGE A FEE.
THE MASCARA IS DRYING MY EYES OUT.
KLUB KLUB
SARUMARU HAS NERVES OF STEEL.
True.
What do you want to eat, Suzume?
Huh?
Grilled squid and okonomiyaki to start?

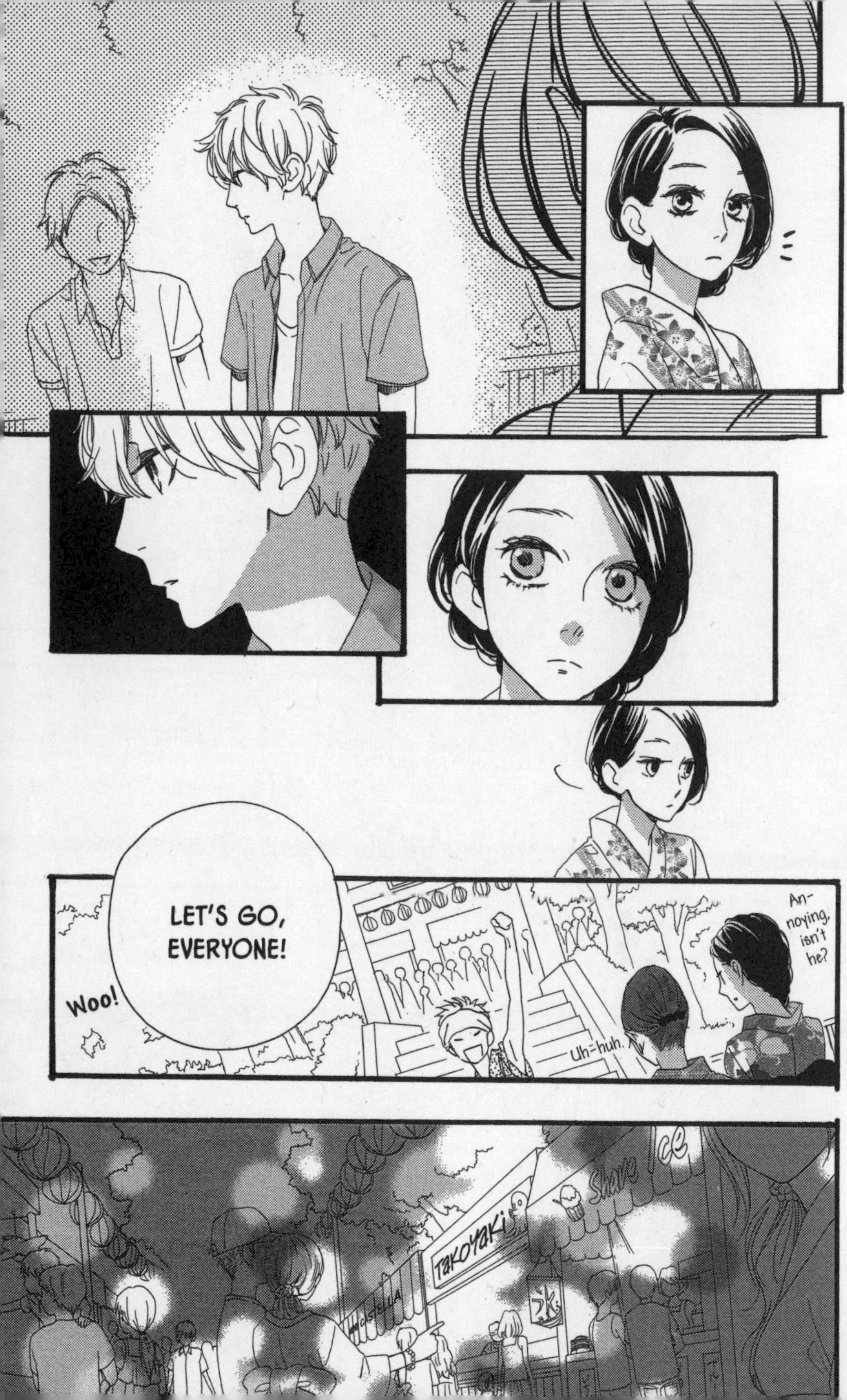
LET'S GO, EVERYONE!
An-noying, isn't he?
Uh-huh.
Woo!
Shave Ice
TAKOYAKI
CASTELLA

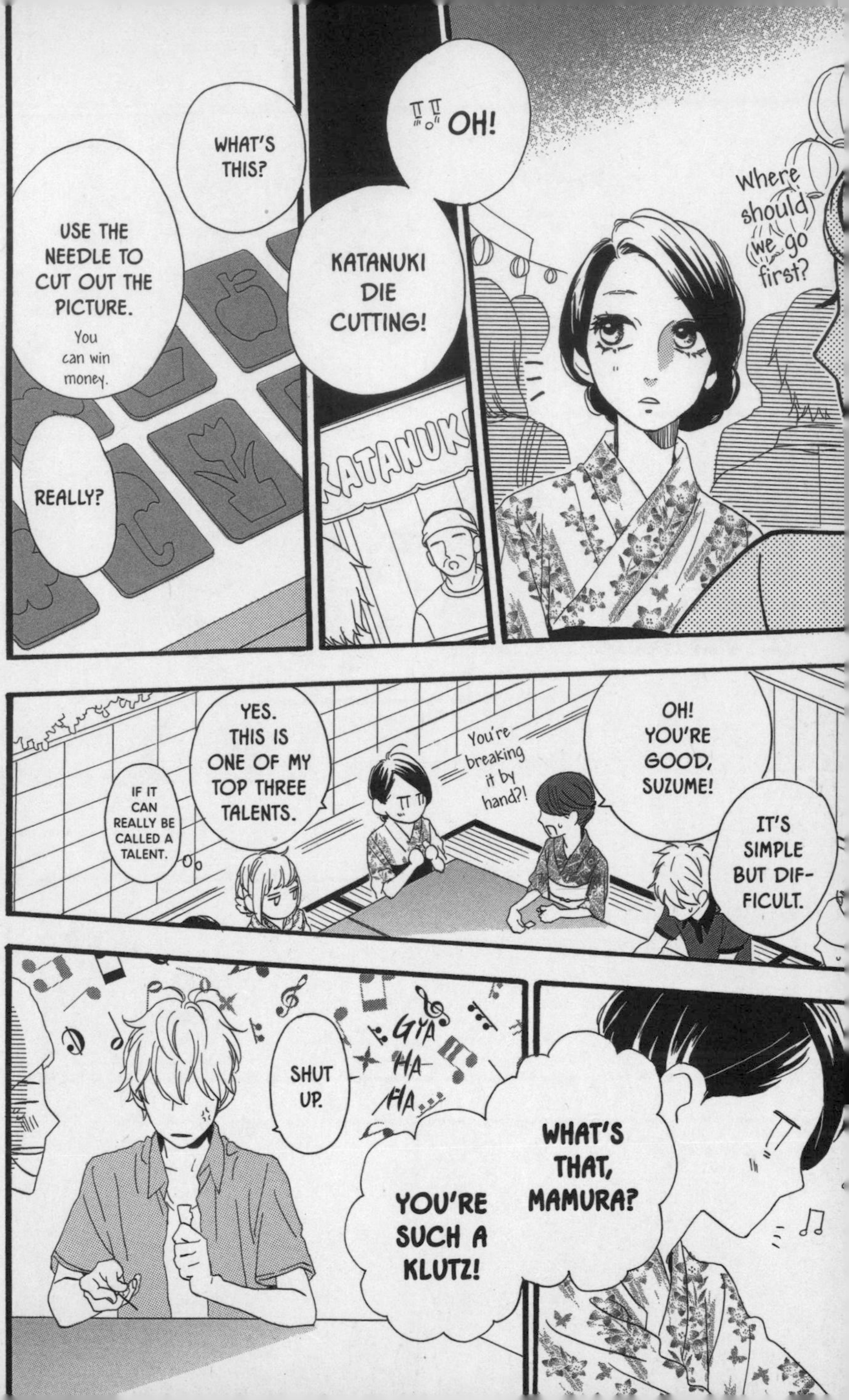
Where should we go first?
OH!
KATANUKI DIE CUTTING!
KATANUKI
WHAT'S THIS?
USE THE NEEDLE TO CUT OUT THE PICTURE.
You can win money.
REALLY?
OH! YOU'RE GOOD, SUZUME!
IT'S SIMPLE BUT DIFFICULT.
You're breaking it by hand?!
YES. THIS IS ONE OF MY TOP THREE TALENTS.
IF IT CAN REALLY BE CALLED A TALENT.
WHAT'S THAT, MAMURA?
YOU'RE SUCH A KLUTZ!
GYAHAHA...
SHUT UP.

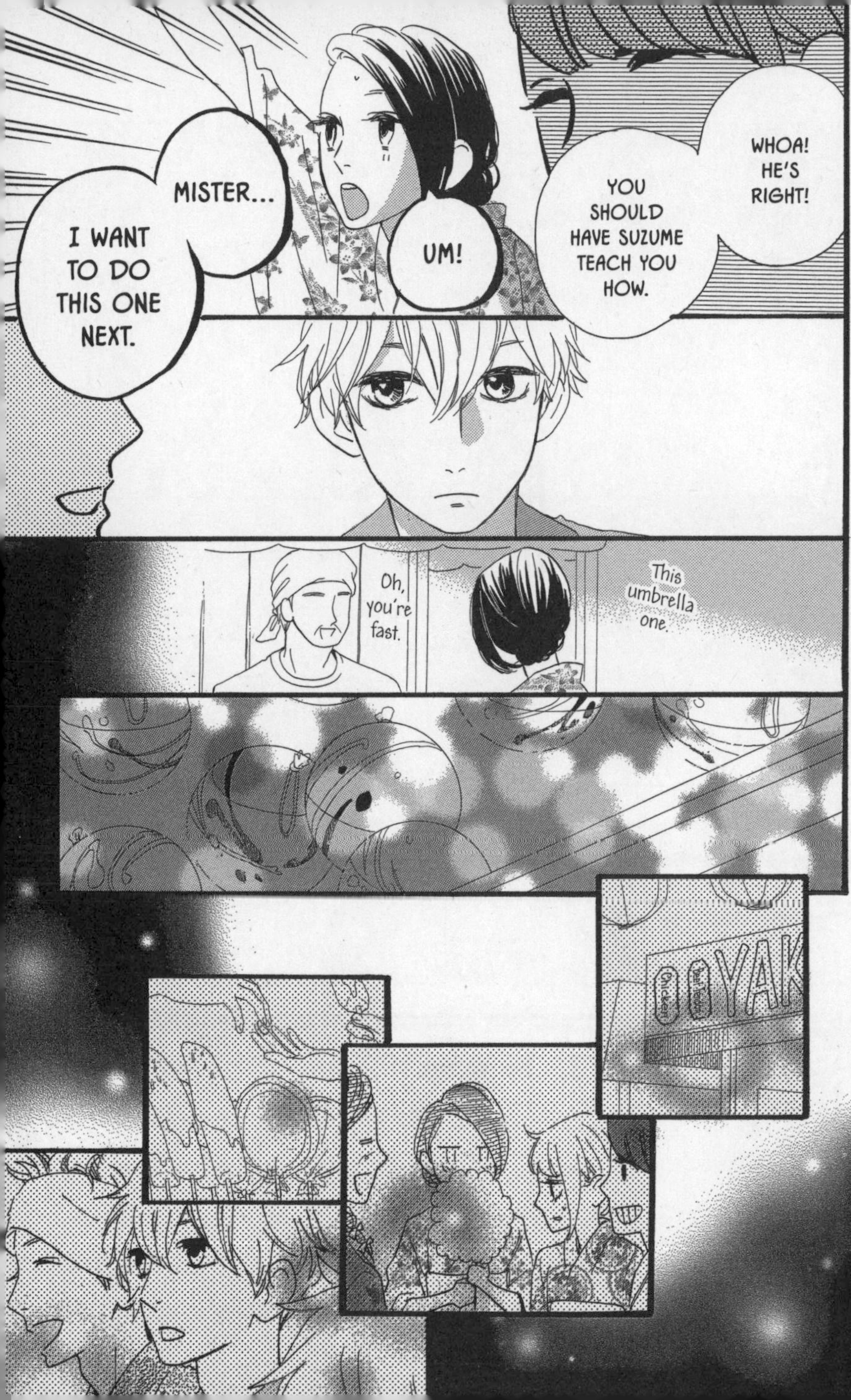
WHOA! HE'S RIGHT!
YOU SHOULD HAVE SUZUME TEACH YOU HOW.
UM!
MISTER...
I WANT TO DO THIS ONE NEXT.
This umbrella one.
Oh, you're fast.
YAK
Chicken

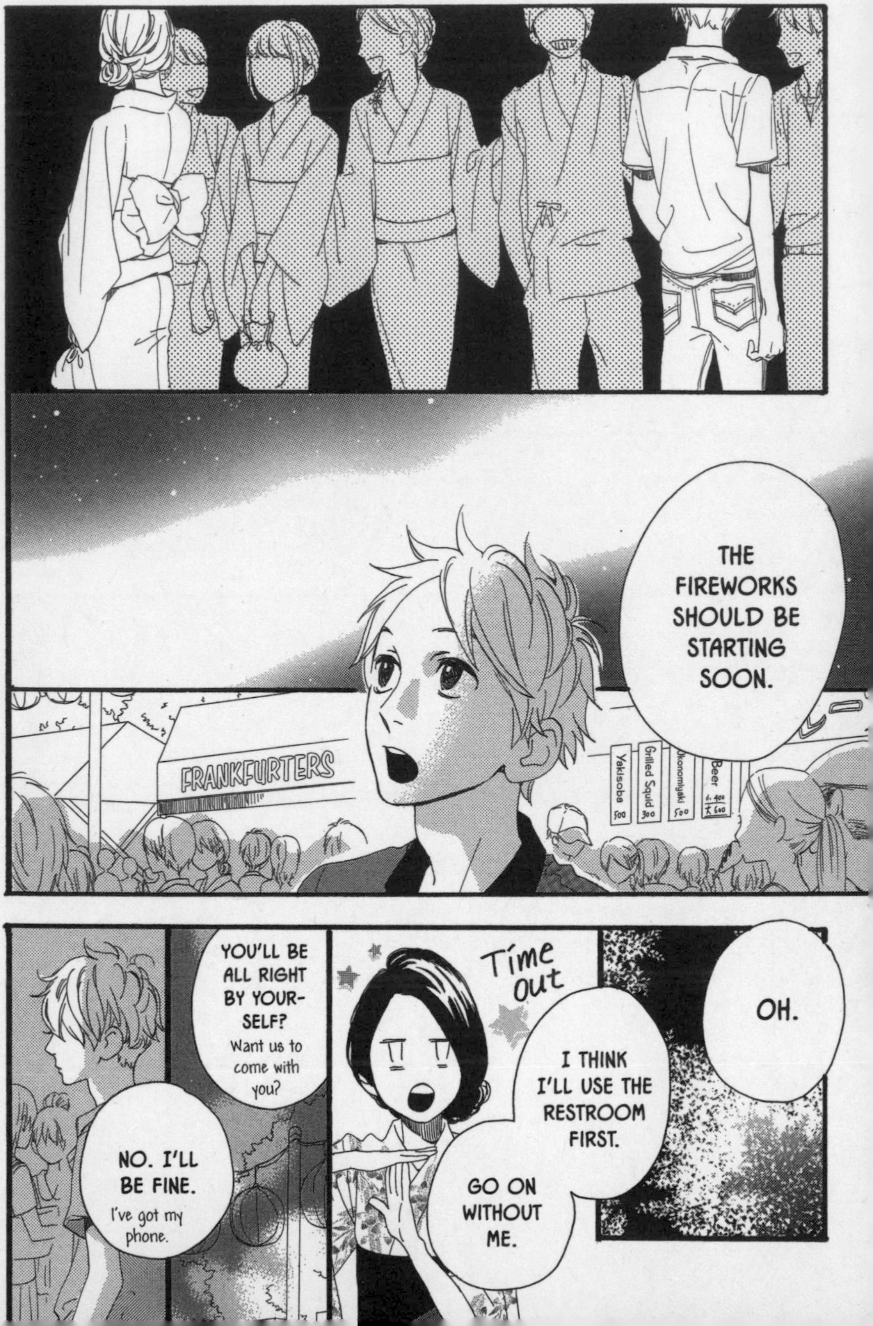
THE FIREWORKS SHOULD BE STARTING SOON.
FRANKFURTERS
Beer
Okonomiyaki 500
Grilled Squid 300
Yakisoba 500
OH.
Time out
I THINK I'LL USE THE RESTROOM FIRST.
GO ON WITHOUT ME.
YOU'LL BE ALL RIGHT BY YOUR-SELF? Want us to come with you?
NO. I'LL BE FINE. I've got my phone.

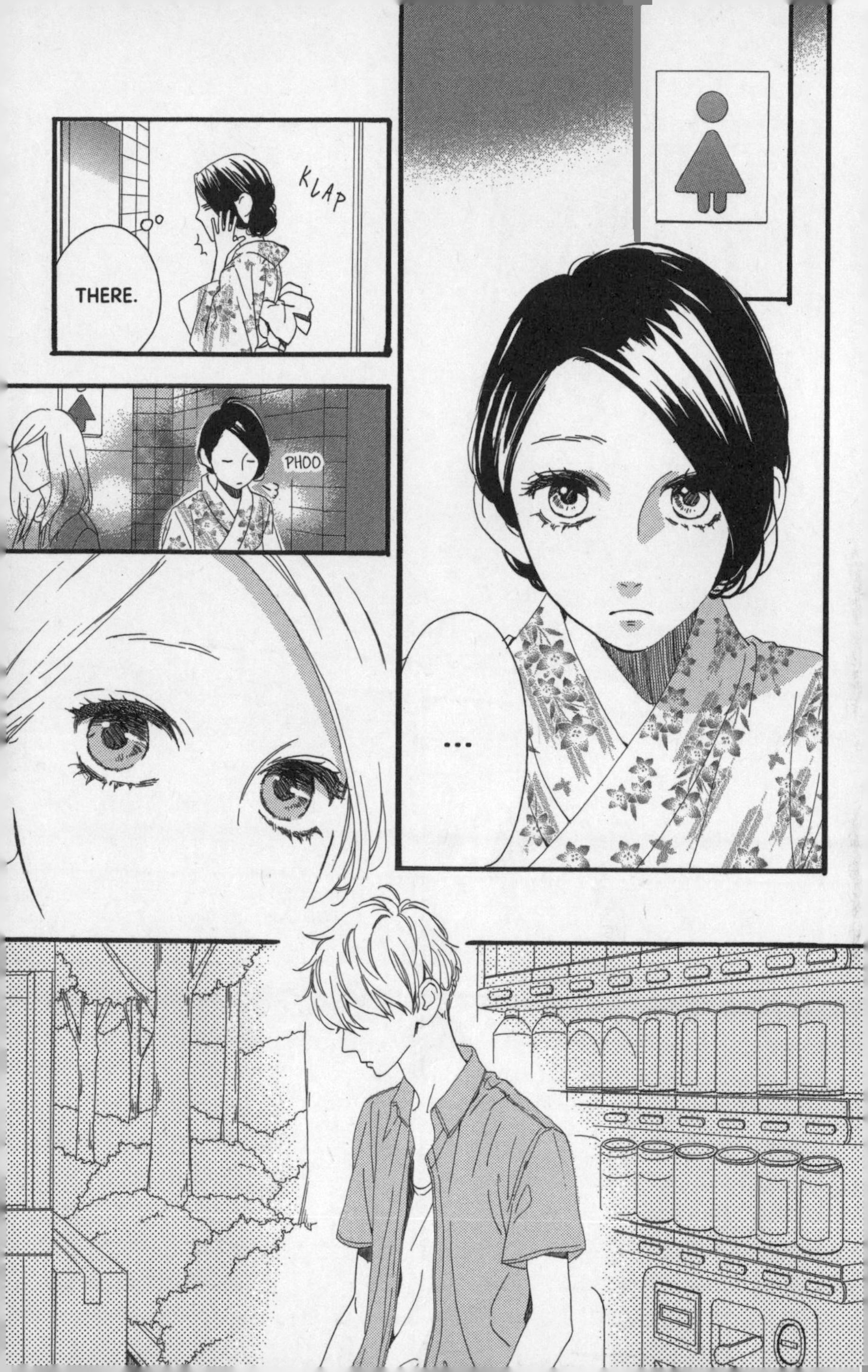
...
KLAP
THERE.
PHOO

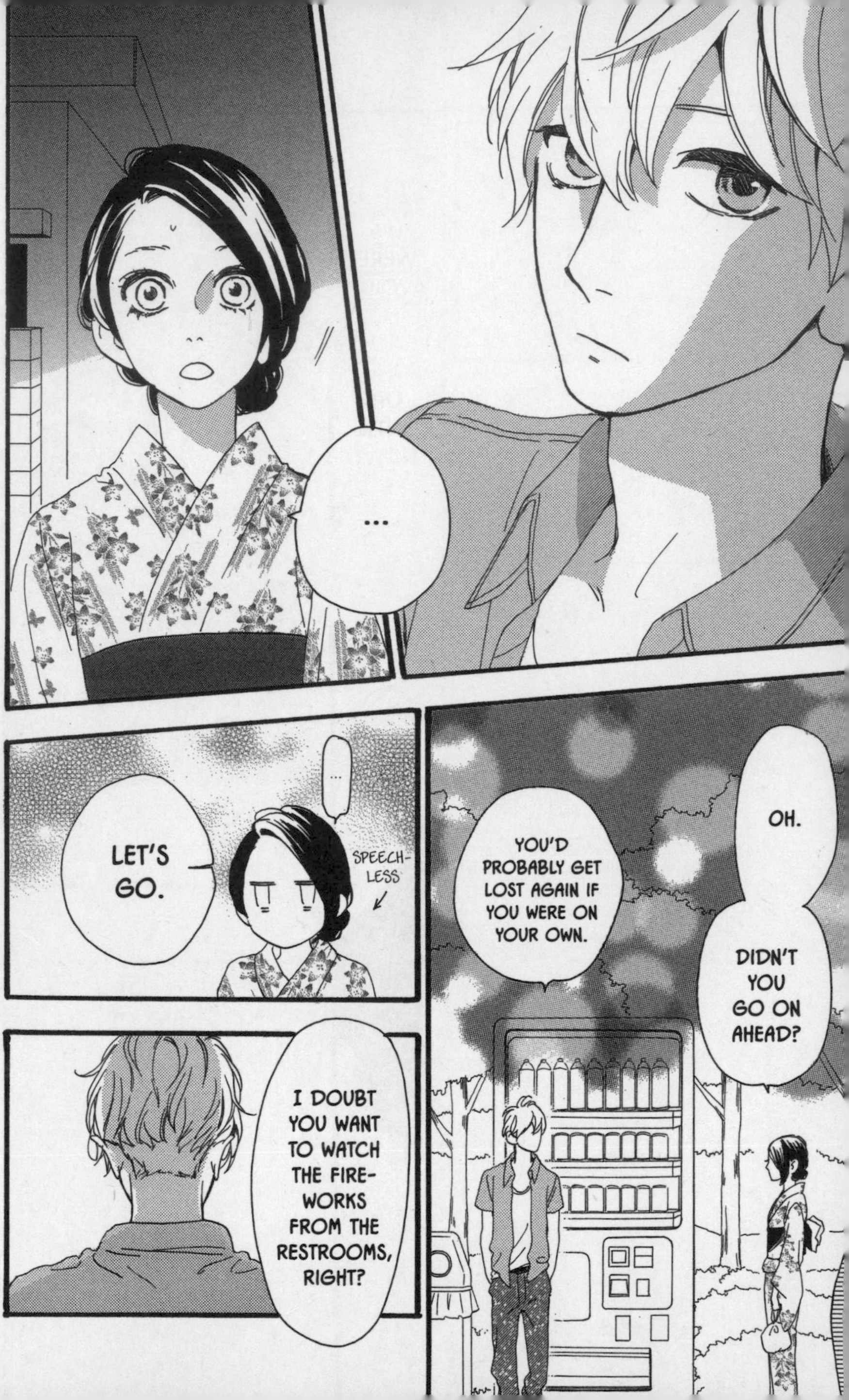
...
OH.
DIDN'T YOU GO ON AHEAD?
YOU'D PROBABLY GET LOST AGAIN IF YOU WERE ON YOUR OWN.
...
SPEECH-LESS
LET'S GO.
I DOUBT YOU WANT TO WATCH THE FIRE-WORKS FROM THE RESTROOMS, RIGHT?

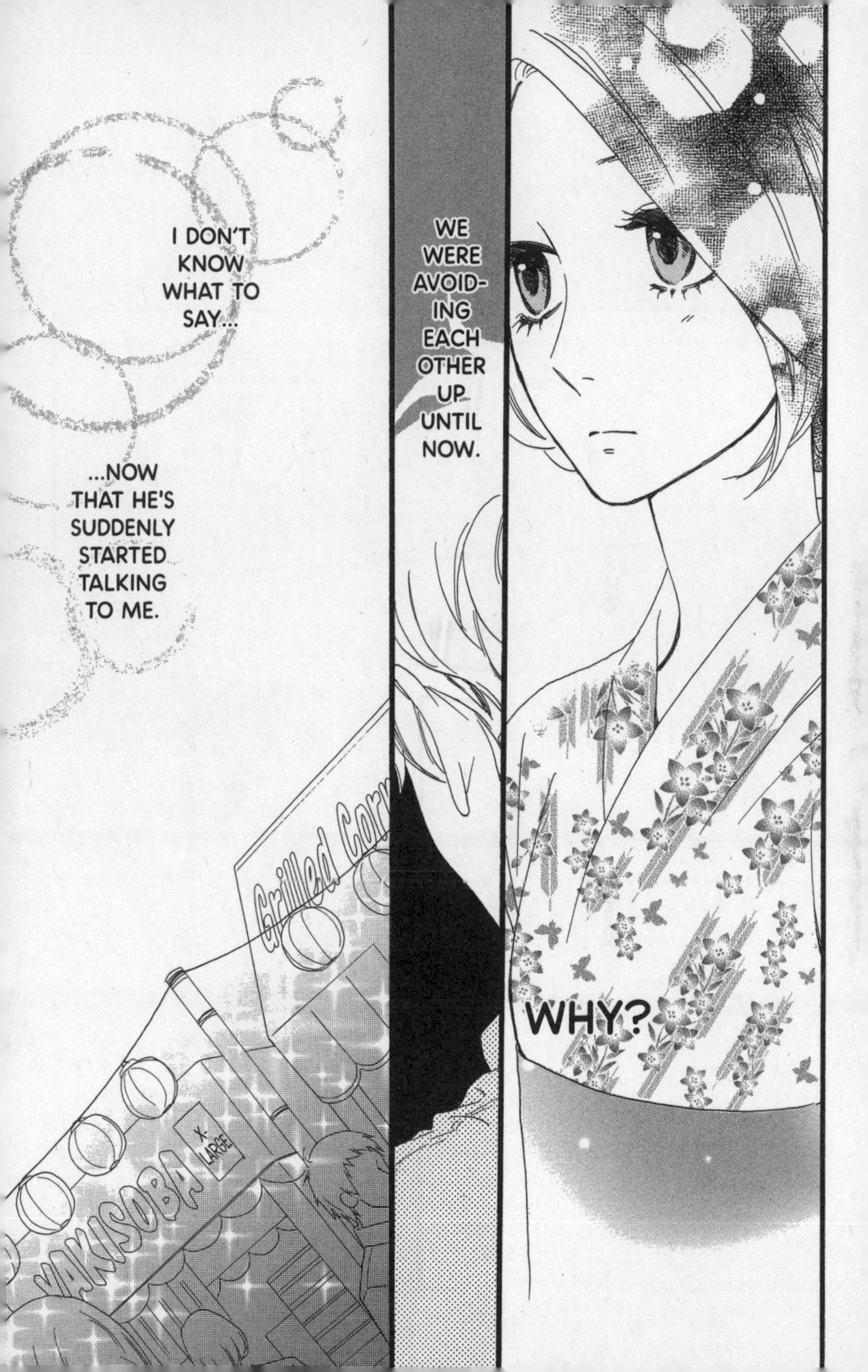

WHY?
WE WERE AVOIDING EACH OTHER UP UNTIL NOW.
I DON'T KNOW WHAT TO SAY...
...NOW THAT HE'S SUDDENLY STARTED TALKING TO ME.
X-LARGE
YAKISOBA

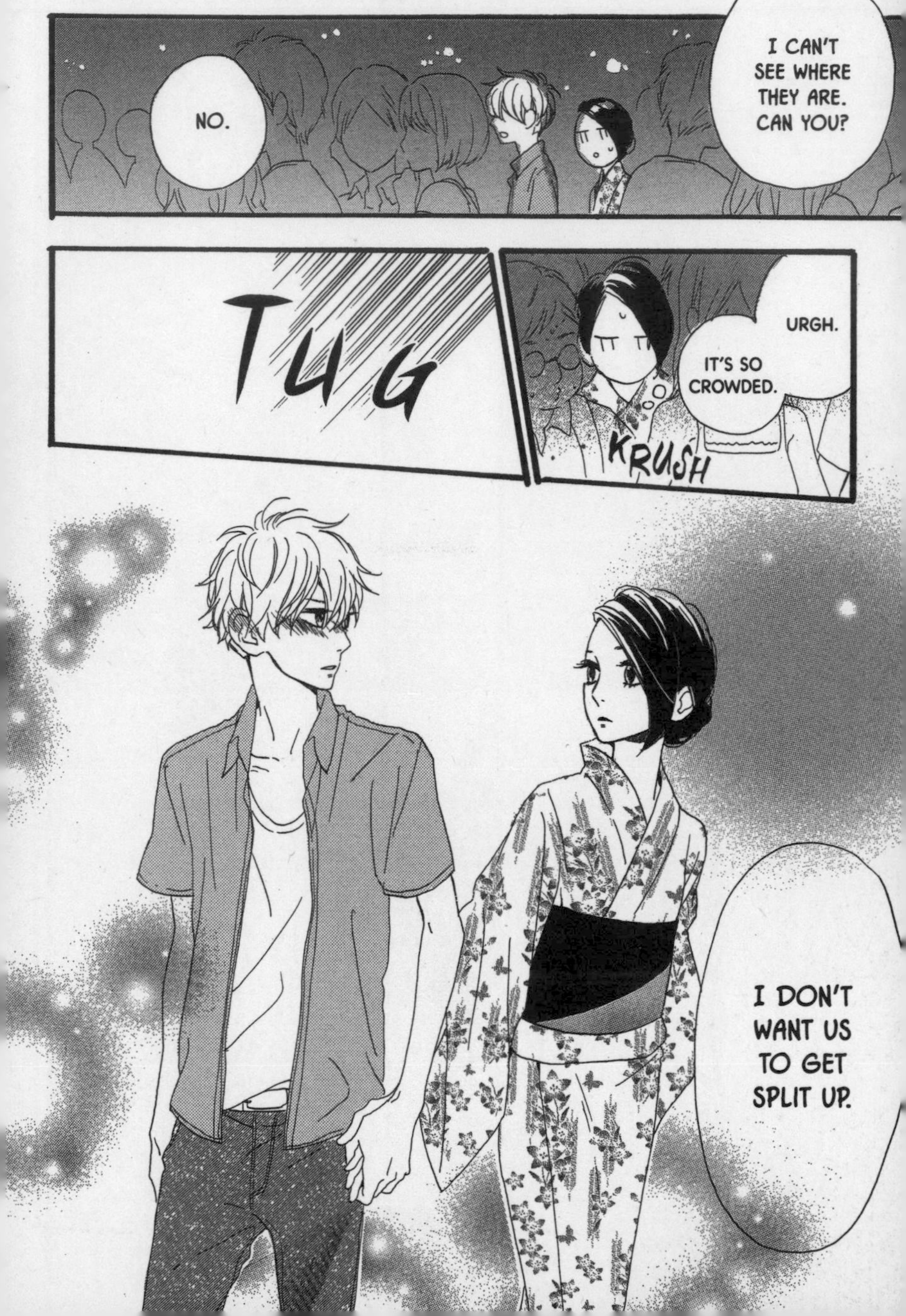
I CAN'T SEE WHERE THEY ARE. CAN YOU?
NO.
URGH.
IT'S SO CROWDED.
KRUSH
TUG
I DON'T WANT US TO GET SPLIT UP.

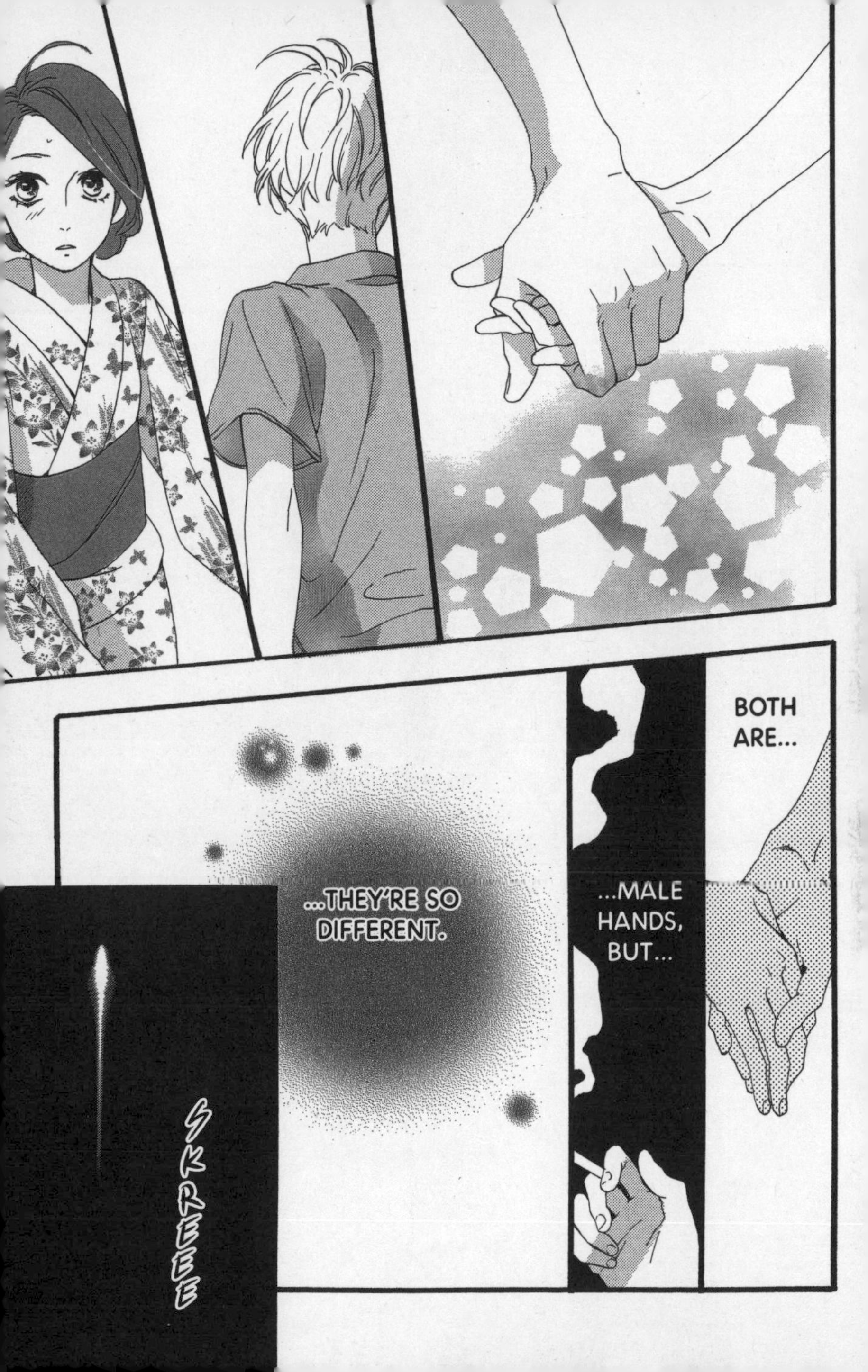
BOTH ARE...
...MALE HANDS, BUT...
...THEY'RE SO DIFFERENT.
SKREEE

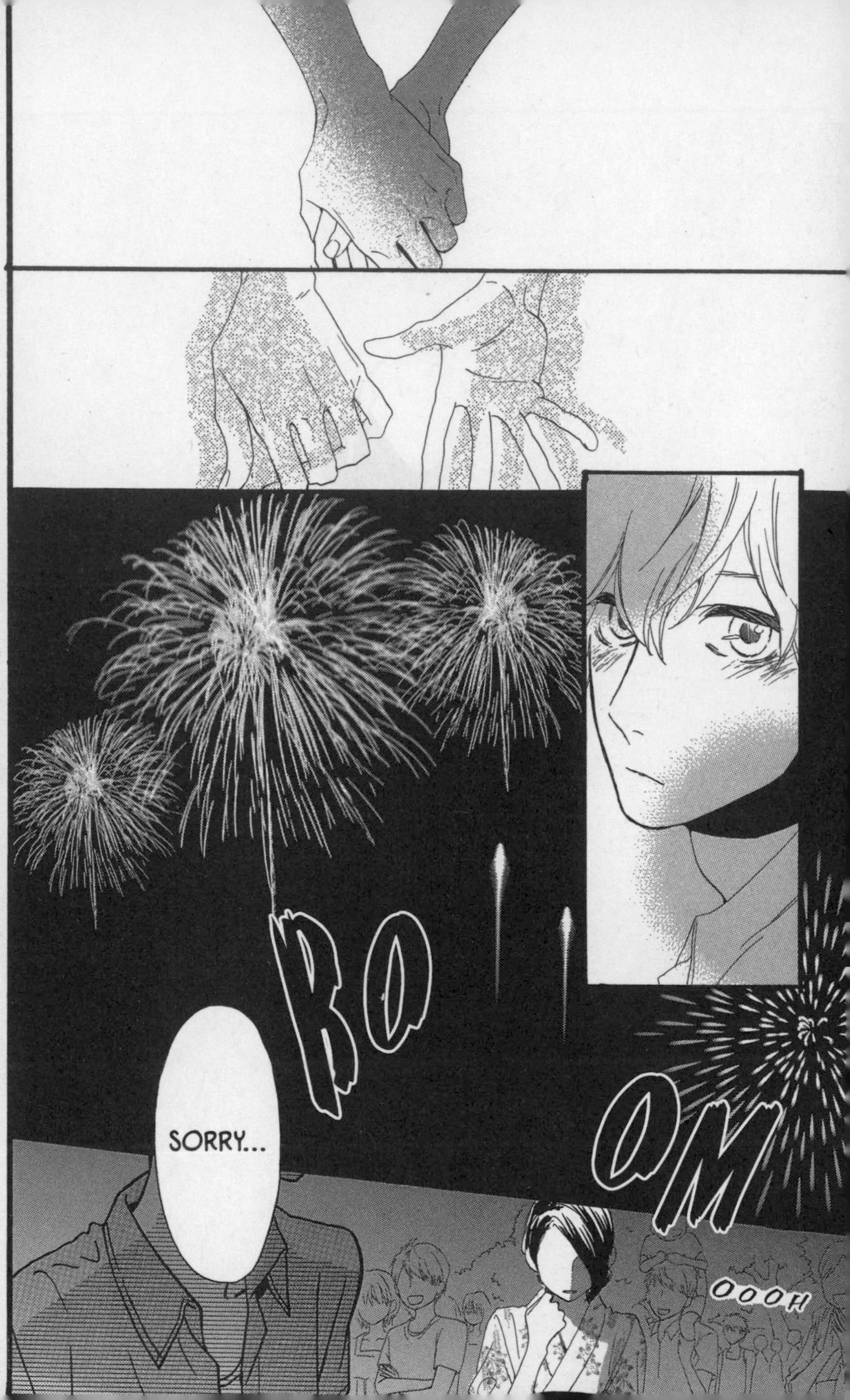
BOOM
SORRY...
OOOH

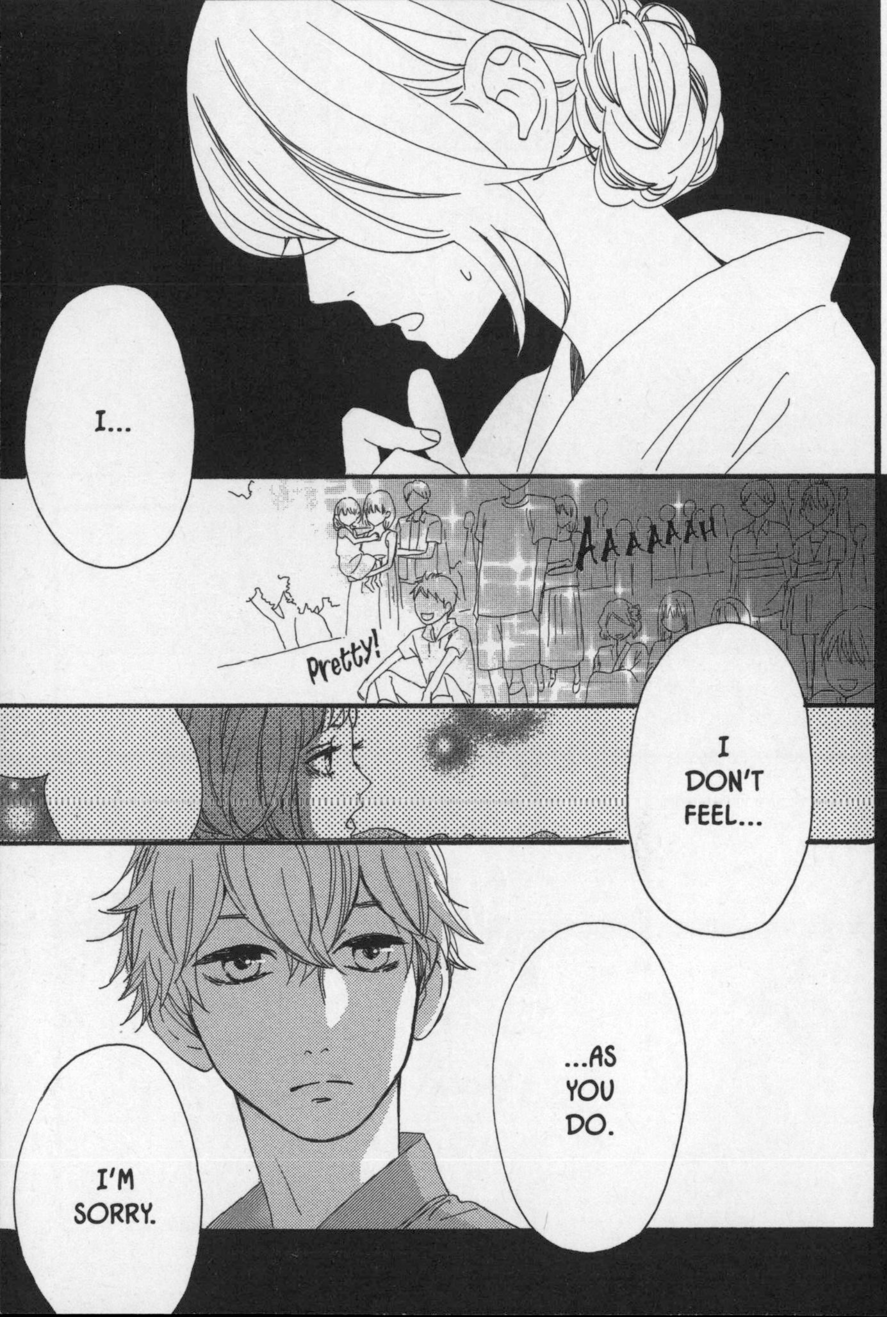
I...
AAAAAAAH
Pretty!
I DON'T FEEL...
...AS YOU DO.
I'M SORRY.

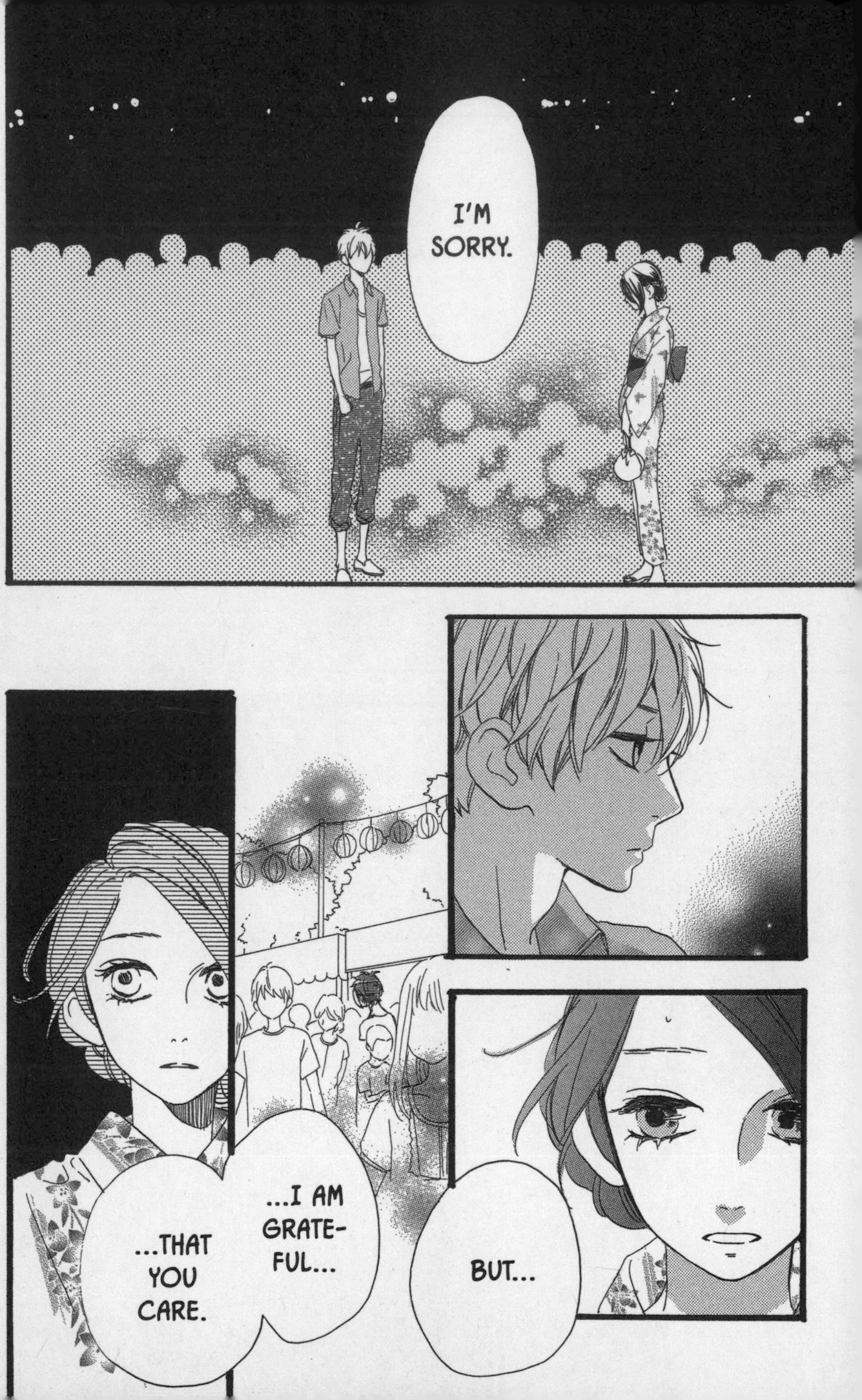
I'M SORRY.
BUT...
...I AM GRATE-FUL...
...THAT YOU CARE.

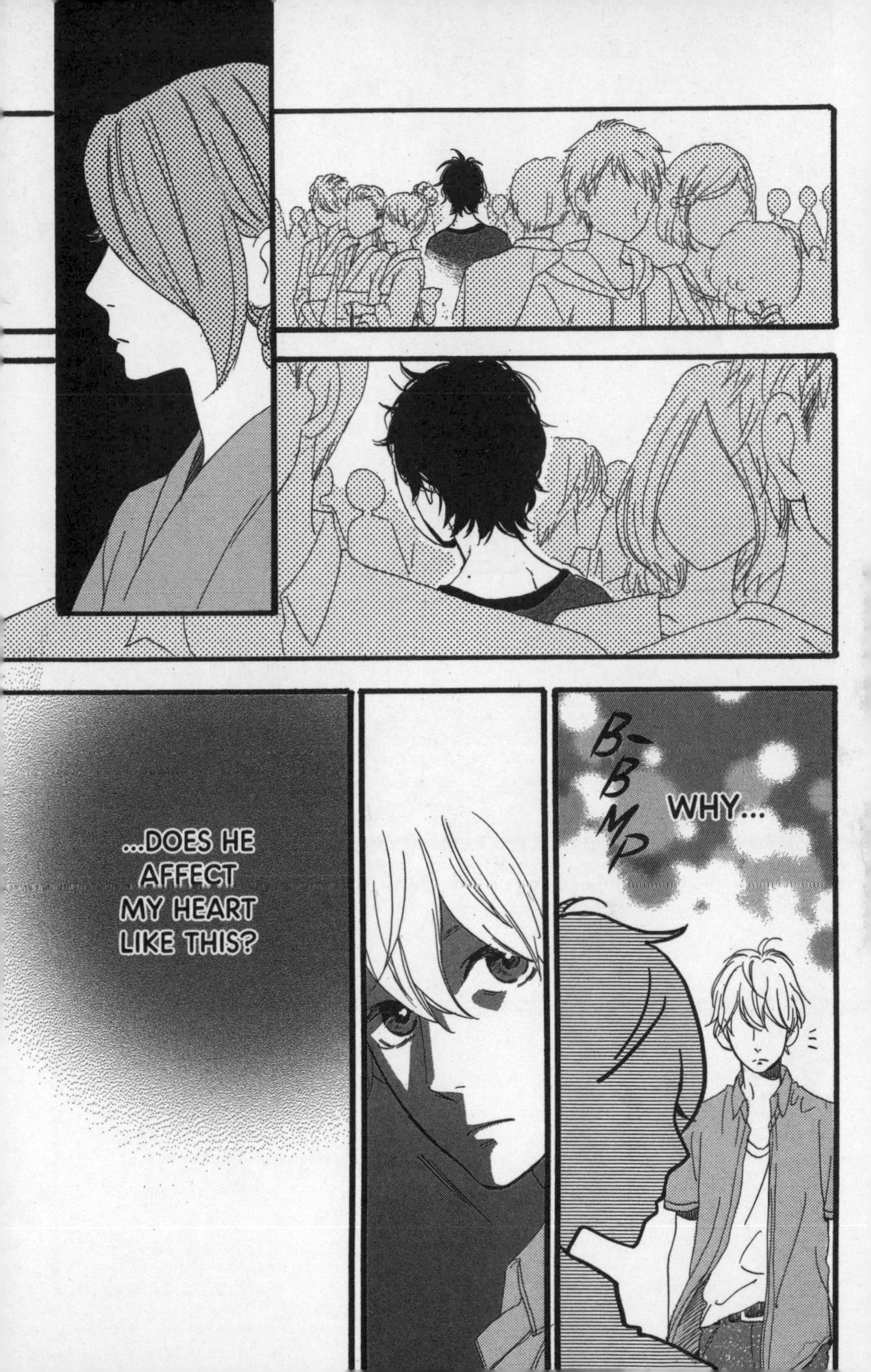
B-BMP
WHY...
...DOES HE AFFECT MY HEART LIKE THIS?

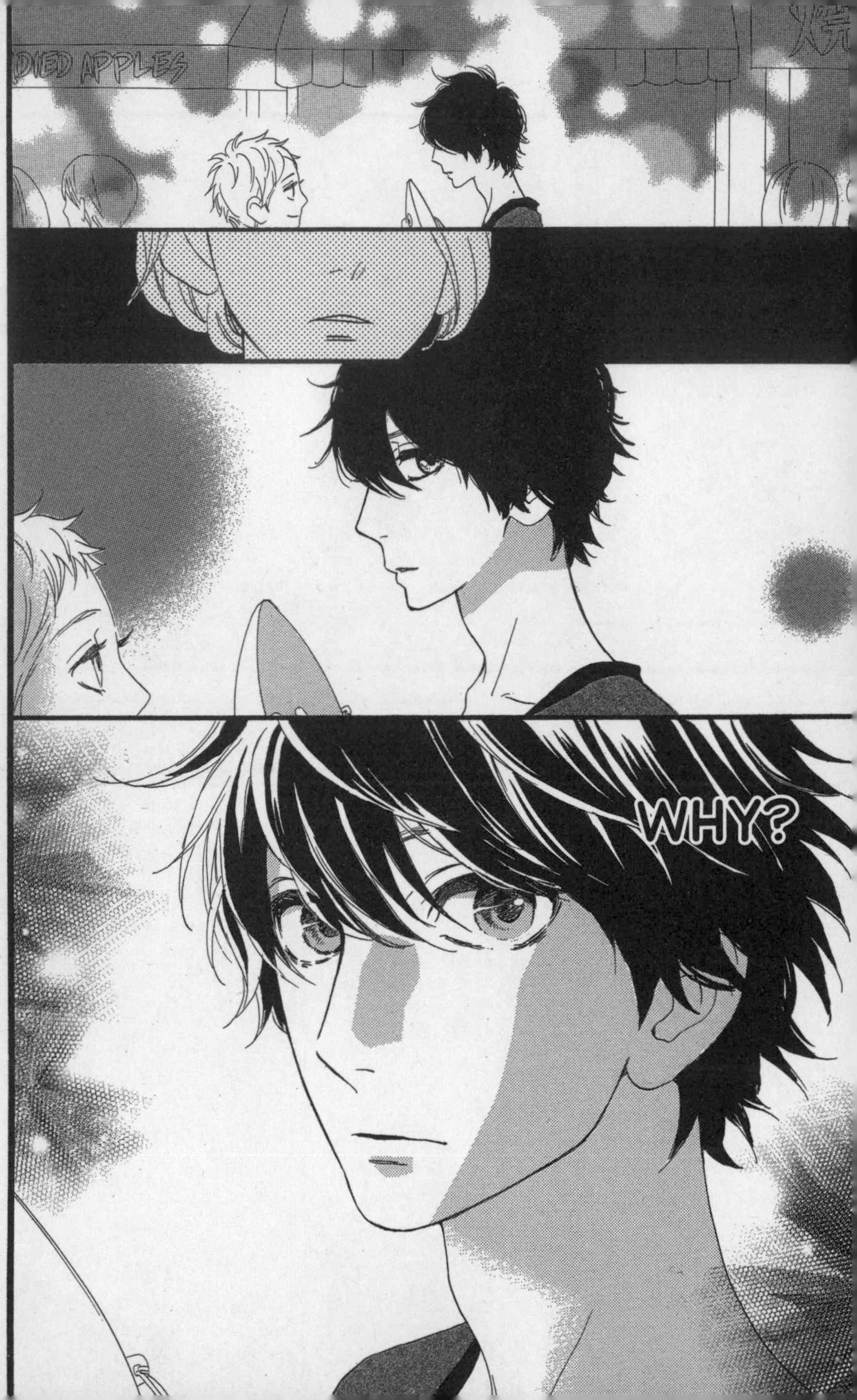
DIED APPLES
WHY?

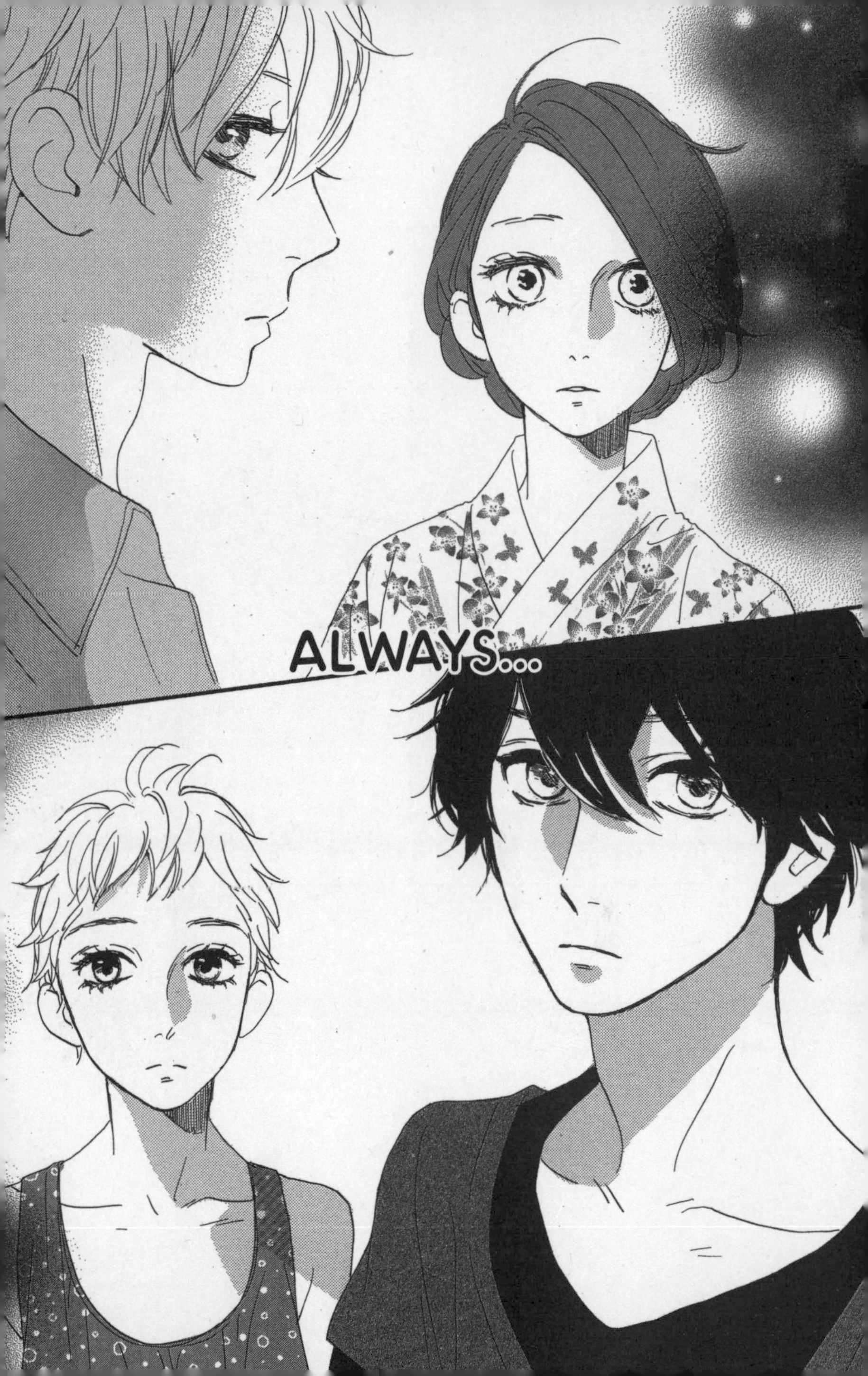
ALWAYS...

More Simple Scribbles

I have nothing else to write about, you see.

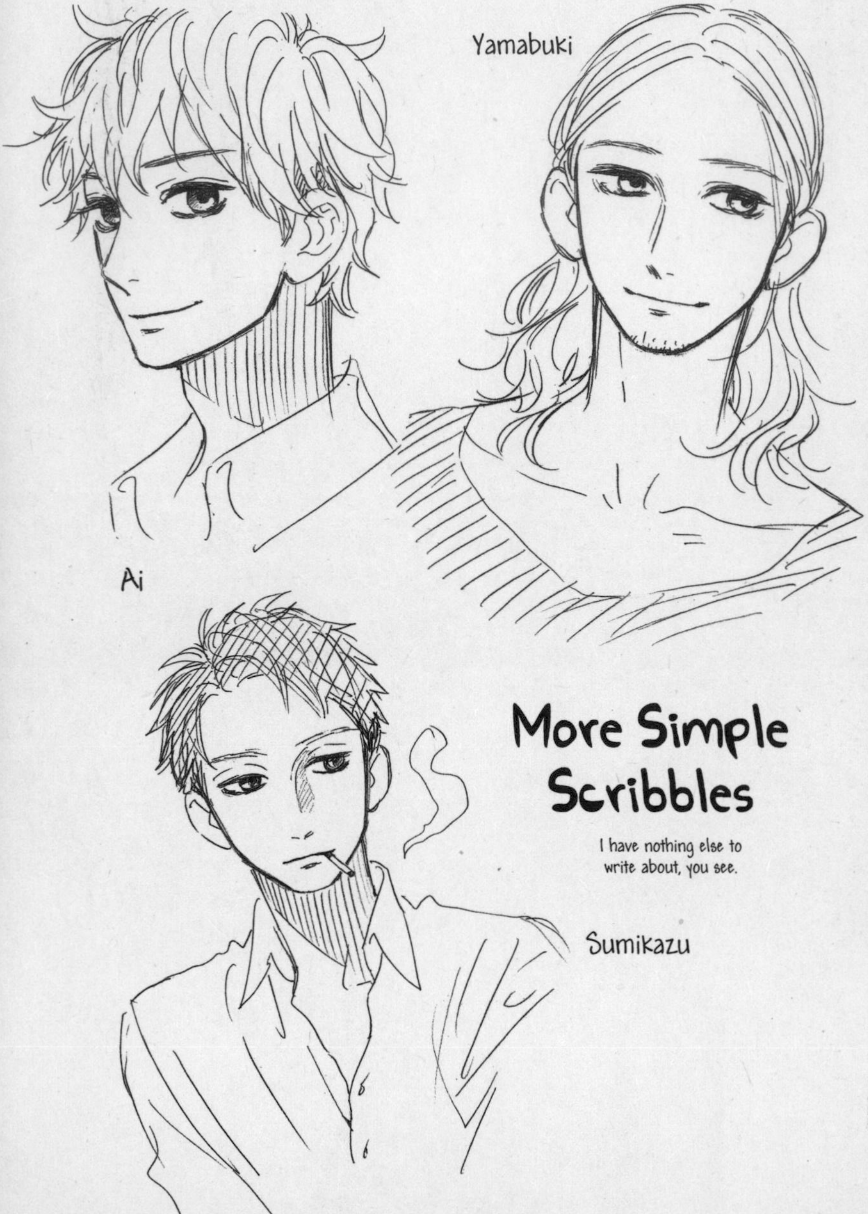
Yamabuki
Ai
Sumikazu

Day 20

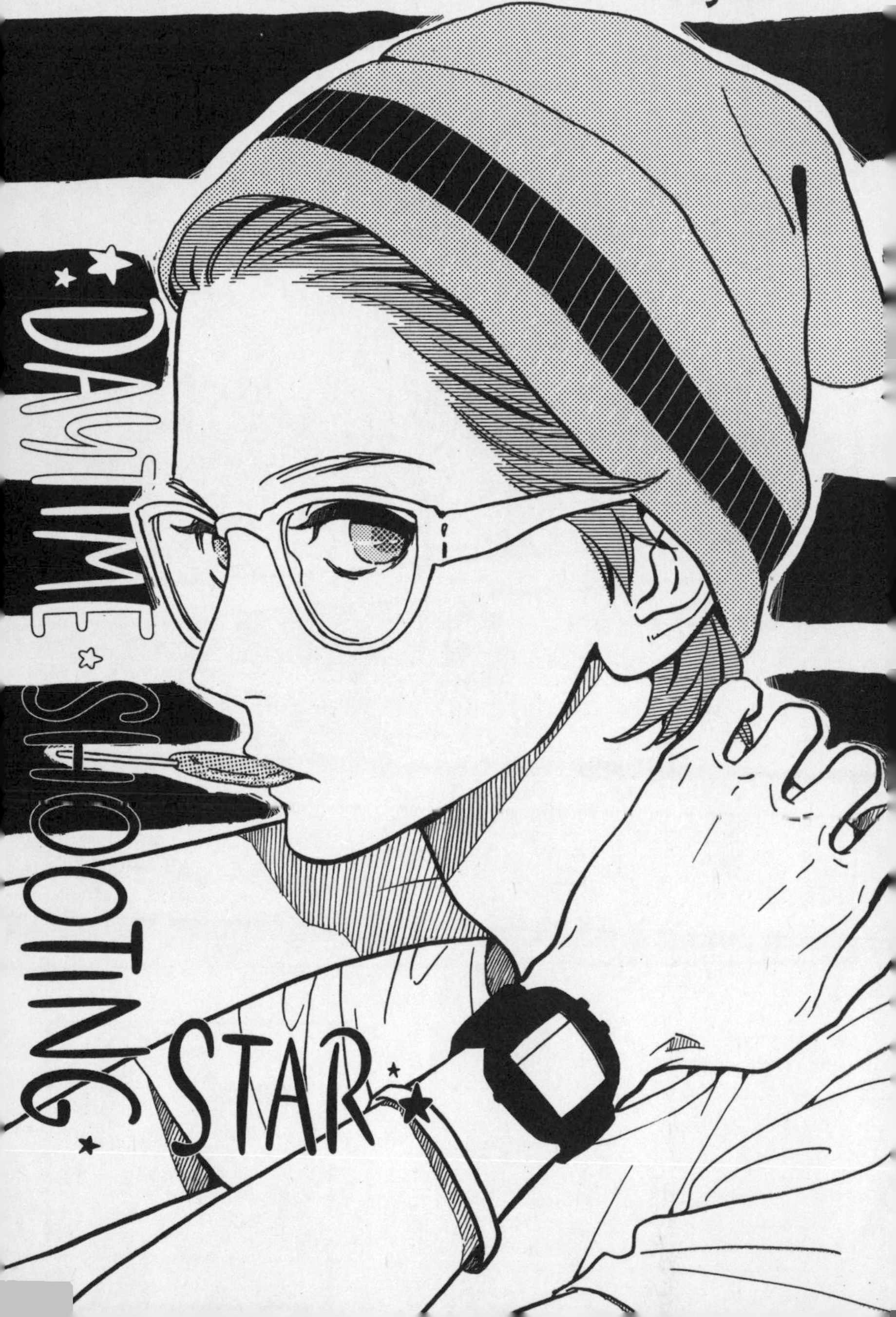
DAYTIME SHOOTING STAR

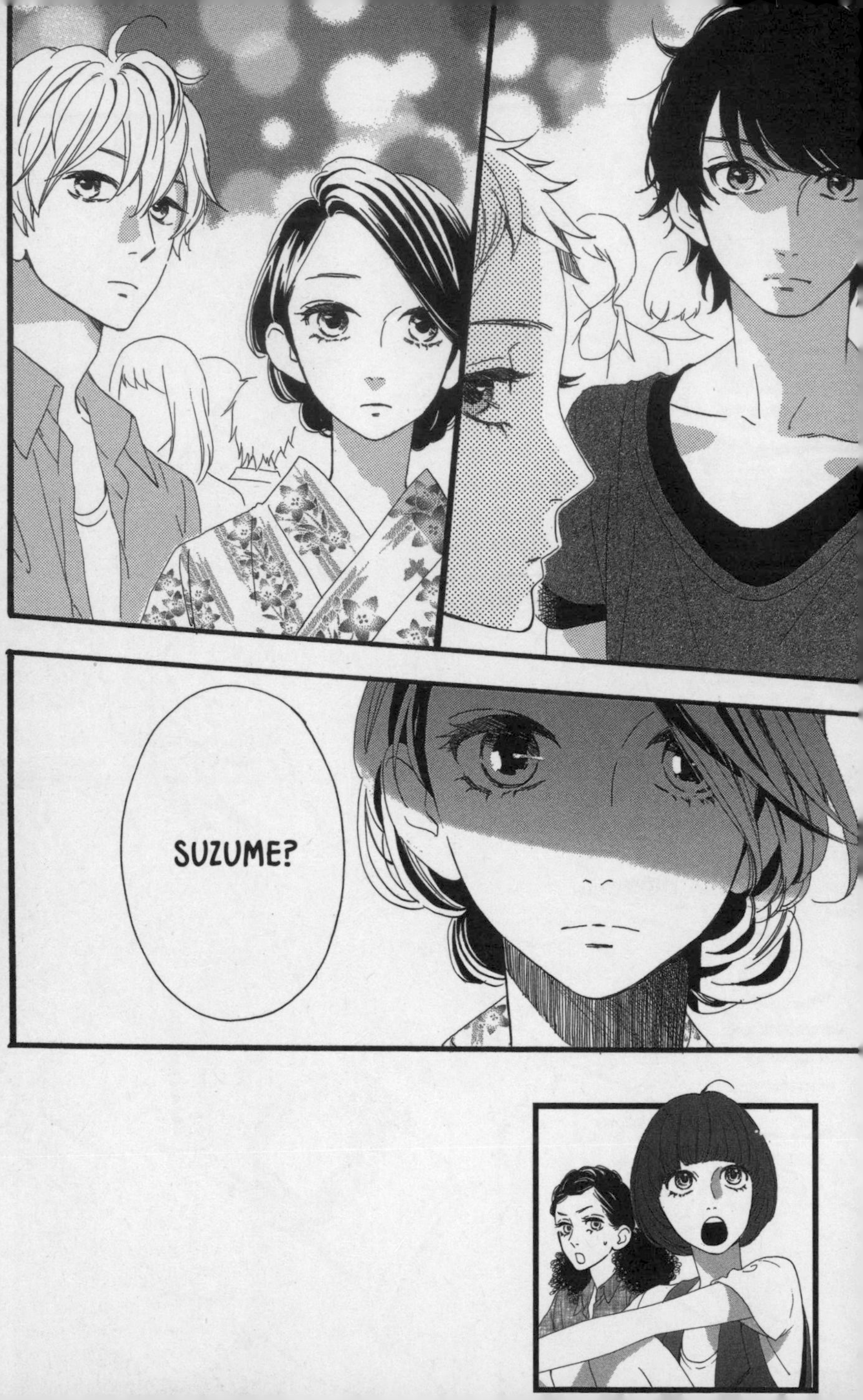
SUZUME?

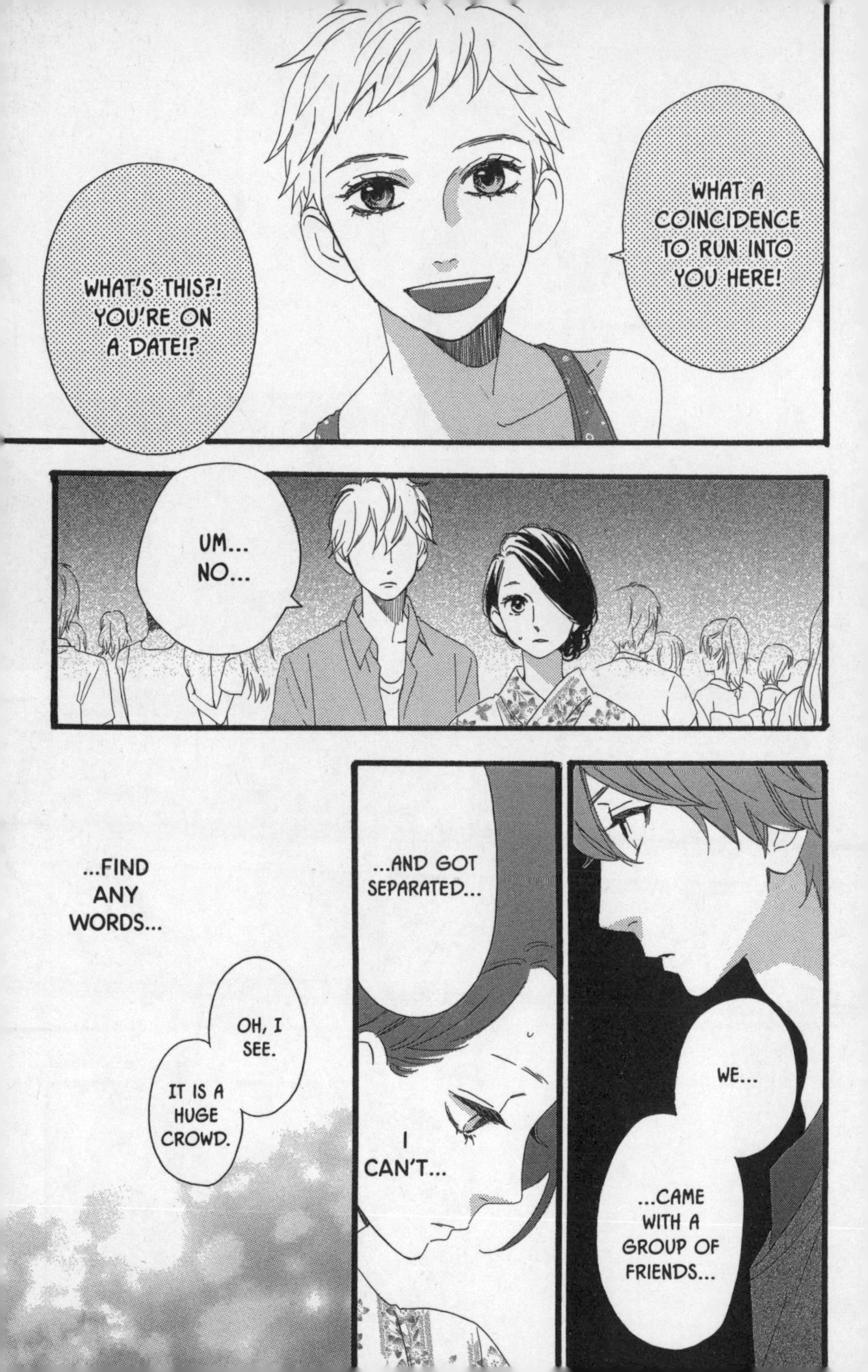
WHAT A COINCIDENCE TO RUN INTO YOU HERE!
WHAT'S THIS?! YOU'RE ON A DATE!?
UM... NO...
WE...
...CAME WITH A GROUP OF FRIENDS...
...AND GOT SEPARATED...
I CAN'T...
...FIND ANY WORDS...
OH, I SEE.
IT IS A HUGE CROWD.

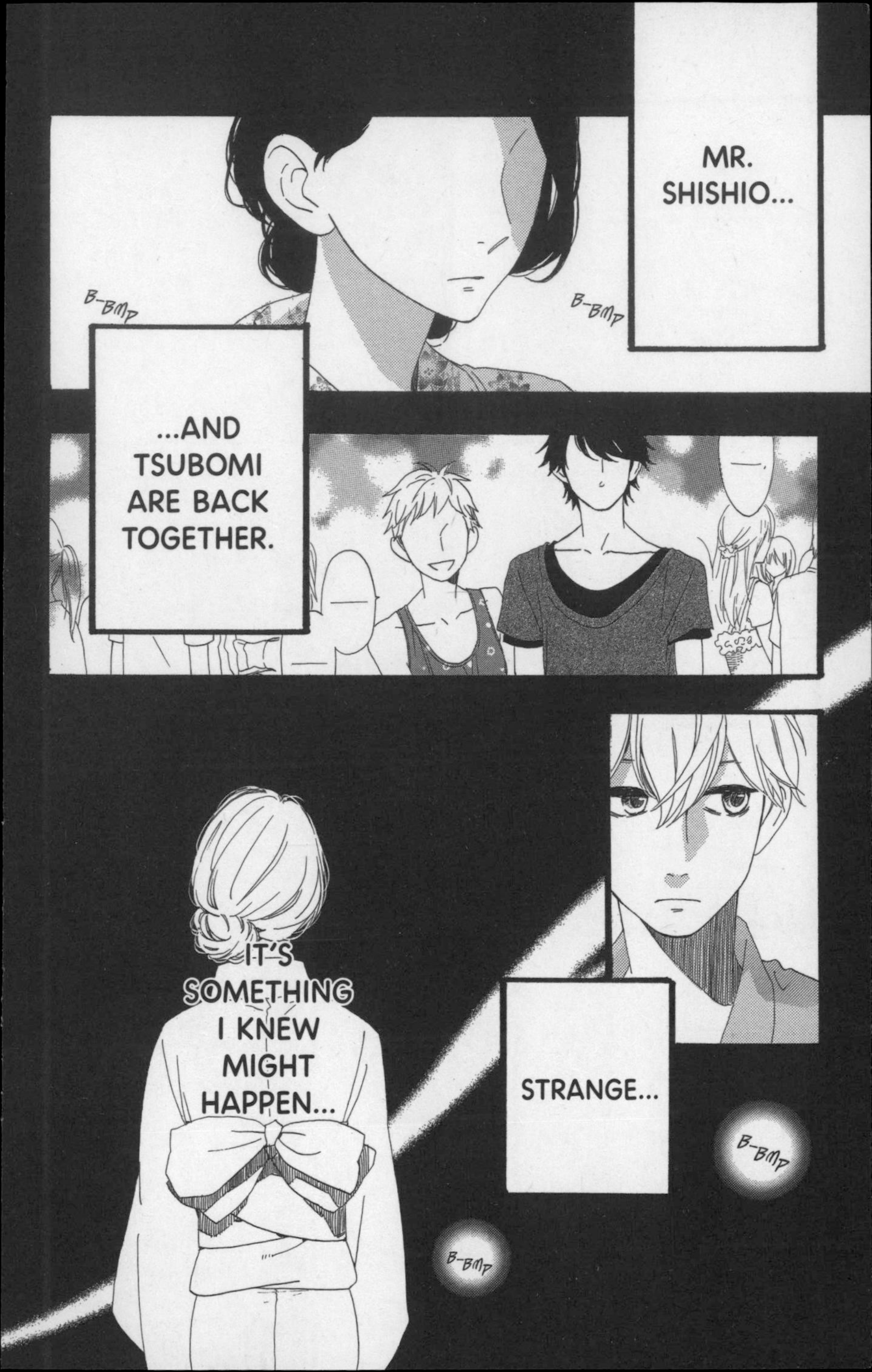
MR. SHISHIO...
B-BMP
B-BMP
...AND TSUBOMI ARE BACK TOGETHER.
STRANGE...
B-BMP
IT'S SOMETHING I KNEW MIGHT HAPPEN...
B-BMP

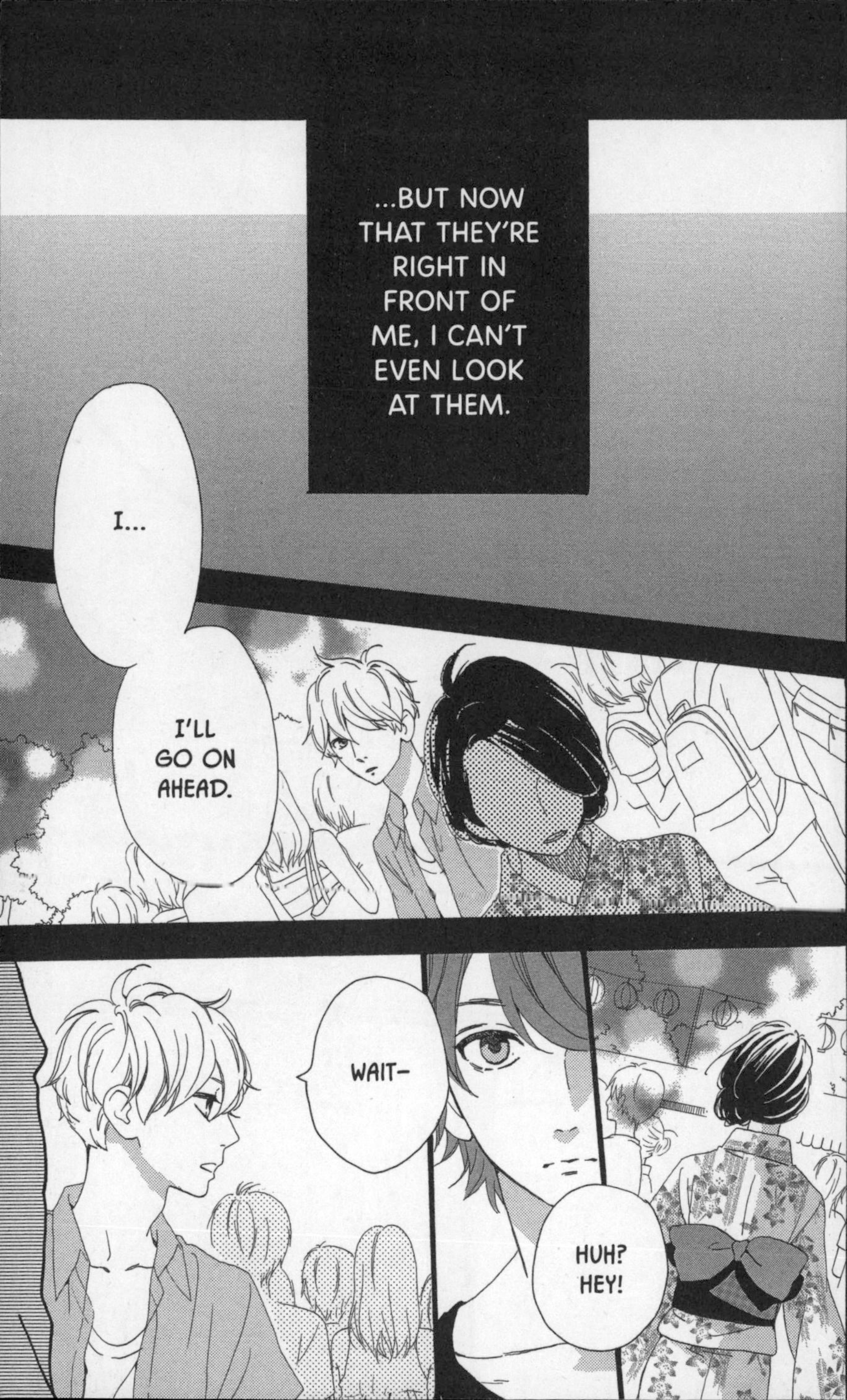
...BUT NOW THAT THEY'RE RIGHT IN FRONT OF ME, I CAN'T EVEN LOOK AT THEM.
I...
I'LL GO ON AHEAD.
HUH? HEY!
WAIT-

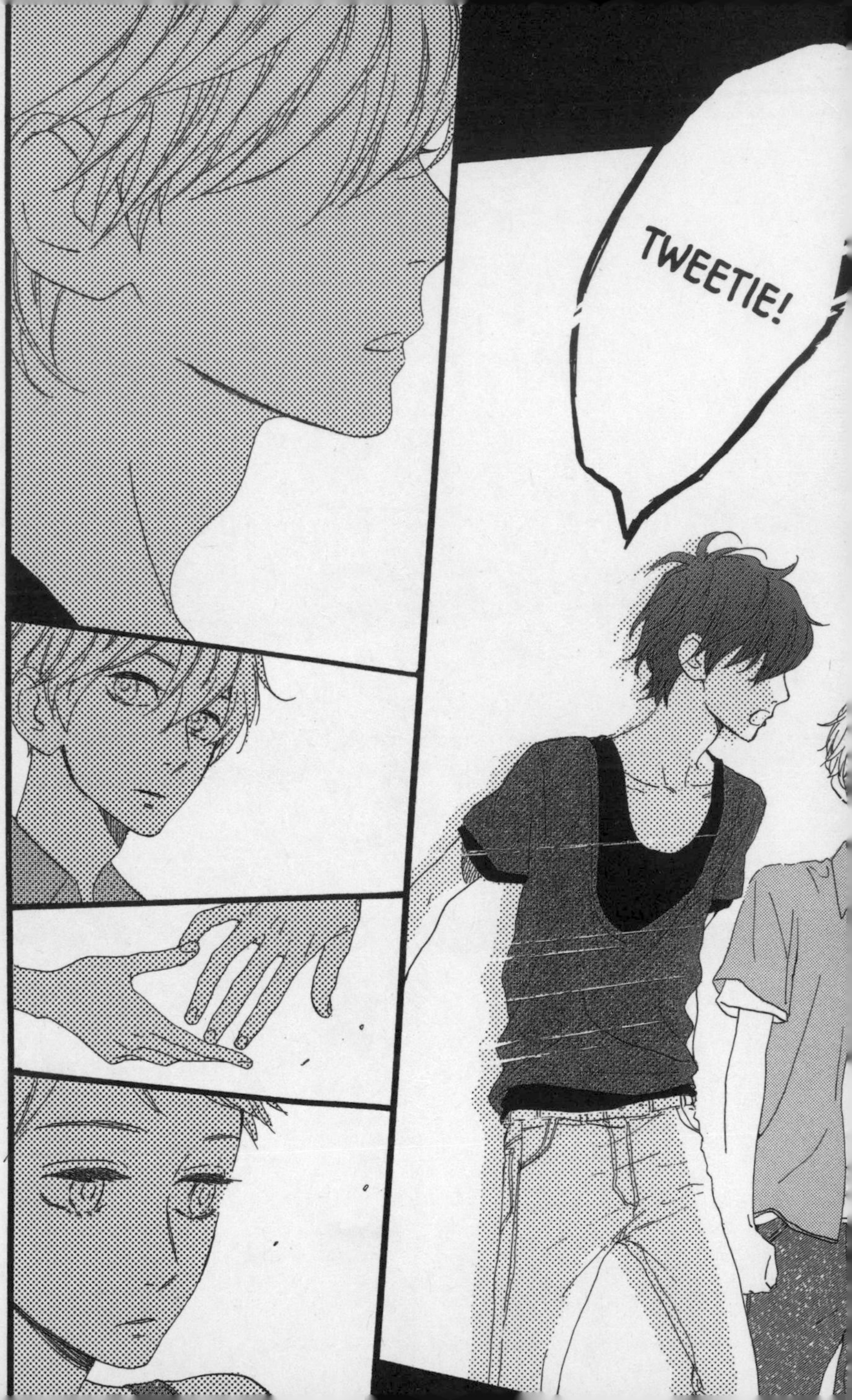
TWEETIE!

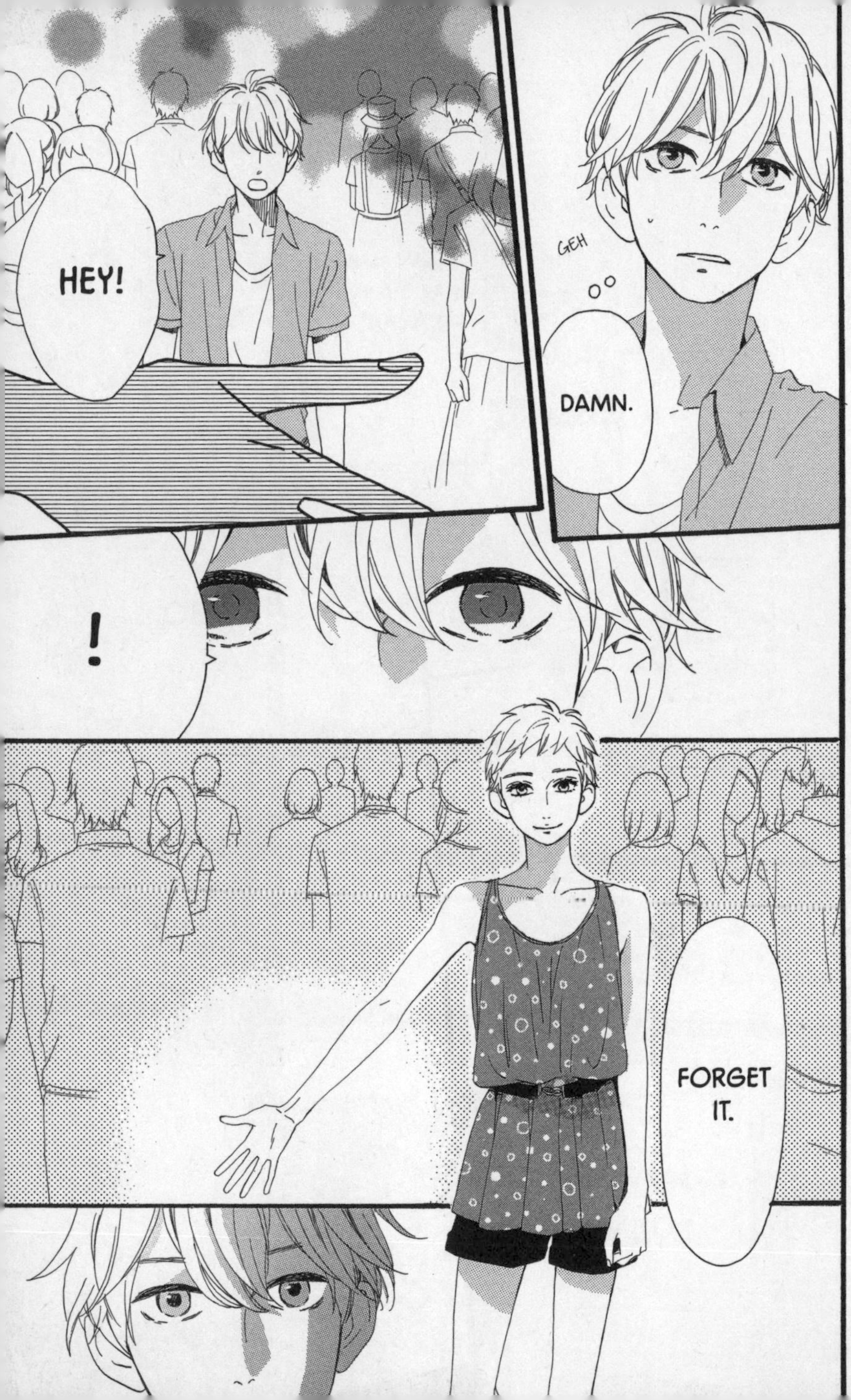
GEH
DAMN.
HEY!
!
FORGET IT.

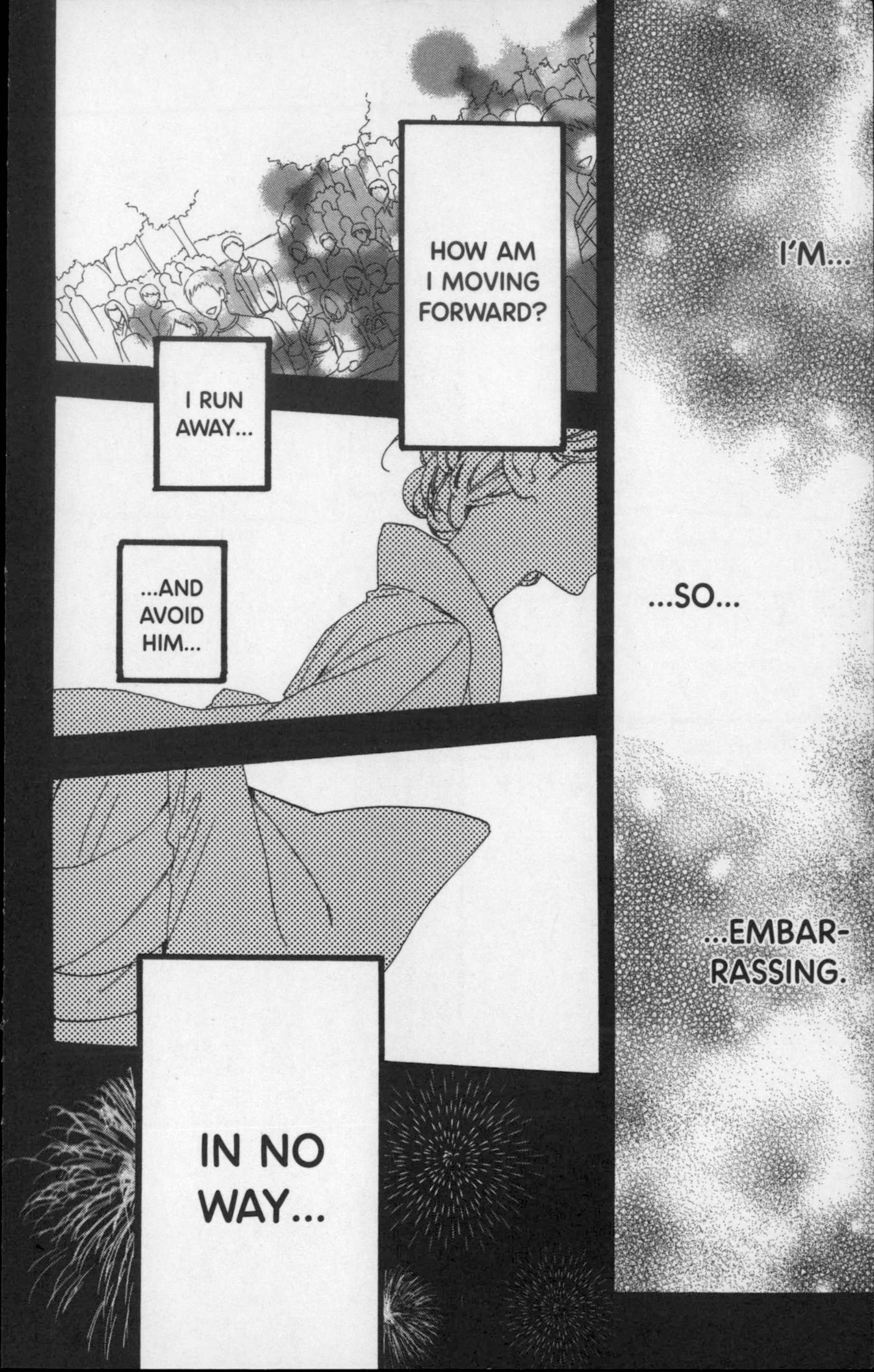
I'M...
...SO...
...EMBAR-
RASSING.
HOW AM I MOVING FORWARD?
I RUN AWAY...
...AND AVOID HIM...
IN NO WAY...

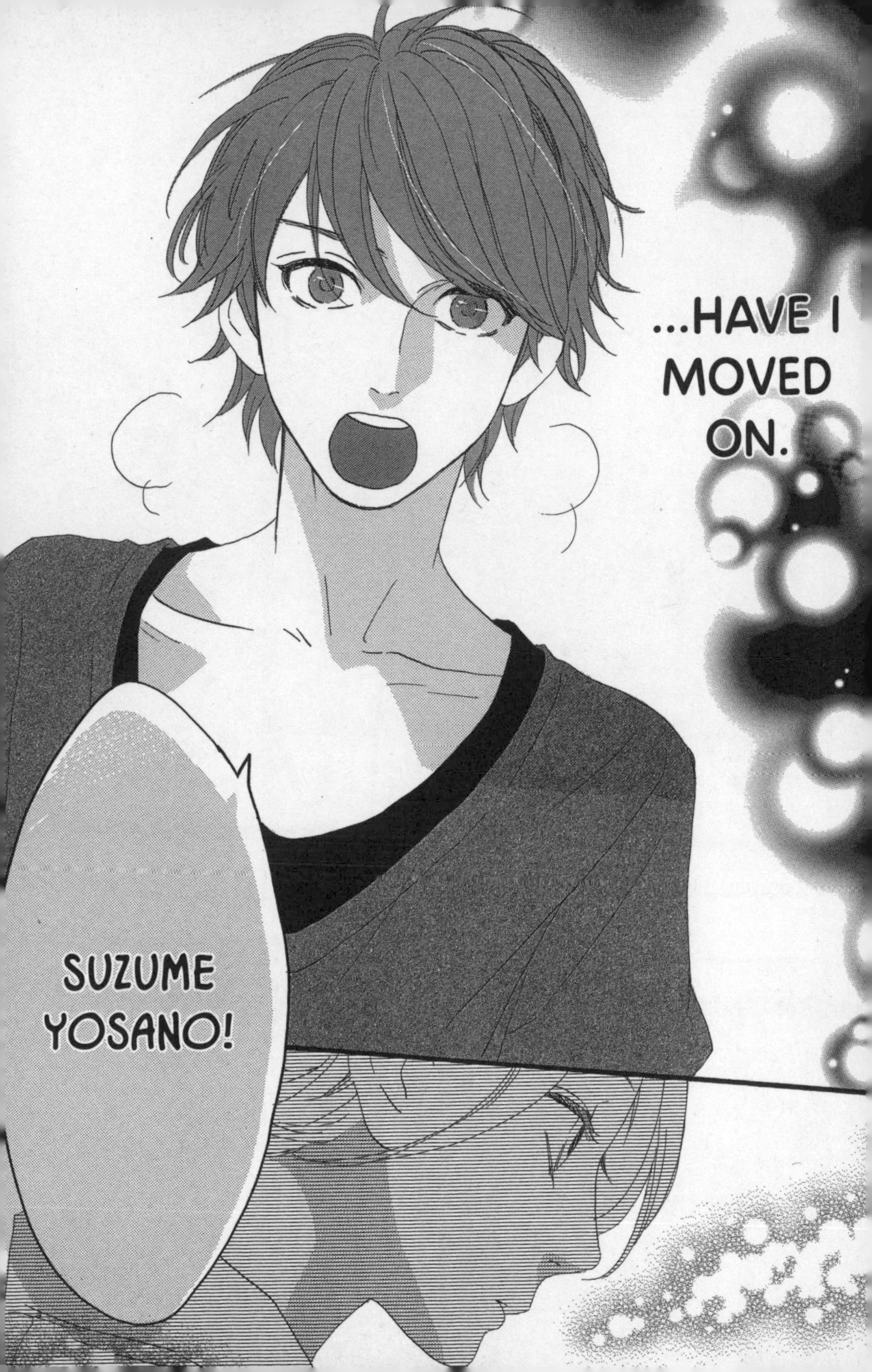
...HAVE I MOVED ON.
SUZUME YOSANO!

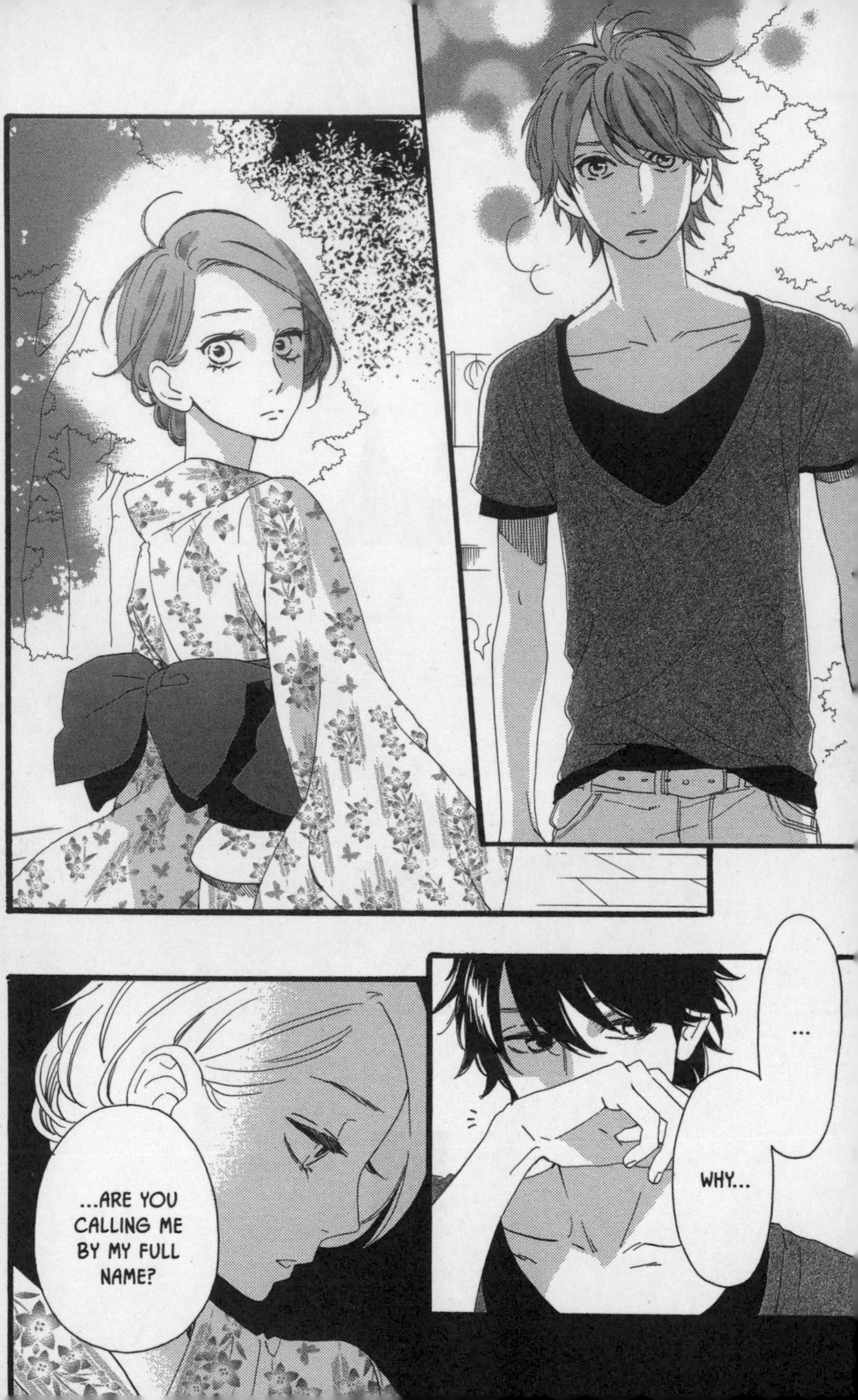
...
WHY...
...ARE YOU CALLING ME BY MY FULL NAME?

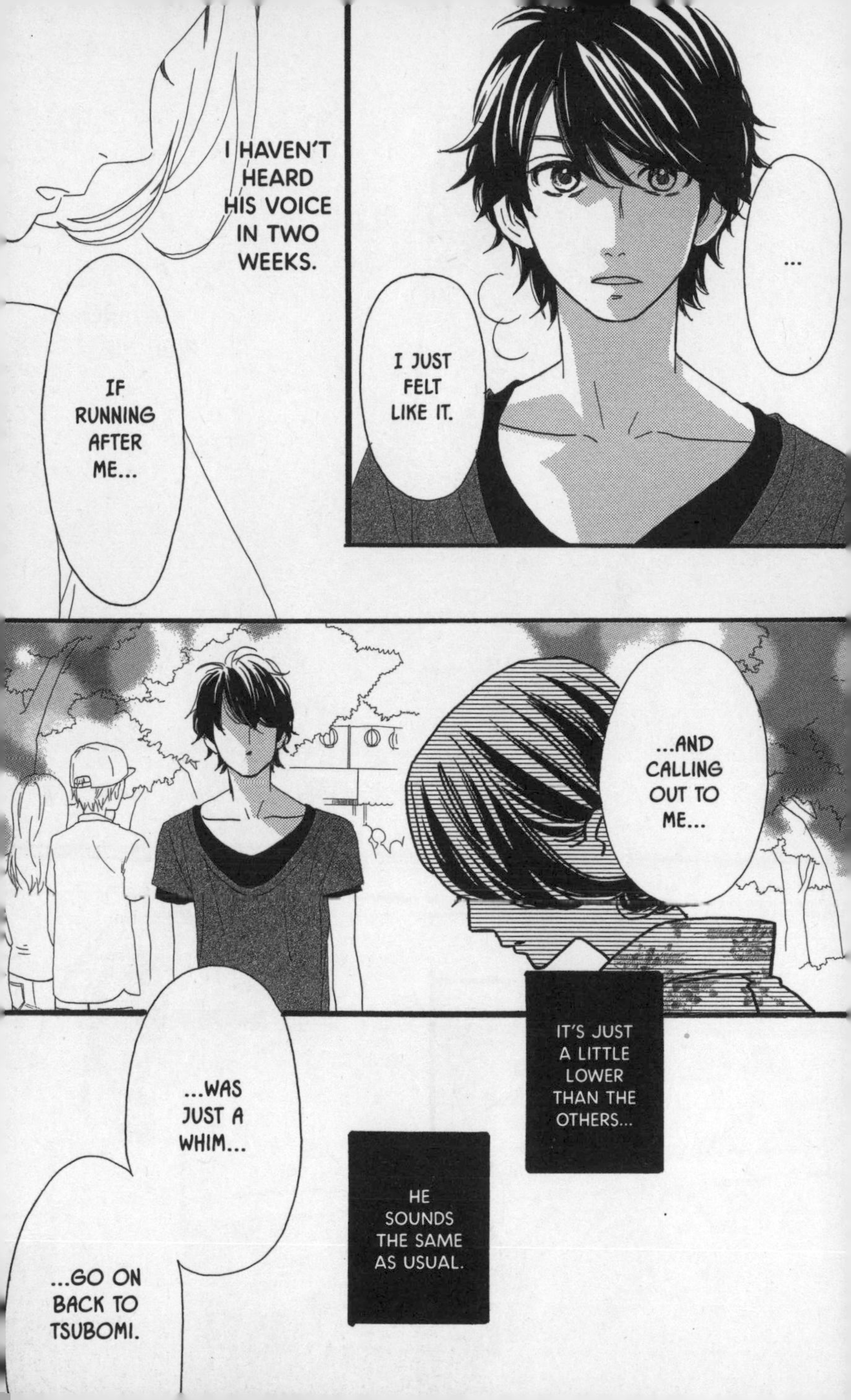
...
I JUST FELT LIKE IT.
I HAVEN'T HEARD HIS VOICE IN TWO WEEKS.
IF RUNNING AFTER ME...
...AND CALLING OUT TO ME...
IT'S JUST A LITTLE LOWER THAN THE OTHERS...
HE SOUNDS THE SAME AS USUAL.
...WAS JUST A WHIM...
...GO ON BACK TO TSUBOMI.

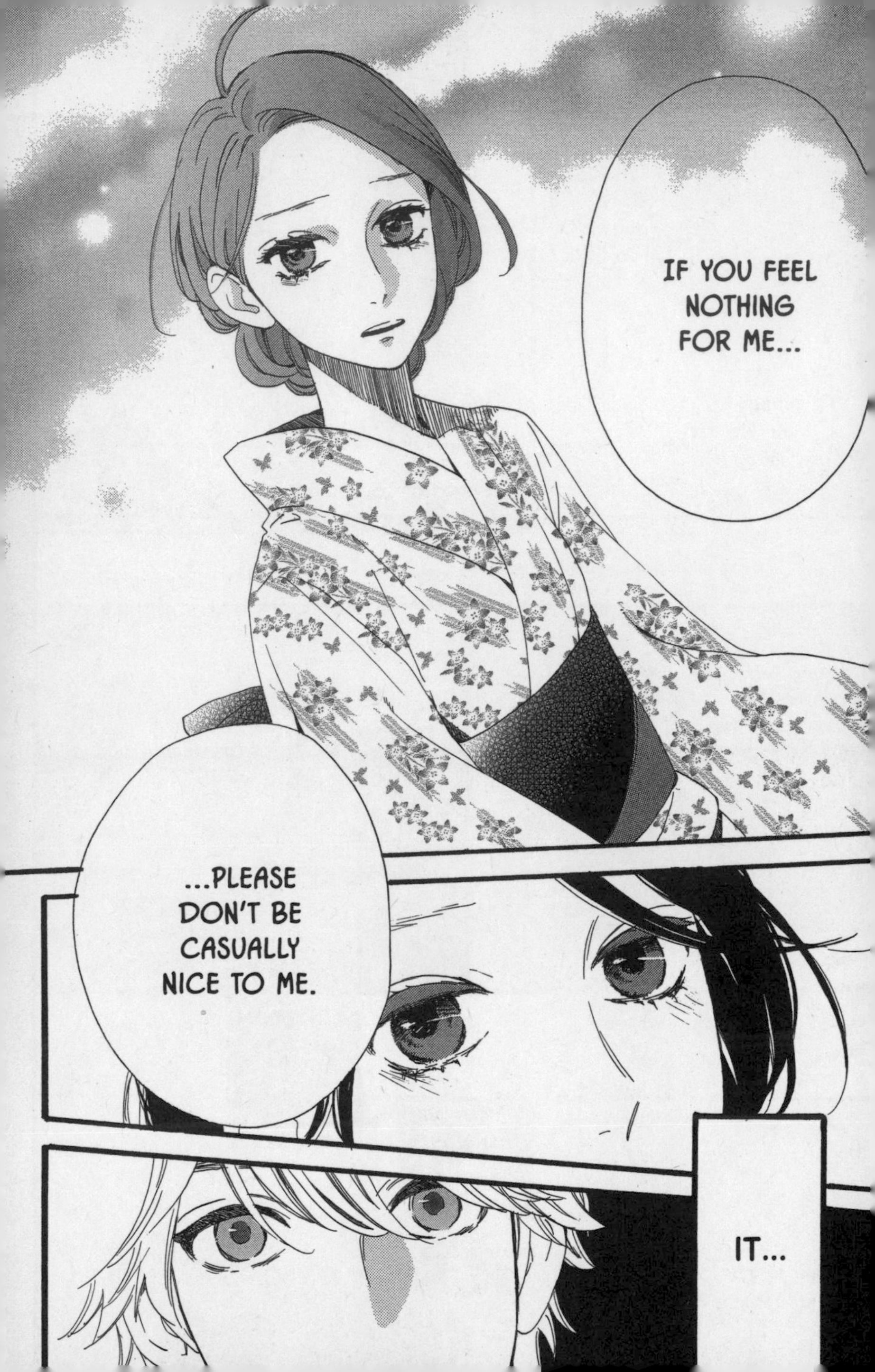
IF YOU FEEL NOTHING FOR ME...
...PLEASE DON'T BE CASUALLY NICE TO ME.
IT...

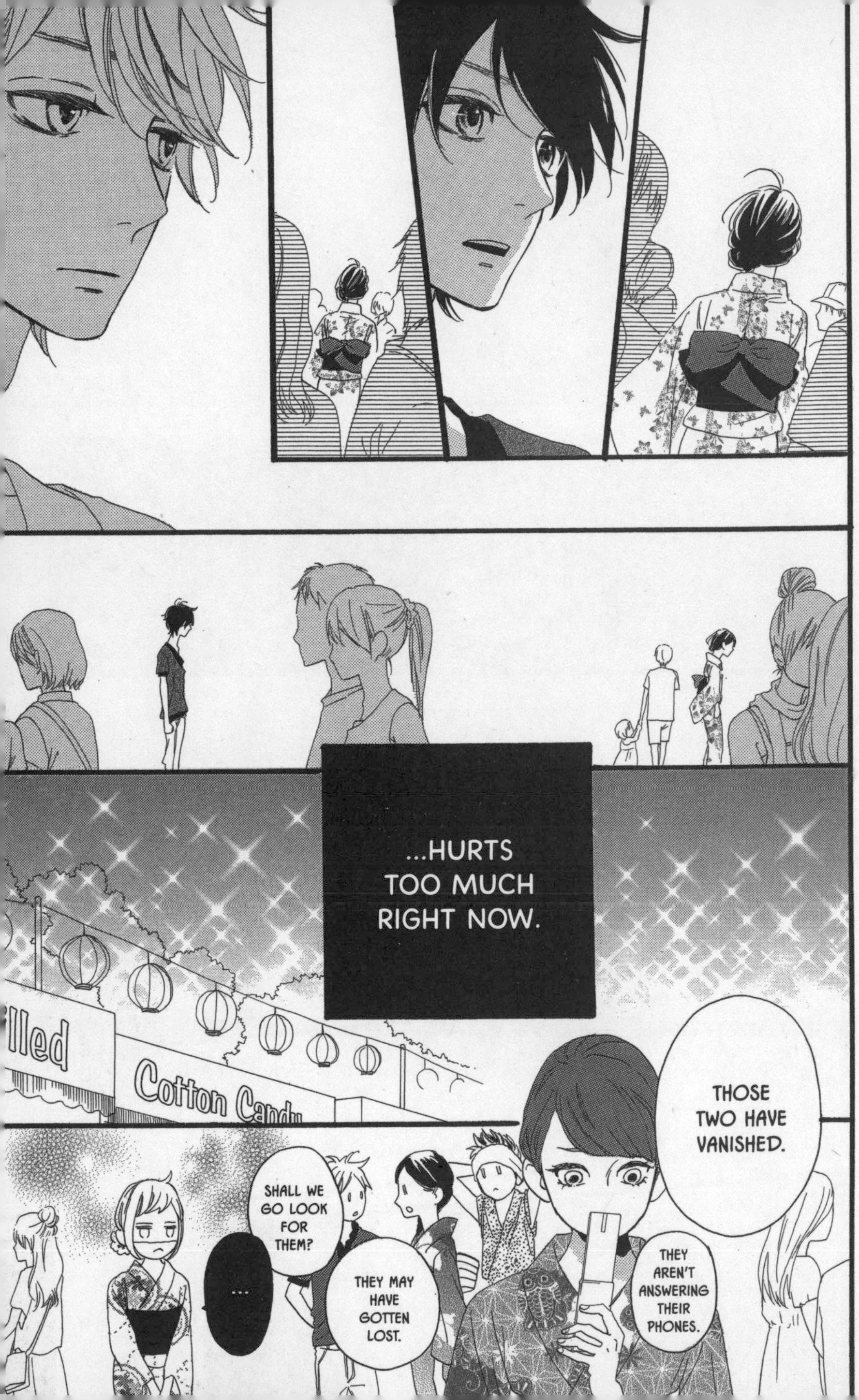

...HURTS TOO MUCH RIGHT NOW.
lled
Cotton Cand
THOSE TWO HAVE VANISHED.
THEY AREN'T ANSWERING THEIR PHONES.
SHALL WE GO LOOK FOR THEM?
THEY MAY HAVE GOTTEN LOST.
...

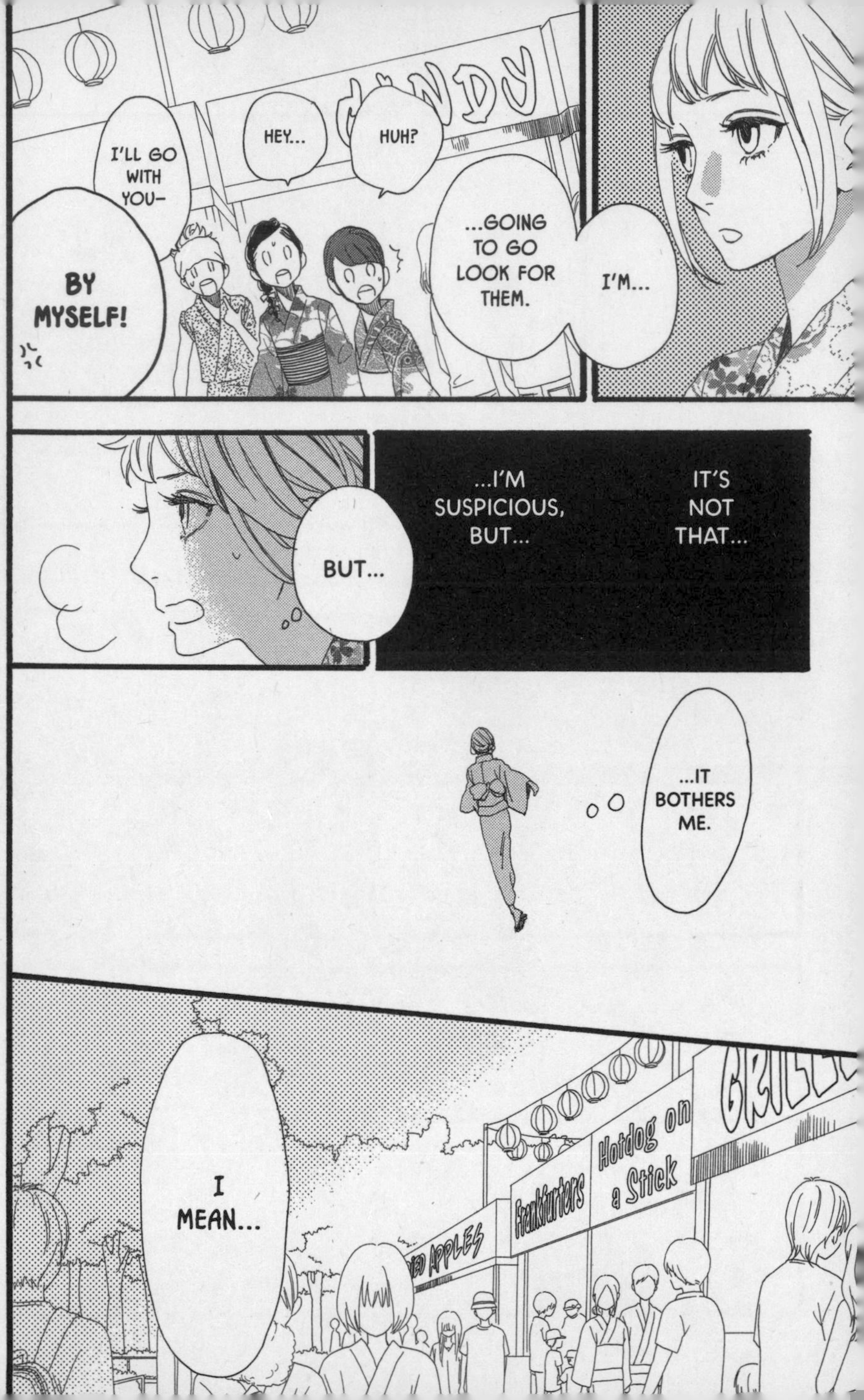
I'M...
...GOING TO GO LOOK FOR THEM.
HUH?
HEY...
I'LL GO WITH YOU–
BY MYSELF!
IT'S NOT THAT...
...I'M SUSPICIOUS, BUT...
BUT...
...IT BOTHERS ME.
Hotdog on a Stick
Frankfurters
I MEAN...

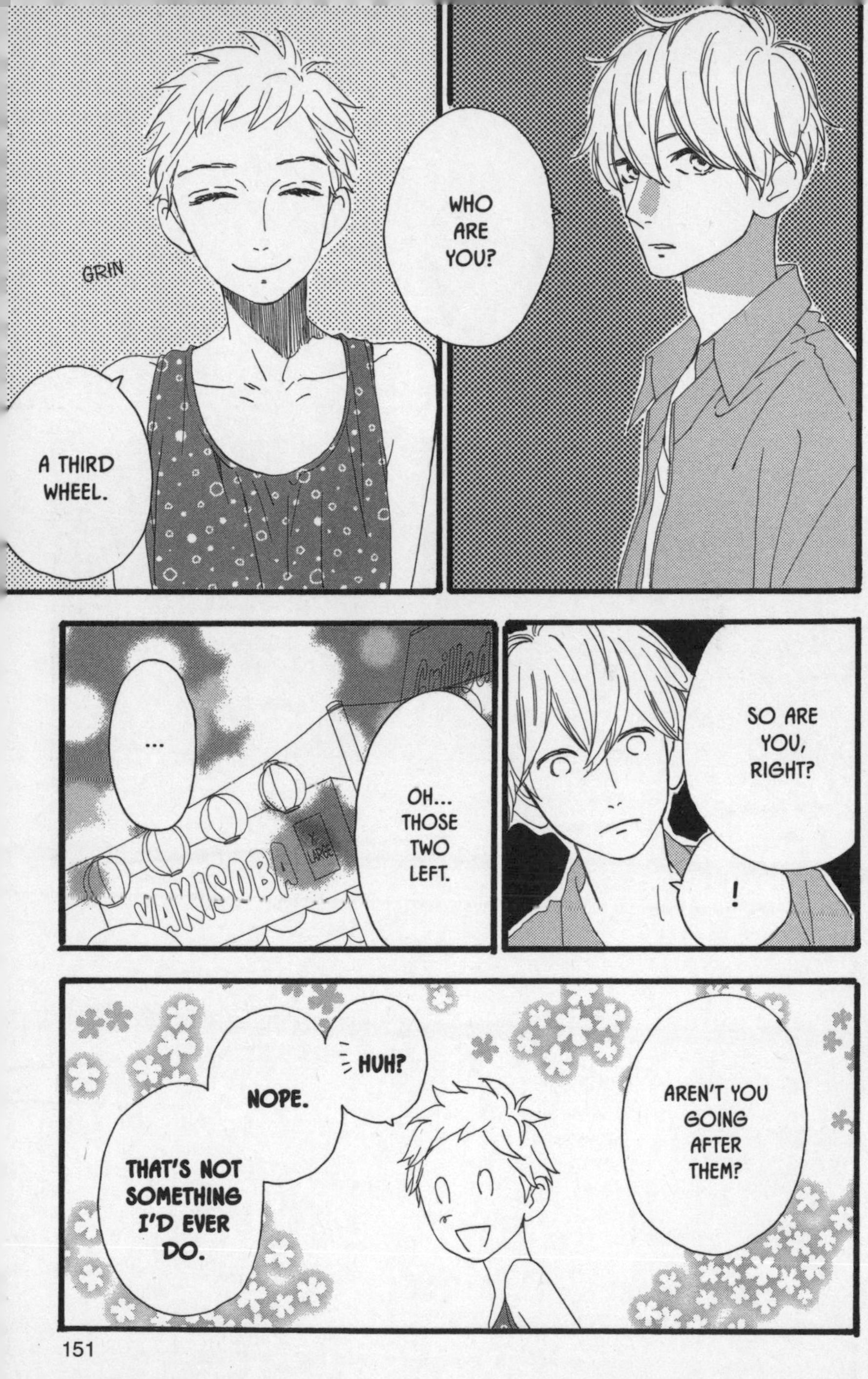
WHO ARE YOU?
GRIN
A THIRD WHEEL.
SO ARE YOU, RIGHT?
!
OH... THOSE TWO LEFT.
...
YAKISOBA
AREN'T YOU GOING AFTER THEM?
HUH?
NOPE.
THAT'S NOT SOMETHING I'D EVER DO.

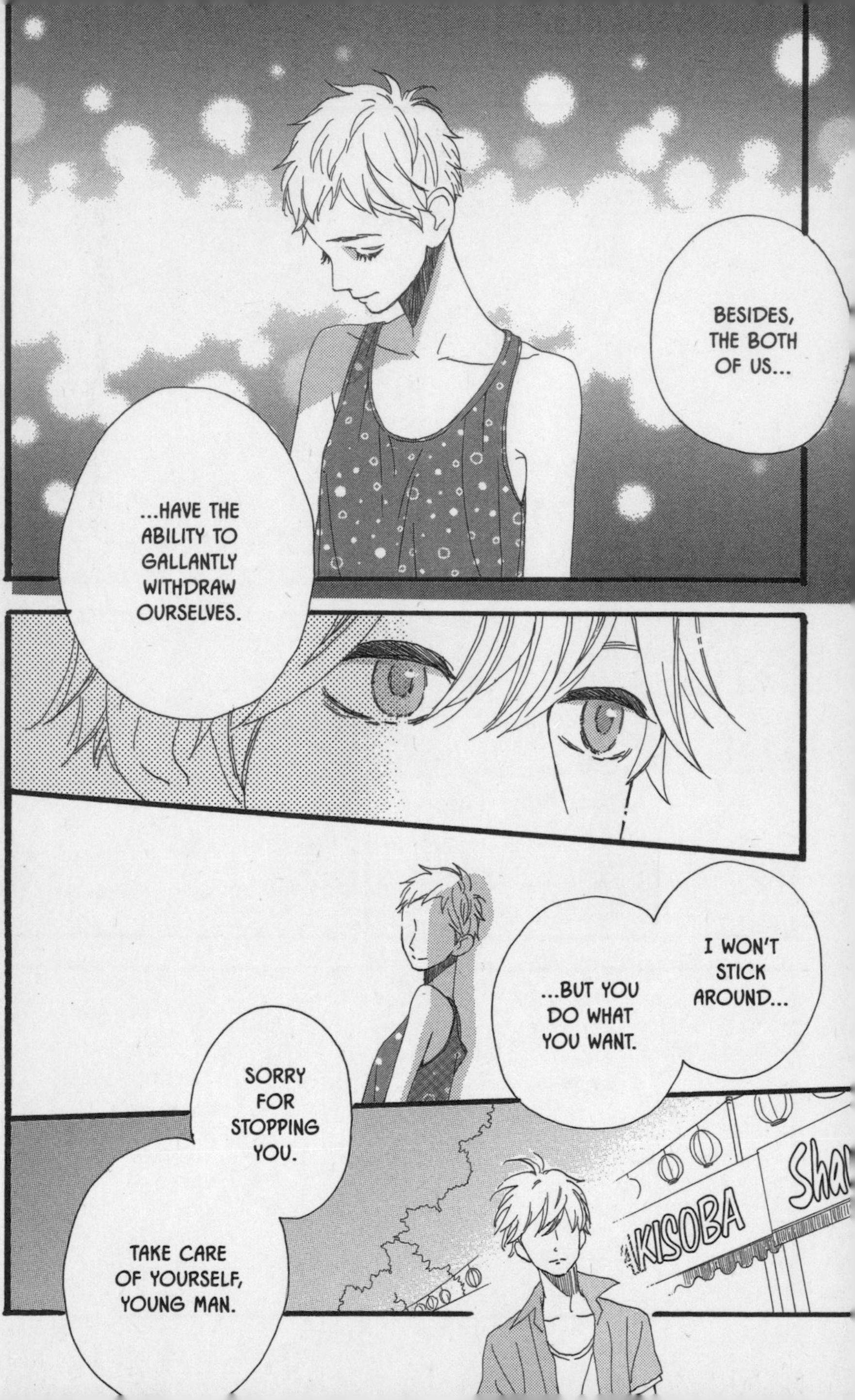
BESIDES, THE BOTH OF US...
...HAVE THE ABILITY TO GALLANTLY WITHDRAW OURSELVES.
I WON'T STICK AROUND...
...BUT YOU DO WHAT YOU WANT.
SORRY FOR STOPPING YOU.
TAKE CARE OF YOURSELF, YOUNG MAN.

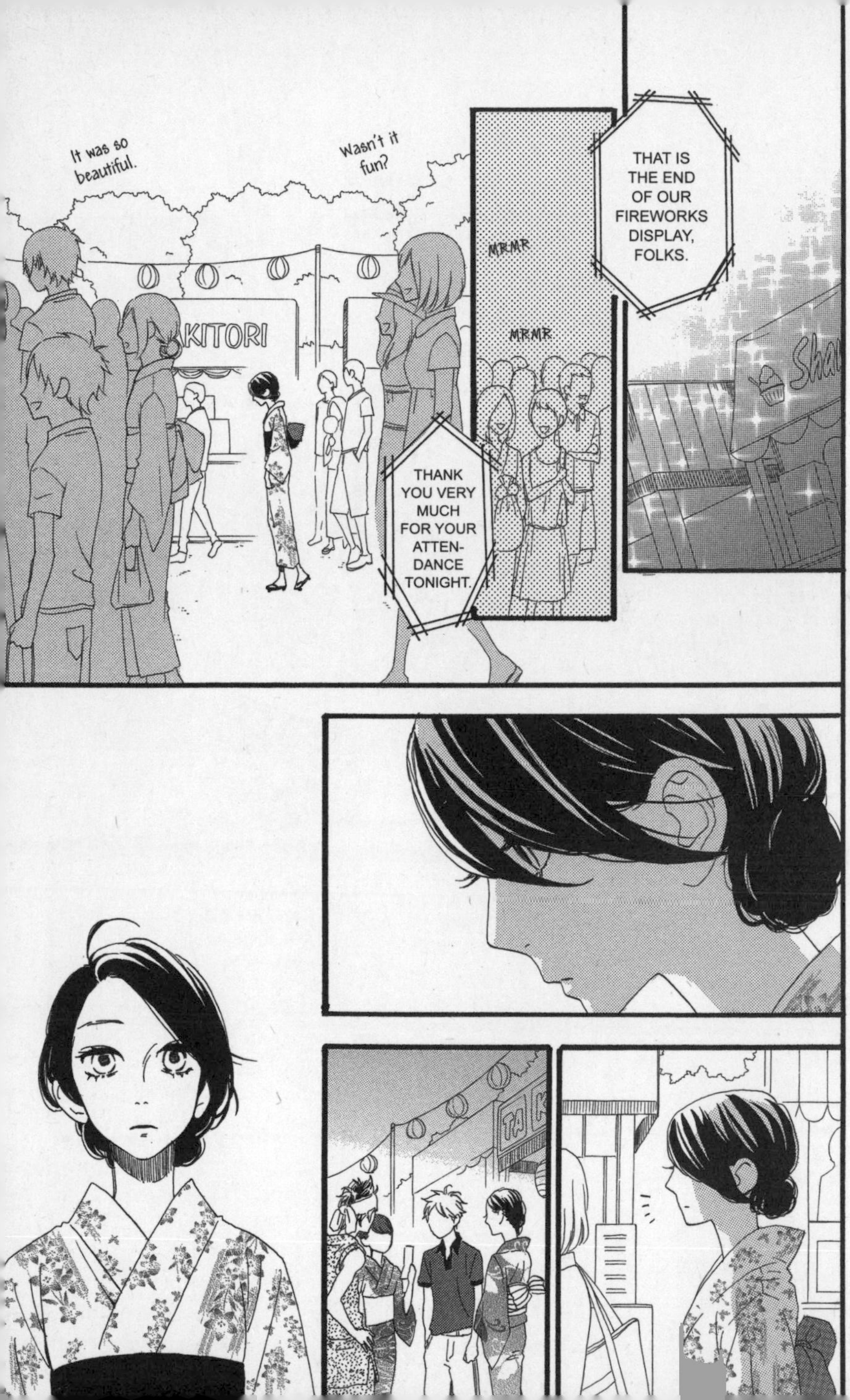
THAT IS THE END OF OUR FIREWORKS DISPLAY, FOLKS.
MRMR
MRMR
THANK YOU VERY MUCH FOR YOUR ATTEN-DANCE TONIGHT.
Wasn't it fun?
It was so beautiful.

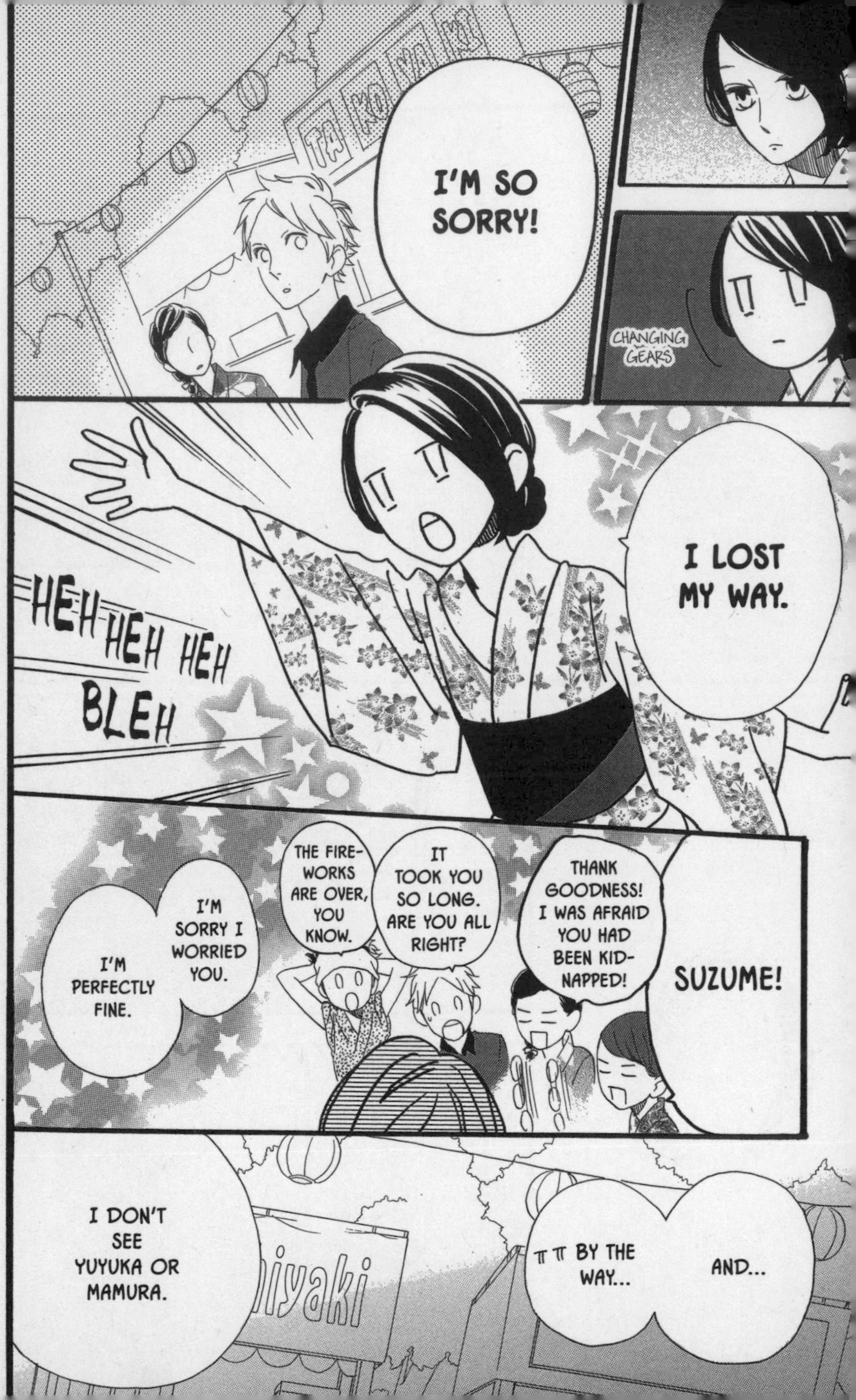
CHANGING GEARS
I'M SO SORRY!
I LOST MY WAY.
HEH HEH HEH
BLEH
SUZUME!
THANK GOODNESS! I WAS AFRAID YOU HAD BEEN KID-NAPPED!
IT TOOK YOU SO LONG. ARE YOU ALL RIGHT?
THE FIRE-WORKS ARE OVER, YOU KNOW.
I'M SORRY I WORRIED YOU.
I'M PERFECTLY FINE.
ππ BY THE WAY... AND...
I DON'T SEE YUYUKA OR MAMURA.

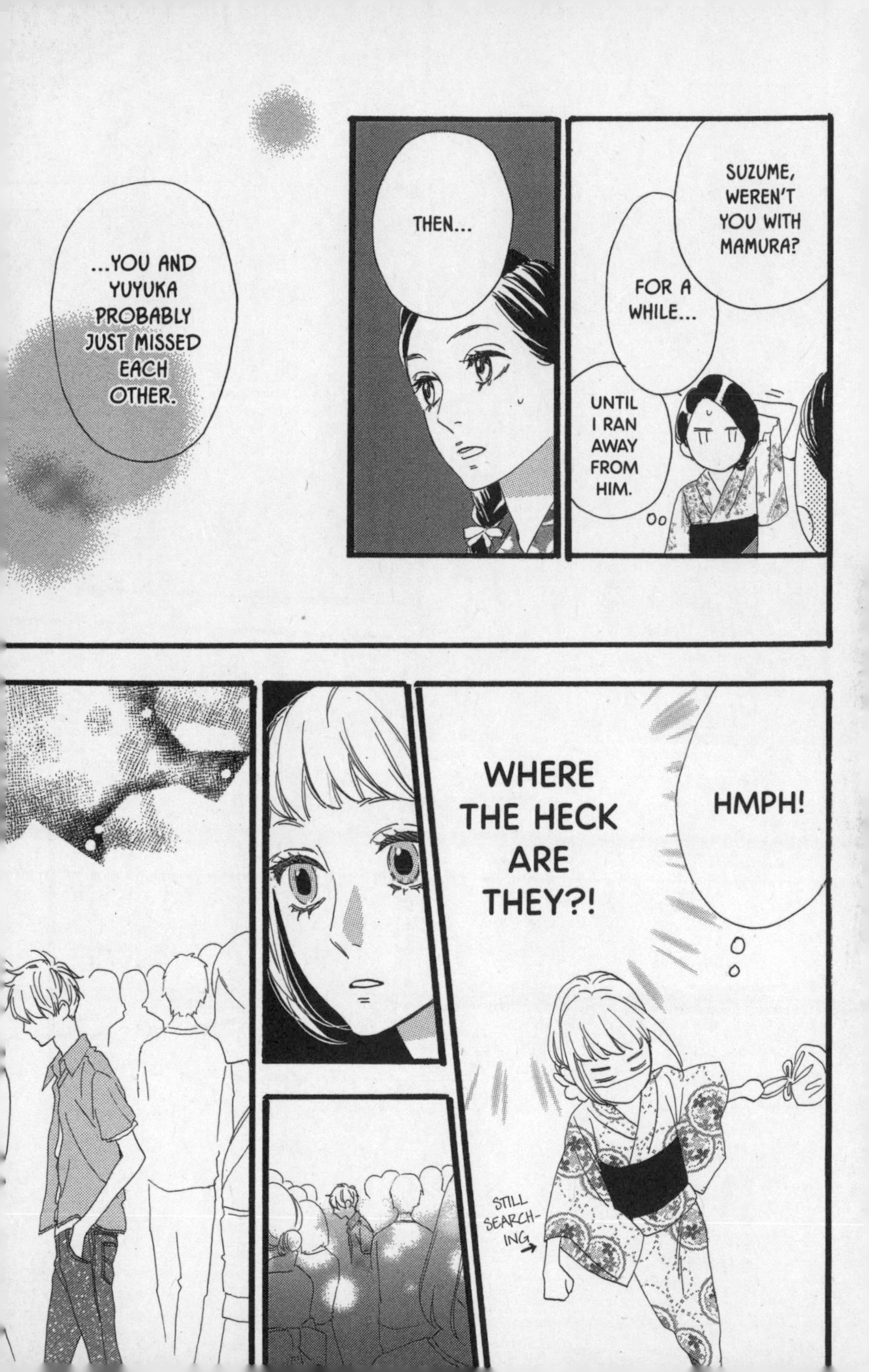
SUZUME, WEREN'T YOU WITH MAMURA?
FOR A WHILE...
UNTIL I RAN AWAY FROM HIM.
THEN...
...YOU AND YUYUKA PROBABLY JUST MISSED EACH OTHER.
HMPH!
WHERE THE HECK ARE THEY?!
STILL SEARCHING

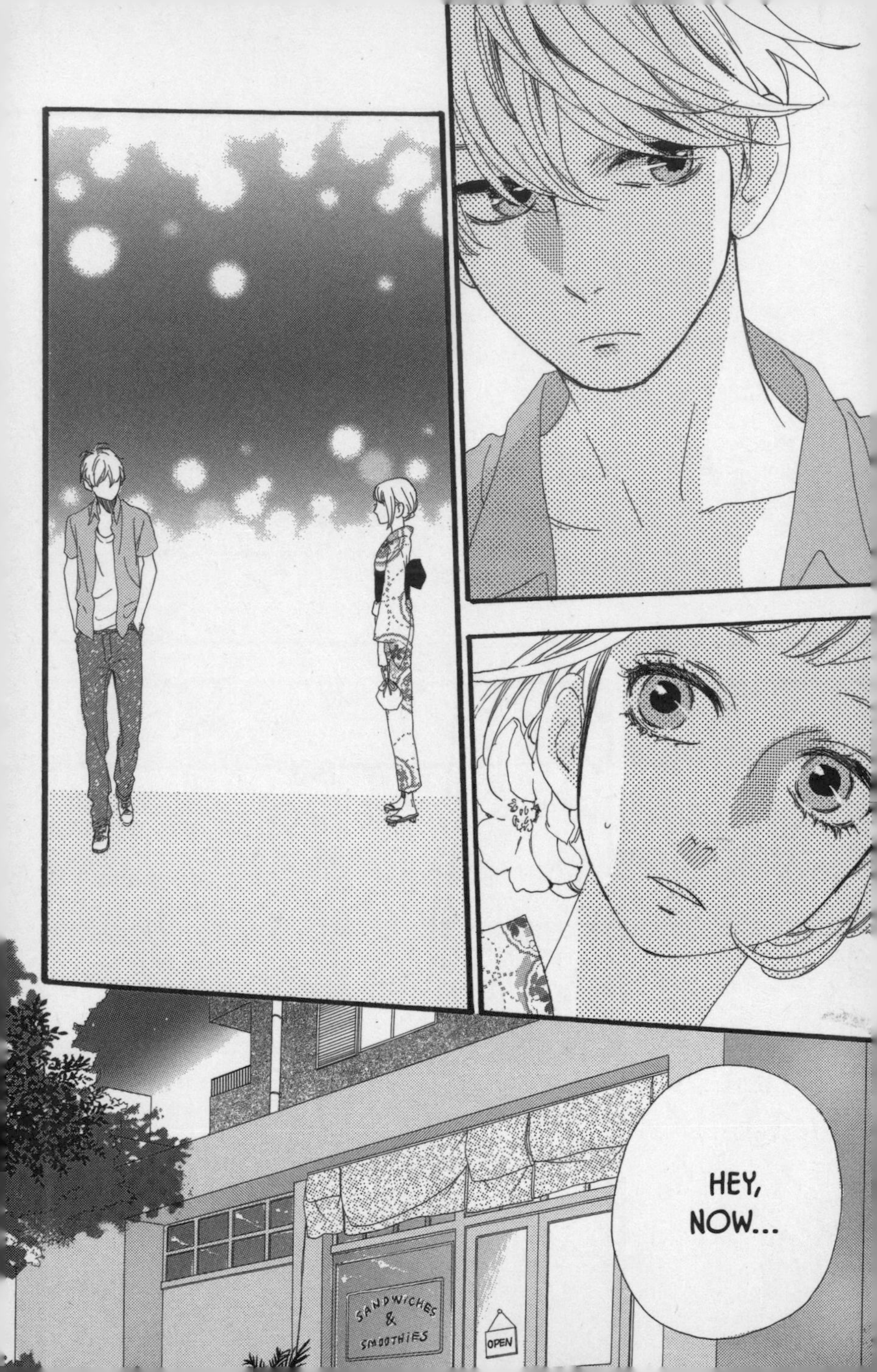
HEY, NOW...
SANDWICHES & SMOOTHIES
OPEN

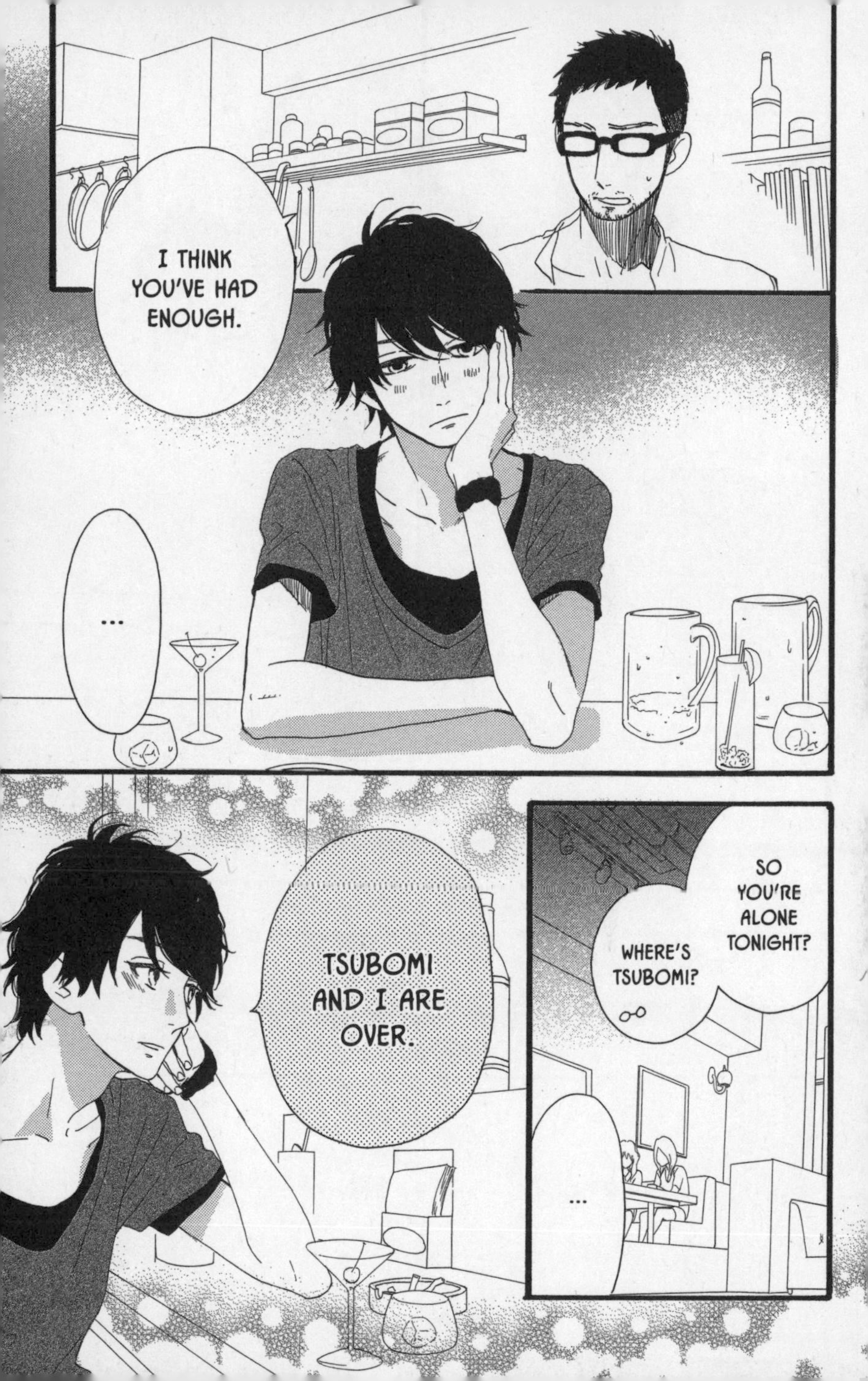
I THINK YOU'VE HAD ENOUGH.
...
SO YOU'RE ALONE TONIGHT?
WHERE'S TSUBOMI?
...
TSUBOMI AND I ARE OVER.

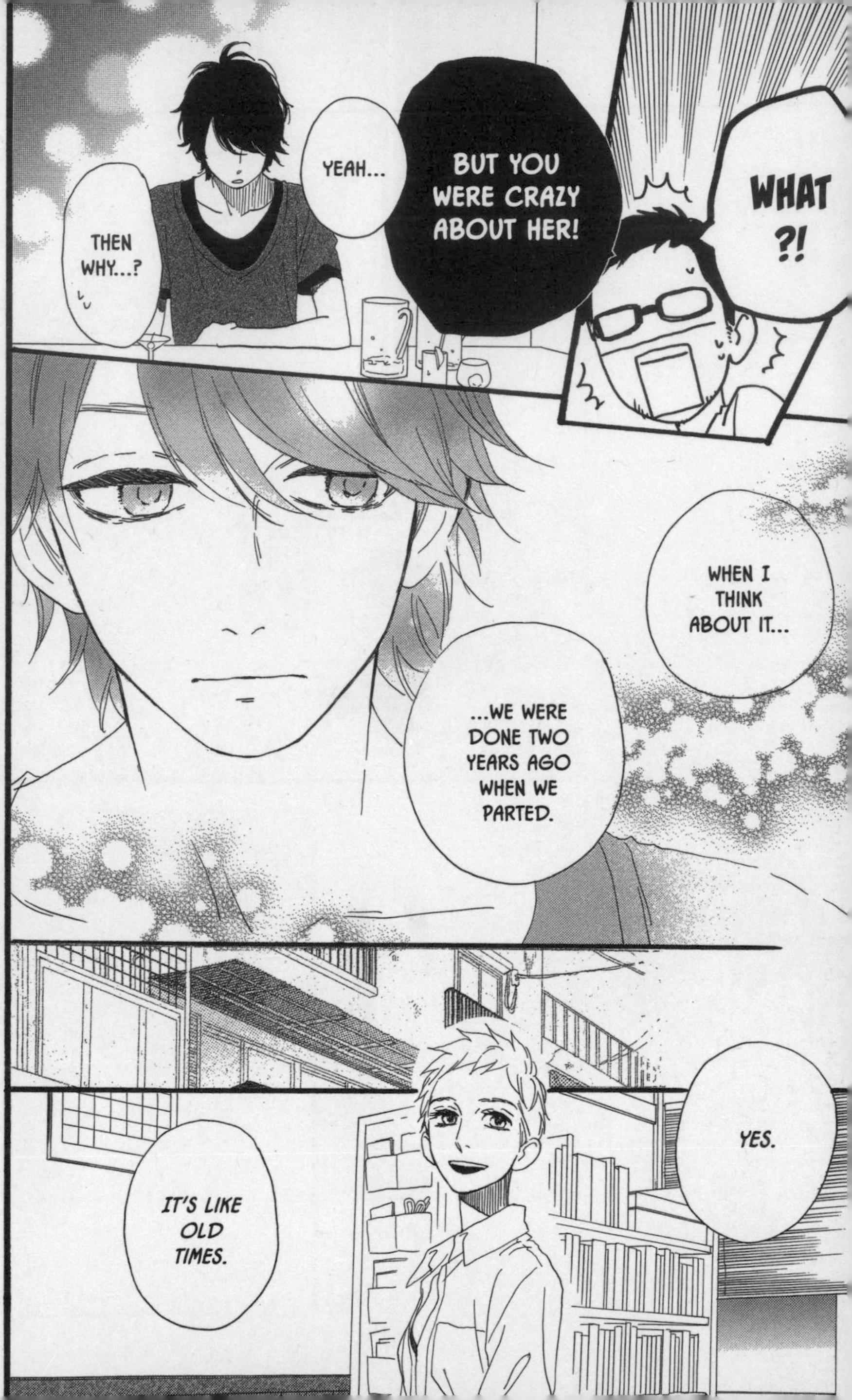
WHAT ?!
BUT YOU WERE CRAZY ABOUT HER!
YEAH...
THEN WHY...?
WHEN I THINK ABOUT IT...
...WE WERE DONE TWO YEARS AGO WHEN WE PARTED.
YES.
IT'S LIKE OLD TIMES.

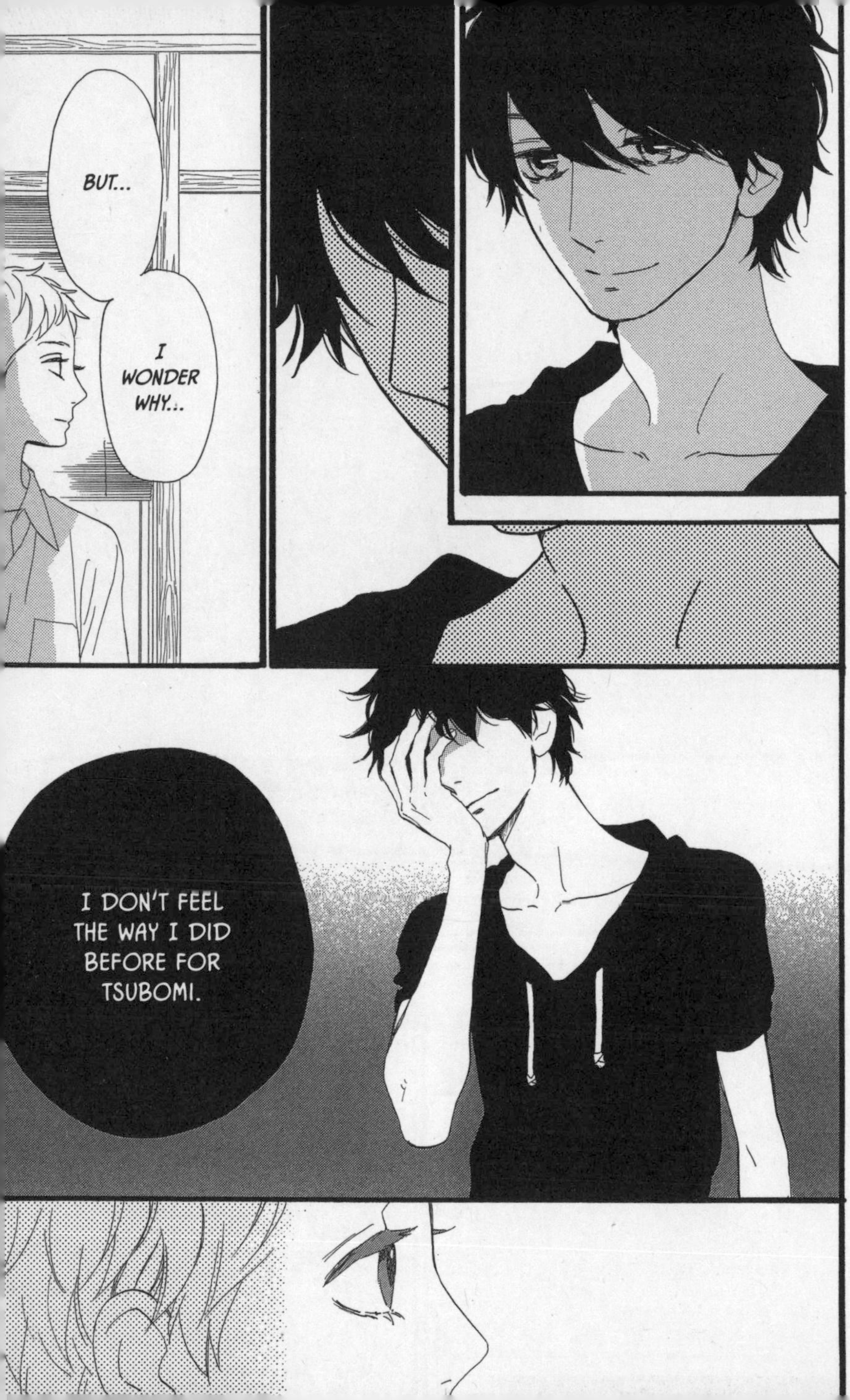
BUT...
I WONDER WHY...
I DON'T FEEL THE WAY I DID BEFORE FOR TSUBOMI.

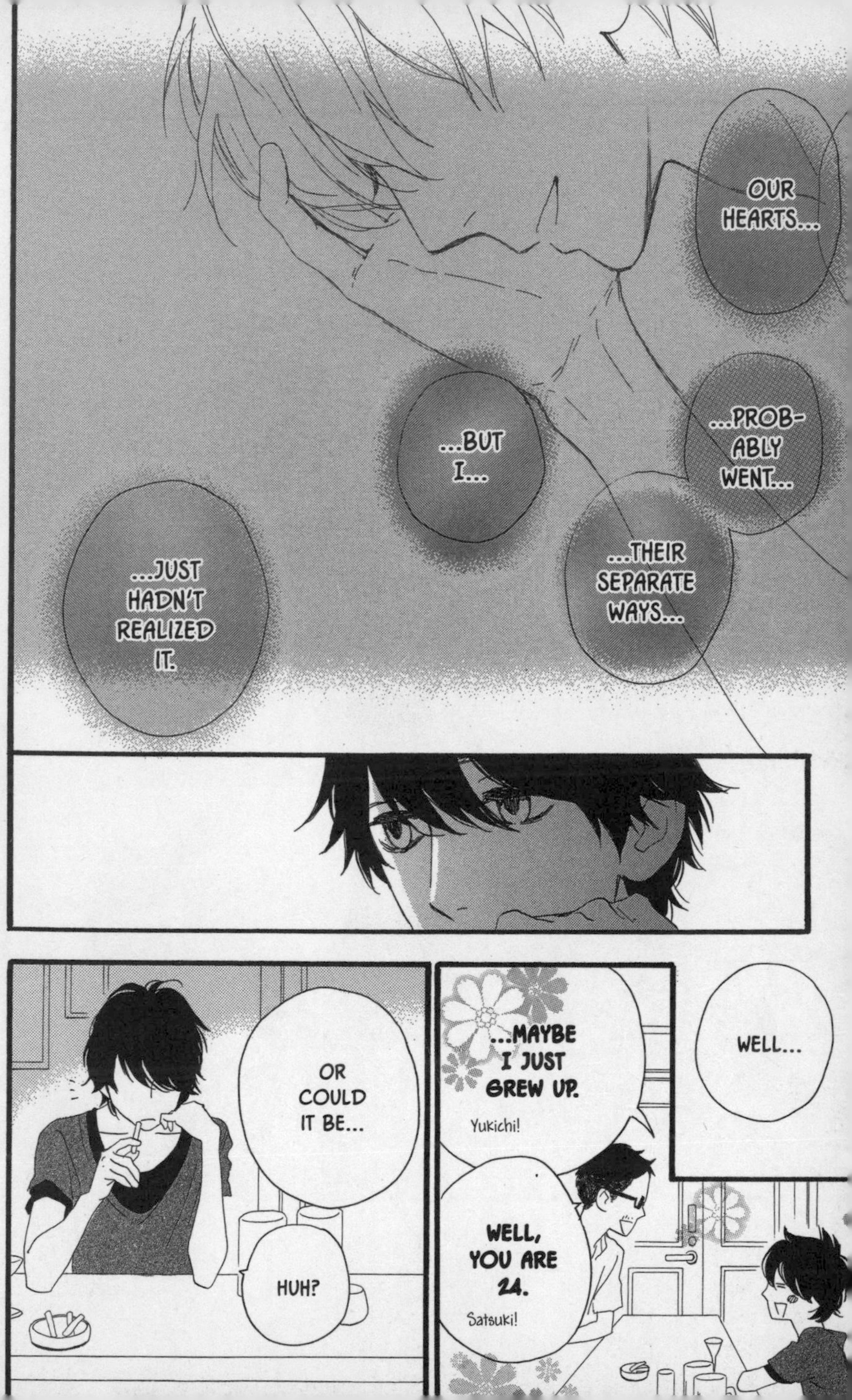
OUR HEARTS...
...PROB-ABLY WENT...
...THEIR SEPARATE WAYS...
...BUT I...
...JUST HADN'T REALIZED IT.
WELL...
...MAYBE I JUST GREW UP.
Yukichi!
WELL, YOU ARE 24.
Satsuki!
OR COULD IT BE...
HUH?

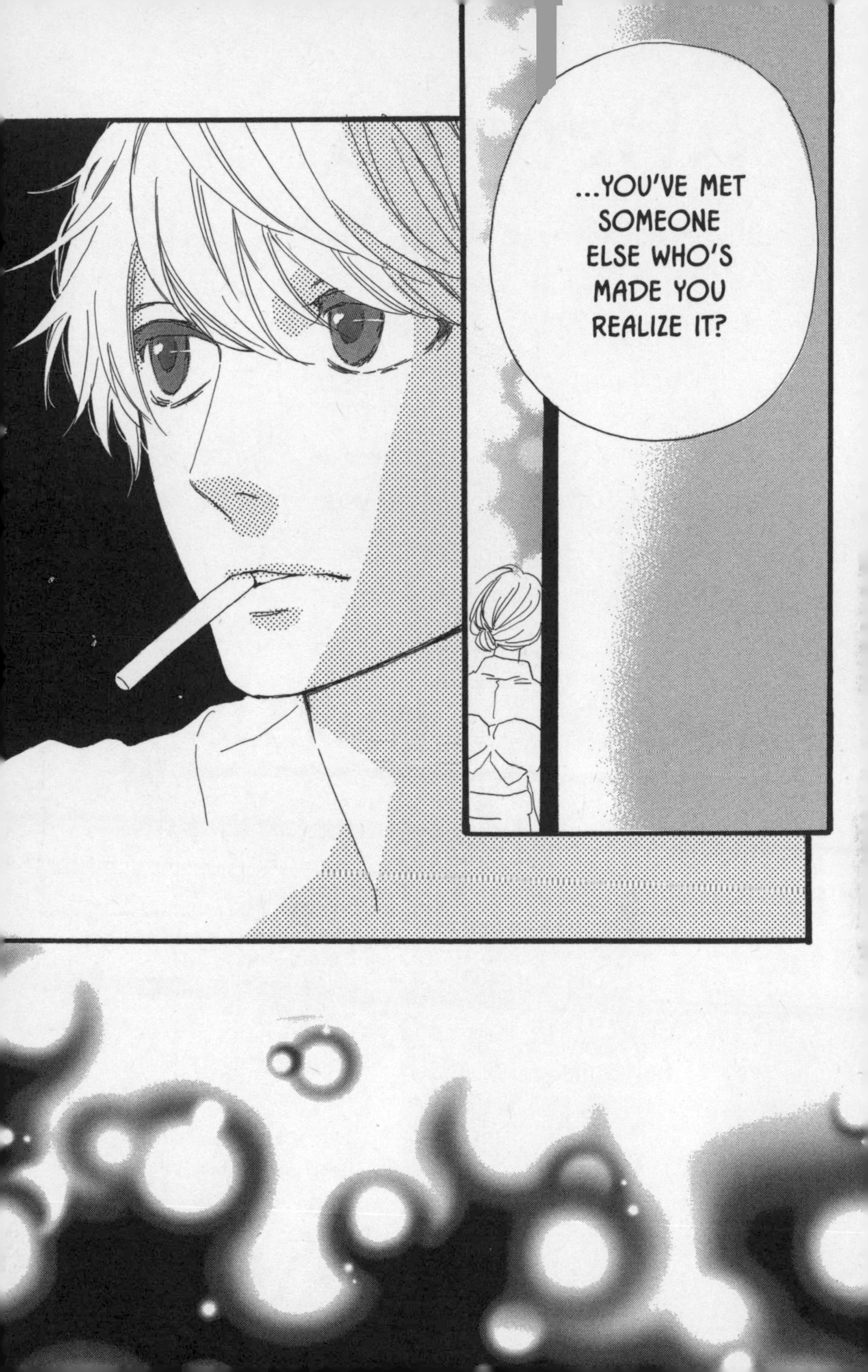
...YOU'VE MET SOMEONE ELSE WHO'S MADE YOU REALIZE IT?

Afterword

"Oh, it's the afterword already," I think as I am writing this. This is because my six-page "Second Kiss" and "Switch Girl Tribute" are included in this volume.

And so, how did you like volume 3 of *Daytime Shooting Star*? I look forward to reading your impressions! ♪

Let's meet again in volume 4. ♧

Special Thanks!!!

Editor K
Sakochan・Ms Noborio
Graphic Designers
The Editorial Department
Printer's Staff
Friends & Family

All My Readers

Bye-

bye!

← Our main character never looks good in her uniform.

I'm not good at drawing hearts.
(These are not Glico candies.)

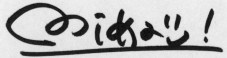

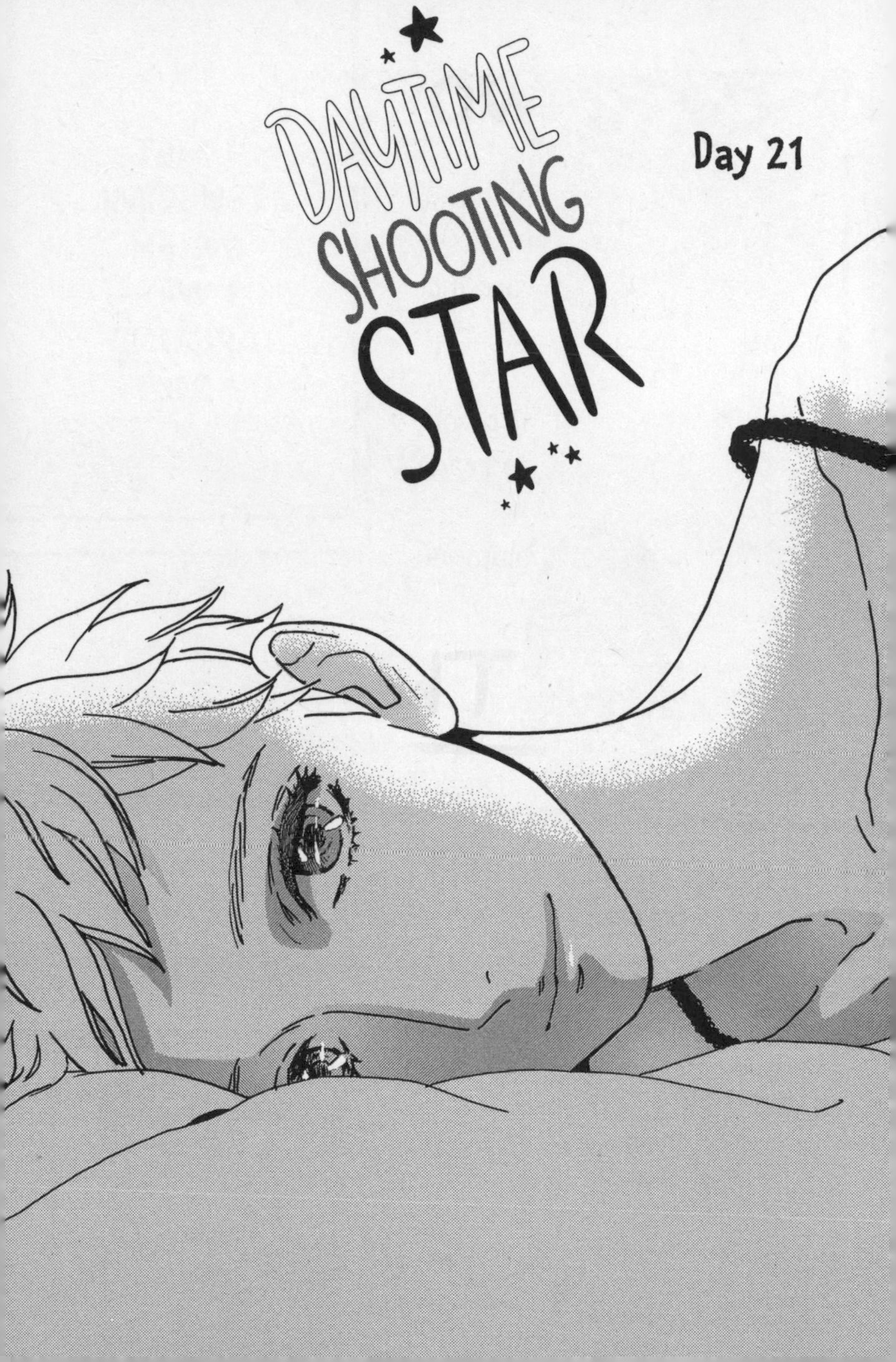
DAYTIME SHOOTING STAR
Day 21

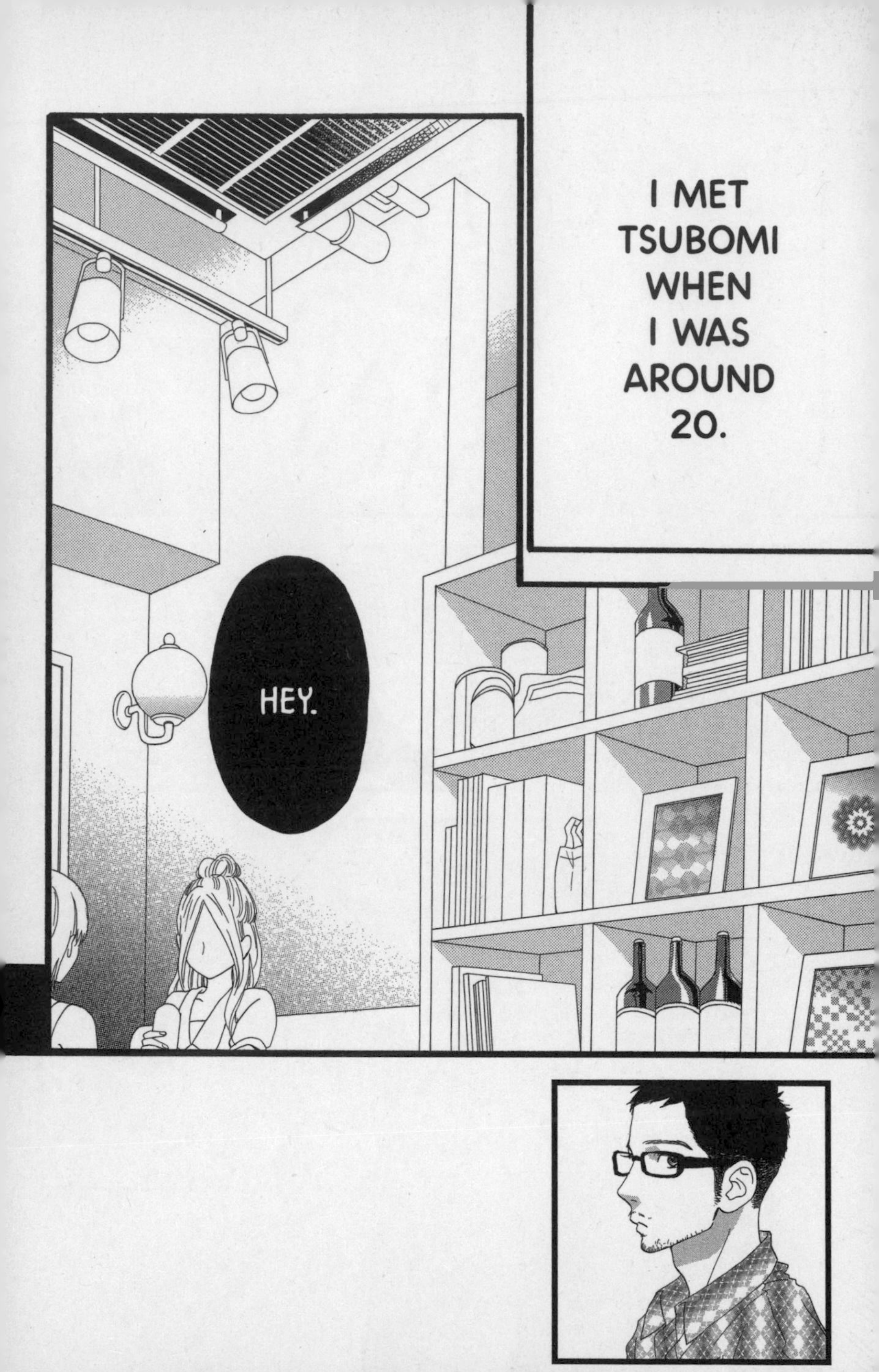
I MET TSUBOMI WHEN I WAS AROUND 20.
HEY.

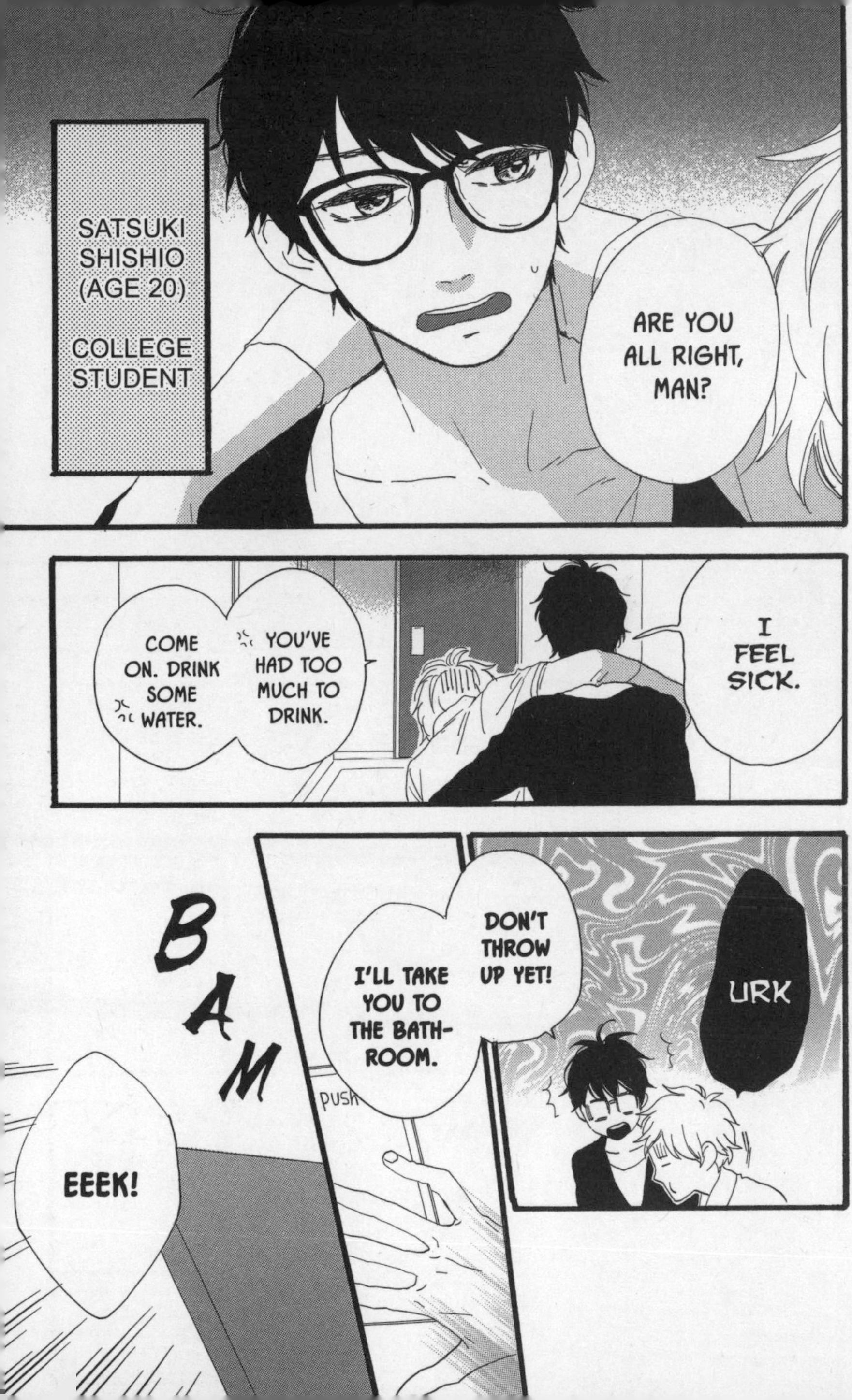
ARE YOU ALL RIGHT, MAN?
SATSUKI SHISHIO (AGE 20) COLLEGE STUDENT
I FEEL SICK.
YOU'VE HAD TOO MUCH TO DRINK.
COME ON. DRINK SOME WATER.
URK
DON'T THROW UP YET!
I'LL TAKE YOU TO THE BATH-ROOM.
PUSH
BAM
EEEK!

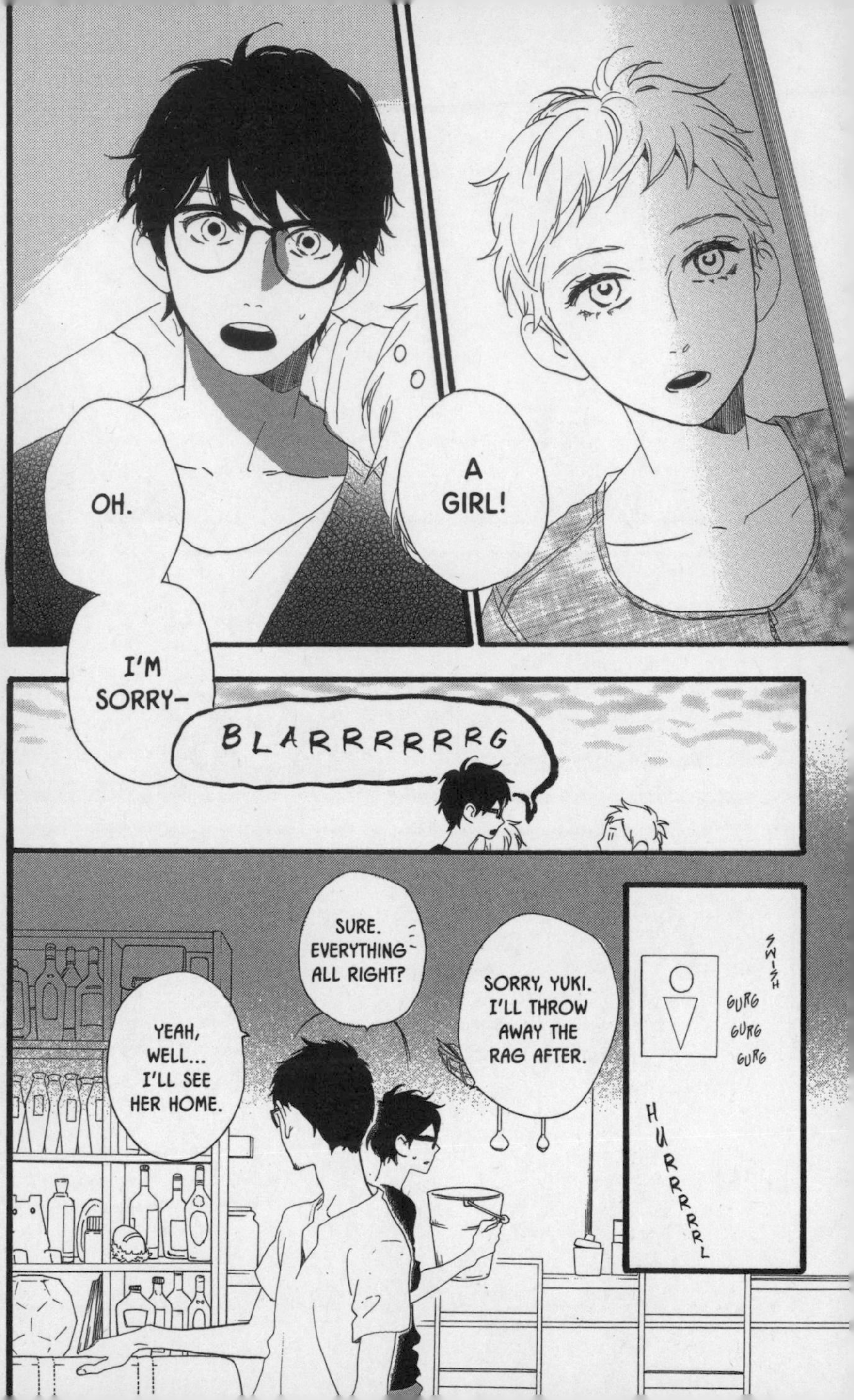
A GIRL!
OH.
I'M SORRY—
BLARRRRRRRG
SWISH
GURG
GURG
GURG
HURRRRRL
SORRY, YUKI. I'LL THROW AWAY THE RAG AFTER.
SURE. EVERYTHING ALL RIGHT?
YEAH, WELL... I'LL SEE HER HOME.

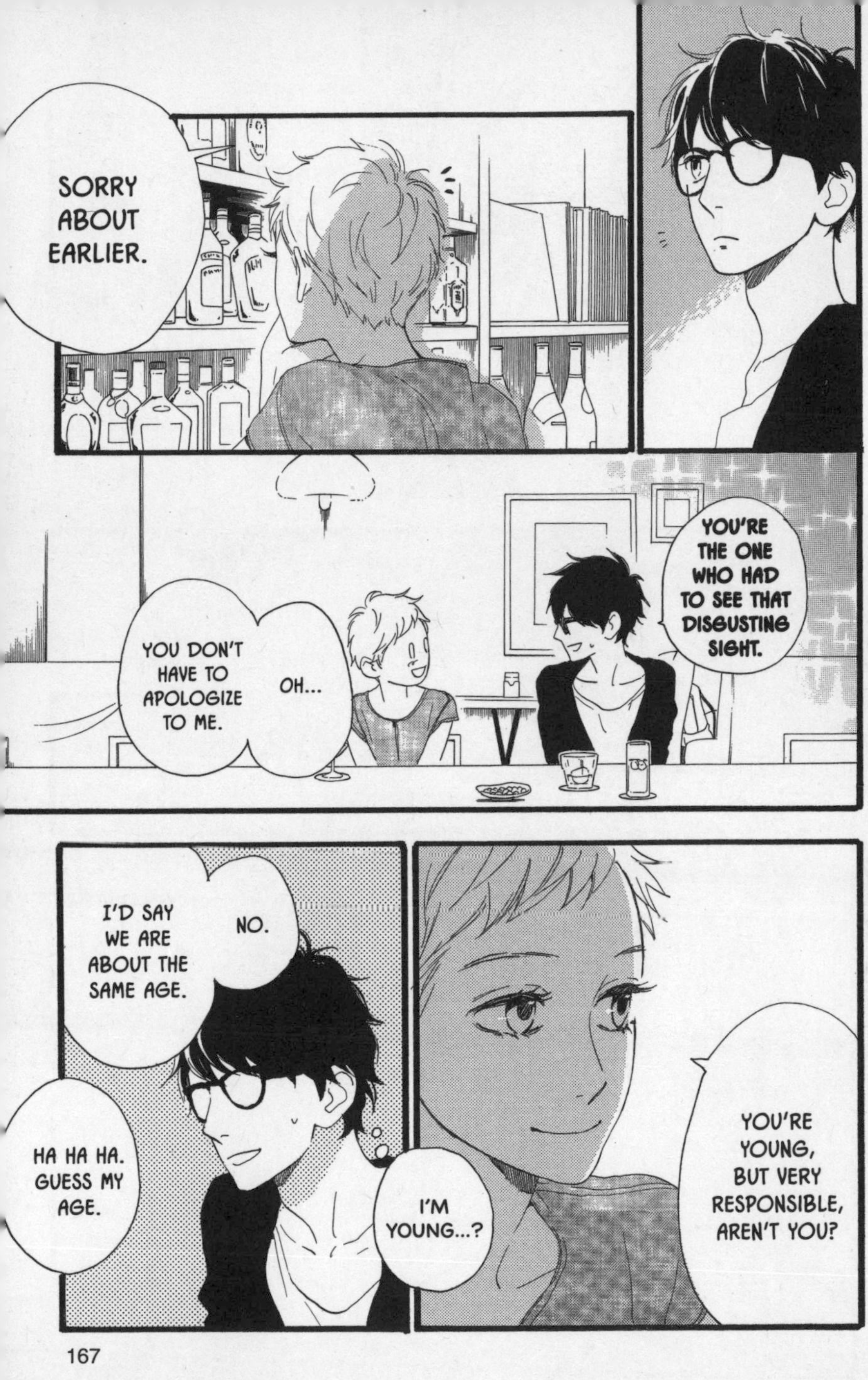
SORRY ABOUT EARLIER.
YOU'RE THE ONE WHO HAD TO SEE THAT DISGUSTING SIGHT.
OH...
YOU DON'T HAVE TO APOLOGIZE TO ME.
YOU'RE YOUNG, BUT VERY RESPONSIBLE, AREN'T YOU?
NO.
I'D SAY WE ARE ABOUT THE SAME AGE.
I'M YOUNG...?
HA HA HA. GUESS MY AGE.

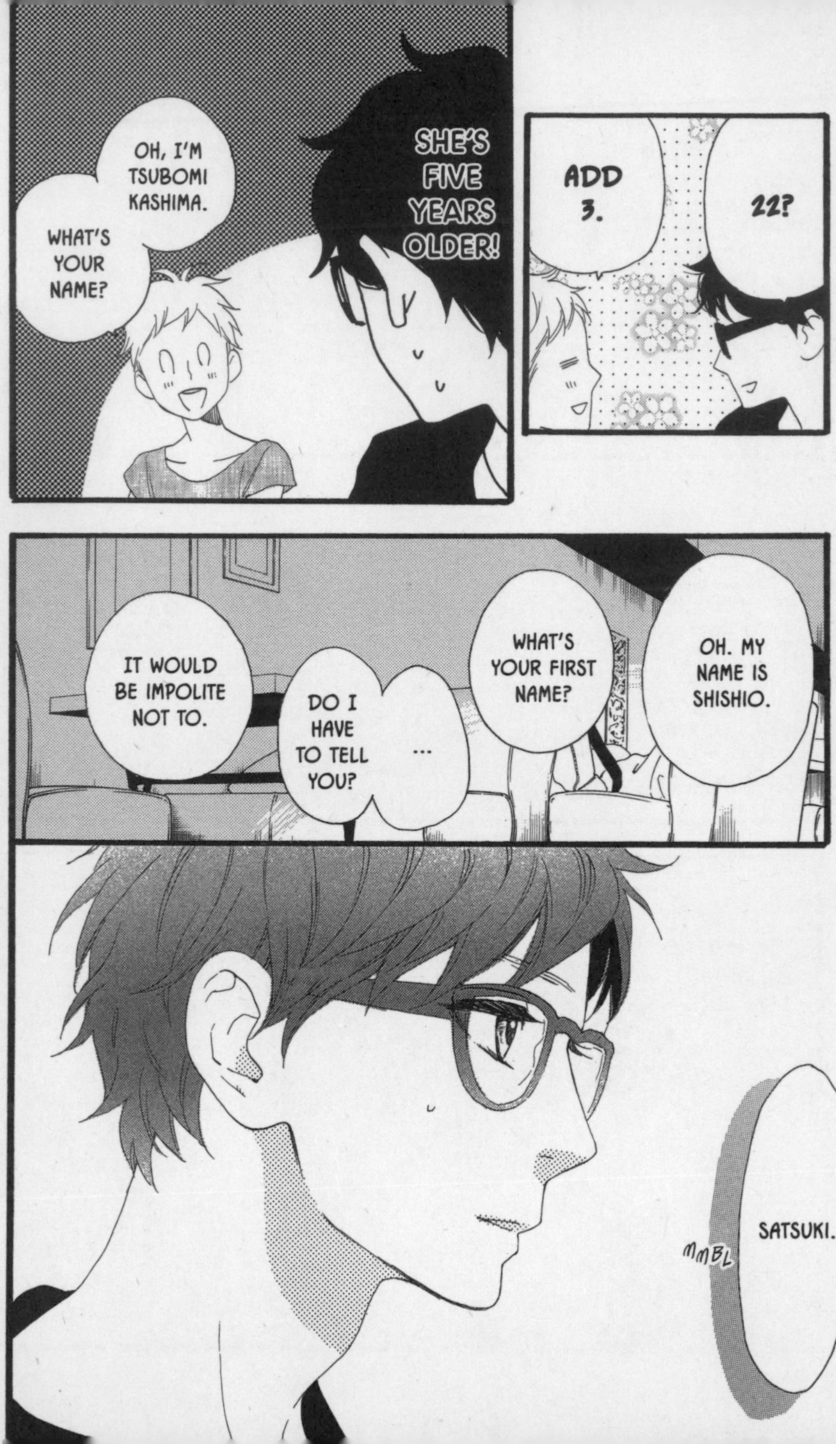
22?
ADD 3.
SHE'S FIVE YEARS OLDER!
OH, I'M TSUBOMI KASHIMA.
WHAT'S YOUR NAME?
OH. MY NAME IS SHISHIO.
WHAT'S YOUR FIRST NAME?
...
DO I HAVE TO TELL YOU?
IT WOULD BE IMPOLITE NOT TO.
SATSUKI.
MMBL

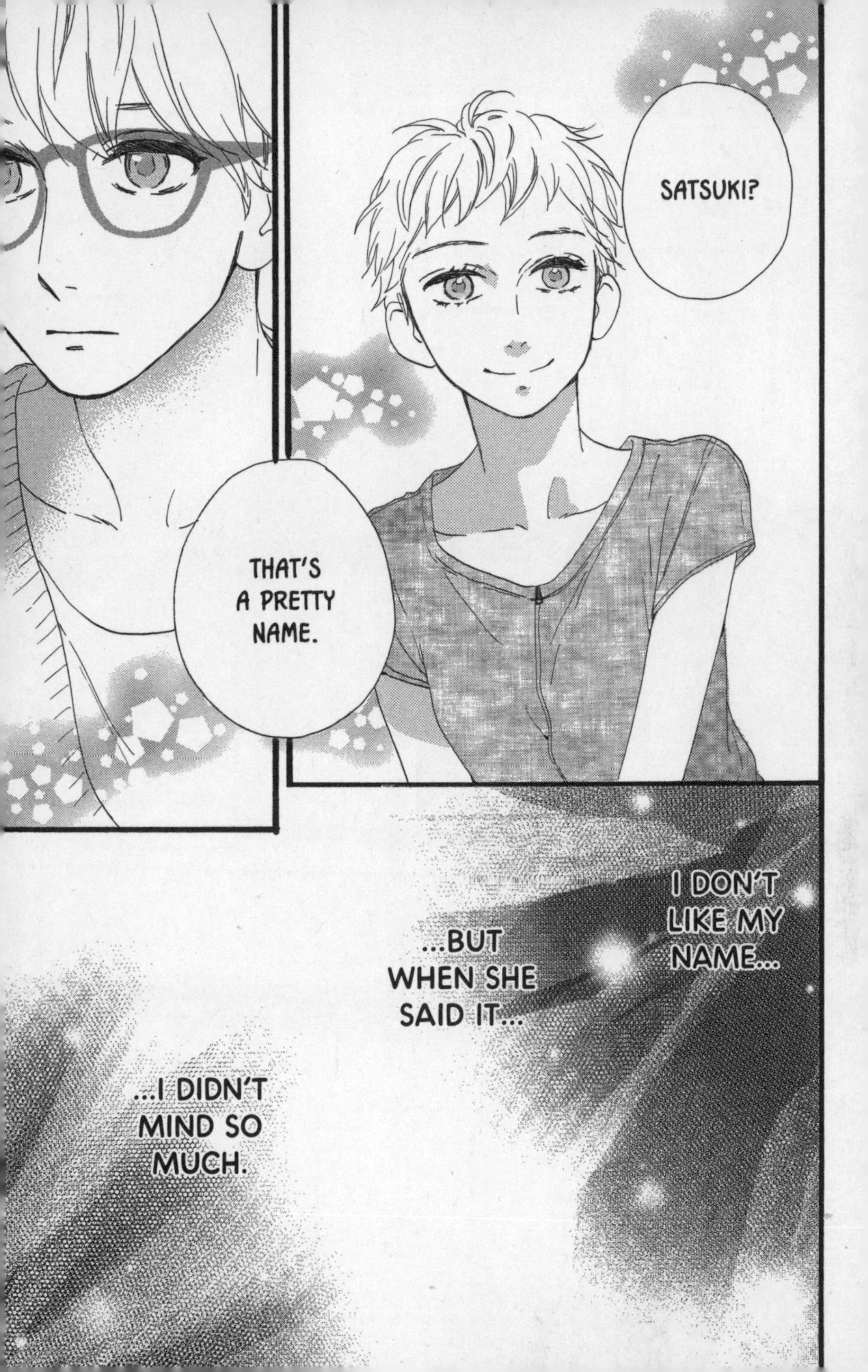
SATSUKI?
THAT'S A PRETTY NAME.
I DON'T LIKE MY NAME...
...BUT WHEN SHE SAID IT...
...I DIDN'T MIND SO MUCH.

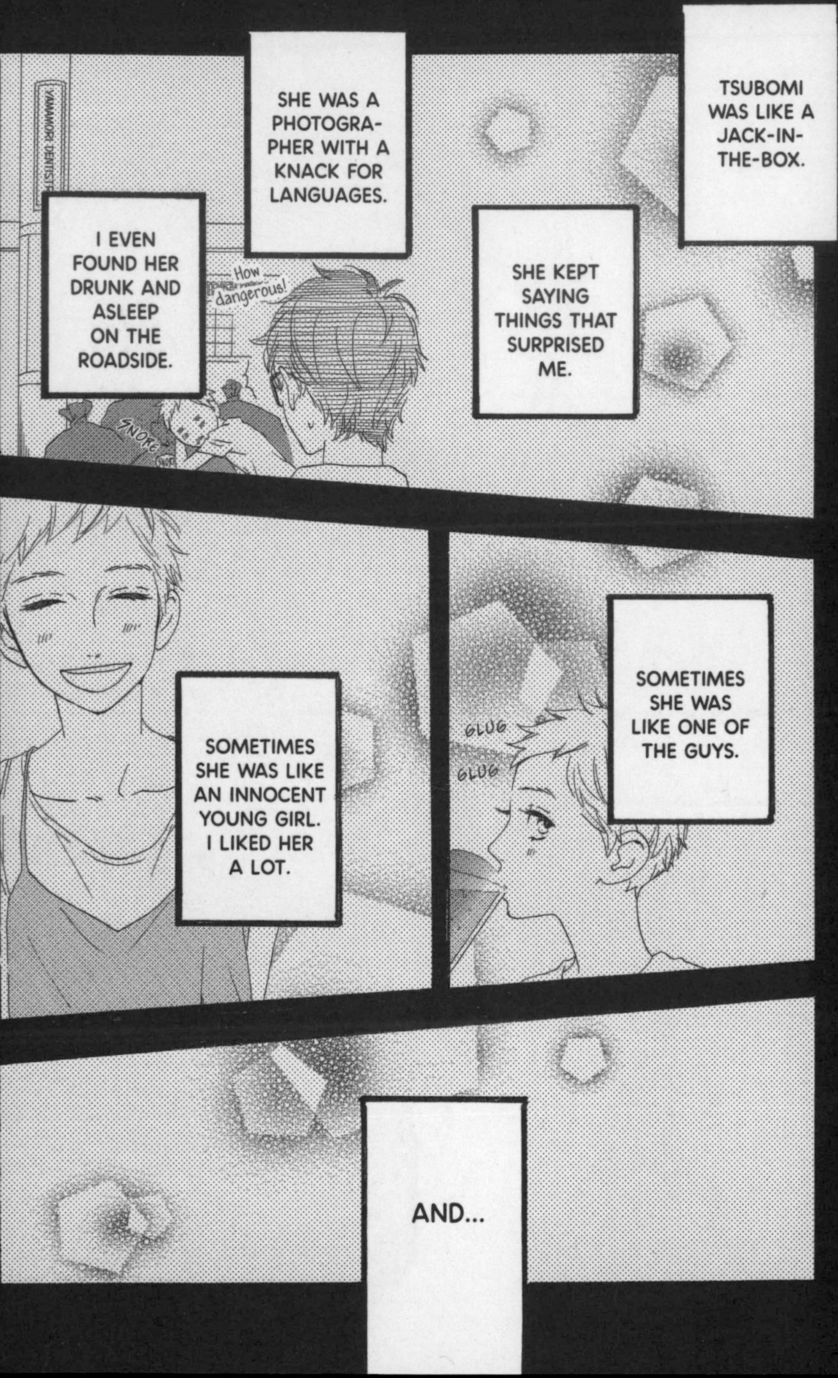
TSUBOMI WAS LIKE A JACK-IN-THE-BOX.
SHE KEPT SAYING THINGS THAT SURPRISED ME.
SHE WAS A PHOTOGRAPHER WITH A KNACK FOR LANGUAGES.
YAMAMORI DENTIST
I EVEN FOUND HER DRUNK AND ASLEEP ON THE ROADSIDE.
How dangerous!
SNORE
SOMETIMES SHE WAS LIKE ONE OF THE GUYS.
GLUG
GLUG
SOMETIMES SHE WAS LIKE AN INNOCENT YOUNG GIRL. I LIKED HER A LOT.
AND...

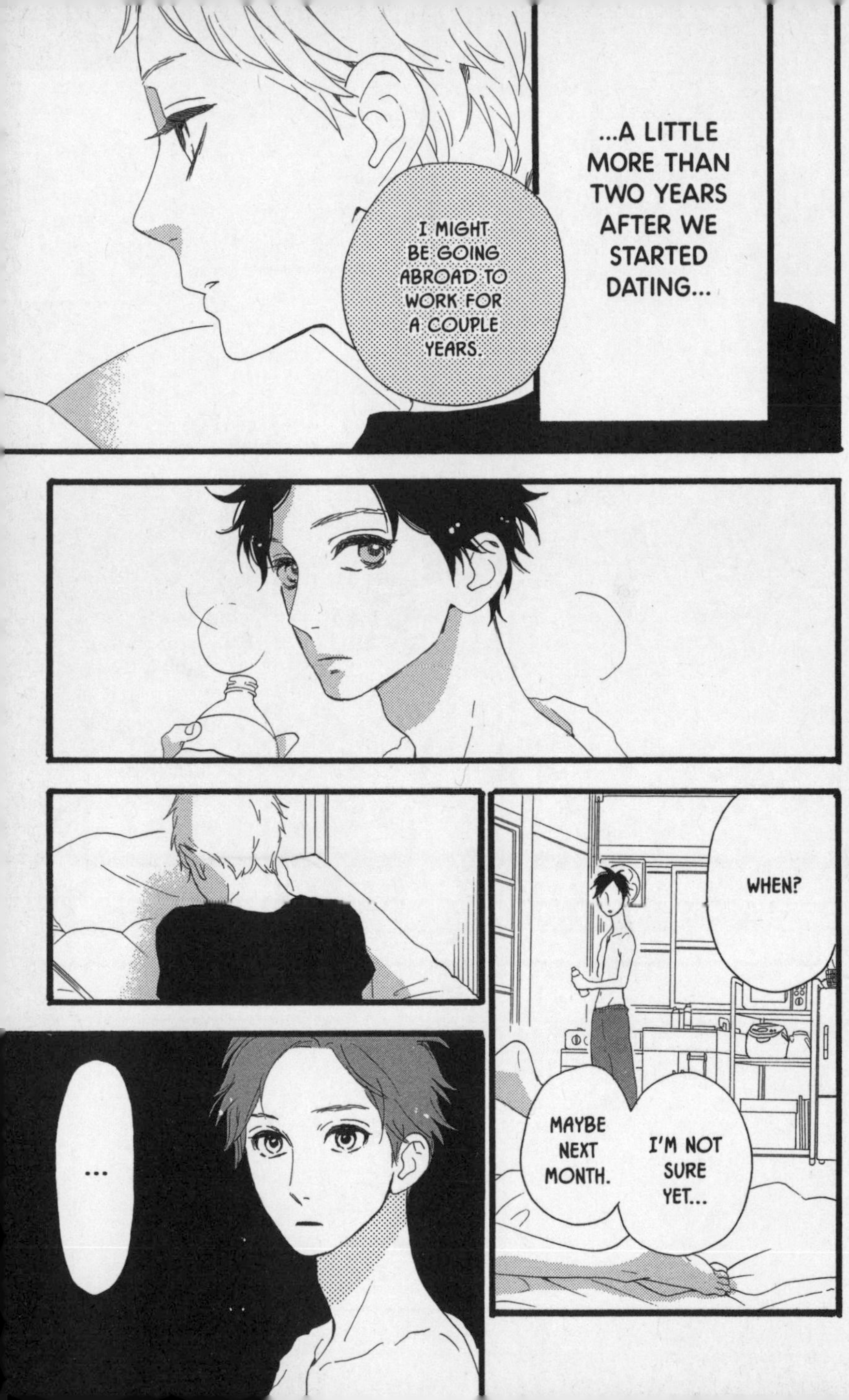
...A LITTLE MORE THAN TWO YEARS AFTER WE STARTED DATING...
I MIGHT BE GOING ABROAD TO WORK FOR A COUPLE YEARS.
WHEN?
I'M NOT SURE YET...
MAYBE NEXT MONTH.
...

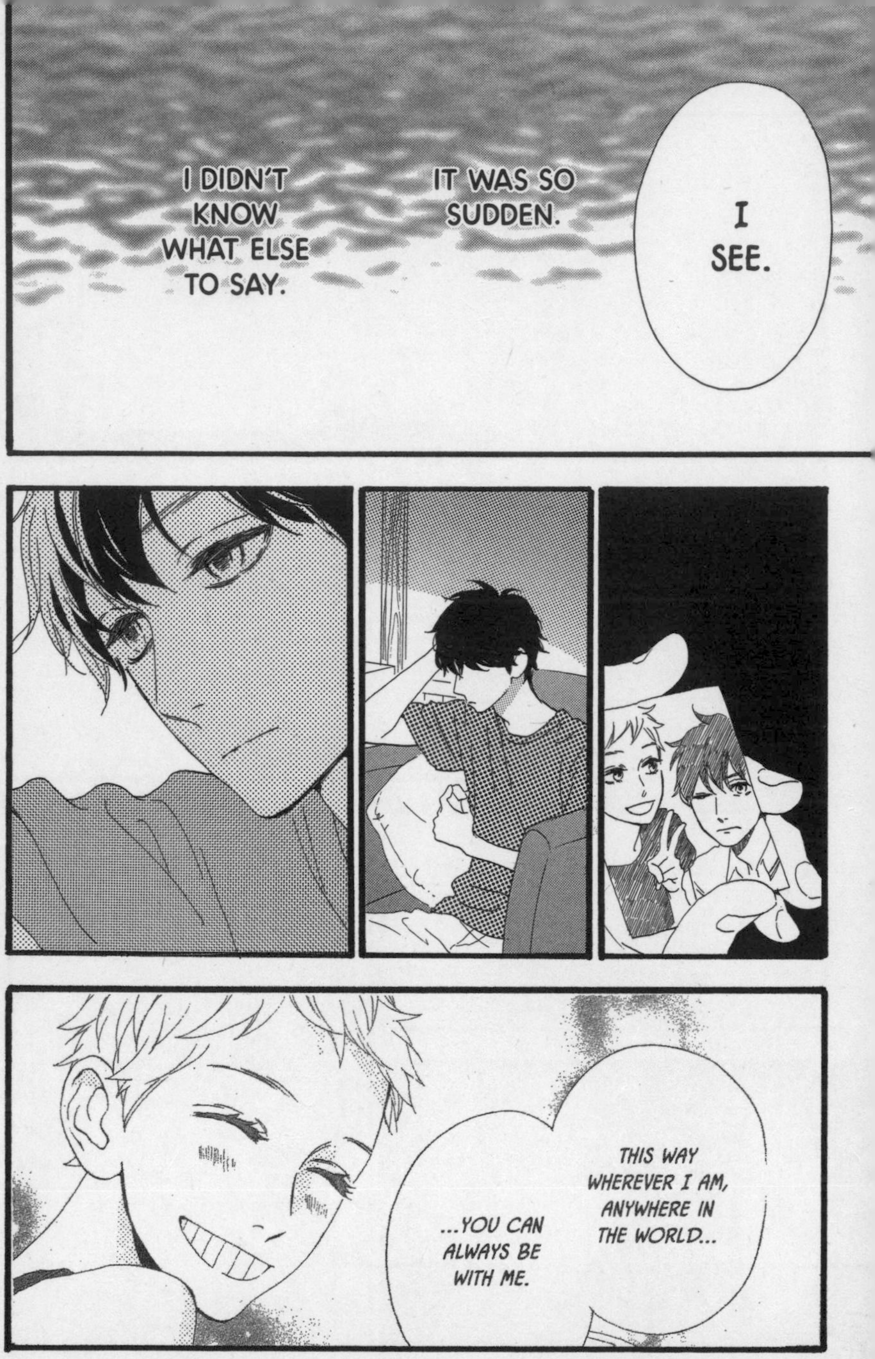
I SEE.
IT WAS SO SUDDEN.
I DIDN'T KNOW WHAT ELSE TO SAY.
THIS WAY WHEREVER I AM, ANYWHERE IN THE WORLD...
...YOU CAN ALWAYS BE WITH ME.

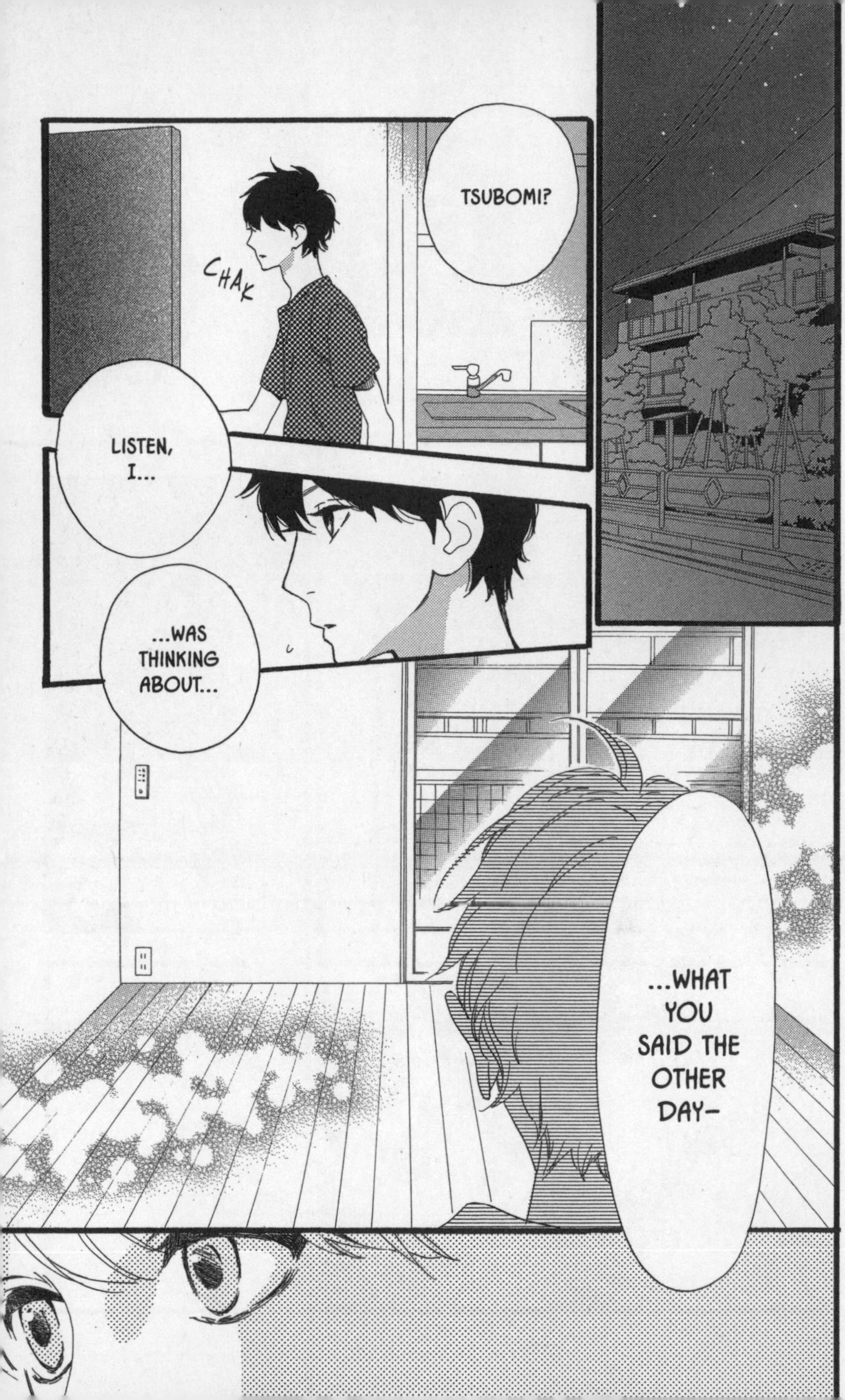
TSUBOMI?
CHAK
LISTEN, I...
...WAS THINKING ABOUT...
...WHAT YOU SAID THE OTHER DAY—

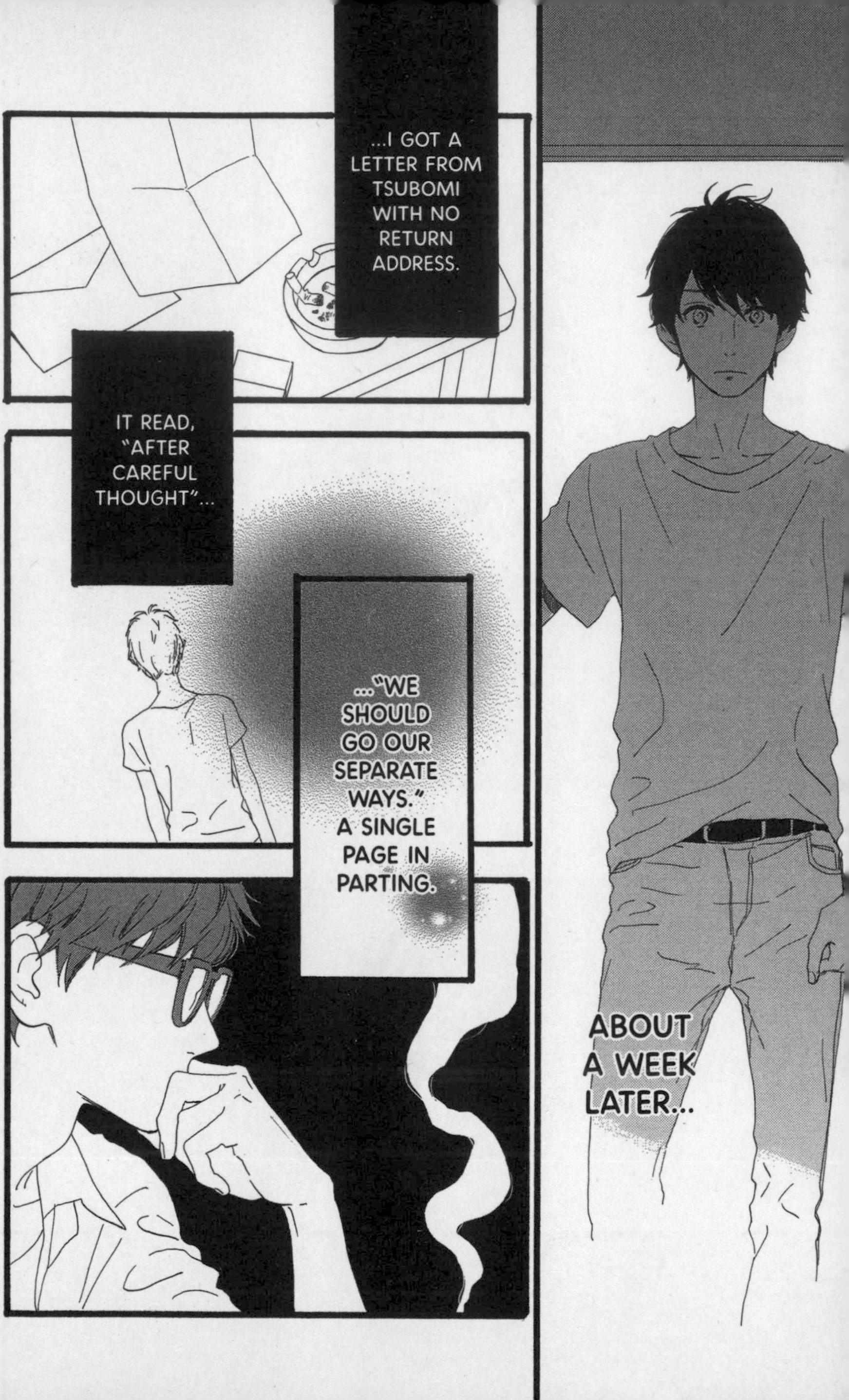
ABOUT A WEEK LATER...
...I GOT A LETTER FROM TSUBOMI WITH NO RETURN ADDRESS.
IT READ, "AFTER CAREFUL THOUGHT"...
..."WE SHOULD GO OUR SEPARATE WAYS." A SINGLE PAGE IN PARTING.

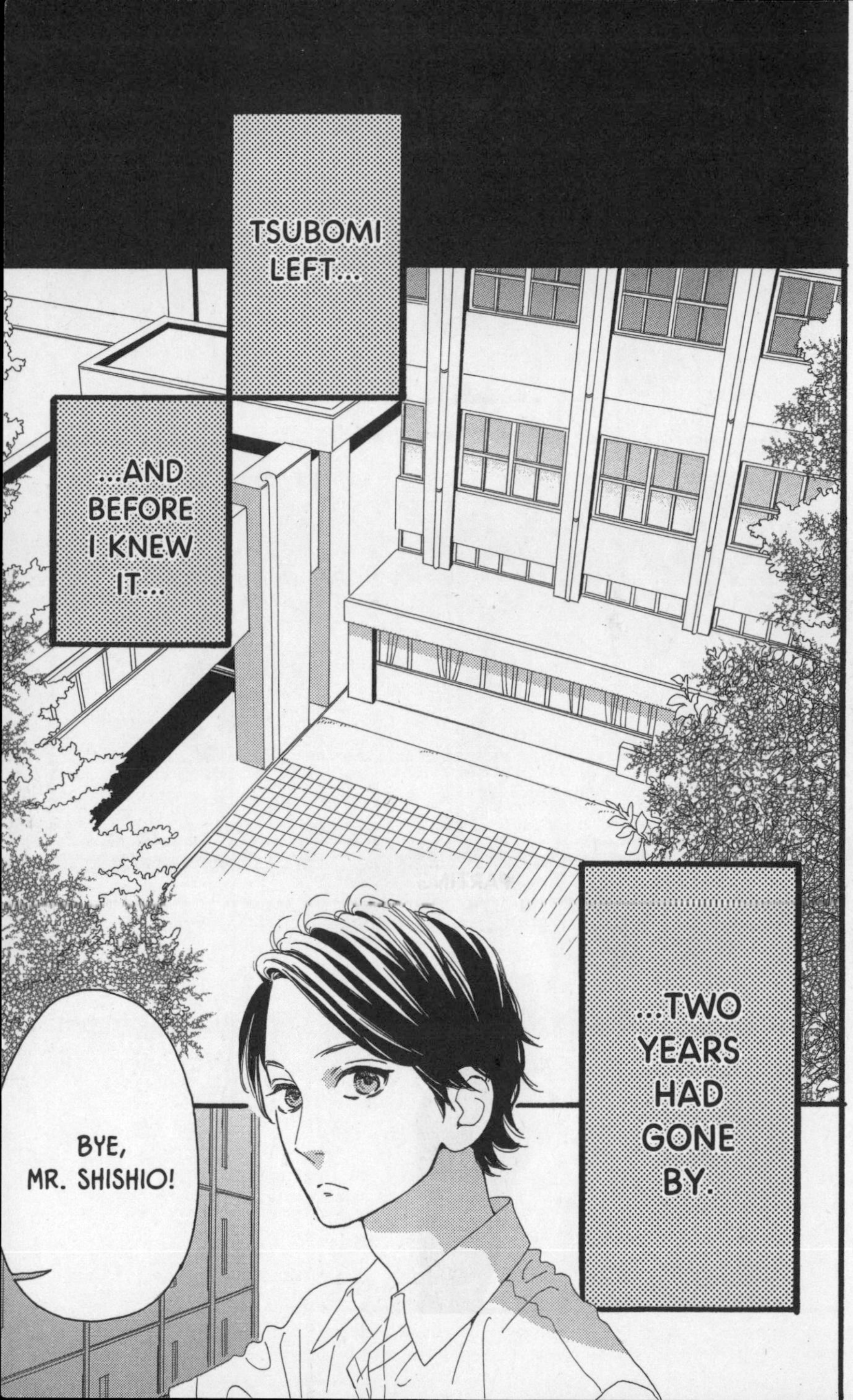
TSUBOMI LEFT...
...AND BEFORE I KNEW IT...
...TWO YEARS HAD GONE BY.
BYE, MR. SHISHIO!

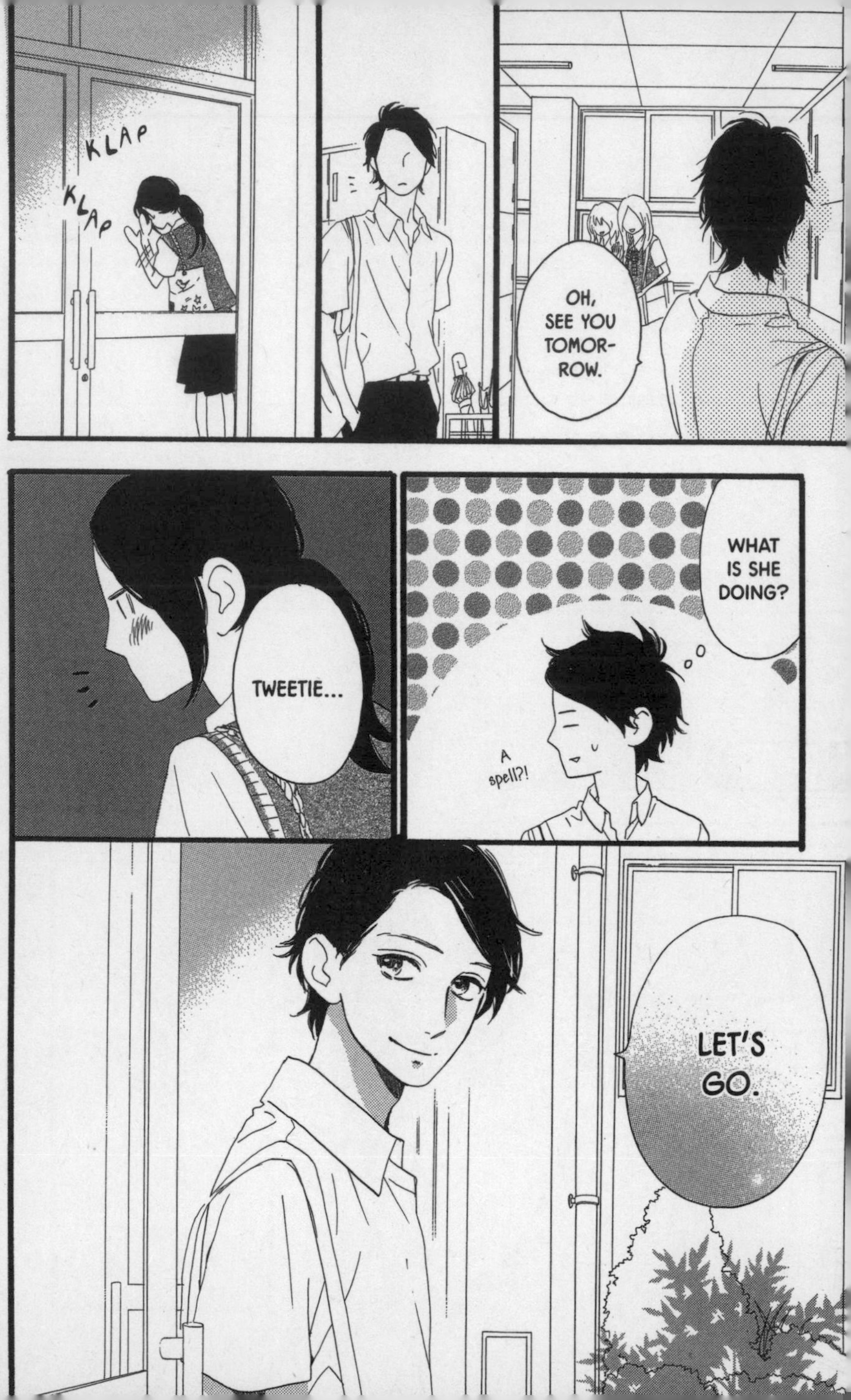
OH, SEE YOU TOMOR-ROW.
KLAP
KLAP
WHAT IS SHE DOING?
A spell?!
TWEETIE...
LET'S GO.

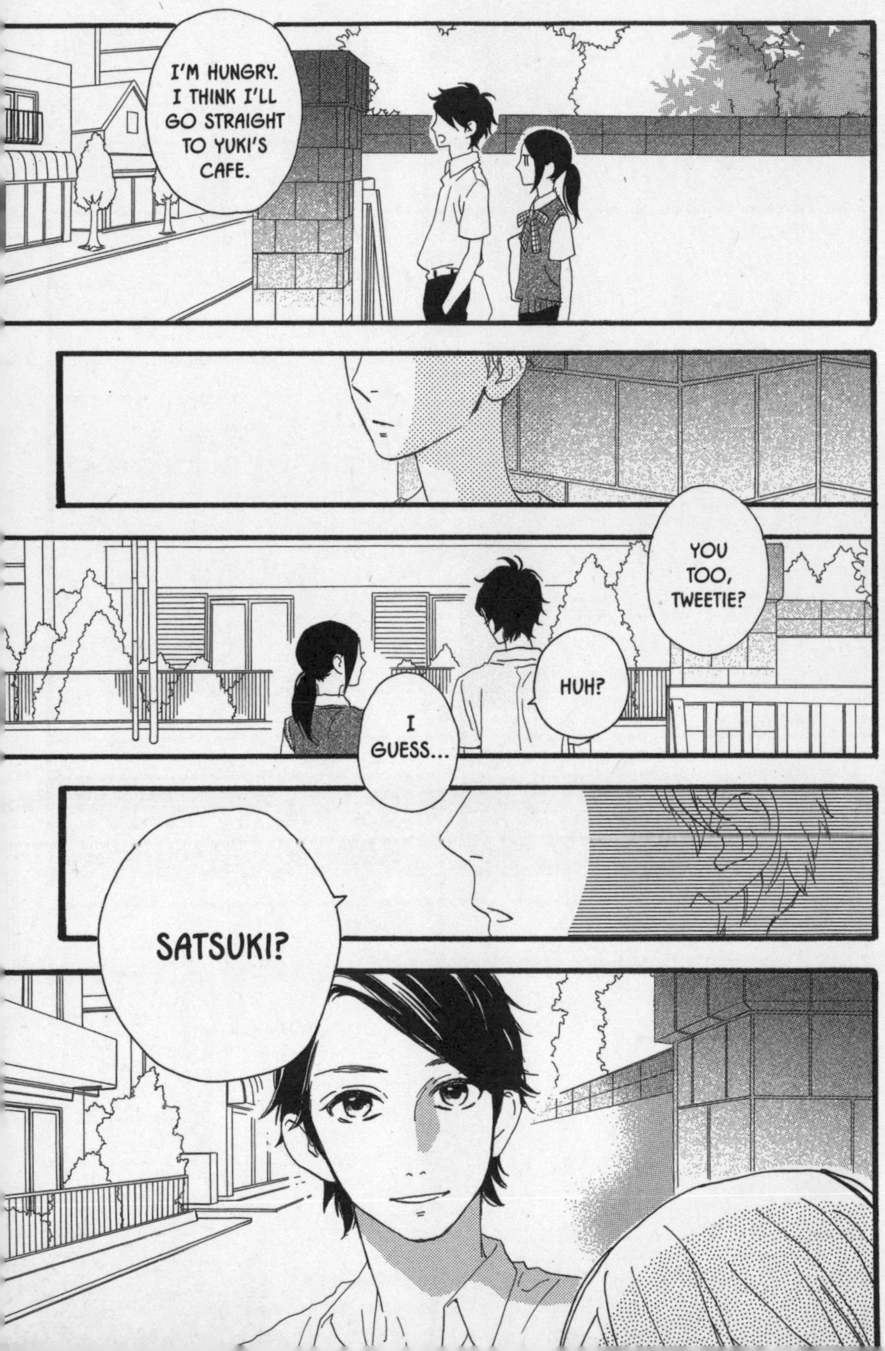
I'M HUNGRY. I THINK I'LL GO STRAIGHT TO YUKI'S CAFE.
YOU TOO, TWEETIE?
HUH?
I GUESS...
SATSUKI?

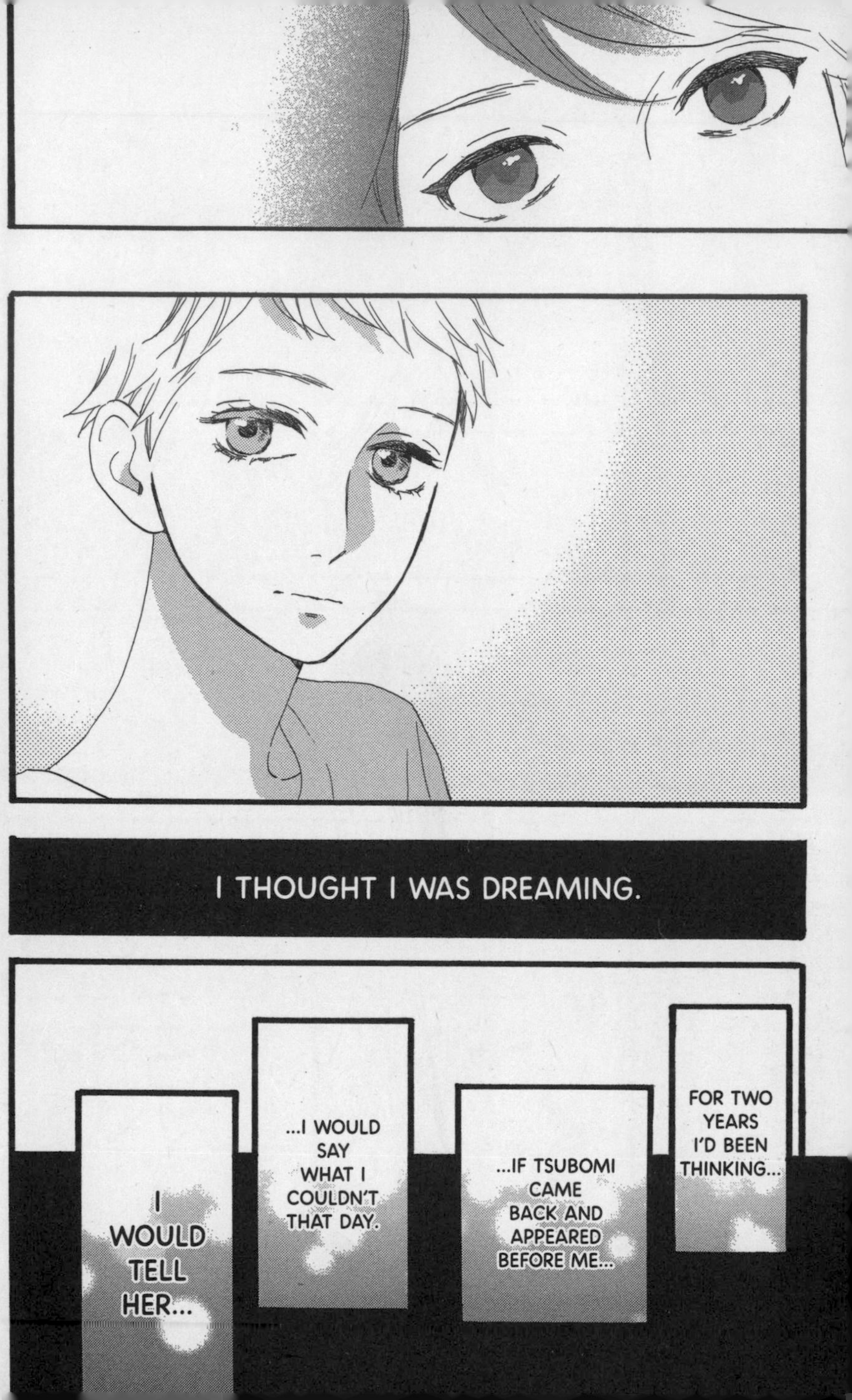
I THOUGHT I WAS DREAMING.
FOR TWO YEARS I'D BEEN THINKING...
...IF TSUBOMI CAME BACK AND APPEARED BEFORE ME...
...I WOULD SAY WHAT I COULDN'T THAT DAY.
I WOULD TELL HER...

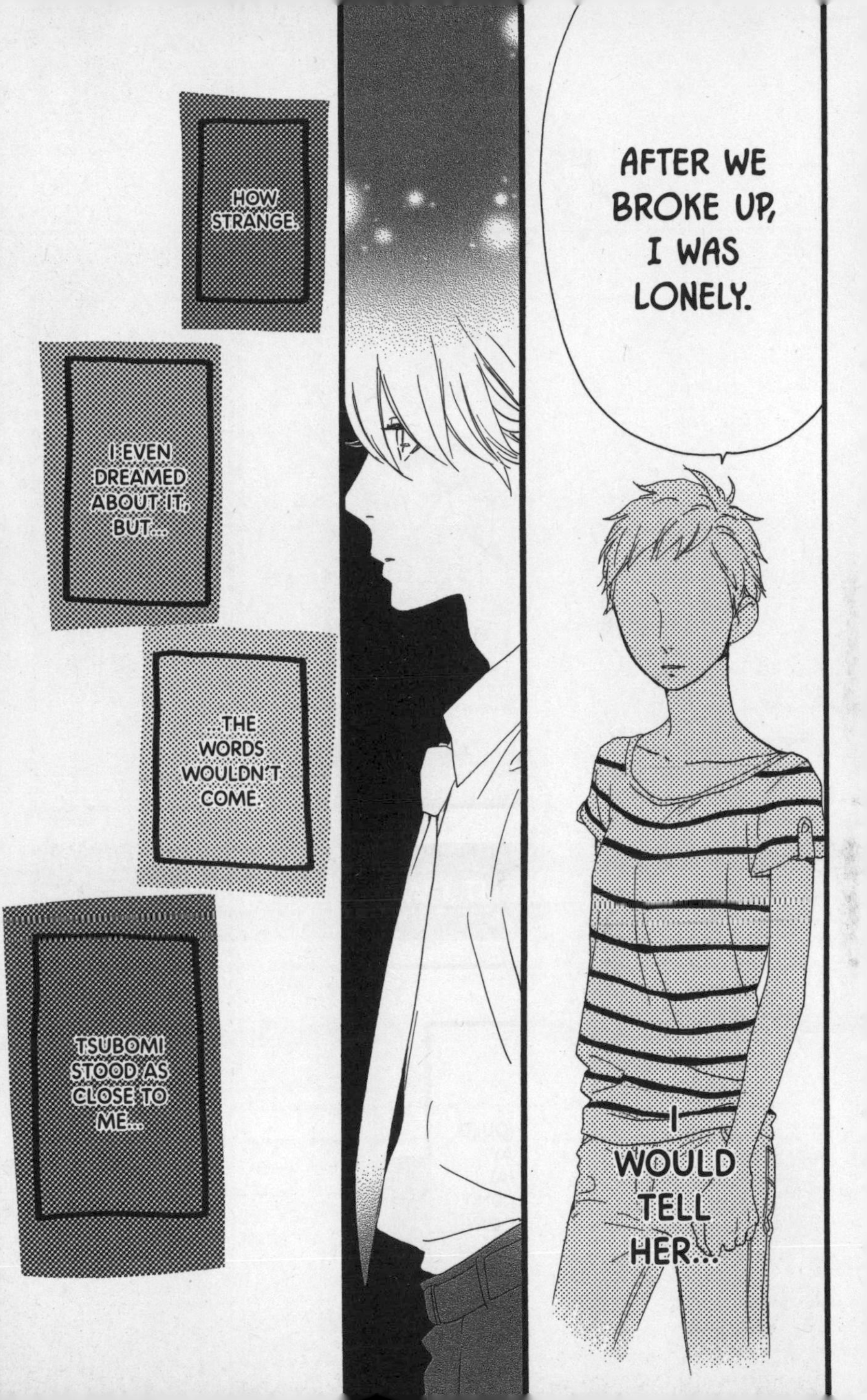
AFTER WE BROKE UP, I WAS LONELY.
I WOULD TELL HER...
HOW STRANGE.
I EVEN DREAMED ABOUT IT, BUT...
...THE WORDS WOULDN'T COME.
TSUBOMI STOOD AS CLOSE TO ME...

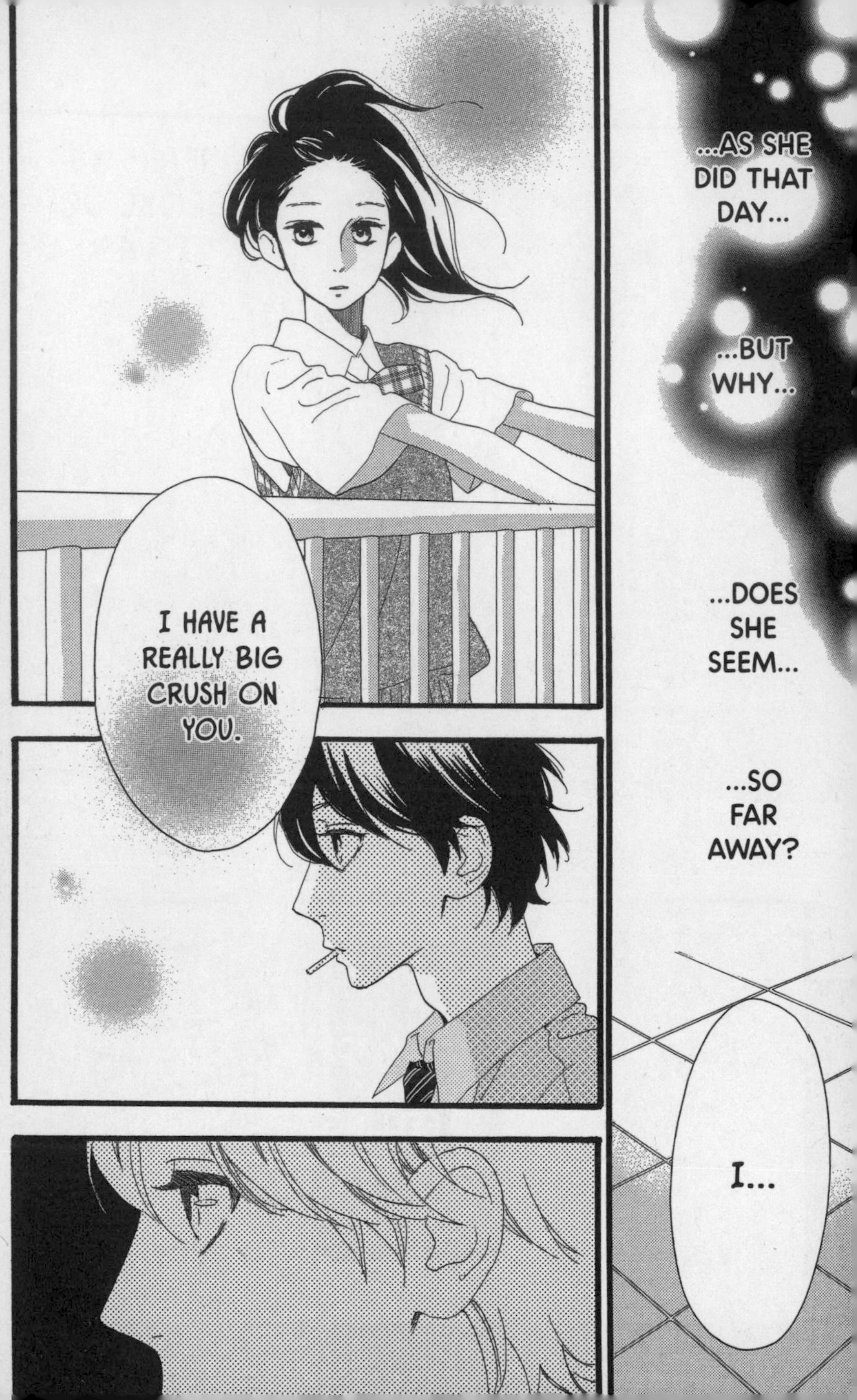
...AS SHE DID THAT DAY...
...BUT WHY...
...DOES SHE SEEM...
...SO FAR AWAY?
I...
I HAVE A REALLY BIG CRUSH ON YOU.

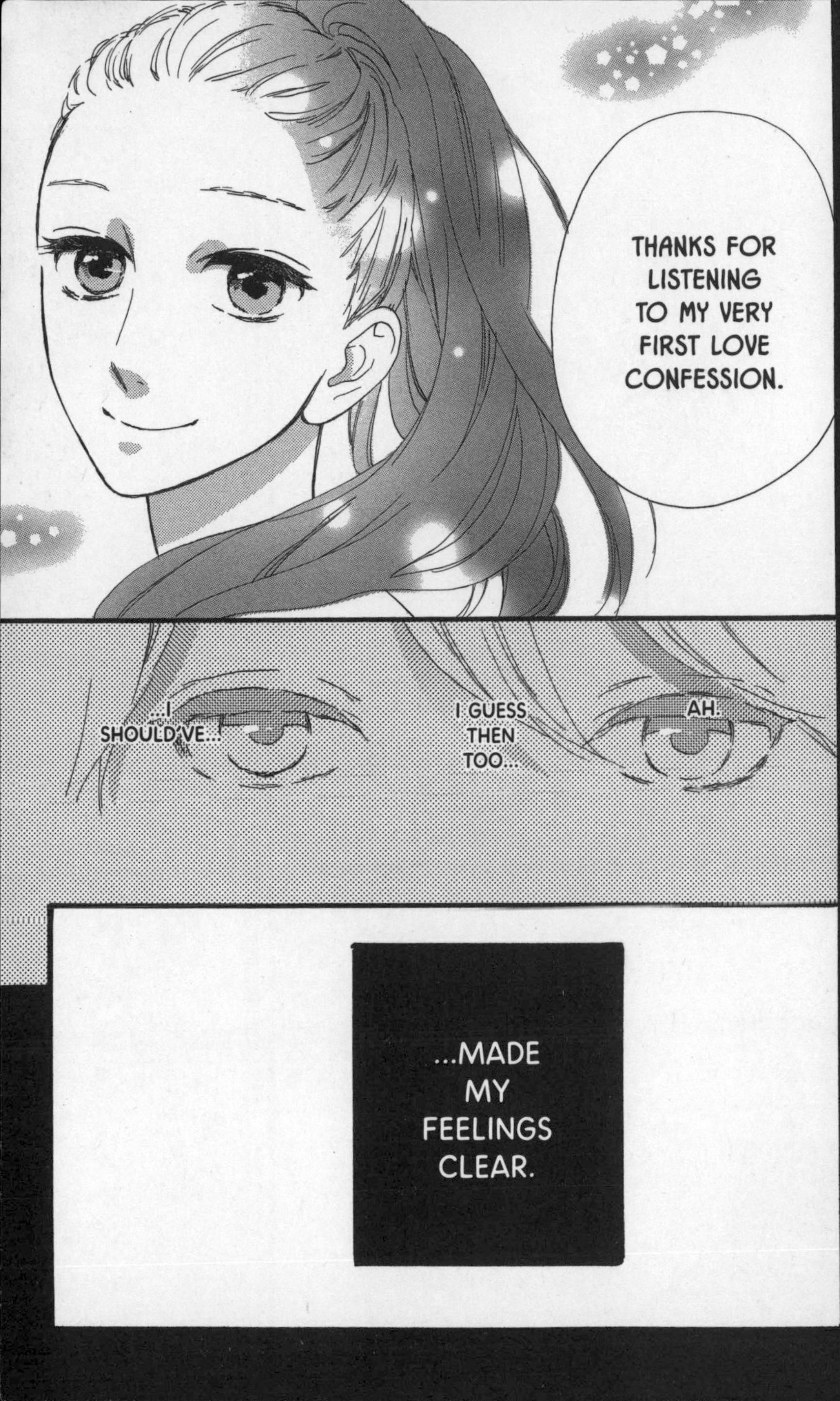
THANKS FOR LISTENING TO MY VERY FIRST LOVE CONFESSION.
AH.
I GUESS THEN TOO...
...I SHOULD'VE...
...MADE MY FEELINGS CLEAR.

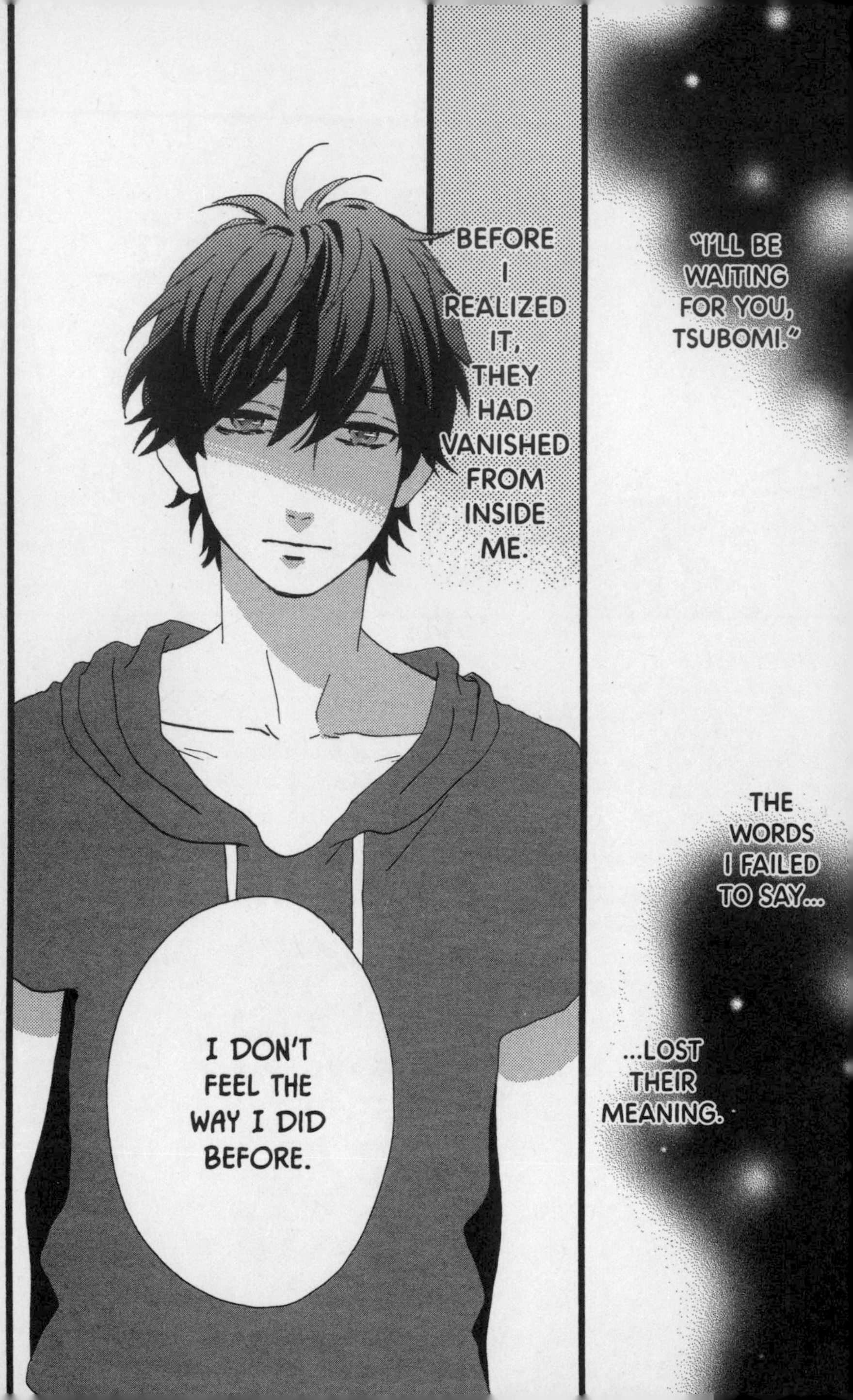
"I'LL BE WAITING FOR YOU, TSUBOMI."
THE WORDS I FAILED TO SAY...
...LOST THEIR MEANING.
BEFORE I REALIZED IT, THEY HAD VANISHED FROM INSIDE ME.
I DON'T FEEL THE WAY I DID BEFORE.

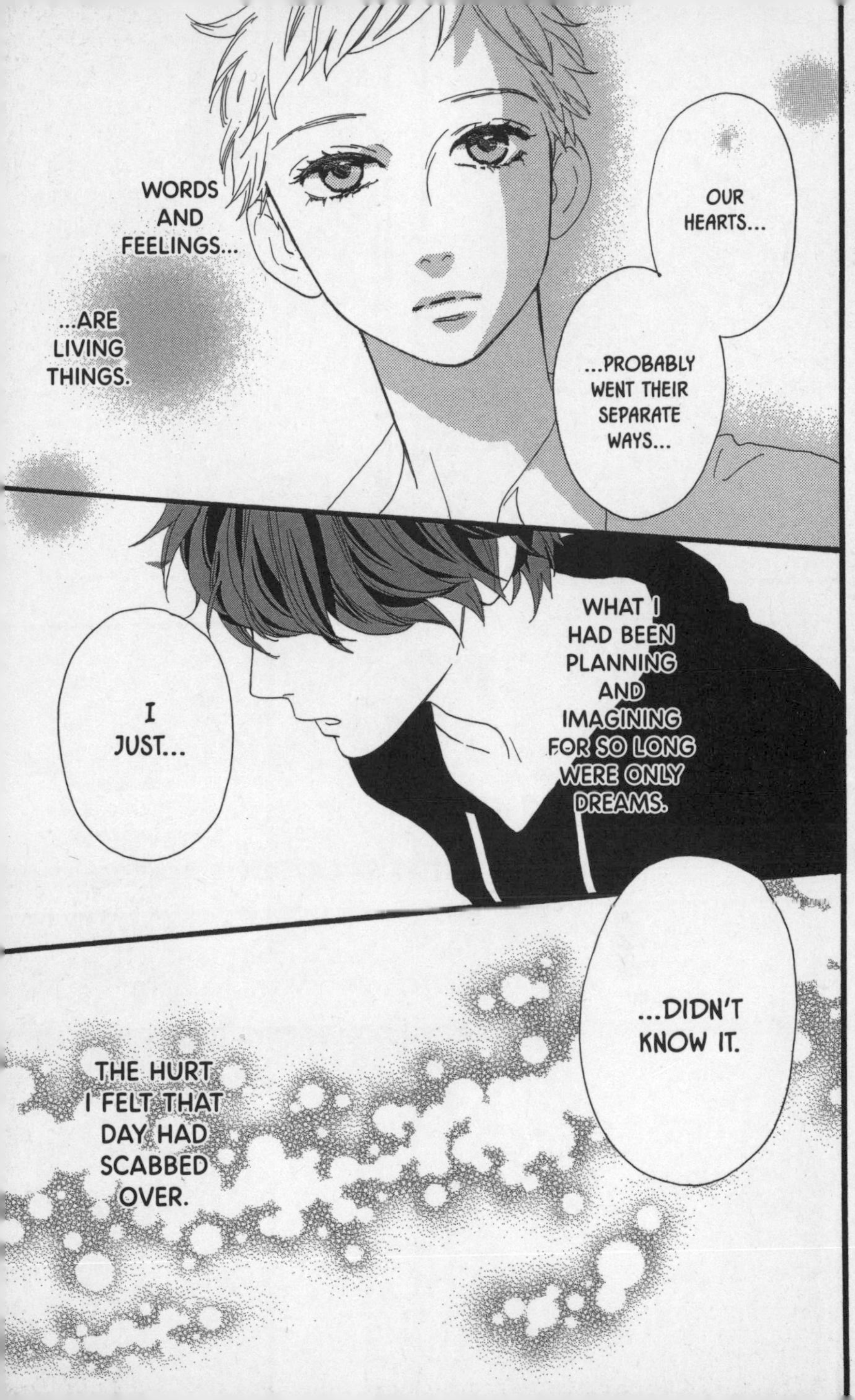
OUR HEARTS...
...PROBABLY WENT THEIR SEPARATE WAYS...
WORDS AND FEELINGS...
...ARE LIVING THINGS.
WHAT I HAD BEEN PLANNING AND IMAGINING FOR SO LONG WERE ONLY DREAMS.
I JUST...
...DIDN'T KNOW IT.
THE HURT I FELT THAT DAY HAD SCABBED OVER.

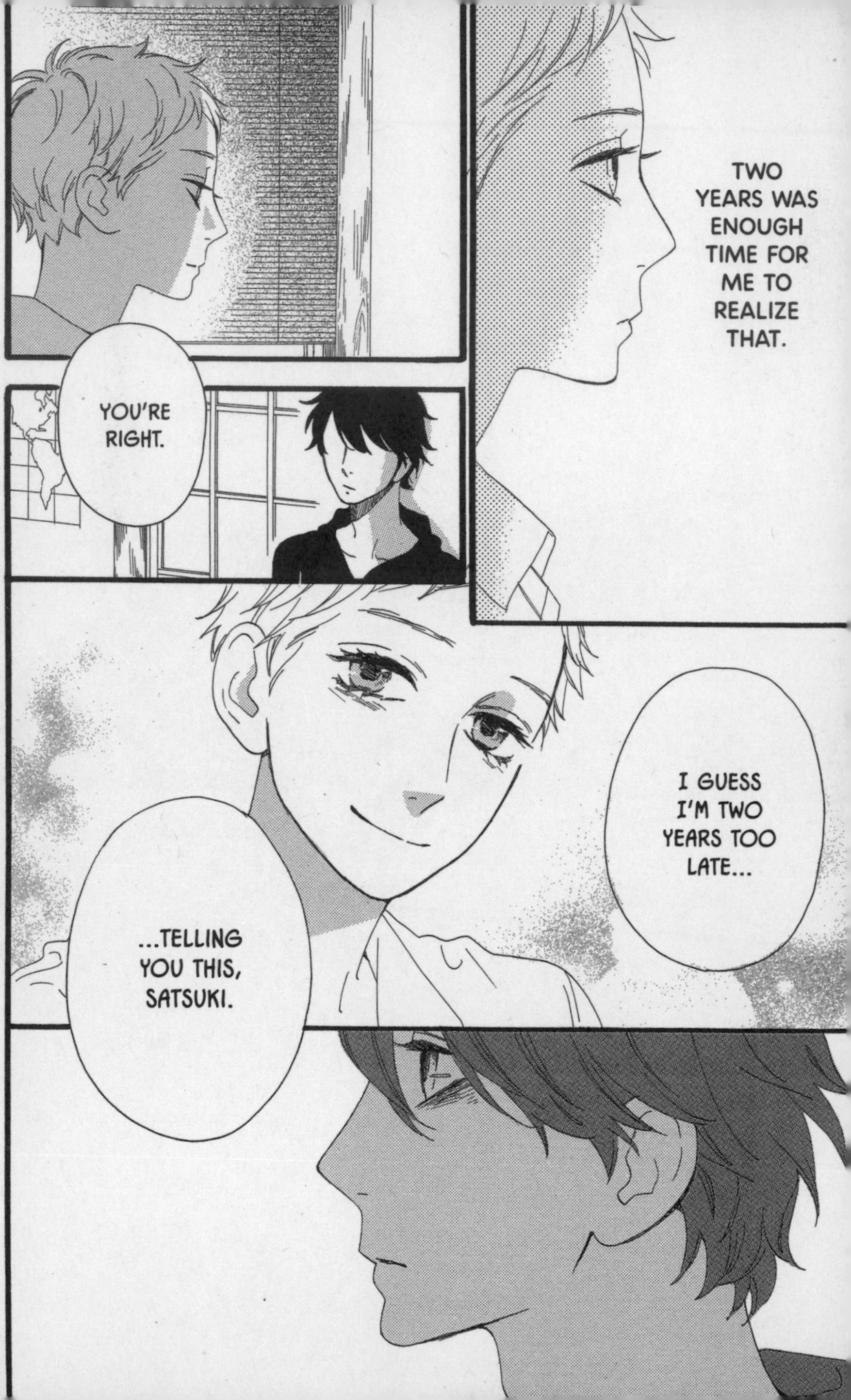
TWO YEARS WAS ENOUGH TIME FOR ME TO REALIZE THAT.
YOU'RE RIGHT.
I GUESS I'M TWO YEARS TOO LATE...
...TELLING YOU THIS, SATSUKI.

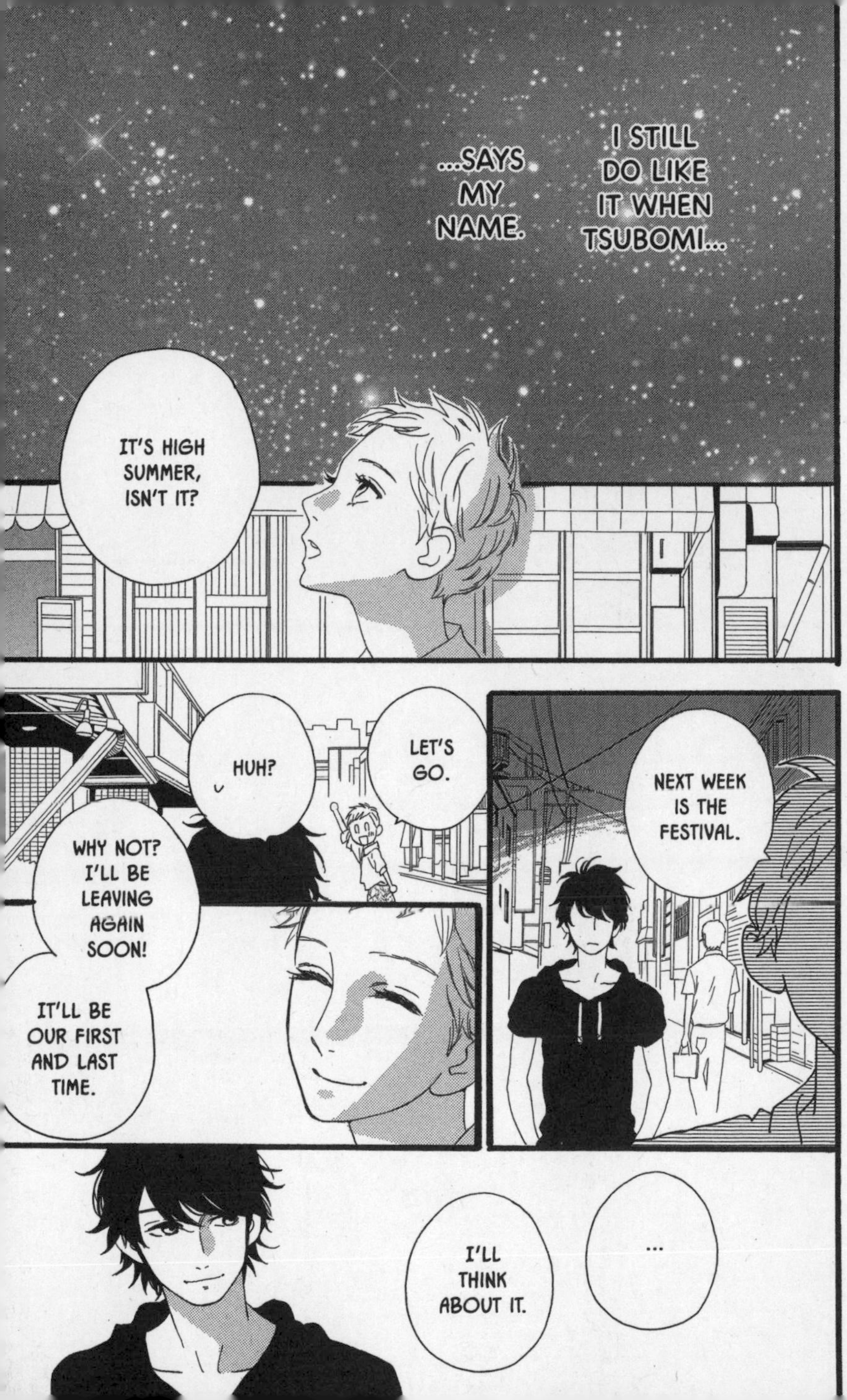
I STILL DO LIKE IT WHEN TSUBOMI...
...SAYS MY NAME.
IT'S HIGH SUMMER, ISN'T IT?
NEXT WEEK IS THE FESTIVAL.
LET'S GO.
HUH?
WHY NOT? I'LL BE LEAVING AGAIN SOON!
IT'LL BE OUR FIRST AND LAST TIME.
...
I'LL THINK ABOUT IT.

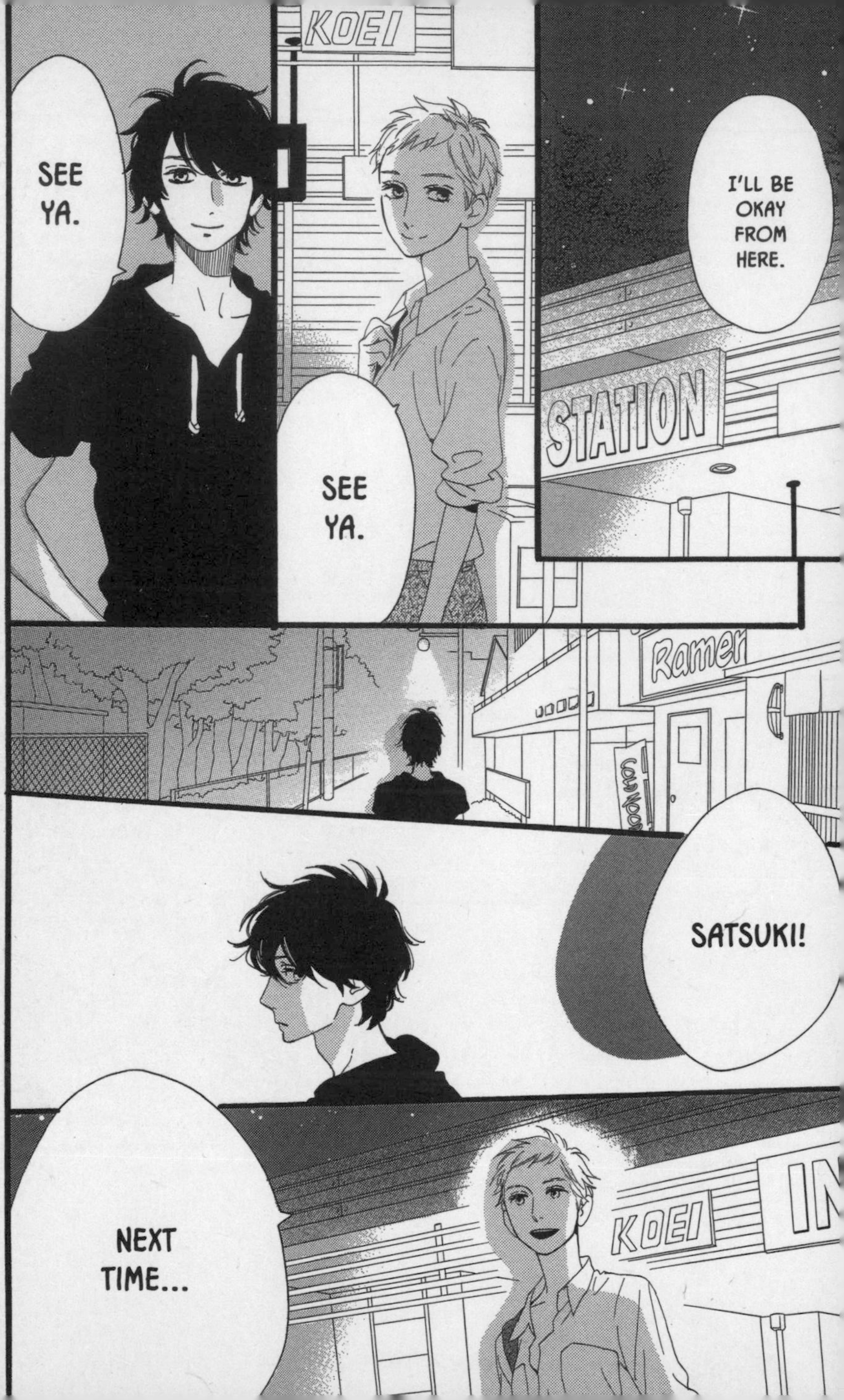
I'LL BE OKAY FROM HERE.
SEE YA.
SEE YA.
SATSUKI!
NEXT TIME...

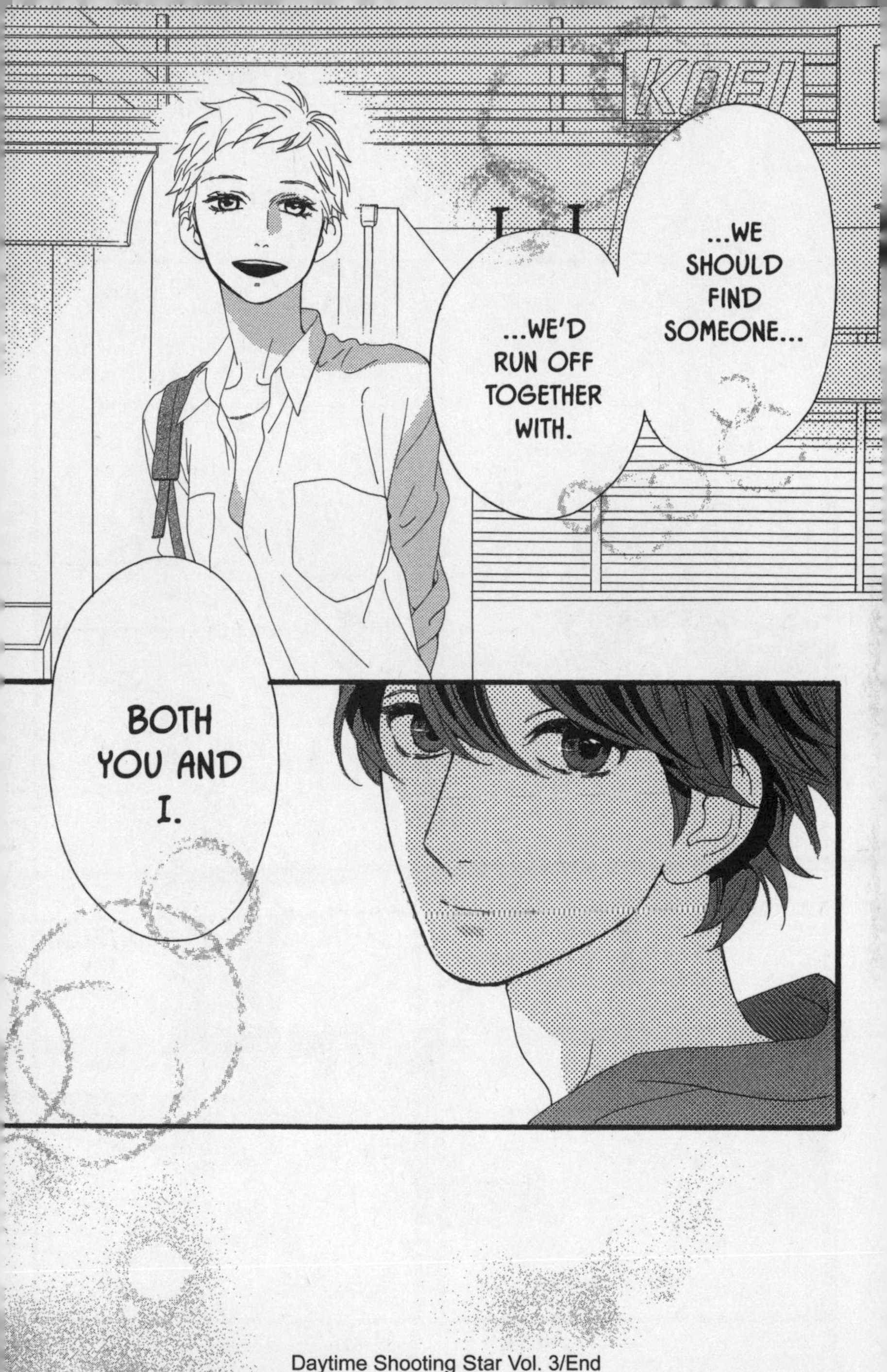
...WE SHOULD FIND SOMEONE...
...WE'D RUN OFF TOGETHER WITH.
BOTH YOU AND I.

Daytime Shooting Star Vol. 3/End

Satsuki Shishio's ON/OFF Modes

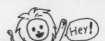

Hey!
OFF
• bedhead
• no hair wax (messy)
• thick glasses for near-sightedness
• unshaven
• smokes Camels
• baggy clothes
• slim-leg pants low on hips
• carries only an ashtray, phone and wallet
• sports watch
• puts everything in his pockets
• clothes look expensive, but they're all old and cheap
• basically wears sneakers
ON
• dresses properly because other teachers complain
• contact lenses (single day)
• uses hair wax to keep hair neat
• suffers from dry eye
• often goes without a necktie
• basically hates ties because they're uncom-fortable
• gets mistaken for a student when wearing hip-huggers or baggy pants, so dresses neatly in a suit
• sports watch
• doesn't spend much on suits
• fine with a cheap suit
• wears slippers in the school building

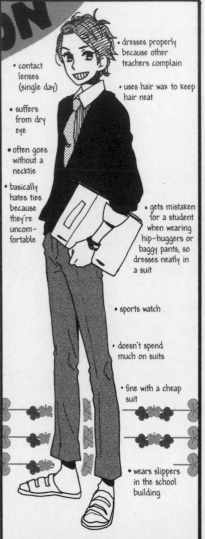

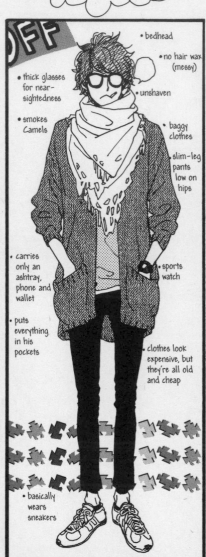

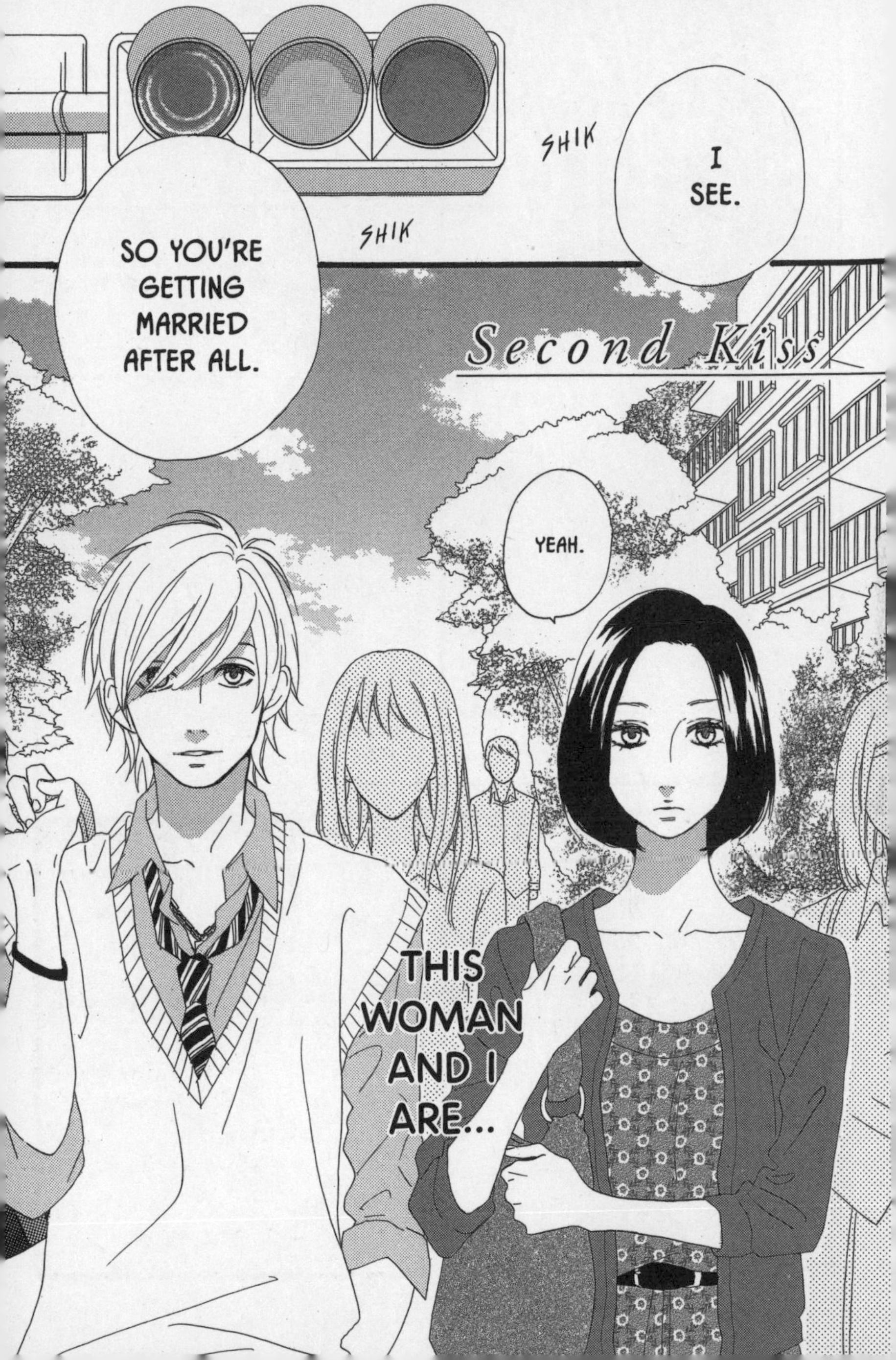
SHIK
I SEE.
SHIK
SO YOU'RE GETTING MARRIED AFTER ALL.
Second Kiss
YEAH.
THIS WOMAN AND I ARE...

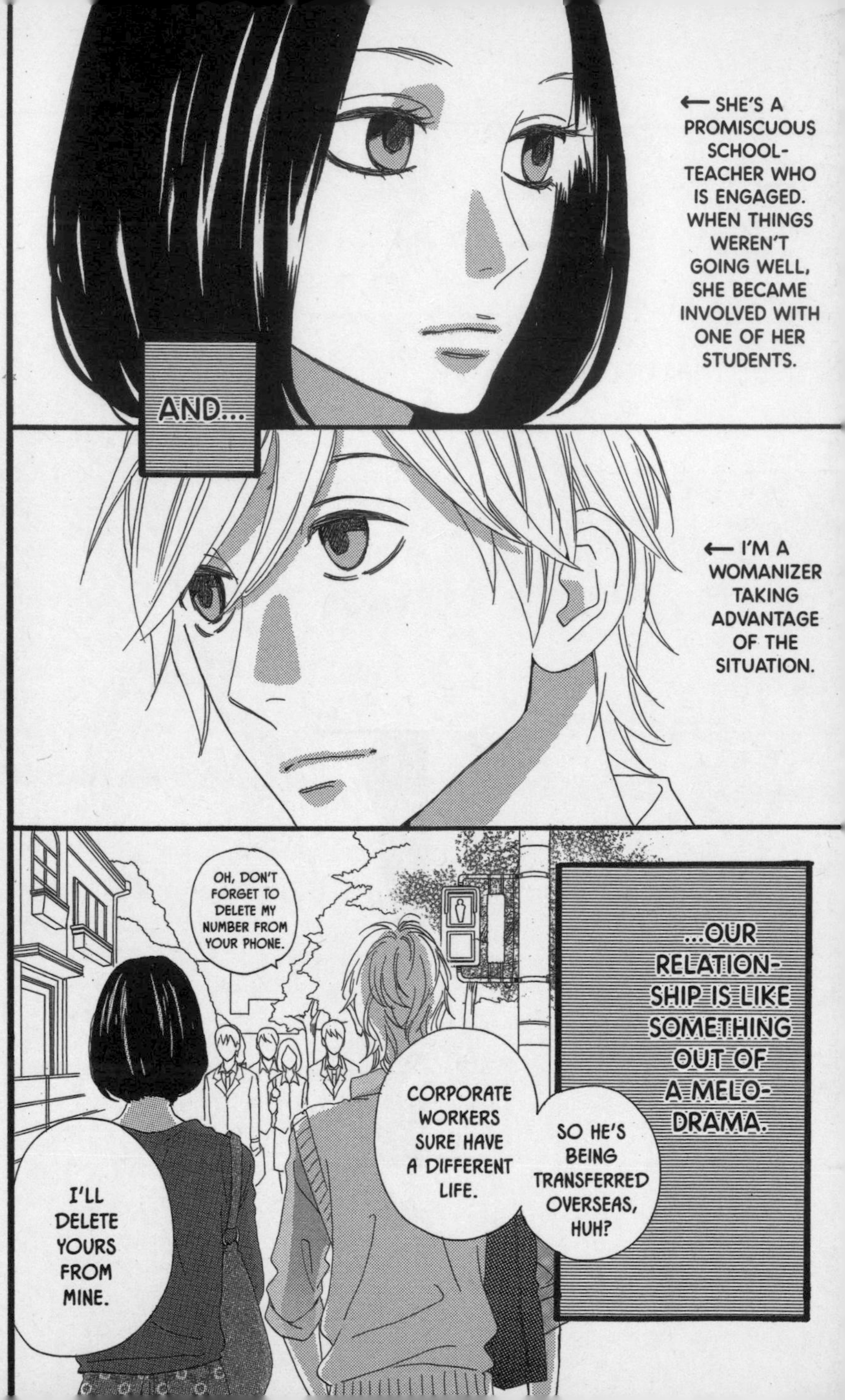
← SHE'S A PROMISCUOUS SCHOOL-TEACHER WHO IS ENGAGED. WHEN THINGS WEREN'T GOING WELL, SHE BECAME INVOLVED WITH ONE OF HER STUDENTS.
AND...
← I'M A WOMANIZER TAKING ADVANTAGE OF THE SITUATION.
...OUR RELATION-SHIP IS LIKE SOMETHING OUT OF A MELO-DRAMA.
SO HE'S BEING TRANSFERRED OVERSEAS, HUH?
CORPORATE WORKERS SURE HAVE A DIFFERENT LIFE.
OH, DON'T FORGET TO DELETE MY NUMBER FROM YOUR PHONE.
I'LL DELETE YOURS FROM MINE.

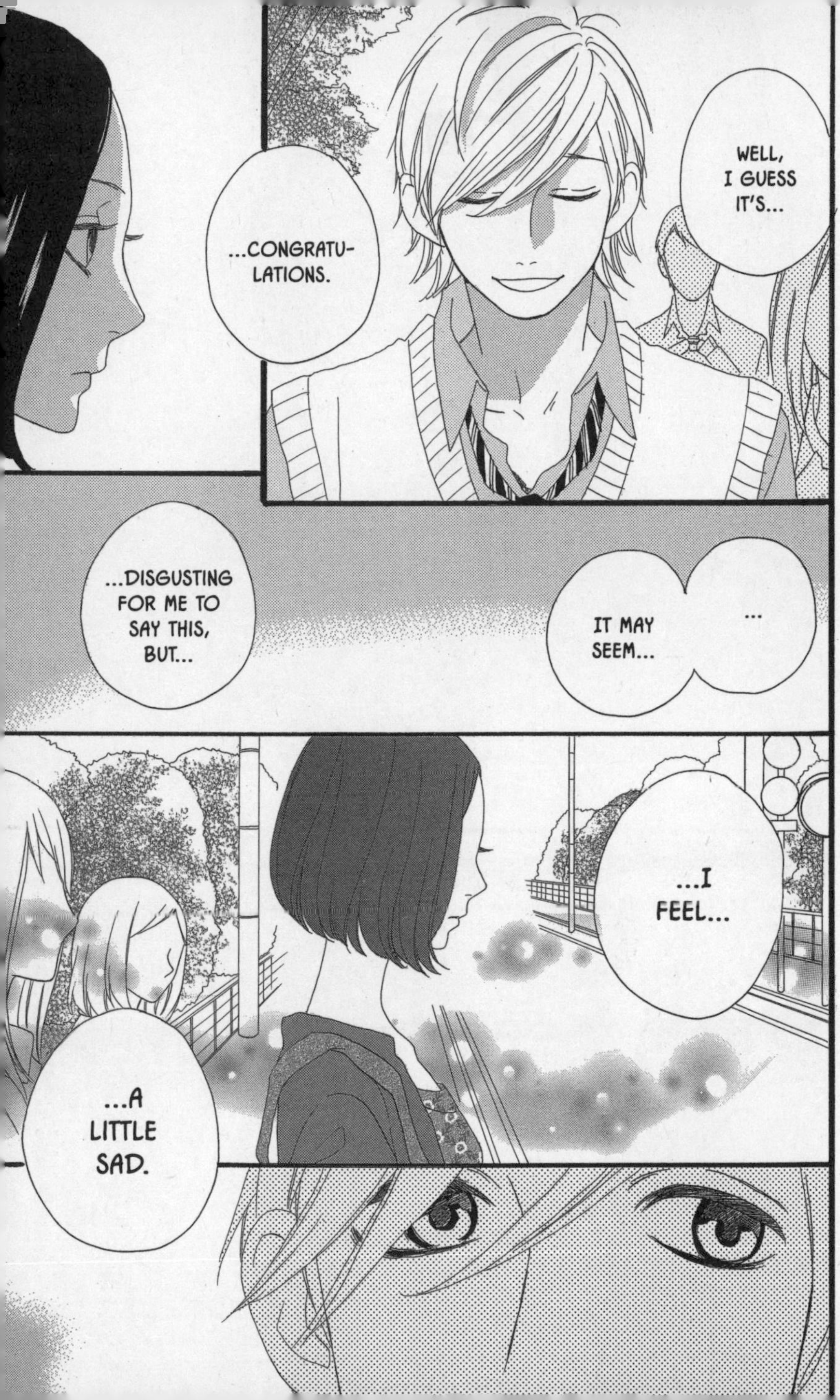
WELL, I GUESS IT'S...
...CONGRATU-LATIONS.
...
IT MAY SEEM...
...DISGUSTING FOR ME TO SAY THIS, BUT...
...I FEEL...
...A LITTLE SAD.

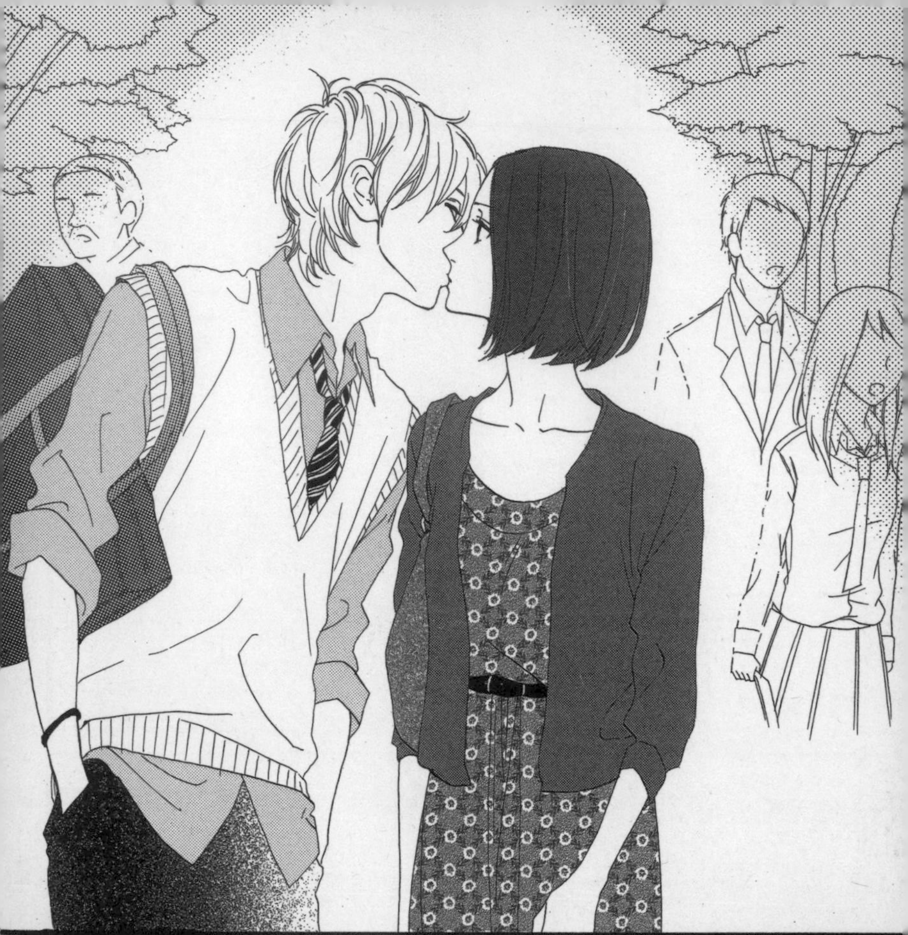

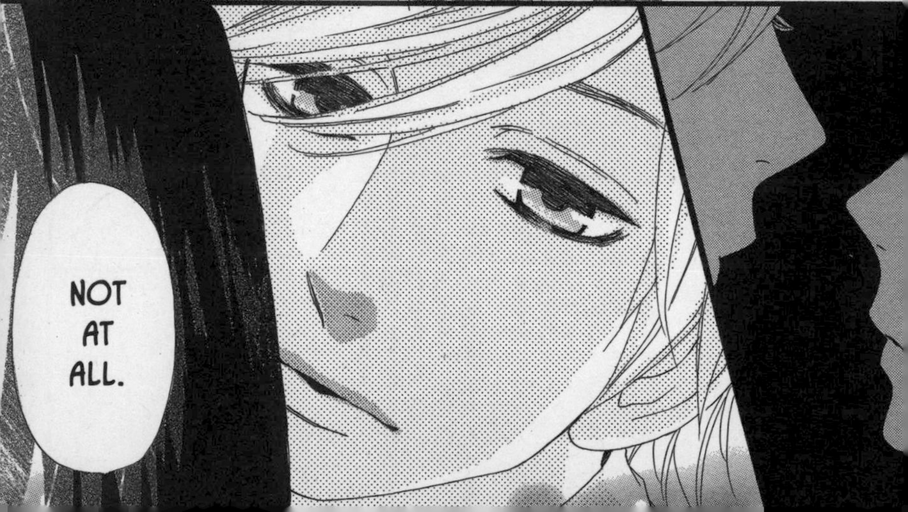
NOT AT ALL.

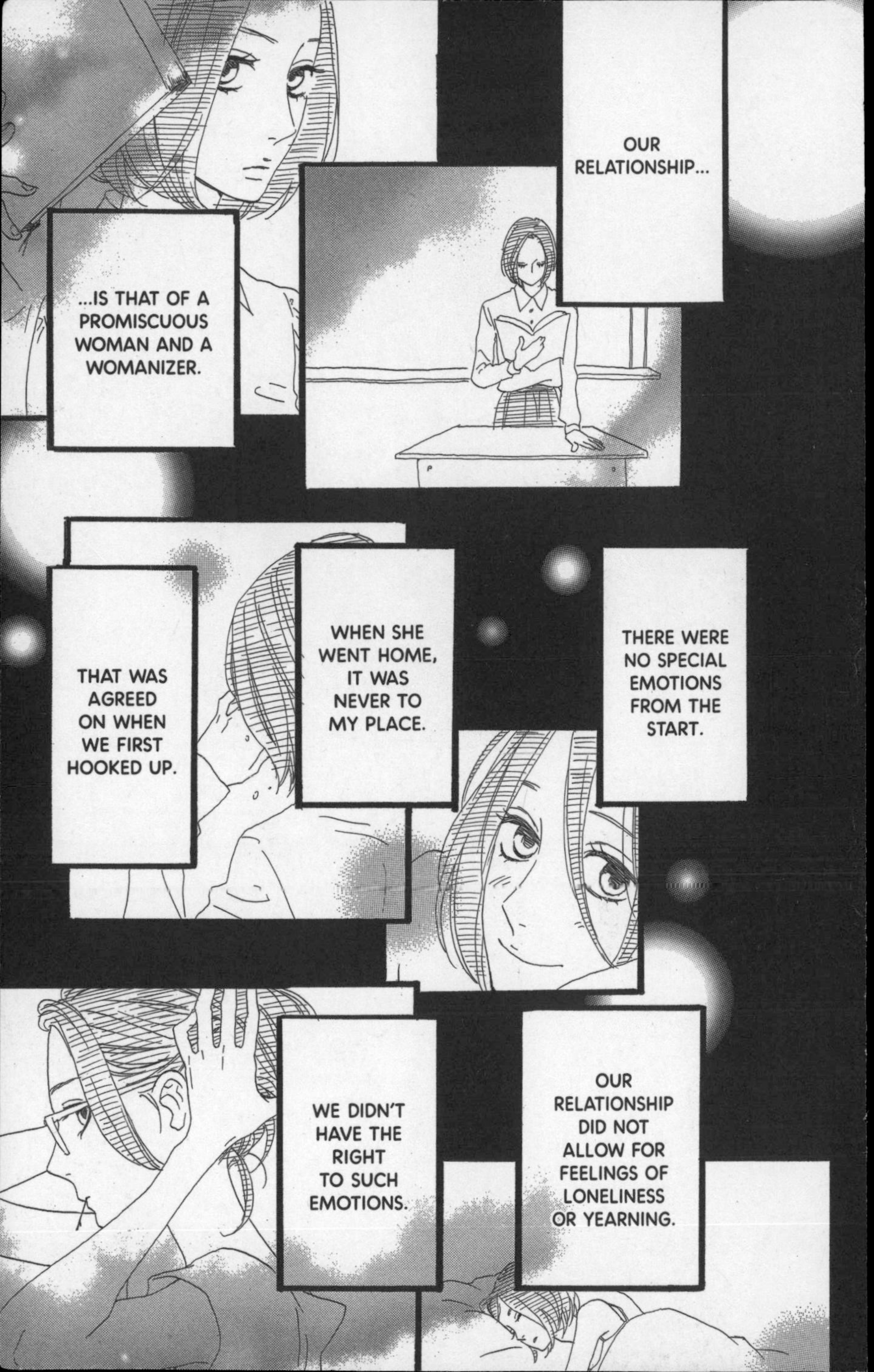
OUR RELATIONSHIP...
...IS THAT OF A PROMISCUOUS WOMAN AND A WOMANIZER.
THERE WERE NO SPECIAL EMOTIONS FROM THE START.
WHEN SHE WENT HOME, IT WAS NEVER TO MY PLACE.
THAT WAS AGREED ON WHEN WE FIRST HOOKED UP.
OUR RELATIONSHIP DID NOT ALLOW FOR FEELINGS OF LONELINESS OR YEARNING.
WE DIDN'T HAVE THE RIGHT TO SUCH EMOTIONS.

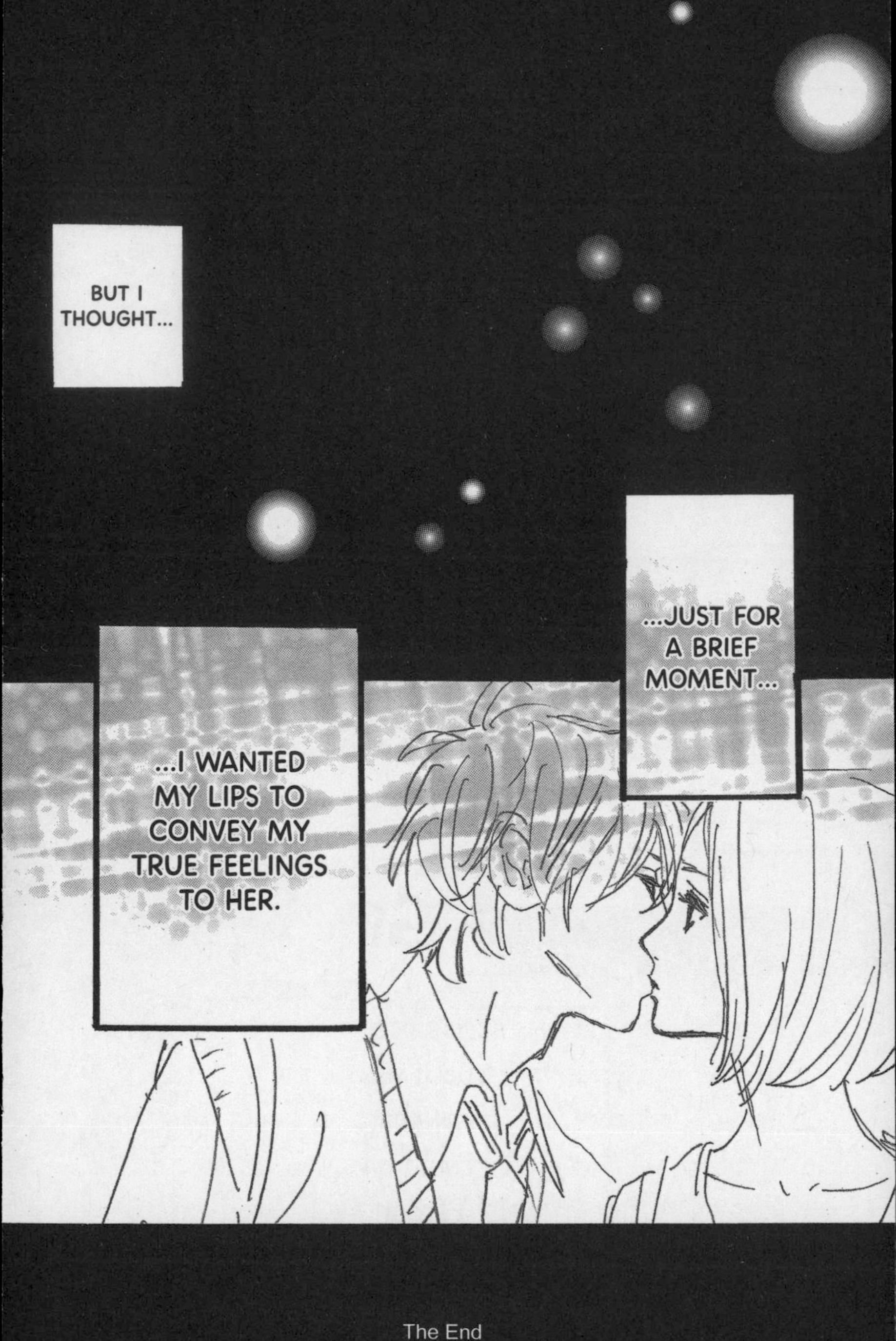
BUT I THOUGHT...
...JUST FOR A BRIEF MOMENT...
...I WANTED MY LIPS TO CONVEY MY TRUE FEELINGS TO HER.
The End

Regarding "Second Kiss"

I created this story back when *Margaret* was doing a bonus "Kiss" feature. Everyone had her own theme, but mine was "A Painful Kiss."

I don't know if you'd call this a painful kiss, but I hadn't drawn a full-on kiss scene in a while, so I felt a little embarrassed.

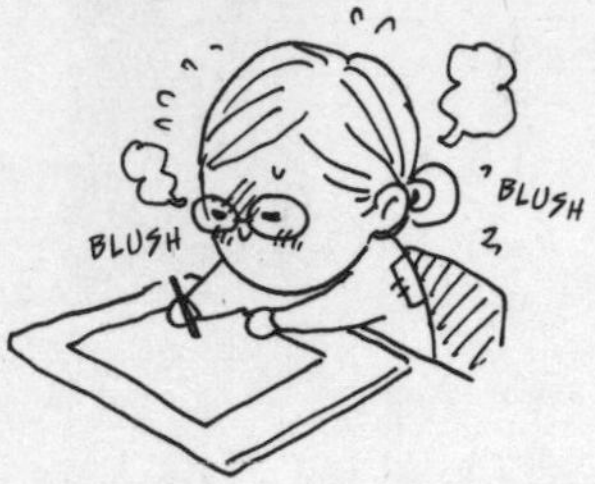
BLUSH
BLUSH

Regarding "Switch Girl Tribute"

Congratulations on the series becoming a TV drama! ♪ How nice! It's great how true it was to the original! Shishio is the only one of my characters with these On/Off modes, so this is all I could give you. Other authors had much better tributes! Pardon me for the sketchiness of my offering...

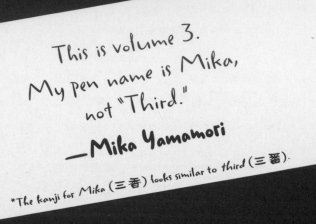

This is volume 3.
My pen name is Mika,
not "Third."
—Mika Yamamori

*The kanji for Mika (三香) looks similar to third (三番).

Mika Yamamori is from Ishikawa Prefecture in Japan. She began her professional manga career in 2006 with "Kimi no Kuchibiru kara Mahou" (The Magic from Your Lips) in *The Margaret* magazine. Her other works include *Sugars* and *Tsubaki Cho Lonely Planet*.

★DAYTIME★SHOOTING★STAR★ ☆3.

SHOJO BEAT EDITION

Story & Art by
Mika Yamamori

Translation ★ **JN Productions**
Touch-Up Art & Lettering ★ **Inori Fukuda Trant**
Design ★ **Alice Lewis**
Editor ★ **Nancy Thistlethwaite**

HIRUNAKA NO RYUSEI © 2011 by Mika Yamamori
All rights reserved.
First published in Japan in 2011 by SHUEISHA Inc., Tokyo.
English translation rights arranged by SHUEISHA Inc.

The stories, characters and incidents mentioned in this
publication are entirely fictional.

Printed in the U.S.A.

Published by VIZ Media, LLC
P.O. Box 77010
San Francisco, CA 94107

10 9 8 7 6 5 4 3 2 1
First printing, November 2019

viz.com

shojobeat.com

STOP!

You may be reading the wrong way!

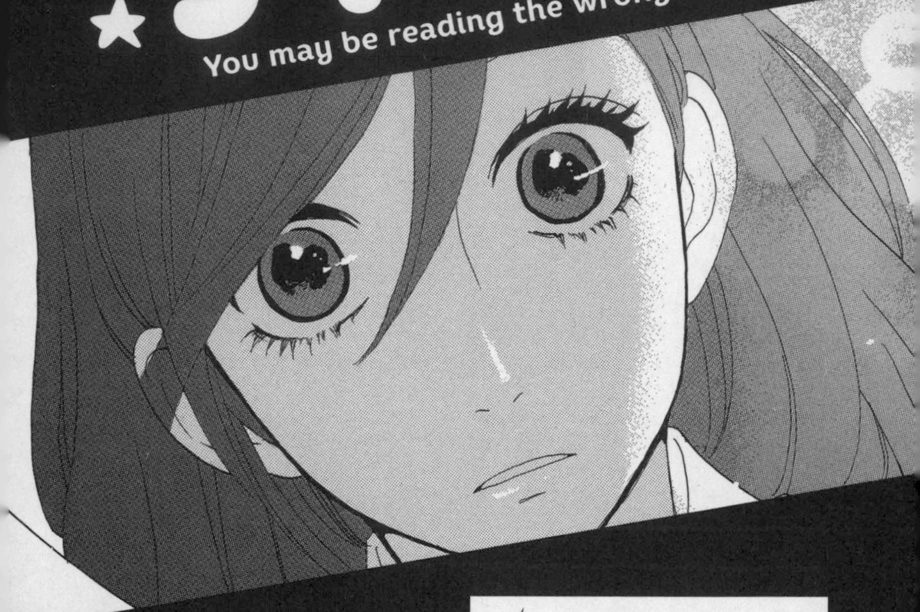

In keeping with the original Japanese comic format, this book reads from right to left—so action, sound effects and word balloons are completely reversed to preserve the orientation of the original artwork.

Check out the diagram shown here to get the hang of things, and then turn to the other side of the book to get started!

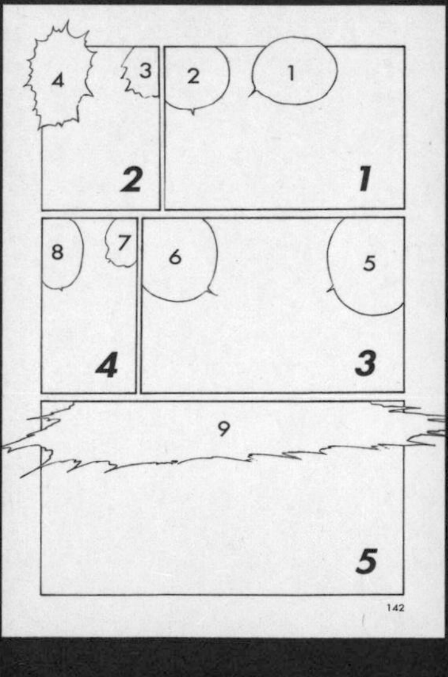

1
2
1
3
4
2
5
6
3
7
8
4
9
5
142